Creating the Cold War University

Creating the Cold
War University

The Transformation of Stanford

Rebecca S. Lowen

University of California Press

Berkeley / Los Angeles / London

University of California Press
Berkeley and Los Angeles, California

University of California Press, Ltd.
London, England

Library of Congress Cataloging-in-Publication Data

Lowen, Rebecca S., 1959–
    Creating the Cold War university : the transformation of Stanford /
Rebecca S. Lowen.
        p.   cm.
    Includes bibliographical references (p.   ) and index.
    ISBN 0-520-20541-3 (alk. paper)
        1. Stanford University—History—20th century.   2. Universities
and colleges—California—Sociological aspects—Case studies.
3. Universities and colleges—Research—Political aspects—
California—Case studies.   4. Universities and colleges—Research—
Economic aspects—California—Case studies.   I. Title.
LD3030.L68   1997
378.794′73—dc20   96-5022
                        CIP

Manufactured in the United States of America
9   8   7   6   5   4   3   2   1

In memory of my mother, Joan Kolberg Lowen,
and for my father, Robert W. Lowen

Contents

Acknowledgments

One of the satisfactions in coming to the end of a project is the opportunity to acknowledge the many people, institutions, and organizations that made its completion possible.

For their financial support, I thank the Center for International Security and Arms Control at Stanford University for a MacArthur fellowship in Peace and Security Studies; the National Science Foundation for a Science, Technology and Society fellowship; the Smithsonian Institution's National Air and Space Museum for a Guggenheim fellowship; and the Center for the History of Physics of the American Institute of Physics for a travel grant. To the administrators and staff of these organizations, I extend my gratitude.

I should also like to thank the historians, students, and staffs of those institutions where, first as a graduate student and then as a postdoctoral scholar, I did most of the work on this book: the history department at Stanford University, the history of science department at Johns Hopkins University, and the National Air and Space Museum's Division of Space History. A number of people deserve special mention. I had the good fortune to have as a graduate advisor a gifted and dedicated teacher and scholar, Barton Bernstein. I thank him for teaching me the historian's craft, for his dependable interest in this project, and especially for his steady faith in my abilities. I should also like to thank Gregg Herken and Robert Smith of the Air and Space Museum for ensuring that I had access to a computer and a place to work and for creating, along with the other members of the space history division, a wonderfully congenial environment in which to think and write. I am especially grateful to Allan Needell for the opportunity to present a portion of this work in the Museum's history of science seminar, and to Sharon Kingsland of the Johns Hopkins history of science department for inviting me to present my work in the department's seminar. I also offer my special thanks to those members of the Johns Hopkins community who welcomed this native Californian into their midst and helped me to make the adjustment to life in the Baltimore–Washington, D.C. area.

A host of archivists and their staffs made possible the research on which this book is based. I am indebted to the extraordinarily capable, dedicated, and friendly staff of the Stanford University Archives, where I conducted the major portion of my research. I thank Archivist Roxanne Nilan for providing access to all relevant archival collections and for accommodating my work schedule; Hilary Shore and Robin Chandler for responding patiently to my countless paging requests; and Linda Long for expertly answering my many questions and sharing her vast knowledge of the Stanford collections. I should also like to thank Margaret Kimball, Karen McAdams, Steven Mandeville-Gamble, Mark Dimunation, and Henry Lowood, Stanford's physics librarian and an historian of science, for their assistance.

Thanks are also due the archivists and staffs of the Hoover Institution, the Stanford Linear Accelerator Center, the Niels Bohr Library of the American Institute of Physics, the Carnegie Institute of Washington, the National Archives, the Library of Congress, and the several university archives that I visited in the course of my research. I should like especially to thank Roger Anders of the Department of Energy for facilitating access to material related to the funding and construction of the Stanford Linear Accelerator; Allan Divack of the Ford Foundation for his cordial assistance with the foundation's collections; and David Van Keuren for mediating between me and the less-than-welcoming staff of the Office of Naval Research's Naval Research Advisory Committee.

I am also very grateful to all those current and former members of the Stanford community who kindly agreed to my requests to interview them. I should particularly like to acknowledge the late Philip Rhinelander, who, although gravely ill, encouraged my visits and my questions. I also extend my very sincere thanks to the Termans—Lewis, Terence, Frederick, Jr., and his wife, Bobbie—who set aside an entire morning to answer my questions and share with me their memories of their father and grandfather and never once asked about, or attempted to control, the content of this project.

Many people kindly read and commented on this book during its various stages of revision. Barton Bernstein, Gordon Chang, Peter Galison, Karl Hufbauer, Robert Kargon, Otis Pease, and David Tyack read the entire manuscript in its earliest incarnation, providing encouragement and many helpful suggestions. I owe special thanks to Bruce Hevly, who took time away from his own work to introduce me to the literature in the history of science and to read carefully every draft of this work that I shared with him.

I also benefited from the comments of those who read the revised manuscript, in part or in its entirety: Brian Balogh, David DeVorkin, Carol Gruber, Christophe Lecuyer, Allan Needell, Larry Owens, Edward Shils, Spencer Weart, and an anonymous reviewer for the University of California Press. I should like especially to thank Michael Bernstein for a helpful reading of the manuscript; Sigmund Diamond for his early endorsement of this project and for sharing with me a useful source; and Peggy Pascoe for her incisive reading of the introduction and her wise counsel over the years. I also owe many thanks to my superlative editor, Elizabeth Knoll (now with W. H. Freeman), for her enthusiasm for this book, for much sensible advice, and for her forbearance in the face of many missed deadlines. This book is the better for the advice and criticisms I received; any remaining inadequacies are the responsibility of the author.

My family and friends assisted me, in ways both concrete and intangible, over the course of research and writing, and I am deeply grateful to them. In those instances when my pursuit of archival material took me away from the comforts of home, I was fortunate to be offered a place to stay and many wonderful meals by Ed and Rhoda Rossinow. I was also hosted innumerable times by Sara Lowen and Tom Omestad, who provided excellent company, moral support, and, when needed, enjoyable diversions from the tasks of research and writing. For their steady support, I also thank: Todd Benson, Gloria Byrnes, Gertrude Kolberg, the late Marillyn Johnson, Chris and Samara Lowen, and Diane Vik. During the writing of this book, I was indulged and cared for by my husband, Douglas Rossinow; I could not have completed this book without him. I thank him for listening, for his many thoughtful comments, for buoying me during low moments, for his fabulous sense of humor, and, not least of all, for doing all the cooking.

Finally, I should like to acknowledge my parents, who had perhaps the greatest, if least easily articulated, influence on this work. Midwesterners by birth, children of the Great Depression, they participated in the geographic and social mobility of postwar America yet remained faithful to the social democratic politics and values of their origins. Among these values is the belief in the inherent worth of education—a belief that helps explain their support for my decision to spend so many years in school studying a seemingly impractical subject. I thank them for their encouragement and generosity, for their appreciation for historical scholarship, and for many other things more important but less easily expressed.

Shortly after I began writing this book, my mother was diagnosed with a rare cancer, and I began taking breaks from this work to spend time with her. The book is no worse for this; I only regret that I did not neglect it more. My mother fought with tenacity an inherently unfair fight, and she accepted her defeat with grace and courage. This book is dedicated to her memory, and to my father, whose loss is the greatest.

Introduction

      With the end of the cold war, the features of American life associated with it—the arms race, a bloated defense budget, the "military-industrial complex," a political rhetoric defined by anticommunism—would seem to be things of the past, characteristics of a discrete period in the history of the United States. Historians of recent American history are already redefining their field, giving an end point to post–1945 U.S. history. Conferences on the cold war and American culture and books on such topics as the cold war and intellectual life and the cold war and American science are further indications of this scholarly trend—as is a book about the "cold war university."

But while America's research universities, just as American science and culture, were undoubtedly shaped by the more than forty years of cold war between the United States and the USSR, other forces, which are not neatly bound by the beginning and end of the cold war, were shaping them as well. The way in which universities, other institutions, and the larger culture responded to the cold war was determined not simply by the tension between the United States and the Soviet Union but also by concerns and conflicts that preceded the cold war. Moreover, many of the characteristics of cold war American society may not necessarily fade as the cold war recedes into history. It is improbable that American universities, for example, will revert to the status and roles that they played before the cold war began.

Despite the complexities of causation and periodization, it is clear that America's research universities were profoundly changed by the cold war, both in relation to their role in society and in terms of the scientific and scholarly disciplines practiced and taught within them. Before World War II, America's universities were peripheral to the nation's political economy. They were committed to promoting the scientific method, to allowing academic scientists and scholars to discover and study "truths," and to developing the character of their students who were, for the most part, the sons of the nation's business and professional elites. While some universities included service to society as part of their mission, none of them conceived of this service as direct assistance to the federal government. Autonomy from the federal government was, in fact, central to the definition of the university as well as of the science and scholarship conducted within it. Similarly, the concept of autonomy from private industry and, more broadly, the world of commerce, distinguished the university from the mere technical institute. Universities were, in their own imagining, ivory towers.[1]

During the cold war, the nation's leading universities moved from the periphery to the center of the nation's political economy. To Clark Kerr, chancellor of the University of California at Berkeley in the 1950s and early 1960s and one of the first to herald publicly this shift, the postwar university was a wholly new institution, one that was uniquely responsive to the society of which it was now very much a part. Kerr recognized the significance of the cold war to American universities. Such military technologies as ballistic missiles, guidance systems, hydrogen bombs, and radar required the expertise of highly trained scientists and engineers. By the early 1960s, the federal government was spending approximately $10 billion annually on research and development, with the Department of Defense and the Atomic Energy Commission contributing over one half of the total. Universities and university-affiliated centers received annually about one tenth—or $1 billion—of these federal research and development funds, more than half of which went to just six universities by the early 1960s. These universities, in turn, depended on federal patronage for over fifty percent of their operating budgets.[2]

But Kerr also saw the postwar university as the product of broader forces that were shifting the nation from an industrial to a postindustrial society, from an economy in which labor and raw materials were the essential inputs to one in which expert knowledge was the key to economic growth and prosperity. Nothing better exemplified for Kerr the centrality of the university to postindustrial society than the shifting industrial geography. High-technology companies were clustering around the Berkeley and Stanford campuses in the San Francisco Bay

Area, around Harvard and MIT in Massachusetts, and around the campuses and research facilities in the Chicago area. These "cities of intellect," or "science regions," as they have since been called, testify to the importance of the American university to the post–World War II economy as do the assiduous, although not always successful, efforts to replicate them.[3]

If the university's relationship to society changed after World War II, the university underwent internal changes as well. Large laboratories staffed with myriad researchers having no teaching duties and working in groups with expensive, government-funded scientific equipment became common features of the leading research universities after World War II. As the organization and funding of science changed, so did the kinds of knowledge produced and taught. Universities made room for new fields of study, such as nuclear engineering and Russian studies, which bore obvious relevance to the nation's geopolitical concerns. Traditional social science disciplines also shifted their emphases, stressing quantitative approaches over normative ones and individual behavior and cultural studies over sociological ones.[4]

Most commented upon, then and now, were changes in the education of students and in the role of university professors. As Kerr readily acknowledged, professional advancement in the postwar university depended wholly on research and publication, which in turn depended on the development of patronage. Thus, undergraduate teaching received short shrift as professors, not surprisingly, showed more interest in and loyalty to their patrons outside the university than to their own institutions and students. If the university before World War II was a community of scholars and scientists, the postwar university was, as Kerr described it, a loose collection of academic entrepreneurs—scientists and scholars perpetually promoting themselves and their research to potential patrons.[5]

That the nation's leading universities changed in the ways that Kerr outlined in the 1963 Godkin Lectures at Harvard (and published later that year as *The Uses of the University*) has never been disputed. What has been a subject of debate, however, is whether these changes represented progress or degradation and decline. As is often the case with valuative questions, the generally accepted answer has tended to change along with shifts in the nation's political and cultural climate. In the 1950s and early 1960s, for example, the consensus was that the metamorphosis of the university was part of a broader progressive trend; *The Uses of the University* remains the classic presentation of this view. While Kerr regretted what was being lost—a sense of the university as a community and a devotion to undergraduate education—this regret was overwhelmed by his appreciation for what was being gained. The university was no longer an ivory tower but a flexible institution with multiple constituencies, a "multiversity."

Kerr's views came under attack in the decade following the publication of *The Uses of the University*. To Robert Nisbet, a conservative sociologist who idealized the prewar academic community, the university had been hopelessly degraded by its emphasis on service and its relationship to the federal government and to private enterprise. Nisbet leveled his most searing criticisms at fellow colleagues, whom he accused of abandoning traditional, if unglamorous, commitments to teaching and scholarship to chase after money and fame. The multiversity was also attacked by the left at this time for its purported dehumanizing approach to education and its collaboration with the nation's war machinery.[6]

The end of the Vietnam War took much of the heat out of the controversy surrounding the university and its role in society, but expressions of dissatisfaction, often quite strident, resurfaced in the mid-1980s. The university was attacked from the right for neglecting undergraduates and introducing curricula emphasizing relevance and cultural diversity instead of transcendent values and traditions. As before, blame focused on university professors who, it was claimed, had been student radicals in the 1960s. Less attention was paid in these years to critics on the left concerned about the increase in defense dollars pouring into university laboratories and the connections between federally supported academic researchers and privately owned, for-profit businesses. Defenders of the cold war university also reemerged to stress the economic benefits derived from universities' collaboration with the federal government and private industry and to insist that state-supported (and, specifically, military-supported) science produced good, not bad, science.[7]

This book aims not so much to take sides in this long-running debate about the American university but rather to explore precisely how the changes that have provoked so much controversy came about. Thus, while this book is generally critical of the cold war university, it does not, for example, challenge the assertion that academic scientists who were supported with military funds were excellent scientists doing world-class research. My interest is not in evaluating the quality of the science conducted but rather in explaining historical change—in understanding why academic scientists began accepting support from the military, how they adapted their understanding of their roles as academic scientists to accommodate this change, and how this new source of patronage shaped the kinds of knowledge produced within the university.

Further, my criticisms of the postwar university should not be assumed to imply a preference for the prewar university, particularly the prewar private university, which was a deeply flawed institution. That institution's sense of community, for example, of which some critics of today's university have bemoaned the loss, derived in large measure from the concerted exclusion of Jews, African-Americans, and women from the faculty and the student body.[8] Finally, I have declined here either to validate or criticize student activists, which is one reason that the history related here stops in the mid-1960s, before the campuses became scenes of organized political protests. It is specious to suggest, however, as have several historians and commentators, that those students politicized American universities. As this book will make clear, politics have always intruded into the affairs of the university, most notably during the Red Scare of the 1950s, but at other times as well, and almost always at the initiative of university administrators and professors, not students. Regardless of whether one approves or disapproves of the methods of student protesters, students clearly were recognizing and responding to, rather than initiating, the politicization of their institutions.[9]

Thus, neither critics nor defenders of the university will find their views fully supported here. Again, my interest as an historian is to understand how and why the university became a service institution, how this change was related to the university's new ties to the federal government and to private industry, and how these new relationships affected the way knowledge was organized, the kinds of knowledge produced, and the role of academic scientists, and more generally, university professors.

Addressing these questions is important to achieving a complete understanding of the development of the cold war political economy. Exploring how American universities changed may also enhance our understanding of American culture during the cold war. Historians have skillfully analyzed the construction of stereotypically gendered social roles and popular cultural presentations of anticommunism; they have also explored the "culture of anxiety" created by the atomic bomb and the arms race.[10] But there has been a tendency both to conflate the 1950s and the cold war in discussions about culture and to overlook less striking but perhaps more persistent characteristics of the broader period, including a pervasive scientism, the triumph of the idea of apolitical expertise, and the popularization of psychotherapeutic ideas and techniques. An exploration of these aspects of American cultural history cannot ignore the postwar university, which was not only the meeting ground of many of the defining features of the cold war but also, in its educative role, the transmitter of particular values and ideas to a younger generation.

My interest in historical context and human agency—in how and why American universities and the knowledge produced within them changed—necessitated an exploration of motives and the precise relationships among academic scientists, administrators, and university patrons. This, in turn, dictated a close study of one university, in the expectation that the details of how one university was transformed would elucidate the larger patterns and forces that affected all universities experiencing similar changes.

Stanford University was an obvious choice for a study of the "federal grant university," in Kerr's nomenclature, or what I am calling the "cold war university." During most of the cold war, Stanford was one of the top recipients of Defense Department patronage; it was also one of the first universities to forge close relationships to private industrial concerns, many of which were developing war-related technologies. By the 1980s, Stanford had become the exemplar of the cold war university. The subject of books celebrating the development of Silicon Valley, Stanford was also the first university to be audited by the federal government in the early 1990s for purportedly misusing overhead monies derived from federal contracts. The budgeting practices of Stanford administrators were hardly idiosyncratic, but the extensive attention that was devoted to Stanford suggests that Stanford is widely perceived as a model of the cold war university, of its purported excesses as well as successes.[11]

To regard Stanford as the archetype of the cold war university is not to claim that Stanford is identical to other leading research universities. As is every university, Stanford is in some ways idiosyncratic. It is a private university, for example, but unlike Harvard and Yale, was founded in the late nineteenth century with the fortune of a robber baron. In this respect, it is similar to Johns Hopkins University and the

University of Chicago. But unlike these universities, Stanford generally lacked prestige and influence in the early twentieth century. In fact, Stanford did not emerge as a prestigious academic institution until the 1960s, when it appeared on lists of the "top ten" universities in America as well as on lists of the handful of universities receiving the most support from the federal government. This swift rise to prominence, understood at the time as related directly to the university's defense contracts and to California's postwar economic boom (itself the product largely of defense spending), is Stanford's most distinctive characteristic. But even in this respect, Stanford is not unique. The University of California at San Diego, for example, experienced an equally dramatic elevation of reputation and influence during the cold war.

This particular combination of representativeness and distinctiveness made Stanford University particularly attractive for a study of the cold war university. Changes that were occurring at all leading research universities were occurring with great rapidity at Stanford; thus, at Stanford, it is possible to see in bold relief what was changing and why. Just as Stanford became a model for universities in the 1970s and 1980s that sought to increase their financial resources and improve their academic standing, Stanford's history offers a paradigm for understanding what was happening, albeit more subtly, at other leading research universities between the 1930s and the 1960s.

To take the institution of the university—rather than individual departments, laboratories, scientists, patrons of science, or a cluster of universities—as the primary object of study represents a departure from historiographic tradition. The history of individual universities has traditionally been left to retired administrators and institutional boosters and treated as a variant of hagiography. Professional historians, while occasionally studying a collection of universities, have generally focused on the professions and academic disciplines or on the relationships between science and patronage and between experts and the state, working around the edges of the university or ignoring it entirely.

The unintended effect of this intellectual division of labor has been to reinforce the reigning view of the multiversity as an institution with weak central authority, dominated by its scientists and scholars who respond not to internal institutional pressures but to their patrons and sponsors outside the university or to the imperatives of the disciplines they practice. Beyond holding and serving the needs of these experts, the multiversity appears to be institutionally insignificant. Viewed as such, the history of the multiversity is conveniently synonymous with the history of the relationships among scientists, experts, and the state, thus helping to explain why professional historians have devoted little attention to the university itself. Further, the transformation of the university appears inevitable rather than problematic; it is understood simply as the natural outcome of the inexorable rise of a powerful, centralizing state increasingly dependent upon scientific knowledge and expertise, and of the attendant growth of a body of scientists and experts committed to professional autonomy and to influencing public affairs.

This was Kerr's interpretation, and historians of science and of the development of the state have generally worked within this framework. While some have traced the origins of the ties between experts and the state as far back as the Civil War and others, to the War Industries Board of the First World War, historians have more recently stressed the deep suspicions held by scientists and experts before World War II of any permanent alliance with the federal government. For most scientists, the relationship was seen as potentially threatening to professional independence, portending the subjection of their work to political agendas. In the years preceding the Second World War, scientists sought patronage from private industry, wealthy individuals, and private philanthropies. The federal government itself showed a distrust of experts whom it could not directly control, rejecting pleas in the 1930s, for example, for federal funding of academic science.

This wariness between academic scientists and the federal government dissolved, so this story goes, with the onset of World War II, when the government once again called upon scientists—most notably, the nation's physicists—for assistance. In the course of developing war technologies, both the military and the physicists recognized fully the advantages of a lasting association. The relationship was then cemented during the cold war, particularly during the Korean War, through federal (primarily military) patronage to academic scientists and through the involvement of these scientists as advisors to the federal government. While most attention has focused on the physics community, the general assumption has been that the relationship that developed between physicists and the state was eventually replicated by other academic scientists and social scientists. The federal government came to recognize the usefulness of a broad array of scientific and social scientific disciplines in fighting the cold war; the scientists, aware of the enormous prestige enjoyed by the physicists, eagerly sought to emulate them by developing ties to state patrons.[12]

Implicit, if not explicit, in this interpretation, is the view that academic scientists and the military reshaped the university and the kinds of knowledge produced within it, pulling the university into a relationship with the federal government and rendering it subject to the interests of the newly empowered academic scientists. Debates among those critical of this development turn on whether military patrons "used" the scientists who accepted the proffered patronage or whether the scientists actively sought and developed military patronage for their own purposes. In either scenario, the university itself is rendered a passive institution, a passivity indicated in the very title—"the uses of the university"—of Kerr's commentary on the multiversity.[13]

This story changes, however, when the university—the home of the scientists and the institution into which patronage flowed—is placed at the center. Focusing directly on the institution and the relationships within it reminds us that although the scientists and scholars within its walls may be independent professionals by training, they are also employees of a corporate entity. This fact once disgruntled Thorstein Veblen, who fulminated against the leaders of American universities, the "Captains of Industry" and the "Captains of Erudition," as he called them, who insisted on treating professionals as mere employees.[14] These Captains of Industry and Erudition did not simply fade from the scene in midcentury to be replaced by supine administrators who were controlled by patrons and scientists. Although some academic scientists and scholars did indeed gain leverage over university administrators by developing extensive patronage, most remained, to varying extents, bound by institutional constraints and rules. Just as in Veblen's day, university administrators, in their capacity to hire and fire and to distribute institutional resources, played a significant role in determining who gained a voice in the academic world and who did not, which kinds of research were emphasized and which were not. One of the arguments of this book is that the leaders of the nation's universities, along with patrons and some scientists, strongly influenced the creation of the cold war university. For both institutional and ideological reasons, they favored and promoted the development of heavily subsidized scientific work and stressed the production of knowledge over the education of students.

Making the university the context as well as the subject of study not only highlights the fact that universities are places of employment and institutions in which all do not have equal power. It also provides an opportunity to broaden the study of science and patronage beyond a single discipline or type of patron to encompass the activities of professors in a variety of academic departments and to include multiple sources of research support. Expanding the focus in this way not only helps correct for the disproportionate attention that has been paid to the history of academic physics but also exposes the error of simply positing a mimetic relationship and imposing on other academic disciplines the pattern of development of postwar physics.[15] At Stanford, for example, the statistics, electrical engineering, psychology, and philosophy departments were among the early, eager pursuers of federal patronage, as were some, but not all, of Stanford's physicists. And the physics department was the last, rather than the first, university department to permit faculty members to be hired with government, rather than university, funds. In the case of the social sciences, private foundations, rather than the federal government, were the most generous supporters of social science research in the early cold war.[16]

None of these findings is easily encompassed by the general theory that physicists established a relationship with federal patrons which was then emulated by other academic scientists. Again, the role of academic administrators, to whose authority all departments in the university were subject, must be considered. This study examines the involvement of university administrators in negotiating with research patrons—both the federal government and private foundations—and in pressuring scientists—physical, natural, and social scientists—to develop external support for their work.

By focusing on the activities of academic administrators, particularly in relation to the social sciences, it is also possible to bring together the literature on the postwar patronage of academic science and the literature on McCarthyism and American universities. The most recent work on universities and the Red Scare has stressed the role of top university administrators in collaborating with congressional committees or intelligence agencies in the establishment of intellectual conformity on the nation's campuses. Historian Ellen Schrecker has suggested that individual social scientists, responding to the general climate of repression, adopted "apolitical" and "scientific" approaches to the study of society to protect themselves from political controversy and possible accusations from red-baiters. Historians of science have also noted the prominence and popularity of quantitative and scientistic approaches to studying society in this period but have suggested that the interests of patrons explains this development.[17]

There is, however, another (and not incompatible) explanation that takes into account both patronage and the relationships between academic administrators and scientists and connects individual motivation directly to observable institutional pressure. University administrators clearly had a stake in eliminating potentially controversial teachers from their campuses, sometimes for ideological reasons, but also for practical ones—they sought to avoid controversies that might alienate patrons of the university. They additionally had a strong stake in maintaining (or achieving) national prestige for their institutions. With respect to disciplines such as political science, these concerns dictated an emphasis on quantitative and behavioral methods, which were deemed both apolitical and scientific and for which generous external support was available. Thus, while surely there were particular instances in which individual social scientists freely chose to adopt a quantitative approach to their work, this study shows as well how university administrators at Stanford sought to channel intellectual efforts to meet the concerns of trustees and patrons. This result was achieved not so much by coercing particular individuals (although this did occur) as by applying pressure in favor of quantitative and subsidized work at the departmental level through the exercise of administrative power over faculty hiring, promotions, and salaries. This shaping of the academic disciplines to reflect the interests and values of patrons cannot be seen in studies that look primarily at the relationships between patrons and individuals within the university. Similarly, by focusing on those periods of crisis when ideological conformity was achieved through selective dismissals of faculty members, we overlook the subtler but perhaps more consistent way in which intellectual channeling occurs.

In addition to examining developments across disciplines, taking the university as the context of study makes it possible to look at the prominent members of a discipline along with their lesser-known colleagues and their interactions as members of a common department. The tendency among historians of science has been to give a predominant voice to those scientists whose work and methods were deemed "nationally significant" or became the standard, and to highlight the activities of so-called academic entrepreneurs. Intentional or otherwise, this approach leaves the impression of inevitability and consensus. This is misleading. We need both to recognize the historical context of definitions of academic "success" and "national significance" and to listen to the voices of those who questioned these definitions.

Dissent is not a feature usually associated with the university of the

1940s and 1950s. A search for open political debate in this period, for example, and particularly for vocal moral opposition to the university's involvement in weapons research in peacetime, will yield little. But the university of this period was, in fact, riven with conflict. This conflict included occasional disagreements between scientists and their research patrons about control—over the direction of the sponsored research, over the workplace, over security restrictions. Most dissent at Stanford, however, focused on the university itself and, more specifically, on the institution's leaders. It was the university's administrators, rather than the patrons of academic research, who were accused of devaluing teaching and the life of contemplation, of seeking to impose upon the faculty the priorities of external patrons, and of violating professorial and departmental autonomy.

The dissenters, of course, constituted a minority of the faculty and were most often, but certainly not always, professors who were in some way marginalized within the university. Recovering the voices of those who were in open disagreement is important, however, for they make clear that the creation of the cold war university did not proceed smoothly. While its development may have been overdetermined, it was not predetermined. This study emphasizes the conflicts that occurred, not because internecine academic battles make for good historical gossip, but in the belief that illumination of these conflicts will clarify what those at the time believed was at stake and what would be lost as well as gained in the transformation of the university.

Finally, studying closely one university, rather than a group of institutions, makes it possible to understand better the relationships both within the university and between the university and its various patrons. Those studies, both historical and sociological, that have examined a group of leading universities have, because of their scope and the vast amount of data available, tended to rely on functional or structural analyses.[18] While helpful in identifying broad trends, these works have been less successful in explaining the dynamics of change. The focus on functional groups—trustees, administrators, professors, patrons—as having separate and well-defined interests and spheres masks the shared interests, political ideologies, and even personal relationships that cross functional categories and link, for example, some trustees to some patrons and some administrators to some professors.[19] Further, the emphasis on group identity as defined by institutional function masks disagreements within the group and inequalities based on access to external funding as well as on professional status.

This study makes clear that while academic administrators played an important role in transforming Stanford University, they were not acting alone. They worked closely with some scientists and scholars who shared their interests and goals (and in a number of cases went on to become university administrators themselves), as well as with the patrons of academic science. Had these groups not overlapped or shared interests and had professors, for example, strongly identified themselves as a distinct and separate group, the postwar university might have developed very differently than it did.

To illuminate why university administrators and some academic scientists would engage in transforming their own institutions requires an understanding not just of the opportunities provided by the appearance of federal support for academic science after the Second World War but also of the circumstances under which scientists and their universities operated in the decade preceding the war. Serious consideration of the earlier period presents a challenge to those studies that suggest that the collaboration of academic scientists and the military during World War II is in itself sufficient to explain the postwar transformation of the university.[20] This book argues that the development of the postwar university cannot be understood fully without taking into account the responses of university administrators to the collapse of the American economy in the 1930s and to Franklin Roosevelt's New Deal.

The Great Depression affected the nation's universities and their scientists; it was particularly devastating for private institutions. For the politically conservative leaders of most of the nation's universities, problems of finance paled in comparison to feared changes that the New Deal might impose on the nation's political economy. A number of university administrators, imagining the specter of federal assistance and control, sought to solve institutional financial problems by forging close alliances with private industry. Among this group were Ray Lyman Wilbur, president of Stanford, and Herbert Hoover, the former president of the United States, who was also a Stanford trustee and Wilbur's close friend and advisor.

Recognition of the constraints of depending on industrial patronage—limited interest on the part of industry and patrons' challenges to the scientists' professional autonomy—coincided not just with the mobilization of science for the Second World War but also with the development of a relationship between American universities and the federal government based on the federal contract. Historian Larry Owens has perceptively pointed to the significance of the contract, both symbol and instrument of the marketplace, in bringing about an alliance between the state and institutions traditionally mistrustful of the state.[21] While the contract alone might have sufficed to reassure wary university administrators that they could enjoy federal patronage *and* insulation from democratic control, it was the offer to subsidize the universities themselves through the payment of indirect, or overhead, costs—an offer made first by the wartime National Defense Research Committee, administered by the conservative Vannevar Bush—that proved irresistible to university administrators.

The generous contractual terms provided universities by the federal government during World War II made university administrators eager to perpetuate the relationship with the federal government after the war. Even so, the first years of the postwar period were not marked by the immediate emergence of the federal-university relationship that predominated during the cold war. The period between the end of World War II and the onset of the Korean War was one of negotiation, between universities and the federal government and within universities, over the form that the federal-university relationship would take, and particularly how universities would integrate federal contracts into their financial and academic structures. At Stanford and other universities that had not been sites of federally sponsored wartime laboratories, the acceptance of federal patronage after the war did not simply indicate a willingness to perpetuate a war-born relationship; it required an explicit decision.[22]

Among the advocates of untempered exploitation of postwar federal patronage was Frederick Terman, an electrical engineer by training and for most of his academic career an administrator at Stanford. As others have recognized, no examination of Stanford can ignore Terman's role in guiding the university along the path it took and helping bring it to national prominence. It is important to remember, however, that Terman was not solely responsible for reshaping Stanford, nor was he unique among university administrators generally. Moreover, it is inaccurate to view Terman simply as an academic entrepreneur. This is a much-used term but one that is inadequate for fully explaining the behavior of those members of the university who avidly seek patronage.[23] First, the term creates the erroneous impression of an individual acting independently, making and seizing opportunities unconstrained by institutions. Most professors, however, engaged in entrepreneurial behavior precisely in response to institutional constraints. Terman and his counterparts at other universities, by contrast, may best be understood not simply as academic entrepreneurs but as administrators consciously working to make entrepreneurship the normative behavior of university professors.

Entrepreneur has also come to be used as a description of motivation as well as of behavior, implying that the academic entrepreneur is in search of personal or institutional wealth and aggrandizement. Undoubtedly true for some, this term is entirely insufficient for comprehending Terman and others who were strongly guided by ideological conviction. Recognizing the importance of ideology, Terman becomes much more than an administrator avidly seeking patronage in order to make Stanford the Harvard or the MIT of the West. By situating him within the historical context of Progressive Era and cold war ideas about politics and science, we can see how these ideas shaped his vision of the university and its relationship to society.

It is in this context that Terman becomes an interesting historical personage. An admirer of Herbert Hoover and the son of Lewis Terman, a noted developer and promoter of intelligence tests, Frederick Terman carried into the cold war particular features of corporate progressive ideology—a passion for quantifying and rationalizing behavior and processes, a belief in expertise, and a vision of social and economic organization in which independent experts guide and serve the needs of private corporations and advise those agencies of the federal government that promote and assist private enterprise.[24] For Terman, the cold war provided the opportunity for realizing this model of society and for making the university an essential part of it. The university, he believed, should be a highly rationalized and efficient producer of scientific and technical knowledge and trained "manpower," autonomous from but essential to both private industry and the federal government. This was to be a three-way institutional partnership, or a "win-win-win" relationship, as Terman called it.[25] The extent to which relationships among Stanford, industry, and the federal government after World War II conformed to the ideal society conceived by prewar corporate progressives was less an inevitable culmination of earlier, prewar tendencies than it was the result of powerful members of the university community seeking to build and develop such relationships as required by institutional needs and inspired by ideological convictions. These individuals made common cause with those within the federal government and industry whose interests meshed with their own.

The result, for Stanford, was national influence, academic prestige, and wealth. For some, this is a story of one university's rise to "greatness," a tribute to a handful of resourceful and determined administrators and scientists. For others, it is a story of decline, of scientific talents misdirected by a warfare state, of greatness purchased at the price of dependence on the military-industrial complex. Perhaps, however, this narrative is best understood neither as the story of a rise to prominence nor as a fall from grace but rather as a story of evolving institutional contradictions, which assumed a particular form in midcentury and which, in the post–cold war period, will be reshaped rather than resolved.

I

The Thirties

On March 4, 1933, under gray skies before the nation's Capitol, Franklin Roosevelt, newly inaugurated as the nation's thirty-second president, addressed a country ravaged by its worst depression in forty years. Fifteen million Americans, one-quarter of the nation's workforce, were jobless in 1933. In the previous year, the country's net income had fallen from $90 billion to $42 billion, and by inauguration day thirty-eight states, including New York and California, had declared bank holidays. According to a reporter on the scene, President Roosevelt exuded confidence as he promised to use the powers of the federal government to spur economic recovery and assured Americans that they had nothing to fear.

Herbert Hoover, sitting on the platform behind the president, listened, stiff and impassive. His face, according to a reporter on the scene, was white and drawn. Highly sensitive to criticisms that his administration had been ineffectual and indifferent to the nation's suffering and deeply antagonized by Roosevelt's political style and proposed expansion of federal power, Hoover would become an outspoken and persistent critic of the New Deal. Immediately after the inaugural ceremony, he left Washington, accompanied by his former secretary of the interior and loyal friend, Ray Lyman Wilbur. They would head soon for Palo Alto, California, to resume, after a four-year hiatus, direction of Stanford University—Wilbur as president and Hoover as a member of the board of trustees.[1]

As would the leaders of other universities, both public and private, Wilbur would face the challenge of raising money and running a university during a severe economic depression. Along with Hoover, he would also watch closely and with deep skepticism the activities of the Roosevelt administration and join the debates within the academic world spawned by the depression and the New Deal about the university's proper role in society, specifically about the relationship between universities and the federal government. At the same time, leaders of Stanford would confront a problem specific to their institution: a widely recognized decline in Stanford's academic reputation.

It was in this context—of changes, both real and feared, in the political economy, in the patronage relations of science, and in the hierarchy of universities—that the leaders of Stanford and some faculty members determined that Stanford needed a new source of patronage to support academic research and that the proper ally of the private university was private industry. While this conviction would receive fullest institutional expression after World War II, industrially sponsored research began at Stanford in the late 1930s. It would prove to be a development far more satisfying to Stanford's administration than to the faculty members involved.

Prologue

A week's train ride from Washington, D.C., Stanford was a small university of a few hundred faculty members and several thousand students in 1933, surrounded and dwarfed by huge expanses of undeveloped land once owned by Jane and Leland Stanford. Leland Stanford—California's Republican governor during the Civil War, later a senator, and one of the "big four" partners in the Central Pacific Railroad—had amassed one of the huge industrial fortunes of the Gilded Age, $17 million of which had provided an endowment for Stanford University, created by Stanford and his wife as a memorial to their son.[2] The university had opened in 1891, at the peak of the post–Civil War movement that was transforming America's denominational colleges, such as Harvard, into universities and was spawning wholly new institutions, including Stanford, the University of Chicago, and Johns Hopkins University.

Pushing forward the transformations in higher education were the members of a new business class interested in practical education for their sons. The richest of this industrial class, including men like Stanford, provided the funds necessary to create new institutions and transform the old. The leaders of America's colleges themselves directed the transformation of their institutions. Guided by the examples of German and English universities, they abandoned a curriculum based on rote memorization, expanded offerings in science, and instituted programs for advanced training. By the 1890s America's institutions of higher education embodied, to varying degrees, the goals of advancing scientific research, providing practical training, and socializing the sons of a new middle class. According to Stanford's first president, David Starr Jordan, a natural scientist and progressive interested in educational reforms, Stanford would not cloister undergraduates, as had the old denominational colleges, but would prepare them for life in the "real" world.[3]

This educational orientation suited Herbert Hoover, a midwesterner and Quaker of modest means, who entered with Stanford's first freshman class and began studying geology under John Caspar Branner. After graduating, Hoover became a consulting engineer to mining companies in Australia and China and in less than two decades was a millionaire and Stanford's richest alumnus. The efforts of two Stanford trustees familiar with Hoover through their mutual involvement in a California-based oil company brought Hoover on to Stanford's board of trustees in 1912.[4]

Although Stanford's president Jordan had been one of the founding members of the Association of American Universities (AAU), an organization of the fourteen leading public and private research universities that was formed in 1900, by the time Hoover became a trustee in 1912, it was clear that Stanford had not developed the commitment to research that characterized most of the AAU's members. Jordan's interests had been focused elsewhere, but the university also lacked the necessary resources. Stanford's financial problems were manifold and had developed shortly after the university opened its doors in 1891. Legal problems relating to the Stanford endowment, the decision not to charge tuition, the disastrous impact of the 1906 earthquake, and a dearth of patrons had together placed stringent limits on the university's operating budget, thus damaging faculty recruitment and inhibiting research. The Stanfords' decision to locate the university fewer than sixty miles from the already well-established University of California had meant severe competition—which Stanford could not meet—for the limited resources and college-bound students in California's Bay Area. From the 1890s through the 1910s, a period when institutions of higher education were expanding the size of their faculties and placing greater emphasis on research, Stanford's trustees, most of them conservative businessmen, retained tight control of the university's budget. President Jordan's requests for additional operating funds were usually met with challenges that he reduce expenditures; the effect, according to Jordan, was to keep Stanford University in the "stone age."[5]

Hoover, whose devotion to engineering principles made him the most progressive of the businessmen who dominated Stanford's board of trustees, was eager to reform Stanford, both to bring it into line with developments at the other research universities and also to rationalize its operations and set it firmly on the path toward research and training of practical value. Hoover worked immediately to modernize the university's bookkeeping and to raise the salaries of the faculty members to levels commensurate with their status as professionals. He also encouraged Jordan, who by the 1910s was less interested in reforming Stanford than in committing himself fully to the cause of world peace, to retire. In 1913, the trustees made Jordan chancellor of the university, a position which Hoover likened to that of a "consulting engineer." To fill temporarily the role of president, or "general manager," as Hoover put it, the trustees chose Hoover's former mentor and friend, Stanford geologist John Branner.[6]

Despite Branner's apparent compatibility with trustees interested in the practical applications of geological knowledge, he quickly ran afoul of Hoover's commitment to practical training when he attempted, with widespread faculty support, to disband the university's medical school and use the budgetary savings better to support the arts and sciences faculty.[7] The trustees immediately began the search for Branner's replacement. Again, Hoover's interests prevailed. Arguing strongly against appointing an "old-line President" who could "preside at Sunday School Conventions and make choicely classical orations on public occasions," Hoover urged the trustees to select a leader committed to education and research with practical applications, a "westerner," in Hoover's terms.[8] The trustees approved Hoover's candidate for the position, Ray Lyman Wilbur, the dean of Stanford's medical school and a friend of Hoover since their days as undergraduates at Stanford.

When Wilbur became the president of Stanford in 1916, Europe was entering the third year of devastating war; within a little more than a year, the United States would also formally enter the First World War. Mobilization for war had an immediate impact on America's institutions of higher education, quickly emptying campuses of both scientists and students. (Wilbur himself traveled between the West and East

Coasts during the war in his position as chief of the conservation division of the Food Administration, a wartime agency under Herbert Hoover's direction.) Patriotic fervor swept the campuses, leading to the repression of pacifists, German sympathizers, and other dissidents. Stanford dropped its motto, "Die Luft der Freiheit weht" (the wind of freedom is blowing), lest the university be thought insufficiently anti-German. Finally, in the last months of the war, the U.S. Army commandeered the campuses, turning them into military training grounds for enlisted college students.[9]

The research universities were also affected by the war in less direct but more lasting ways. The federal government's need to reorganize the political economy for war and to develop new techniques and weapons within the armed services brought together government officials, representatives of industrial enterprises, and leaders of America's scientific community. This wartime mobilization did not, as some have suggested, mark the beginning of a military-industrial complex.[10] But by placing authority in particular organizations, it did bring to prominence a particular group of scientists, industrialists, and statesmen whose views and activities helped shape the postwar patronage and social relations of academic science and, indirectly, the universities. The National Research Council (NRC) was one such organization, a branch of the National Academy of Sciences created in 1916 and authorized by President Woodrow Wilson to organize and promote scientific research—academic, governmental, industrial—for national security and welfare.

Those involved in the NRC's mobilization and coordination of scientific research for the war—George Ellery Hale, noted astronomer and director of Pasadena's Mount Wilson Observatory; Robert Millikan, Nobel laureate in physics and professor at the University of Chicago; Elihu Root, former secretary of state under Theodore Roosevelt and a trustee of the Carnegie Institute of Washington; and representatives of General Electric, AT&T, and DuPont—came to this task believing that basic scientific research was essential not just to the U.S. war effort but also to postwar industrial and commercial progress. Thus, scientific research, even of the more abstruse, academic variety, needed to be organized, coordinated, and generously supported. This outlook was shaped in part by their admiration for German science, which enjoyed an international reputation and had also provided the basis for Germany's industrial and military strength. Political conservatives like Hale and Root, who were also, of course, eager to see the Allies defeat Germany, rejected the German model of organizing and centralizing science under state direction. Instead, they believed that the coordination and support for American science should remain in private hands. Further, the "best" science, as they understood it, should be conducted under private auspices, primarily in America's universities.[11]

This view—that scientific research was ultimately useful, if not essential to industrial progress, but that direct state involvement in sponsoring or coordinating basic scientific research was inappropriate—became the dominant one after World War I. The contributions of scientists to the development of technologies used during the war, from I.Q. tests to poison gas, were widely heralded after the war as evidence of the link between academic science and technological progress. At the same time, proponents of a more active role for the state were being effectively marginalized by the conservative backlash against real and imagined socialists and radicals. In this climate the leaders of the scientific, industrial, and philanthropic communities worked effectively both to celebrate and develop private patronage for academic science. Leaders of the NRC, including Hale, argued vigorously with the few industrial leaders who favored government subsidies for academic research after the war. They also worked to defeat congressional legislation that would have provided federal support for engineering research in the state universities after the war, and they convinced both the Rockefeller and Carnegie philanthropies to contribute generously to the support of academic science, beginning with large grants in 1919 to the NRC.[12]

Herbert Hoover, back in the United States after his wartime organization of food relief efforts in Europe with a national reputation as a great yet efficient humanitarian, shared Hale's views regarding science, industrial progress, and the federal government's proper role in relation to both. To historians, in fact, Hoover has come to exemplify the early-twentieth-century interests of some corporate capitalists, government officials, scientists, and reformers in rationalizing industry, eliminating wasteful competition, and reducing labor unrest. Positioning themselves in the broad middle between those supporting state intervention in the economy and conservatives resistant to any change, Hoover and others advocated instead a role for the state that did not include legal coercion or publicly owned enterprises but involved providing information and guidance to facilitate voluntary reforms. Integral to this outlook was a reliance on "experts," whose commitment to scientific rationalization and social engineering seemingly transcended ideological commitments; these experts would gather and process the information needed to guide, coordinate, and promote private efforts. Between 1921 and 1928, Hoover worked to put these ideas into practice as secretary of commerce.[13]

Hoover also shared Hale's belief that scientific research was of value to industry and that it was best conducted in universities free of government subsidies and of political influence. He thus accepted Hale's request in 1925 that he lead a campaign to solicit $20 million in large contributions from private corporations to endow a National Research Fund. Income from the fund was to be used to support academic research, with the NRC allocating the money to deserving scientists. Working with Hoover, who was by this time also a trustee of the Carnegie Institute of Washington, were fellow Carnegie trustee Elihu Root, the leaders of the NRC, prominent scientists, including Millikan and Hale, and representatives from AT&T and General Electric.

Hoover and the others failed to convince industry to contribute to the fund, largely because they could not guarantee that any one industrial concern that donated money would be the sole beneficiary of the research supported by the fund.[14] But industrial concerns did provide support for fellowships and for research of specific interest to them throughout the 1920s. Numerous wealthy individuals did as well. And during these years the major philanthropic foundations committed themselves to promoting the advancement of knowledge, chiefly in the physical and biological sciences, through research grants to the leading universities. Private donations to universities reached almost $82 million in 1923–1924 and peaked in 1929–1930 at over $148 million.[15] In comparison, support from the federal government remained exceedingly modest, restricted to small grants to the state universities for agricultural research.

The 1920s were thus marked by a huge philanthropic outpouring for academic science. The research universities did not share equally in the prosperity, however; just four universities—Harvard, Chicago, Columbia, and Yale—received one-quarter of the total support available from private foundations in these years.[16] Although not one of the greatest beneficiaries of postwar philanthropic largess, Stanford, too, enjoyed a significant share of the benefactions flowing to universities in the prosperous 1920s, due largely to the influence of Hoover, who by 1921 had embarked on a national political career as President Harding's secretary of commerce. Shortly after the war, Hoover met with Henry S. Pritchett, a trustee of the Carnegie Corporation, James R. Angell, the president of the corporation, and Elihu Root to spark their interest in supporting an institute at Stanford that would be devoted to research on economic issues related to food. In 1921 the Carnegie Corporation granted Stanford $700,000 for the establishment of a Food Research Institute, which was to be guided by an advisory committee headed by Hoover. Also in the early 1920s Hoover collected almost $500,000 from private sources to establish the Hoover Library to collect and organize material relating to his wartime Commission for the Relief of Belgium and, more broadly, to the recent war.[17]

Hoover also helped Stanford draw support from San Francisco businessmen in the early 1920s, convincing them of the importance of establishing on the West Coast a business school like the one at Harvard, which at that time was the only university-affiliated business school in the country. By 1925 businesses had pledged sufficient support for the school, and Stanford's trustees formally approved its establishment. And in 1927 Stanford, along with several universities, including Caltech and MIT, received a large grant from the Daniel Guggenheim Fund to promote research in aeronautical engineering.[18]

Hoover's efforts through the 1920s to establish and fund new institutes represented the commitment of both Hoover and President Wilbur to fostering research and specialized training at Stanford. At this time Hoover also insisted that the university begin charging tuition to permit an increase in the university's operating budget and enable Wilbur both to raise faculty salaries and to establish a small yet significant fund for faculty research. But the elaboration of research institutes separate from traditional university departments also reflected Hoover's disregard for the university's departmental structure and its tradition of departmental autonomy, both of which he viewed as impediments to efficient and rational organization. In 1915 Hoover had written a long letter to president-elect Wilbur complaining of Stanford's system of "faculty control." He encouraged Wilbur effectively to abolish the Academic Council, an organizational body of the university's faculty with "ultimate authority" over the internal policies of the university and to institute instead a clear chain of command that insured that the "best brains" within the university prevailed. Hoover also suggested that "exceptional" professors be identified and rewarded with salaries significantly above the norm.[19]

President Wilbur followed some of Hoover's suggestions. He organized departments into schools after the war and appointed deans, thus establishing an administrative structure intermediate between the president and department heads. (In 1925 Hoover's brother, Theodore, a specialist in illumination, was named dean of the School of Engineering.) Wilbur ignored Hoover's advice, however, when it involved challenges to the autonomy of academic departments and to the traditional powers of the faculty. He did not, for example, abolish the Academic Council, nor did he rely very much on the advice of his newly appointed deans.[20]

Wilbur also resisted Hoover's suggestions that he penalize those faculty members who expressed views contrary to those held by Hoover. In the mid-1920s Hoover had become particularly upset by an "outbreak of LaFolletism" on campus; some faculty members in the engineering and the economics departments had, it seems, voiced support for the public ownership of utilities. To Hoover these professors, "who are experts and *should* know the *truth*," were either being "deliberately untruthful" or else were "incompetent in *their* profession"; in either case, they did not belong in the university. Since President Wilbur's actions were restricted by "that well established form of blackmail on Universities called Academic Freedom," Hoover suggested that Wilbur might instead deny promotions and advancements to the faculty members in question.[21]

In this instance, Wilbur, as Stanford's president, found himself in the middle of a conflict between a trustee and some faculty members, the one interested in seeing Stanford represent his own interests and views, the others committed to unrestricted inquiry and to promoting their own views of the truth. This was a situation familiar to presidents of American universities, institutions with avowed commitments to free inquiry but controlled, ultimately, by wealthy industrialists or state legislators who were often less concerned with professors' desires for professional autonomy and academic freedom than with suppressing criticisms of their own interests and commitments. The well-known academic-freedom cases of the turn of the century—at the University of Wisconsin, Brown University, the University of Chicago, and Stanford—had illuminated this institutional contradiction and had also made clear that university presidents in fact served ultimately as the trustees' chief administrative officer. At Stanford, President Jordan had failed to withstand insistent pressure from founding trustee Jane Stanford to remove Edward Ross, an outspoken sociologist with socialist leanings, from the faculty in 1900.[22]

In subsequent years, the unmistakable conflicts revealed in incidents like the Ross case subsided not only because the incidents had been instructive to those tempted freely to voice their opinions but also because professors organized to press university presidents to recognize a commitment to academic freedom and establish a system of tenure. University presidents also helped mute tensions in the first decades of the century by permitting considerable professorial autonomy at the departmental level. Such autonomy, engendered largely by the growth and specialization of university faculties, left the hiring and supervision of faculty members in the hands of the individual university departments rather than in those of the president. The university president hired the departmental chairperson, but even here, the views of the department's members often carried weight.[23]

Wilbur supported this tradition of departmental autonomy throughout his tenure as Stanford's president and in doing so seems not to have damaged his personal relationship with Hoover or Hoover's reliance on Wilbur's professional assistance. Both men met regularly as members of an informal fishing club headed by Wilbur; both also belonged to the exclusive Caveman Camp of the Bohemian Grove, an influential private club north of San Francisco.[24] And in 1928 Herbert Hoover, as newly elected president of the United States, called Wilbur to Washington, D.C., to be the secretary of the interior.

The Depression and the New Deal

When Wilbur and Hoover returned to Stanford in March 1933, the prolonged economic depression, the reason for Hoover's defeat at the polls, had just begun seriously to affect America's leading universities. Students, themselves hurt by the economic collapse and unable to pay tuition, had failed to enroll in their usual numbers in the fall of 1932 at both public and private universities and colleges. State governments, seeking to meet increased demands for public relief and to balance budgets, substantially cut appropriations for their universities that same year. The University of California sustained a 15 percent reduction in appropriations; the University of Michigan, a crushing 44 percent cut. The private, endowed universities suffered smaller, yet still significant, losses of income as yields from invested endowment, a primary source for operating expenses, declined sharply. Harvard's 18 percent reduction in expendable income from investments was typical. At Stanford, income from investments fell $300,000, or about 20 percent.[25]

In early May 1933, two months after his return to campus, President

Wilbur reported gravely to the university's trustees that Stanford faced a financial emergency. Wilbur responded to the straitened circumstances as did the presidents of other research universities. Rather than lay off faculty members, he cut all salaries by 10 percent, delayed promotions indefinitely, left vacancies on the faculty unfilled, postponed improvements to plant and buildings, and reduced the university's small research budget.[26] With the trustees' approval, he also lifted the limit of five hundred that had been placed on the enrollment of women by Jane Stanford, hoping to take advantage of a "surplus of women" interested in attending college to increase income from tuition.[27]

Stanford and other private universities faced more than temporary financial problems in the 1930s, however. Roosevelt's New Deal and, more broadly, the political climate during the depression portended a change in the patterns of scientific and academic patronage that Hale, Hoover, and others had worked to establish after World War I. President Wilbur and the presidents of other private universities feared both a permanent decline in endowment income and private philanthropy, the traditional sources of support for the private universities, and the appearance of a new source of support—the federal government. These concerns, misplaced in many instances, were heightened at universities, such as Stanford, where the leadership was ideologically opposed to the New Deal.

The private universities typically depended for about half of their operating income on returns from invested endowment, and the inflation that occurred in the 1930s threatened the value of these investments. While Herbert Hoover railed publicly against Roosevelt's fiscal policies as ruinous to those dependent on investment income, university financial officers met and weighed their options. Schools were warned against spending endowment principle, although some, in desperate financial straits, had no other options. Others urged following the leads of Harvard and MIT—diversifying investments and buying common stocks, previously considered an unacceptable risk but now seen as a necessary hedge against inflation. Stanford took timid steps in this direction.[28]

Fearing that yields from endowments would continue to decline, university presidents and business officers all agreed on the need to intensify the search for philanthropic support. But their hopes of tapping excess private wealth seemed threatened by the political climate of the 1930s. Huey Long, the populist senator from Louisiana, had begun attracting national attention and a core of devoted supporters for his

Share the Wealth plan. In California in mid-1934, socialist author Upton Sinclair had won the Democratic gubernatorial nomination and was expected to win the race for governor against his conservative Republican opponent. Alarmed at the implications of Sinclair's EPIC (End Poverty In California) plan, California's conservatives, including Herbert Hoover, staged a massive propaganda campaign against Sinclair. They ensured his defeat but could not assure themselves that there would be no further challenges to the status quo.[29]

By June 1935, in response to pressure from his political left, President Roosevelt urged Congress to pass "soak-the-rich" tax legislation. He proposed sharply graduated corporate income taxes, higher rates on the incomes of the wealthiest, increased taxes on inherited wealth, and a gift tax.[30] To James R. Angell, president of Yale and former president of the Carnegie Corporation, the proposed taxes presented a "menace" to America's private universities. In fact, they were "potentially far more sinister" than anything the universities had yet experienced in the depression.[31] Although hardly radical in final form, the Revenue Act of 1935 did raise gift and inheritance taxes and further feed the fears of university presidents and financial officers that the result would be a decline in donations and bequests to their institutions.[32] By 1937 Thomas S. Gates, president of the University of Pennsylvania, warned his colleagues in the AAU that economic and social forces were "rapidly molding a new environment" that was hostile to the private university.[33]

The problem was not simply that inflation and taxation apparently threatened traditional sources of support for the private universities. Additionally, public universities were rebounding from their lowest point of economic insecurity to such an extent that by the mid-1930s enrollments in some were higher than they had been before the depression began. While the surge in enrollment reflected the lack of jobs for college-age students, it also showed the increased drawing power of the public universities, which offered an inexpensive education compared to the private schools. (Tuition at Stanford in the 1930s was about $115 per academic quarter, in comparison with roughly $25 per quarter at the neighboring University of California.) Also, many of the public universities had responded to the progressive political climate with an increased emphasis on adult and vocational education. Some schools, such as the University of Minnesota, had also reached out to nontraditional students by creating new curricula shaped to be relevant to their concerns and needs.[34]

In addition to rising enrollments, which brought income from tuition, federal funds for relief programs had eased pressure on the state budgets and permitted the restoration of earlier budgets for public higher education. Federal funds, administered through the Works Progress Administration, also provided support for a small but significant number of researchers at the state universities and for the construction of new buildings. And in 1935, Congress passed the Bankhead-Jones Act, which provided over $19 million to the land-grant colleges and experiment stations for agricultural research, effectively doubling the amount of federal money flowing to tax-supported institutions of higher education. Given the increasing support for and popularity of public higher education, as well as the likelihood of a continued decline in support for private universities, Gates concluded that the private universities faced a "grave dilemma."[35]

For President Wilbur and Stanford's trustees, Stanford's particular experiences seemed clearly to confirm the dilemma facing the private university during the depression. In 1932 Stanford's administration finally abandoned its campaign to raise several million dollars for Stanford, an effort that had gotten off to a slow start in the 1920s and that by the first years of the depression clearly stood no chance of success. This fund-raising failure meant the loss of $750,000 in matching funds pledged by the General Education Board of the Rockefeller Foundation to improve the sciences at Stanford and of $2.5 million in matching funds for the medical school. The significance of the loss was heightened by the realization that there seemed to be no possibility of raising funds from other sources in the 1930s.[36]

The efforts of individual faculty members to raise funds to support their research similarly met with little success in the 1930s. In 1935, for example, Stanford's physicists solicited support from the Carnegie Corporation and the Rockefeller Foundation, both generous patrons of academic science in the 1920s, seeking $100,000 to develop a powerful x-ray tube for explorations of the spectra of heavy elements. But during the depression, the foundations cut appropriations and made the medical and biological sciences their main concern. They refused the physics department's request for support, and, lacking funds, the physicists abandoned their project.[37]

The dearth of patronage was particularly worrisome when Stanford's faculty and administrators compared their institution to other universities that had developed private patronage for elaborate scientific equipment, which was setting a new standard of research in fields such as physics. For example, across the San Francisco Bay at the University of California at Berkeley, physicists led by Ernest O. Lawrence had successfully attracted both patronage and popular acclaim for Lawrence's cyclotron, an accelerator of atomic particles. Despite the depression, Lawrence, skilled in salesmanship as well as science, raised $275,000 from private foundations, individuals, and corporations for his laboratory in the 1930s and, at the end of the decade, a pledge of $1.15 million from the Rockefeller Foundation for the construction of yet another, bigger "atom smasher."[38] Stanford's physicists were twice offered equipment in the 1930s for a cyclotron, but both times they had reluctantly refused because they lacked the additional resources necessary for building and operating the machine.[39] The physicists' inability to enter the world of high-energy physics, or even to develop an organized, large-scale physics program in x-ray research that could attract patronage, relegated their department, as they recognized ruefully, to "a rather poor third" in comparison with the departments at Berkeley and Caltech.[40]

Other departments, and Stanford as a whole, were compared unfavorably with other public and private universities in the 1930s. In June 1935, the same month that Roosevelt had called on Congress to raise taxes, the *Atlantic Monthly* published an article ranking the leading universities in America. Stanford, to the dismay of its trustees, was not among the leading eleven institutions, a list that included four public universities. That Stanford was an active contestant for twelfth place, along with the University of Illinois, the University of Iowa, and Ohio State University, was small consolation.[41] The judgment that Stanford was on the decline was echoed throughout the decade, as some of the best departments in the university received warnings from former students, potential patrons, and colleagues at other universities. An alumnus well placed in the oil industry warned the geology department to expect no support from his industry; there was "general concurrence" among the oil companies that Stanford's program in geology was no longer first-rate. A dean at the University of Maryland expressed concern that the reputation of Stanford's biology program, once one of the best in the country, now lagged behind at least twenty other biology departments. Apologizing for his pessimism, he posited that Stanford was in danger of becoming a "third-rate institution in ten years."[42]

These warnings of imminent decline and the concomitant difficulty of attracting the funds needed to maintain, much less improve, the quality of the university created foreboding among Stanford administrators and trustees in the 1930s about the fate of their institution. As the general secretary of the university admitted to an alumnus in 1937, Stanford had "a problem of first magnitude."[43] To President Wilbur and the trustees, Stanford's problem was merely an extreme version of the dilemmas facing all private universities during Roosevelt's administration. Their own institutional difficulties confirmed their negative estimation of the New Deal.

Wilbur's pessimism about the fate of Stanford, about the private universities in general, and about the New Deal were exacerbated by signs that the federal government might take an interest in institutions of higher education, private as well as public. Most upsetting to Wilbur were hints that the federal government might provide financial support to the private universities. To Wilbur, higher taxes coupled with offers of governmental support represented Roosevelt's method of forcing the private universities into the "arms of the government," part of his larger plan for eliminating the private sphere.[44] Other less conspiratorially minded university presidents shared Wilbur's fears that the private universities, which were in serious economic trouble, would turn to the federal government for assistance and thus provide the opening wedge for governmental involvement in, and perhaps control of, private higher education.

Wilbur's worry that private universities would accept federal funds was not unfounded. In May 1933, the same month that Wilbur declared a financial emergency at Stanford, President Roosevelt had announced the first of the New Deal's relief programs, the Federal Emergency Relief Administration (FERA), which was authorized by Congress to spend $500 million in grants to states. In response to a request by Minnesota's State Emergency Relief Administration, the FERA had approved the use of federal funds to subsidize needy college students. In February 1934 the program was extended to public and private colleges and universities in every state, and by the 1934–35 school year, over 1,450 schools were receiving collectively $11.5 million in federal money to support a total of 100,000 students with part-time work.[45]

Over 130 private institutions rejected federal aid, however, including the nation's wealthiest and most prestigious universities, Harvard and Yale. In refusing federal support, President Angell of Yale and President James B. Conant of Harvard set an example: private institutions, if they were truly "private," were free of all possible political influence; thus, they did not accept governmental support, even on a temporary, "emergency" basis. But despite this example and his own anti–New Deal sentiments, Wilbur, like the presidents of most other public and private universities facing serious reductions in income, had begun accepting federal relief funds for the support of needy Stanford students as soon as the money had been made available. In the spring of 1934 Stanford received almost $14,000 in federal funds through California's State Emergency Relief Administration for the support of three hundred needy students. In the 1934–35 school year, four hundred students (about 12 percent of Stanford's student body) were on federally financed work relief.[46]

Wilbur's own inability to refuse federal support no doubt contributed to his anxiety about the motives of the federal government with respect to private institutions of higher education. Other developments fed his unease. Under Roosevelt's administration, the Office of Education, located in Harold Ickes' Department of the Interior, had doubled in size, declared a commitment to progressive educational ideals, and expanded the collection of statistics on higher education while also seeking to standardize the data to facilitate national comparisons. Administrators at many private universities and colleges, including Stanford, regarded the data-gathering as intrusive and aimed at centralizing control of higher education, and they participated reluctantly or not at all. To one of several requests from the Office of Education for statistics on the costs of education at Stanford, Wilbur angrily advised Stanford's comptroller not to comply. "We are in no way seeking standardization. . . . We want Stanford to go on about its own affairs in its own way. I hope that no effort will be made to help out in these studies."[47]

Much more worrisome than the activities of the Office of Education or the emergency assistance provided by FERA were the efforts of some in Congress in the late 1930s to legislate further increases in federal support for university-based research. In 1937 Congress created the National Cancer Institute as a branch of the National Institutes of Health (NIH); unlike the NIH, which did all research in-house, the Cancer Institute was authorized to award research grants to academic scientists. Also that year, Congress began considering a bill, backed by Karl Compton, president of MIT and one of the younger, less stodgy members of the conservative National Research Council, to allocate funds for research to the Bureau of Standards. The bureau, with the advice of the NRC, was to use some of these funds to provide grants for research to scientists in both the public and private universities.

To Compton, the proposed legislation (which did not pass) maintained the essential tradition of the NRC. The support for academic science would be distributed to the scientists whose work, in the opinion of the leaders of the scientific community, most deserved it; the funds would not, as members of Congress often advocated, be distributed on a state-by-state basis or to public universities alone. That the source of funds in this case was the federal government did not particularly worry Compton. He was already familiar with agencies of the federal government, having formulated a plan in 1933 for a board of experts to advise the federal government on important areas of scientific research. Compton's willingness to seek federal patronage may have reflected his position as president of a technological institute that was well acquainted with industrial patronage and comfortable with an institutional emphasis on practical, rather than "pure," research. Compton's goal was to ensure that the funds, whatever the source, were distributed in a manner that conformed to the needs and interests of his institution. In this case, his own organization, the NRC, would help determine who received federal support.[48]

But to Wilbur, Compton's willingness to court federal patronage was worrisome; it represented a break with tradition that portended serious consequences for the private university. As president of the AAU in 1937, Wilbur set the agenda for the annual November meeting—a discussion of the relationship between the federal government and institutions of higher education. University representatives at this and subsequent AAU meetings agreed with Wilbur that, at a minimum, federal support posed problems. Robert Millikan, president of Caltech and a senior member of the NRC, and Harold Dodds, a social scientist and president of Princeton, were among those who believed that federal patronage threatened the very nature of the private university. As Dodds explained, the private universities differed fundamentally from the public universities because they did not accept taxpayer support. Free of governmental patronage, the private universities were insulated from political forces that might try to regulate admissions standards, influence the curriculum, and direct the work of academic scholars and scientists. From this perspective, the private universities were the only true havens where scholars and scientists could search for and pass on "truths"; they were, essentially, the proverbial ivory towers, remote from the pressures of democratic society. Thus in seeking or accepting federal support, the private universities threatened their very purpose. "Let us be sure not to barter [our freedom] away to any external control in a moment of fright," Dodds concluded with dramatic flourish at a subsequent AAU meeting.[49]

This elitism evoked objections from at least one public-university president, who suggested that the private university was no freer than the public university but was just controlled by private patrons rather than by a state legislature.[50] Others, including Charles Seymour, president of Yale (who had succeeded Angell in 1937), and James Conant of Harvard, questioned whether, given the growing importance of the public universities, whose charters included the aim of serving society, the private universities could afford any longer the pose of remoteness from society that Dodds had affirmed. As Seymour warned, "[I]solation from the life and the needs of the nation spells sure death" for the private institutions. But Seymour's suggestions for bringing the private universities to the service of the nation were, in fact, merely rephrased affirmations of the traditional aims of these universities. He stressed, for example, that the private university provided its greatest service to society by preserving the ideals of scholarship and imparting to students habits of thought and culture rather than technical skills. The private universities could "render no greater service to the commonwealth," Seymour advised, than by remembering that "their first duty should be faithfully to mind their business."[51]

Few representatives of either the private or the public universities demurred to Dodds's harsh judgment of federal patronage.[52] In various forums in the 1930s, many representatives of the public universities receiving federal patronage for agricultural research, including the progressive Lotus Coffman, president of the University of Minnesota, expressed dissatisfaction with federal patronage and urged that it not be viewed as an alternative to state or private support. Federal support, these university administrators complained, was more restrictive than state support; it also involved excessive red tape, made the universities subject to "long distance management," in the words of the comptroller for the University of Wisconsin, and skewed research away from problems of local significance toward problems defined by the federal government.[53] The experiences of the public universities no doubt heightened the concerns of the leaders of the private universities, such as President Wilbur, about the dangers inherent in federal patronage.

For James Conant, the real problem was not the availability of federal patronage for academic science, which the private universities could simply refuse, as Harvard had done, but rather the ebbing of alternative sources of support. As he had explained before the 1937 meeting to Wilbur, who had written of his fear that the federal government was bent on destroying the private universities, "[I]f and when private institutions pass under government control," it would be "because they were forced there as a result of their begging policy for money."[54] With private philanthropy seemingly endangered by the New Deal and with governmental patronage an unpalatable alternative for many, Conant suggested that the universities reconsider their relationships with private industry. This would mean emphasizing "rather more direct connections between discovery and use than we have cared to advocate in the past," Conant acknowledged. But this new emphasis would supplement, not replace, the tradition of pure research and would be instrumental in attracting industrial patronage to the university.[55]

Ideology and Industrial Patronage

Conant's call in 1937 for a "thoroughgoing renovation" of the relationship between private industry and the university and for the "wider deployment of the philosophy of utility" resonated deeply with Stanford's president and trustees and reinforced conclusions that they were already drawing themselves. Industrial support seemed to offer a solution to their need for funds to support the research that was essential for maintaining Stanford's reputation as a research university. Moreover, industrial support was ideologically appealing to Hoover and Wilbur who already viewed private industry as an ally against the political forces that they believed were pushing the nation toward a statist, planned economy.

Traditionally, industrial support and the philosophy of utility had been held at arm's length by the nation's leading private universities. Many academic scientists and university presidents, including Conant's predecessor, A. Lawrence Lowell, viewed applied research as sullied by material concerns. Its proper place was a technical institute such as MIT, not a university such as Harvard. Stories of the unhappy experiences of some MIT scientists confirmed this view. The noted chemist A. A. Noyes, for example, left MIT in the early 1920s, deeply frustrated with the emphasis there on applied work and service to industry. Perhaps for this reason, Conant, a chemistry professor at Harvard before becoming the university's president, drew back from the full implications of his call in 1937 for rethinking the industry-university relationship. He merely suggested resurrecting the National Research Fund, which had failed in its earlier attempt to garner donations for research from industrial firms.[56]

A significant number of Stanford's faculty members were similarly suspicious of involvement in industrially sponsored research. Stanford's aeronautical engineers, for example, had a long-standing policy of refusing "commercial work." Although Caltech's aeronautical engineers had proved that undertaking testing work in return for fees from aeronautics firms could be lucrative (industrial funds supported graduate students who conducted the tests), the engineers at Stanford rejected such work as tedious and routine, acceptable practice for a technical institute, perhaps, but a misuse of the talents of Stanford's aeronautics specialists and a distraction from their own research interests.[57] Others at Stanford were also wary of industrial patronage. According to Donald Tresidder, who succeeded Wilbur as president of Stanford in 1943, "[C]onsiderable numbers of faculty to date are unwilling to see any possibilities in the field [of industrial patronage]; others actively oppose any efforts to interest industry."[58]

But a few members of Stanford's faculty were receptive to soliciting industrial patronage, including Robert Swain, chair of the chemistry department, and Frederick Terman, chair of the electrical engineering department, both of whom were favorites of the administration. Academic chemists and electrical engineers had long, if not always happy, traditions of service to industry. Rather than shun industrial patronage, Swain and Terman were interested in encouraging support from industry according to modes that did not conflict with the interests of academic scientists and engineers.

Swain, a close friend of Hoover who had served as acting president of Stanford during the years that Wilbur was in Washington, began planning with Hoover in the late 1930s to create an institute for industrial research. (The Stanford Research Institute, or SRI, would be founded in 1946.) Swain and Hoover may have had in mind as a model the Armour Research Foundation, which had been established in the mid-1930s as part of an agreement between Chicago businessmen and the Illinois Institute of Technology. To Swain, such an institute would allow the university to take advantage of industrial patronage while separating the sponsored research from the academic research within university departments. In this way, Stanford could avoid the conflicts that had characterized MIT's chemistry department in the 1920s, when direct industrial support for departmental research had led to interference in professors' choice of research problems as well as to restrictions on publishing.[59]

Terman, too, wanted to bring industrial support to Stanford. His interest in developing relations with industry was largely driven by his desire to build the reputation of his department and make it competitive with the leading departments in the country at Caltech and MIT. After careful study of his rivals in 1937, Terman concluded that industrial contacts were the key to their reputations. Fellowships provided by industrial firms enabled both MIT and Caltech to attract the best available students, whose subsequent successful careers in industry helped establish the significance and influence of the departments that had trained them. Contacts with private companies might also lead to research support and to information about issues of interest to industry, both of which were necessary for training students for eventual employment. While acknowledging that some at Stanford "might wish to make fun of the Institute's [Caltech's] set-up," Terman clearly hoped to develop similar relationships between private industry and his department at Stanford.[60]

Terman thus became an adroit and indefatigable developer of industrial contracts in the late 1930s, seeking fellowships, research support, and access to useful information but with mixed success. For example, to attract a fellowship from the Gilfillan company, Terman used pictures and information about the company's radios when he revised his widely used textbook, *Radio Engineering,* in 1937. The stratagem failed, however; times were bad for the radio business and Gilfillan could not afford to donate money to the university. Terman got a similar response from the electrical manufacturing companies he solicited in the late 1930s. Terman offered five businesses first use of an impulse generator he was building in return for lump-sum payments of $500 from each company. But only two of the five companies agreed to participate, and only one of the two offered the full $500.[61]

The university's most extensive experience with industry in the 1930s developed in response to the invention by members of Stanford's physics department of a patentable microwave tube, the *klystron.* The inventors—William Hansen, an assistant professor of physics and friend of Terman; Russell and Sigurd Varian, unpaid researchers in the department (who in later years would found a successful Silicon Valley company); and David Locke Webster, chair of the department—knew that the klystron might be used to develop a blind-landing device for airplanes. This was a matter of great interest to Sigurd Varian, a commercial airline pilot familiar with the dangers of flying at night and in bad weather, and to Webster, a pilot in World War I, who was convinced that a second world war was likely.[62] Although the impetus for seeking patronage to support the development of the klystron first came from the physicists, Stanford's administration was quick to exploit the situation. Largely in response to the invention, Stanford's president and the board of trustees established a policy at the end of 1937 that gave the university ownership of all patents emanating from research conducted at Stanford, clearly hoping to generate income for the university from the licensing of the klystron patent. This practice was frowned upon by many in the academic world as inappropriate and crass, but it was one that had been validated for others by the University of Wisconsin's successful exploitation of patents in the 1930s. By the late 1930s, while other universities were still experiencing financial difficulties, Wisconsin was receiving about $160,000 annually in royalties.[63]

News of the klystron attracted the interest of the Sperry Gyroscope Company, an East Coast manufacturer of searchlight equipment interested in being the sole promoter of a device that in other hands might pose a threat to their business. Early in 1938 Stanford and Sperry agreed to a contract that committed Sperry to pay royalties to the university (which in turn would pay a percentage of the royalties to the klystron's inventors) and to donate $20,000 per year (a substantial amount at that time) to the physics department for research related to developing the klystron. In return, Stanford agreed to make available the physics department's laboratory and two of its physicists—Hansen and Webster. As the owner of the patent, the university also granted Sperry an exclusive license to make, use, and sell the klystron and promised to seek Sperry's approval before allowing the physicists to publish any of their research.[64]

The arrangement pleased Stanford's administration. Sperry had agreed to handle all litigation relating to patent infringements for the university, which was too strapped for funds to hire its own patent attorney. Additionally, the university stood to earn significant royalty payments. By the early 1940s, Stanford had earned almost $30,000 in royalties, an amount roughly equal to the salaries of five full professors at that time.[65]

But for Stanford's physicists, the arrangement with Sperry soon raised troubling issues. The initial decision to accept industrial patronage had been controversial. Hansen, the department's youngest member, was the only physicist at Stanford with few reservations. Like his contemporary and friend, Frederick Terman, Hansen was ambitious and eager to establish his reputation. He was extremely proud of his "inventive ability," which he believed his department chairperson did not properly appreciate, and of his versatility as a physicist. In preparation for asking President Wilbur for a raise, Hansen enumerated his talents in a memo to himself, concluding half-jokingly, "And now I think I'll go buy a hat. On second thought, maybe I won't. They don't make 'em big enough." Hansen was thus delighted with the funds from Sperry and the prospect that the Varian-Hansen invention was going to be "exploited to the limit." He worried only about Stanford's agreement with Sperry to restrict the physicists' publishing activities; without publications, he might have difficulty advancing his career.[66]

But others expressed greater wariness. The theoretician Felix Bloch, a refugee from European fascism, doubted the wisdom of the proposed "entanglements with Big Business." Another member of the department who, like Bloch, was not involved in the klystron research worried that the motives behind the klystron research were commercial rather than intellectual ones.[67] Webster, who had made theoretical contributions to the klystron work but had declined his share of the royalties, also expressed serious reservations about the plan to conduct research under Sperry's sponsorship. To Webster, who had obtained his Ph.D. from Harvard in the 1910s, the goal of the academic physicist was to uncover new laws of nature, not to apply already discovered laws with commercial ends in mind. But as the head of the department, Webster was also concerned about his department's low morale after years of comparatively meager research support and difficulty attracting good students (who chose to study at the better funded, more prestigious departments at Caltech and Berkeley). The arrangement with Sperry seemed to promise the opportunity to do research with generous financial support on a topic of interest to some of the physicists and the hope of making a name for the department. Still, Webster worried that the proposed shift from basic to applied research and the restrictions on sharing information, if viewed outside the context of the constraints faced by his department in the 1930s, might diminish rather than enhance both the department's reputation and the careers of its members. He thus insisted that President Wilbur acknowledge in writing that his and subsequent administrations would not penalize the physicists with respect to promotions and raises for embarking on a course of applied research in the late 1930s and thus contributing little to the advancement of pure physics.[68]

The perceived hazards of engaging in research under industrial sponsorship were not so easily averted, however. The physicists first ran into trouble with Stanford's comptroller, who in early 1938 began seeking to change the agreement with Sperry in an effort to reduce the percentage of the royalties that the university had promised the Varians, who were not Stanford employees.[69] While Webster intervened successfully on the Varians' behalf, the physicists soon became embroiled in conflicts with their corporate sponsor. Throughout the eighteen months that Sperry sponsored work on the klystron (withdrawing support at the end of 1940 to concentrate on war-related research at its Long Island laboratory), the physicists and the company clashed continually over who should control the physics laboratory and who should direct the work on the klystron: the company, which was funding the work, or the physicists, the experts without whom the work could not proceed.

Trouble began almost immediately when Sperry's director of research, Hugh Willis, sent three engineers to work in the physics laboratory at Stanford. As part of the agreement between Sperry and Stanford, the company had promised to provide the physicists with research assistance. But Webster had not anticipated having no say in the choice of staff. Both he and Russell Varian agreed that the Sperry engineers were "nearly useless because of a lack of research instinct."[70] But equally troubling to Webster was Willis's presumptuousness. Willis was not a member of the physics department or the university; he thus had "no authority to appoint any men to our staff," Webster fumed privately. He did not, however, challenge Sperry's action, noting during another clash with the company, that "it is the Sperry company's money that pays for the research."[71]

The physicists were soon embroiled in other disagreements with Willis. Sperry had a large financial stake in the klystron and the desire to develop it quickly, before Sperry's competitors, General Electric and Westinghouse, entered the field. Thus, Willis was eager to change both the pace of work in the physics department and to influence the direction of the physicists' research. Hansen, in particular, was interested in studying and experimenting with alternative designs of the klystron and other microwave devices and was thus especially disturbed when Sperry's representatives directed the physicists to pursue the design that promised the speediest development. In this case, too, Webster accepted Sperry's demands and prodded Hansen to do as Sperry wished: "Whatever may be said about the loss of academic freedom in the choice of research jobs . . . we do not want this industrialization to go so far as the introduction of any time-clocks," he warned.[72] Sperry's eagerness to put a model of the klystron into production produced other conflicts between the physicists and the company. In mid-1939 Willis directed an engineer from Sperry to initiate the production of klystrons in the physics laboratory at Stanford. Webster, who did not challenge the company's interest in engineering work, did object to Willis's effort to put a portion of the physics department's facilities under the control of a Sperry engineer.[73]

Long and heated negotiations between the physicists and Sperry's president and director of research eventually produced a truce between the company and the physicists, but it was short-lived. In late 1939 Sperry directed Stanford's physicists to forgo research on the development of the klystron and instead to think up patentable variations on the klystron in order to strengthen Sperry's patent position. For Webster, that directive was the company's final affront. He regarded the work as demeaning and saw it as serving no purpose other than to help Sperry make money. Even Hansen, who, unlike Webster, stood to earn royalties from klystron sales, was aggravated and suggested that the physicists appeal to Stanford's president for support. But he rejected the idea as quickly as it occurred to him. "If [Wilbur's] reaction is as expected," Hansen wrote, "I expect he will say—do the work. . . . [M]y guess is that the president would find a way of doing most anything that would bring in money."[74]

Hansen's judgment was unduly cynical, perhaps, but it accurately reflected the disparity between the views of Stanford's administration and those of the physicists with respect to industrial patronage. To Stanford's administration, the arrangement with Sperry meant much-needed funds from an ideologically acceptable source. For those physicists who were willing to consider working under industrial sponsorship, Sperry's support proved problematical. At best, it had meant sacrificing, at least temporarily, professional independence in return for uncertain future gain. This was the view of Hansen. He had found working under Sperry's sponsorship to be restrictive but he had a material stake in the klystron and, equally important, had already expressed disdain for university traditions that seemed to inhibit the advancement of his career. As mobilization for war began, Hansen, along with Russell Varian, left Stanford for Sperry's Long Island laboratory to pursue military applications of the klystron.

For Webster, however, the sacrifice involved in working under industrial sponsorship had proved too great. Sperry had challenged both his sense of the proper role of an academic physicist and his authority as the chairperson of a university department to determine who worked in the department's laboratory and what kind of work was done there.

Thus in late 1939 Webster quit as director of the klystron research, explaining to President Wilbur that he was suffering from eye problems but noting privately that "science and patents don't mix any more than oil and water."[75] He had concluded that in accepting patronage from industry, or more generally, engaging in research of a commercial nature, the academic scientist placed professional autonomy at unacceptable risk.

In the 1930s most of Stanford's faculty members would have agreed in large measure with Webster's views. Yet industrial patronage and research of commercial value were of growing interest to Stanford's administrators, who, along with some faculty members, had become deeply concerned about their university's flagging reputation as a research institution. To Wilbur and Hoover, support from industry was preferable to funds from the federal government. These concerns—Stanford's academic reputation, research support, and faculty autonomy—were first raised in the 1930s but would emerge again, amplified, in the next decade.

Even before Webster had left the klystron project, Stanford University had begun accepting funds for research from the federal government. Financial need and ideological opposition to New Deal policies remained unchanged. But by 1939 the political climate was shifting in ways that affected both how the federal government offered funds to institutions of higher education and why conservative administrators like President Wilbur did not hesitate to accept them.

2

Stanford Goes to War

By 1939 President Roosevelt had begun shifting his attention from his plans for domestic reform to the disturbing portents of war in Europe. After the German invasion of Poland that September, he began seriously contemplating how to move Congress and the nation, overwhelmingly in favor of neutrality, toward mobilization for war. Among those who shared Roosevelt's view that American involvement in the war was necessary, if not inevitable, was Vannevar Bush, the president of the Carnegie Institute of Washington and the head of the National Advisory Committee on Aeronautics (NACA), a federal agency providing technical advice to the nation's air forces.

Bush and Roosevelt shared little beyond agreement on the urgency of modernizing and rebuilding the nation's air forces. Bush was a conservative Republican and an acquaintance and admirer of Herbert Hoover (who was a Carnegie Institute trustee). An engineer by training and for years an administrator at MIT, Bush shared Hoover's deep faith in the idea of the expert, highly trained and disinterested, guiding and shaping technological solutions to the nation's problems. In Bush's view, Roosevelt's New Deal had been an affront both to the idea of the apolitical expert and to free enterprise. But ideology mattered less to Roosevelt than Bush's interest in mobilizing scientific resources for war. In mid-1940, after the German army had conquered most of western Europe and forced the British off the continent, Roosevelt authorized Bush to organize and sponsor both academic and industrial research for national defense. "Dr. New Deal" was indeed giving way to "Dr. Win-the-War."

The mobilization of the scientific community, and most notably of physicists, resulted in the development of technologies—radar, the atomic bomb—of consequence for the war and postwar years; it led, too, to changes in the relationship between academic scientists and the federal government.[1] But the universities, as well as their scientists, were mobilized for war, and university administrators as well as professors became accustomed to dealing with a new patron—the federal government. Much of the research sponsored by the agencies headed by Bush—the National Defense Research Council (NDRC) and, later, the Office of Scientific Research and Development (OSRD)—was conducted on university campuses, and universities administered most of the major wartime laboratories. By the war's end, the OSRD had expended over $325 million in support for research in American universities, a sum unimaginable half a decade earlier.[2]

Federal patronage, shunned at least rhetorically during the New Deal, was accepted with alacrity by administrators at Stanford and other universities. Concerns for the fate of the nation certainly played a role in reversing the view that the proper relationship between the universities, particularly the private ones, and the Roosevelt administration was a distant one. But this reversal was not dictated solely by patriotic sentiment, nor did it signal an embrace of the idea of an activist state.[3] Concerns for the nation's defense, however real, mixed easily with concerns for the fate of institutions of higher education. The financial dilemmas of the 1930s persisted and took new forms as the federal government began mobilizing the political economy for war. At Stanford, accepting support from the federal government, beginning in 1939, was first an institutional necessity and then a patriotic duty.

Similarly, the political ideology espoused by Hoover and other conservative university administrators was not abandoned as the federal government mobilized the economy for war. Rather, Stanford's administrators carried into the war years their opposition to the New Deal and the view that federal patronage potentially threatened the autonomy of American universities. So did Vannevar Bush. As head of the NACA and then of the NDRC and of the OSRD, Bush included in the policies and practices of his agencies special consideration for the interests—financial and ideological—of the leaders of the nation's universities. Both the use of the contract to mediate the relationship between the federal government and universities and the OSRD's policies concerning the reimbursement of universities' indirect, or overhead, costs were intended to protect those interests.

Financial Need

While federal support for academic science became available in the context of preparations for war, financial need first prompted Stanford faculty members to embark upon a program of research sponsored by the federal government. In 1939 the university's aeronautical engineering program, rated as one of the top three in the country by the American Council on Education, was bankrupt, having exhausted the generous grant from the Daniel Guggenheim Fund, which for twelve years had covered the salaries of the engineers and the expenses of operating a wind tunnel. With the university's general budget still tightly constrained, President Wilbur could promise no assistance to the aeronautical engineers beyond putting them in touch with the university's volunteer fund-raisers. In May 1939 Everett P. Lesley, Stanford's senior aeronautical engineer, wrote to Harry F. Guggenheim, the son of Daniel Guggenheim as well as a friend of Hoover (he had been Hoover's ambassador to Cuba) that the future of aeronautics at Stanford had become "problematical."[4]

Lesley was seeking a gift from Guggenheim, as he had begun seeking gifts from other wealthy individuals, including a Stanford trustee who was an amateur pilot. But Guggenheim's response, like the others, was prompt and disappointing. Stanford was only one of many universities finding it difficult to maintain its aeronautics program, he wrote. With private funding elusive, the only hope was support from the federal government. Germany had subsidized academic research in aeronautics with impressive results, Guggenheim noted.[5]

Federal support for aeronautical research had indeed become a possibility by 1939. Concerned about the military buildup in Germany, the NACA had already begun advocating military preparedness. Under Bush the agency proposed to sponsor research in educational institutions, the most economical and efficient way, in Bush's view, to expand quickly the nation's supply of the aeronautical engineering experts who he believed should guide the modernization of the air forces. With Roosevelt's backing, Bush approached Congress in early 1939 for an increase of $500,000 in his agency's budget. Although a suspicious Congress rejected his request, Bush persisted, giving Guggenheim and others hope that federal support for sponsored research would be available within the year. (By the end of 1939, through manipulations of his own budget, Bush had found $50,000 for academic research.)[6]

In light of these developments, in mid-1939 Stanford's dean of engineering, Samuel Morris, presented President Wilbur with the available options. The engineers had failed to attract private support, and Wilbur might thus choose to disband the entire aeronautics program. But Morris warned that doing so would be "a serious set-back" at a crucial time for Stanford's reputation in engineering and, more generally, for the university. Alternatively, the aeronautical engineers could seek federal support from the NACA. These were stark choices for Wilbur, who had long feared that financial problems would drive Stanford into dependence on the federal government but who also worried that Stanford's academic reputation had begun to slide dramatically. In weighing the alternatives, institutional need took precedence over principle, as it had when Wilbur accepted funds from FERA during the depression. Rather than endorse federal patronage directly, however, Wilbur took the notion of departmental autonomy to its logical extreme and informed the aeronautical engineers that their program would have to begin to "pay its own way" with whatever support was available. In late 1939 the engineers began negotiating a contract with the NACA for research on propellers, the department's area of expertise. At the engineers' insistence, the contract for over $10,000 included not just the costs of the research but also the salaries of the department's professors and secretaries.[7]

The hazards of depending on outside support quickly became clear to the engineers. Without warning, the NACA, facing its own budgetary dilemmas, reduced the size of the Stanford contract by one-third, leaving the aeronautical engineering department with salary obligations it could not fulfill. Still short of the funds necessary to keep the department in operation, the aeronautical engineers lifted their earlier, self-imposed prohibition against doing commercial testing work for fees. They had, in the words of one, been forced into "taking in washing" to support themselves. If conducting testing work was disagreeable, the aeronautical engineers also found working under NACA's sponsorship trying. The aeronautical engineers disagreed with the NACA over who should determine the research agenda, and despite assertions that they were the experts on airplane propellers, the aeronautical engineers' views were overridden by the wishes of the NACA.[8] The NACA was, after all, paying the bill, a constraining situation that Stanford's physicists working under industrial sponsorship understood well.

For Stanford's administrators, however, accepting support for academic research proved less troubling than they had imagined it would be. Although a division of the university had become dependent on federal support, the funds were being proffered by an agency that Wilbur and Hoover viewed as benign in comparison with, for example, a cabinet department in the Roosevelt administration. In fact, the NACA was generally esteemed by the academic community. Established during World War I, the agency embodied ideas similar to those of the NRC about the proper relationship between the scientific community and the federal government. It was headed not by bureaucrats or political appointees but by academic "experts." At one time, one of Stanford's own engineers, William Durand, had served on the NACA, and Elliott Reid, an expert in aerodynamics, had worked at the agency's Langley Field laboratory before coming to Stanford. Stanford's aeronautical engineers kept in close touch with the NACA, often encouraging students to write directly to the agency's director of research for suggestions for thesis topics. Moreover, Stanford's engineers had accepted small contracts for research on propellers from the NACA since the 1920s; however, these contracts had not been used to pay the engineers' salaries, nor had graduate students been involved in the research.[9]

Becoming dependent on support from the NACA represented a change in Stanford's relationship with the agency, but it was not a change that seemed to trouble Wilbur or Hoover greatly. Not only were they familiar with the NACA, but they also held NACA director Vannevar Bush in high esteem. Bush, they knew, was opposed to an activist state and supportive of private enterprise and private institutions. Moreover, rather than distribute grants to selected facilities or institutions, which Bush and others on the NACA briefly considered in 1939, the members of the NACA had decided to offer research funds through contracts with individual researchers. To those such as Wilbur, who worried that governmental support for private institutions represented an encroachment by the state, the contract was a reassuring symbol of the marketplace. It suggested, in form if not in fact, that the university was not a supplicant to the government but that the parties involved had reached a mutual agreement.[10]

Even more significant, the NACA's charter allowed it to offer contracts for research unhampered by requirements that it distribute funds equally between institutions or that it solicit competitive bids. Contracts could thus be negotiated by representatives from the NACA and Stanford who were already professionally and sometimes personally acquainted, far removed from the political arena where issues of fairness or conflict of interest might be raised. As a Stanford engineer, Arthur Domonoske, explained simply, the university appreciated contracts with the NACA because they involved "no political complications." (The engineers, Domonoske suggested, preferred a grant or "direct subsidy," which meant to them both "steady support" and protection from interference in their work.)[11]

The sponsored research for the NACA also proved unexpectedly lucrative for the university. By mid-1940, Stanford's administration had collected payments from the NACA that exceeded the aeronautical engineers' expenses by almost $4,000. Together with the excess from the engineers' industrial contracts, the university's comptroller had set aside over $7,000, deemed "profits," in a separate university account.[12] It is unclear who was allowed to draw on these funds or how administrators envisioned using them. What *is* clear is that, in addition to meeting the desires of Stanford's administrators for insulation from a politics of egalitarianism, contracts with the NACA also provided financial benefits. Thus, while Stanford's administrators might have preferred private patronage, by the 1940s they had begun to depend upon a particular kind of federal patronage that they found both acceptable and profitable.

While the NACA provided funds for academic research in a way that appeased university administrators and assured them that they were not accepting a handout, the agency's aim was the expansion and improvement of the nation's military capabilities. This goal had not motivated the initial search for federal patronage at Stanford, but it was one that Stanford's administrators and aeronautical engineers were aware of and supported. The administrators could believe that they were not taking a handout from the federal government and at the same time recognize that their university was contributing to the nation's military defense. The engineers, while dependent on the funds for their livelihood, could accept support from the NACA, as well as the less-than-ideal working conditions, realizing that they were, in the words of one, aiding the nation to "regain aeronautical supremacy."[13]

Thus, Stanford's institutional needs quickly became connected to and intertwined with national concerns through participation in the research sponsored by the NACA. And because the NACA was esteemed by the academic community, despite its status as a federal agency, institutional prestige conjoined with financial need and national concerns to form the complex of motives that impelled university administrators and their faculty members to accept federal patronage. This interweaving of concerns for the fate of the nation and for the fate of institutions of higher education prevailed at other universities as well. According to a survey of schools in the western United States conducted in the spring of 1940 by the NACA's coordinator of research, almost every school wanted research support from the NACA, "both from a prestige standpoint and also in order to help support their faculties and extend their equipment." [14]

World War II and the Search for Federal Contracts

By mid-1940 institutional needs and concerns had become more deeply bound up with impulses toward service to the nation as university administrators at Stanford and elsewhere recognized that Roosevelt was not merely preparing the nation defensively but was also preparing for war. In June of that year, Roosevelt authorized Bush to mobilize the nation's scientific resources. That same month, he appointed Henry Stimson, in favor of intervention in the war in Europe, as secretary of war, replacing the isolationist Harry Woodring. With Roosevelt's encouragement, Stimson mounted a campaign for a peacetime draft.

These developments were troubling to Wilbur and the presidents of other universities. However necessary for national defense, they meant upheaval for the nation's universities, many of which were just beginning to operate normally after years of financial stringency. (In 1940 Wilbur had finally succeeded in raising salaries at Stanford to their pre-1933 level.) Wilbur, who had been president of Stanford during the First World War, knew well that mobilization would draw academic scientists into wartime service, leaving the campuses bereft of teachers. Further, the university would lose substantial tuition income as students became subject to a draft. Writing to the president of the American Council on Education in July 1940, Wilbur worried about the fate of the nation's educational institutions and urged that action be taken to prevent them from being "interfered with or mutilated" by the mobilization for war. With the help of the council, Wilbur and other university and college presidents began lobbying Washington for draft deferments for college students. [15]

Wilbur's concern that academic scientists would soon be drawn away from campus to centrally located laboratories run by the federal government was allayed, however, by the policies of the NDRC. Bush and the others on the council—James Conant, Karl Compton, and Frank Jewett, president of the National Academy of Sciences—had taken into account the needs and concerns of university administrators as well as the traditions favored by the conservative leaders of the scientific and political establishments when they had shaped their agency's policies. The NDRC, it was decided, would not centralize war research in laboratories under governmental control but would instead follow the practice of the NACA and place contracts for research with individual scientists and their universities.[16]

This practice was meant to appeal to university presidents, as was the NDRC's policy regarding the payments for the costs incurred by the NDRC's academic contractors. As had the NACA, the NDRC reimbursed universities for the direct costs of research and for the universities' indirect expenses. But the members of the NDRC determined to depart from the way the NACA had calculated and reimbursed overhead costs, both broadening the definition of overhead and abandoning the NACA's policy of itemizing the expenses. In Bush's view, overhead needed to include such costs as depreciation on buildings and equipment and general administrative expenses—costs that, while real, were difficult to calculate with precision. Bush thus decided that universities would be reimbursed for their indirect expenses at a flat rate, established by him somewhat arbitrarily as 50 percent of the direct costs of research. (The NDRC's industrial contractors charged 100 percent; Bush halved the figure to account for the fact that, as tax-exempt institutions, universities had fewer costs than private industry.) Not required to itemize their overhead costs, administrators at some universities regarded the overhead payments from the NDRC as virtually unrestricted funds, the type most useful to them.[17]

The overhead policy was generous, both in strict monetary terms and in the freedom it accorded university administrators. And it was meant to be, according to James Conant, who as one of the original members of the NDRC had helped establish the policy in the mid-1940s. Given that the nation was not yet at war, the members of the NDRC had chosen a generous overhead rate in order to lure university administrators into undertaking research for the NDRC at a time when they might otherwise have hesitated because of the "bother and nuisance" involved.[18]

But Stanford and other universities hardly needed luring in 1940. With faculty members both in favor of U.S. intervention in the war and eager to contribute to a war effort, Stanford administrators saw research contracts with the NDRC as a way to keep professors from leaving campus for war work elsewhere. Additionally, they saw contracts with the NDRC as they had regarded the contracts with the NACA—as a much-needed source of income at a time when traditional sources of funding seemed likely to disappear. Wilbur responded to the creation of the NDRC as did other university presidents, establishing a university committee on national defense. Led by Samuel Morris and composed of the heads of Stanford's science and engineering departments, the committee was asked to survey and provide a list to the NDRC of faculty and facilities available at Stanford for defense-related research.[19]

But nine months after Stanford had offered its resources to the NDRC, the organization had placed only two research contracts totaling about $12,000 at Stanford, both for research in the chemistry department. A significant sum by depression-era standards, it was woefully small compared to what other elite universities had received by that time; MIT, for example, had almost $900,000 worth of contracts by the spring of 1941.[20] Concerned that Stanford was being left out of the war effort, the head of Stanford's national defense committee prodded the NDRC: "Nearly a year has passed without any calls or communications from you. . . . Again we wish to offer our personnel and facilities."[21]

The failure to attract significant support from the NDRC was a disappointment both to Stanford's administrators and to the university's scientists. While President Wilbur had hoped that contracts would hold faculty members on campus and bring in funds to make up for an expected loss of tuition, university prestige was also at issue. By early 1941, administrators and faculty members recognized that institutional prestige no longer inhered in maintaining distance between Stanford and the federal government. Moreover, of the various types of federal support becoming available to universities in the course of mobilization for war, contracts with the NDRC were the most prestigious. Like the NACA, the NDRC was headed by civilian scientists and administrators, men esteemed by the leaders of the academic and scientific communities and believed to be independent experts interested in seeking out and supporting meritorious scientists. Thus, to have been left out of the NDRC-OSRD research program meant to Stanford administrators and faculty members that Stanford had been placed in a different league from the private and public universities to which it had traditionally been compared, another blow to those already concerned about Stanford's academic reputation.

The disappointment of Morris and others at Stanford revealed an initial naiveté about the operations of the NDRC. Despite announced policy, the leaders of the NDRC had, in fact, only partially decentralized wartime research. While administrative control over wartime laboratories had been placed with universities, the preponderance of contract support for academic research went to a select group of universities, much as the bulk of wartime industrial contracts would go to a few industrial firms. In placing research contracts, personal allegiances and professional contacts, as well as merit, clearly influenced Bush, Conant, Compton, and others heading the NDRC and, later, the OSRD, which was established in June 1941. Thus, Compton's MIT, which was the NDRC-OSRD's largest academic contractor and which administered the Radiation Laboratory (primarily devoted to research on radar), received almost $117 million in contracts over the course of the war; Conant's Harvard, which oversaw the Radio Research Laboratory (RRL) (responsible for developing countermeasures to enemy radar), received almost $31 million. Other specialized research and development work was similarly concentrated in laboratories at Caltech, the University of California, the University of Chicago, and Columbia.[22]

The eventual realization that contacts were important in attracting contracts from the NDRC did not lead Stanford administrators to criticize the NDRC and its methods of distributing federal funds. Rather, they embraced the tacit rules of the game, of which they would try later to take advantage themselves. Indeed, the understanding of the importance of connections, as well as a desire to participate in the research sponsored by the NDRC-OSRD, may have played a significant part in the decision of Stanford's board of trustees to offer the presidency of Stanford to Vannevar Bush in December 1941. (Wilbur was over sixty-five years old and had indicated his wish to retire.) But the trustees' timing was bad. Hoover wrote Bush of the offer on 5 December, two days before the bombing of Pearl Harbor. Even in other circumstances, Bush might have declined the offer, but with the nation embarking on a full-scale war, he did not even consider it. He advised Hoover to postpone the search for a president for Stanford until after the war.[23]

Without a major wartime laboratory and with few contracts for research (by December 1941 contract support at Stanford had grown to about $36,000), Stanford had lost over forty professors to war-related work by January 1942, including Frederick Terman, who was chosen by Bush, his former graduate-school advisor, to head the RRL.[24] Terman's move to Harvard prompted engineering dean Samuel Morris to warn President Wilbur that Stanford was "in great danger of losing our top men to central research establishments." With fewer professors and virtually no opportunities for research, Morris feared that Stanford's graduate program would collapse. He also feared, correctly, that Terman, who was responsible for staffing a laboratory that at its peak would number eight hundred, would recruit Stanford's best students to the RRL, further weakening the university's graduate program.[25] Even the undergraduate program seemed in doubt, with enrollments falling due to enlistments. Wilbur did not doubt that Stanford would experience severe upheaval as a result of war mobilization. In April 1942 he gloomily predicted to a friend that many of America's colleges and universities would not survive the war. He began to hope for "another SATC [Students' Army Training Corps]," the program initiated in the last months of World War I, which had turned the campuses over to the army for use as military training grounds. Disliked by some university presidents at the time, the SATC had at least ensured that the campuses were funded and full of students, albeit in military dress.[26]

Wilbur settled for contracts with the army and the Office of Education for training thousands of civilians and "soldier students" in physics and engineering. For those who had dreaded the prospect of teaching just "the women and the 4F's," as one professor put it, the military training programs were welcomed.[27] Administrators and professors were also relieved by the visible evidence that they and their university were doing their share to defeat the Axis powers. As Paul Davis, general secretary of the university, wrote approvingly to Terman, "the leisurely walk of professors about the campus first changed to a dog trot and it has increased to a canter."[28] University administrators also, of course, appreciated the new source of income. President Wilbur was so eager to accept training programs that he contracted to train more soldiers and officers than the army believed the university's dormitory and classroom facilities could reasonably accommodate. Dismayed by the conditions at Stanford, the army ordered an investigation of the campus in 1943, during which Stanford administrators were asked to refute the charge that they were interested in the army training programs primarily for the money.[29]

Undertaking training programs helped prevent the university from operating at a large deficit, but offering classroom instruction in elementary engineering and science to soldiers was hard, often unstimulating work for the professors involved. It was also considerably less prestigious than conducting research aimed at developing new war technologies in well-funded, OSRD-sponsored laboratories headed by eminent scientists. Paul Kirkpatrick, acting chairperson of the physics department during the war, was initially angered when President Wilbur accepted a major training program without consulting the physicists, recognizing that the president was seeking ways to occupy him lest he decide to seek opportunities for war research elsewhere, as had many of the department's other physicists. With "hundreds to shoot through the production line" each academic quarter, Kirkpatrick sought assistance from professors in Stanford's humanities and social science departments who themselves had no war-related research or training obligations.[30] The electrical engineering department was similarly understaffed and its professors "working to the dropping point" in an effort to handle their new teaching obligations. Karl Spangenberg, a leading expert in radio engineering who had hoped to maintain his research program during the war, found the new situation exasperating. "If the research here is going to quit so do I," he warned at one point, calling himself a "victim of technological unemployment."[31] Samuel Morris was also disappointed by the absence of a government-sponsored research program at Stanford. "Personally I should like very much to see Stanford undertake . . . a major war research project," like those at the University of California and Caltech, he wrote midwar. "I believe it would give many members of the faculty and the Stanford family a feeling that Stanford was assuming leadership in the war effort."[32]

Morris's concern that he and others at Stanford were not as deeply involved in the prestigious aspects of the war effort as were their colleagues at other universities had led him, as head of Stanford's national defense committee, to suggest that Wilbur dispatch representatives to Washington, D.C., to seek out the desired contracts from the NDRC-OSRD and other federal agencies. Wilbur, however, had ignored the proposal. Already worried about the university's budget, the president seems to have been concerned about the costs of establishing a presence in Washington. He had already suspended the university's fund-raising program out of budgetary concerns, to the dismay of Paul Davis, who was deeply involved in Stanford's fund-raising efforts. Davis had planned to take advantage of a wartime fear of death and death taxes and a corresponding increase in the writing of wills to press the case for donations and bequests to Stanford. Further, while Wilbur was quite willing to bring Stanford to the service of the nation's military, he seems to have regarded the launching of an organized effort to seek federal contracts as perilously close to "begging" the federal government for financial assistance.[33]

But by mid-1942 others in Stanford's administration had reached conclusions similar to those of Morris. One of those most active in promoting the idea of sending representatives to Washington in search of research contracts was Paul Davis. Davis knew Wilbur well from his days as a student at Stanford. After graduating with a degree in electrical engineering in 1923, Davis had been asked by Wilbur to become the director of the Board of Athletic Control, which raised money from alumni. He then moved on to become the director of San Francisco's Community Chest and to manage a railway in Brazil and a ranch in northern California. In 1936 he was named the university's general secretary. Davis was also a member of the Wilbur-Hoover fishing club as well as of the Bohemian Grove. Once an admirer of Wilbur, whom he described later as "very practical, very wise," by the early 1940s Davis was frustrated with what he saw as Wilbur's intransigence. Wilbur, he would recall later, "didn't seek [his advice] or make it work."[34]

Davis thus began to promote his plan to the president of Stanford's board of trustees, Donald Tresidder. Tresidder, like Wilbur, was an anti–New Deal Republican and an admirer of Herbert Hoover. A Stanford alumnus, he had joined the board in 1939 at Hoover's invitation and had risen rapidly, partly because Hoover supported his strong interest in dramatically reforming Stanford, both to improve the university's academic reputation and to find new sources of financial support. Shortly after the United States joined the war against the Axis powers, Tresidder had met with Hoover at the Bohemian Grove, where they discussed privately Stanford's "inadequacies." To a receptive Hoover, Tresidder had stressed that he favored "unorthodox solutions" to Stanford's problems, as well as more direction of university affairs by the trustees themselves.[35]

In response to Davis's concerns that Stanford was "not at a maximum effort" with respect to the war effort and that "aggressive action needed to be taken quickly," Tresidder created a committee on university services to consider how Stanford might become more fully engaged in war-related research. In addition to several faculty members, the committee included Davis and was headed by Paul Hanna, a professor of education.[36] The new committee recommended sending representatives to Washington, emphasizing that involvement in the government's research program would bring prestige to Stanford and help the university hold onto its faculty members as well as its graduate students, who if engaged in war-related research might be granted draft deferments. Finally, contracts with the federal government would provide the university with "substantial additional income."[37]

Additional income had become particularly important after the decision by Congress in early November 1942 to lower the draft age from twenty-one to eighteen. Facing dramatic tuition losses, some universities had considered laying off faculty members, according to the executive secretary of the OSRD. In the interest of aiding the universities financially, the members of the OSRD had agreed to change their policy governing the reimbursement of costs. Universities would be allowed to charge as a direct cost the salary of any faculty member working on a contract with the OSRD. Thus, costs that the universities would have incurred under ordinary circumstances could now be paid with federal funds, allowing universities to realize significant savings during the war.[38] The policy provided further reason for university administrators to hope for contracts with the OSRD. By raising the direct costs of research, the OSRD had also raised the amount universities could receive in reimbursement for the indirect costs since that figure was based on a percentage of the direct costs. Contracts with the OSRD had thus become both more necessary and more desirable than before to Stanford administrators.

Under pressure from the new committee and from Tresidder (who was widely known to be the trustees' as yet unofficial choice to succeed Wilbur as president), a reluctant Wilbur acceded to the plan to send Davis and Hanna to Washington in late 1942 to search for federal contracts. Davis soon wrote to Wilbur to assure him that he and Hanna were not like the hordes of "desperate university presidents" who had flooded Washington and who "sat on every doorstep and with trembling voices pleaded for a handout." Stanford's representatives, he offered in a carefully wrought if disingenuous distinction, were merely providing interested government agencies with brochures, which included well-formulated research proposals and a list of Stanford's research facilities.[39]

Approaching government agencies was, in fact, not quite as simple as passing out brochures. Davis and Hanna soon realized that "a quick harvest in this work is not likely" and that a permanent presence in Washington was necessary to enable them to cultivate a variety of contacts in Washington—faculty members, alumni, friends of trustees— who might help them acquire contracts from the OSRD and other federal agencies. They thus established an office on LaFayette Square and began "pounding the pavements."[40] They turned to Hoover for an introduction to William Donovan, head of the Office of Strategic Services, the precursor to the Central Intelligence Agency, and to Terman, who took time away from Harvard to introduce them around Washington. Terman's name, according to Hanna, was "an open sesame to all the scientific research groups" in Washington.[41] Hanna also relied heavily on contacts made through the exclusive Cosmos Club, of which he and many influential members of the Washington bureaucracy were members. "Most of the leaders of the war effort would gather for lunch [at the club]," Hanna later recalled. "I would listen and ask questions and find out where research or training needs . . . were. . . . And then I would come back [to Stanford], and write up a [research] proposition and take it back [to Washington]."[42]

The efforts of Davis and Hanna paid off. The Office of Strategic Services, for example, offered them a contract worth several thousand dollars for a study of the "feed economy" of Germany, and the State Department's Office of Coordinator of Inter-American Affairs provided a contract for more than $10,000 for revisions of *Who's Who in Latin America*. The War Department agreed to provide funds to Stanford, through the Hoover Institute, to train designated administrators of occupied territories in the pertinent languages, cultures, and histories.[43]

Most significant, Davis and Hanna succeeded in obtaining additional contracts with the OSRD. By the end of the war, Stanford had twenty-five contracts with the NDRC-OSRD totaling just over $500,000. While this sum did not place Stanford among the agency's top twenty academic contractors, it was roughly equivalent to the combined prewar budgets for Stanford's departments of biology, physics, and chemistry and thus significant to university administrators. Moreover, almost $125,000 of the total amount of contract support was reimbursement for Stanford's overhead expenses, funds that administrators considered virtually unrestricted as to use. Short of traditional sources of income, the university used overhead during the war to cover the expenses of the offices of the dean of students, the registrar, the dean of women, and the director of the summer quarter, as well as costs that had a more obvious bearing on the overall expense of conducting research for the OSRD. According to administrators at the OSRD, Stanford's use of overhead funds was not strictly correct. But the university's administrators "felt rather strongly" that the expenditures should be allowed, and the OSRD did not press the point.[44] It is not surprising, then, that Stanford administrator Paul Davis regarded the OSRD as "a godsend" to the universities.[45]

The Origins of Contract Overhead

To some within the federal government, and even to some within the OSRD itself, the OSRD's policies stretched the bounds of acceptable practice, even during a wartime emergency. Objections centered on the agency's policies for reimbursing overhead costs and were raised by those who believed that a federal agency was ultimately responsible to the Congress and to the American taxpayer. Vannevar Bush defended the policies, as, not surprisingly, did the OSRD's academic contractors. These wartime debates concerning overhead are worth considering briefly because they place Stanford's experience with contract overhead in a larger context and because they reveal much about Bush's views of the relationship between his agency and institutions of higher education, and more broadly, between the public sphere and the private one. Although Bush dismantled the OSRD at the conclusion of the war, his administration of the OSRD established the pattern for relationships between universities and federal patrons of research after the war.

The OSRD's overhead policy was first challenged in early 1942 by a committee that Bush had appointed in response to a complaint from Karl Compton that MIT was not receiving sufficient reimbursement for its overhead expenses. The Jessup Committee, composed of Elihu Root, Jr., and Walter A. Jessup, both trustees of the Carnegie Institute of Washington, and Alan Gregg of the Rockefeller Institute, surprised Bush with its conclusion that the OSRD's overhead rate was, if anything, generous and, at least, inaccurate. The committee advised the OSRD to require universities to itemize their overhead costs. It also suggested that Bush appoint a new committee to recommend specific overhead allowances for all academic contractors with more than $150,000 worth of OSRD contracts. Administrators of institutions with less than $150,000 worth of contracts were merely asked to tell OSRD whether or not they believed they were being overpaid.[46]

While Bush assured the OSRD's executive secretary, Irvin Stewart, that the original overhead rate of 50 percent was accurate, he also admitted privately, "I am not at all disturbed by the thought that we may have been paying more than full costs." According to Bush, if the universities appeared to have been paid too much, this was not because the OSRD's overhead rate was incorrect but because university administrators did not understand how to calculate their overhead expenses. The OSRD did not need to revise its overhead rate as much as it needed to show academic administrators how to keep their books.[47]

Despite these privately expressed views, Bush did take the Jessup Committee's recommendation and appointed a review committee made up of four academic administrators from universities with large amounts of contract support from the OSRD. Robert M. Underhill of the University of California (which ended the war with over $14 million in contracts with the OSRD) was asked to examine the financial records of the California Institute of Technology (which in early 1942 had almost $500,000 in contracts with the OSRD and ended the war as the second largest academic contractor). Horace S. Ford of MIT (which in January 1942 had close to $6 million in contracts) was asked to visit Harvard, Columbia, and Princeton, each with contracts totaling between $500,000 and $1.5 million. R. B. Stewart of Purdue, the only university of the four represented with little in the way of OSRD support, had investigated MIT for the Jessup Committee, and his conclusion that MIT was being overpaid, not underpaid, had played a crucial role in shaping the committee's conclusion. At MIT's request, Stewart was not sent back to MIT but was asked instead to examine the records of the University of California. Floyd Morey of the University of Illinois (which ended the war with over $2 million in OSRD contracts) was dispatched to MIT and to the University of Chicago.[48]

The committee's composition could hardly have inspired confidence in anyone interested in an unbiased analysis of the OSRD's overhead policy. In fact, it evoked criticism from James Conant, president of Harvard, chairperson of the NDRC, and assistant to Bush on the OSRD, who objected that a report rendered by university administrators "cannot help reflecting the point of view which will be favorable to the contracting institutions."[49] This was Conant's conclusion after reading the committee's report, "Proposed Plan of Allowance for Indirect Costs and Contingencies (Now Called Overhead)," in which the committee members had agreed that some of the OSRD's academic contractors were being reimbursed too generously. Stewart, the most critical of the four, had written separately to the OSRD's executive secretary, advising that "overhead should be reduced materially with considerable savings to the federal government" and with no harm to the universities involved. But the committee had rejected the idea that overhead costs should be itemized—the proposal of the Jessup Committee and one that Harvard's treasurer had endorsed. Instead, the group of academic administrators proposed that OSRD continue to calculate overhead on a percentage basis but that it adopt a sliding scale, paying a lower percentage on the larger OSRD contracts. The lowest percentage suggested by the committee (30 percent) was higher than the 20 percent that Stewart of Purdue had earlier recommended to the Jessup Committee.[50] While the OSRD adjusted the overhead rates as recommended, Bush responded to Conant's concern that the new rates might still be overgenerous by requesting the OSRD's fiscal officer, Carey Cruikshank, to examine the OSRD's overhead policy in April 1942.

Rather than settle the debate, Cruikshank's review reignited the disagreements internal to the OSRD and additionally raised the specter of interference in the OSRD's operations by the Congress. According to Cruikshank, the overhead rate seemed unreasonably generous, and the policy of paying a percentage of direct costs was possibly illegal. An informal conversation with an accountant in the auditing division of the General Accounting Office of Congress confirmed his fears. "Ever since I read the first OSRD 'cost' contract I have been somewhat concerned," he explained to Irvin Stewart. "I am afraid that this type of contract comes within the realm of the 'cost-plus-a-percentage-of-costs' ones which are illegal." The contracts that had already been deemed illegal, Cruikshank noted, had allowed an overhead rate of only 5 to 15 percent, in comparison with the OSRD's range of 30 to 100 percent. If the OSRD did not alter its overhead policy, others in the federal government might press them to, Cruikshank advised.[51]

Cruikshank's opinion was unpopular with Bush and Stewart, and after some discussions, Cruikshank withdrew his recommendation that the policy be abandoned. Still believing that the contracts at least bordered on the illegal and convinced that the overhead rate was also too generous in many cases, he agreed that "since we have used this type of contract extensively and have justified, or attempted to justify, it on various occasions we should now stick to it." A change in policy at this point, Cruikshank acknowledged, might look like an admission of impropriety and attract unwanted attention from the Congress.[52] But he became alarmed again when he discovered in mid-1943 just how great the OSRD's overpayment of overhead expenses had been. Some of the OSRD's academic contractors had accumulated excess overhead in "reserve" accounts that totaled as much as $400,000 at MIT and $70,000 at Columbia. Other universities, he suspected, had surpluses but were not offering the information to the OSRD. Cruikshank again warned Bush that "everyone concerned will be subject to censure and criticism," if not to an investigation by the Bureau of the Budget, if the overhead reserves were discovered.[53]

Bush was both unalarmed by the news that some universities held large reserves and irritated by Cruikshank's persistence, in part because the overhead policy had from the outset been intended to be generous. Cruikshank's worries about the OSRD's ultimate accountability to the Congress and the American taxpayer, however, forced Bush to articulate the rationale for the OSRD's overhead policy. While readily granting that the OSRD had "a duty to use care in the expenditure of public funds," Bush insisted that the OSRD also had a duty, "which is unusual and which does not apply to contractual relations generally," to give special attention to the needs of its contractors—the nation's universities. Unlike industrial contractors, university administrators were unfamiliar with contracts and with the concept of overhead expenses. The OSRD, not the universities, was thus the best judge of the universities' needs and expenses, he argued.[54] These were arguments Bush had used before, but now he was more candid. In paying overhead expenses "it would be better to err on the side of liberality," he explained to Irvin Stewart, "for it is a desirable thing for this country" that its institutions of higher education be "in a sound position." He added: "True, this may mean that some of the colleges and universities . . . may find themselves in a better financial position at the end of the war. If so, they will be able to carry on still more effectively in the peace period . . . and this is much to be desired."[55]

American taxpayers and administrators of those colleges and universities left out of the OSRD's wartime program of sponsored research might well have objected to Bush's assertion that what was good for MIT and the OSRD's other academic contractors was good for the nation as a whole. But Bush's views did find resonance with the administrators of those universities with substantial contract support from the OSRD. Almost all those asked to tell the OSRD whether the agency was being too generous in its reimbursement of their overhead costs wrote to say that, if anything, they were being paid too little. The comptroller of the University of Chicago was particularly open in his defense of the OSRD's 50 percent overhead rate. Why, he asked, should academic institutions not be allowed to profit from their governmental contracts? Overhead funds were particularly useful to the private universities, which were already "hard pressed to maintain their budgets."[56] He was, in essence, offering a more blunt version of Bush's own defense of his OSRD policy.

One of the few to dissent from the OSRD's overhead policies was Harvard's treasurer, William Claflin, whose perspective on the overhead issue was no doubt shaped by the fact that Harvard, the nation's wealthiest university, would have been able to manage quite well without government support. In Claflin's view, the OSRD needed to set strict guidelines regarding the use of overhead. Otherwise, given "that vague and nebulous realm of overhead, with no direction as to what should be included other than 'let your conscience be your guide,' " administrators of the nation's universities were bound to respond in a variety of different ways, some reasonably, others opportunistically. Clearly, the "very scrupulous institutions will lose," he predicted. "Others less scrupulous or less wise will profit."[57]

Bush eventually acceded to amending the OSRD's policy with respect to overhead. The agency's academic contractors were asked to return any surplus overhead they might have accumulated, and by 1944 the OSRD had issued to its contractors a loose set of guidelines regarding the overhead expenses they might charge against their OSRD contracts. This did not represent a significant departure from the philosophy that had up to then guided university-OSRD relations, however. Universities were invited, not required, to remit excess overhead. Of an estimated 51 percent of academic contractors with overhead reserves at the end of the war, 28 percent provided refunds to the OSRD, and another 35 percent agreed to reduce their overhead claims. The remaining 27 percent apparently held on to what they had received.[58]

A similar emphasis on voluntarism infected the establishment and enforcement of the overhead guidelines. To determine what might be charged as an overhead expense, representatives of the OSRD consulted with the agency's academic contractors; together they devised guidelines that the contractors regarded as "entirely acceptable, comprehensive, fair and liberal." The liberality was clear in comparison with the overhead policies established by other federal agencies proffering contracts for research during the war. Representatives of the OSRD's academic contractors had stressed to the OSRD that they were "more or less displeased with the Army and Navy," both of which had placed "numerous restrictions, limitations, prohibitions, etc." on their use of overhead payments.[59] Moreover, if Stanford's experience was at all representative, the OSRD did not, ultimately, strictly enforce the guidelines that it had established.

Bush had clearly established the policies and practices of the OSRD with the interests of academic administrators in mind. He was acting out of concern for the financial status of the OSRD's academic contractors and in a way that took account of the wish of university administrators to obtain federal funds on terms that freed them as much as possible from accountability to a patron, especially one scrupulous in safeguarding the interests of the taxpayer. Bush's expenditure of public funds stood in significant contrast to the policies of the New Deal agencies, which in the early 1930s had provided federal funds to aid the nation's financially troubled universities and colleges. In those years, for example, schools that accepted and then invested taxpayers' money were required to return the interest on the investments to the federal government.[60] Bush, however, was less concerned about maintaining strict accountability to the taxpayer than with funding scientific research in a way that he, and not a political body, deemed most beneficial to the nation as a whole.

University administrators responded predictably, if in a way that confused their own political ideologies with their financial concerns for their institutions. Some of the university administrators who had accepted federal funds in the 1930s had disliked the policies governing their use. Conservative university administrators like Wilbur and Hoover charged the Roosevelt administration with attempting to erase the boundaries between the public and the private universities. Many of these same administrators embraced the policies of the OSRD, however. It was these policies that, in eschewing rigorous oversight of the use of public funds, contributed significantly to blurring the distinction between the public realm and private institutions of higher education.

Although the OSRD would be dismantled at the end of the war, the agency had established policies and practices regarding the relationship between the federal government and the universities that were perpetuated. The federal government would become a major supporter of academic science, but it would not support institutions of higher education directly or according to geographic formulas. Contracts, and in some instances grants, would be given to individual researchers, who for the most part were clustered at a handful of major research universities. These universities in turn would draw substantial overhead from contracts and would find, as they had during the war, numerous uses for these funds.

Over the course of the war, administrators at Stanford became appreciative of this particular kind of support from the federal government, and they became open to the possibility that the alliance between the federal government and institutions of higher education might continue after the war if the relationship were to be constructed on the basis of the research contract. But federal patronage joined rather than replaced industrial patronage in the thinking of administrators contemplating postwar financial support for the university. Administrators' willingness to consider both federal and industrial patronage at the end of the war indicated their acceptance, finally, of the demise of the old research economy, which had been based largely on gifts and grants from philanthropists and private foundations, and their embrace of the concept of the university as a provider of services both to government and to business in return for financial support.[61]

This shift was gradual rather than abrupt. It was not provoked by the sudden availability of federal patronage at the end of the war but had commenced during the depression, when administrators at Stanford and other universities had begun anxiously observing changes in the nation's political economy and worrying about institutional finances. At that time, Stanford's administrators began expressing an interest in developing industrial patronage. The wartime activities of the OSRD had convinced administrators that federal patronage might also provide a new and important source of funds to the university without overturning conservative ideas about the proper relationship between universities and the state.

University administrators set to work immediately after the war to ensure that postwar patronage did indeed replicate the patronage relationships that had been established during the war. Under the leadership of Isaiah Bowman, president of Johns Hopkins University, academic administrators and other members of Bowman's "citizens' committee" lobbied Congress in favor of Vannevar Bush's proposal for a National Science Foundation and opposed the version of the foundation proposed by Senator Harley Kilgore, the Democratic populist from West Virginia.

To Bush and university administrators, Kilgore's plan was reminiscent of New Deal reforms and awakened old fears about federal subsidies for academic science. Kilgore proposed that some federal funds be apportioned on a geographical basis, a suggestion that to Bush meant that geographical quotas rather than excellence would determine which scientists received patronage. Kilgore also recommended that the government fund the social sciences as well as the physical and natural sciences. To Bush, the social sciences were not rigorously scientific, and they were thus susceptible to manipulation; federal support, especially from a liberal government, was thus to be eschewed. Finally, Kilgore suggested that the funding agency be headed by an administrator appointed by the president, whereas Bush preferred that decisions about the funding be placed in the hands of a group of supposedly disinterested experts—men like Bush himself, who were drawn from the private sphere, rather than from government, and were thus presumed to be insulated from political forces.

Not all university administrators supported Bush's proposal. The politically liberal Frank Graham, president of the University of North Carolina, wanted to see the New Deal extended to embrace institutions of higher education. As he noted, "The combined endowments of all the colleges and universities in 13 Southern states is less than the endowments of two New England universities." Federal funds offered on a geographical basis represented the only hope for eliminating these inequalities.

The presidents of the nation's leading universities sided with Bush, however. Conant of Harvard, Compton of MIT, Bowman of Johns Hopkins, and Tresidder of Stanford were all close to Bush. They were also political conservatives who shared his elitism and his belief that democratic politics posed a potential threat to both science and the private university. These administrators were not interested in seeing federal support distributed more widely than it had been during the war, as were Kilgore and Graham. They did not want to upset the hierarchy of prestigious universities but to maintain it and, in Stanford's case, to find a place nearer the top.

While clashes over the proposed legislation effectively delayed the creation of the National Science Foundation until 1950, federal support for academic science became available soon after World War II from other sources, principally the armed services. The military origins of this support did not bother Stanford administrators. They were much more concerned about the mechanisms and forms that federal support took than about the kinds of research the federal government supported. Military sponsors were offering contracts for research as had the OSRD; and as had the OSRD, they were providing support not with the aim of distributing funds evenly to all universities but on the basis of personal contacts. For these reasons, support from the military satisfied Stanford's administrators. Additionally, the source of the patronage did not challenge their conception of the university. To administrators, conducting research under contract to the military was Stanford's contribution to the defense of the nation, a contribution that they viewed as nonpartisan and in the interests of all Americans.

While university administrators were satisfied with the nature of postwar patronage available from the federal government, the postwar relationship between universities and federal patrons and between universities and industrial patrons did not simply fall into place after the war. For half a decade after the war, administrators at Stanford would debate and work to define the alliance between the university and its federal and industrial patrons in a way that both benefited their institution and that conformed with, rather than challenged, their ideas about the proper relationship between the state, a private university, and private enterprise. But before Stanford's administrators began debating the form that the postwar relationship between the university and external research sponsors should take, they began making changes *within* the university in order to better position Stanford to take advantage of the new patronage.

3

Eroding Departmental Autonomy

The recasting of the university's role and of its relationship to the political economy was well underway by the end of the war. By 1946 conservative and liberal administrators alike envisioned the university as a "public-service institution." Public service was variously defined. In addition to including service to national security interests or service to American business, the term signaled chiefly that the university was no longer to be thought of as an ivory tower, remote from the needs and interests of American society. The prewar university had, of course, never been solely defined as an ivory tower, but after the war, it was this particular image that was under attack. Commentators linked the concept of "knowledge for the sake of knowledge" to the German university and pointed to that institution and its posture of remoteness from society as partly responsible for the rise of Nazism.[1]

Few challenged this construction or questioned the value of the university's new commitment to serving society. An exception was Harold Stoke, president of the University of New Hampshire and a former dean of the University of Wisconsin. While not advocating a return to the ivory tower, Stoke did fear that the zeal for public service posed dangers both to academic research and to relationships within the university. Universities were in danger of becoming "social and political instrumentalities," Stoke believed, and of sacrificing their role as "havens" where unique perspectives on society could be fostered. If the pursuit of knowledge for its own sake was suspect, Stoke wondered if knowledge pursued instead according to the interests of the patron, whether the militarist or the industrialist, was really preferable.

In addition to his concern that universities had gone too far in their eagerness to serve new patrons, Stoke worried about the changes occurring within the universities. A rift seemed to be developing between those faculty members who had acquired contracts for research and those who had not. He also feared a concomitant devaluation of teaching as that responsibility was foisted onto those faculty members devoid of research patronage.[2] Stoke might also have commented on the diminishing authority of department chairs and the erosion of departmental cohesion in the postwar university. As another university administrator noted approvingly shortly after the war, the age of the "aggrandizement of the [university] department" was coming to an end.[3] These developments—the devaluation of teaching, the appearance of a hierarchy among faculty members based not on seniority but on access to patronage, the weakening of the authority of the department chairperson—are among the recognized changes that took place in American universities after World War II. As did Stoke, later commentators on the postwar university implicitly linked these changes within the university to the shift that had occurred in the university's role in society and in its relationship to the new research economy, focusing on academic scientists (especially academic physicists) as the agents of change. During the war, these scientists had been exposed to new ways of organizing and thinking about research and had begun to enjoy the rewards (notably prestige and esteem) of putting scientific ideas into practice; they returned to their universities after the war with ambitious plans for research and a willingness to provide advice and research results to the federal government in return for patronage. It was these externally supported, research-minded scientists who challenged traditional obligations and authority within the university, according to this story. Absorbed in their research, these scientists had little time or interest in teaching or administrative responsibilities. These traditional departmental obligations, once enforced by the head of the department, could be neglected with impunity as the individual scientist's access to patronage effectively undercut the authority of the department chair. Increasingly, access to outside funds rather than seniority conveyed power and authority within a department, and the individual professor with research contracts replaced the department as the meaningful unit within the university.

This is certainly a fair description of the behavior of some academic scientists after the war; however it is an incomplete explanation of the way in which the changes occurring within the university reflected changes in the research economy. By focusing on the scientists (notably the physicists) who developed postwar federal patronage, the role of federal patronage in stimulating change within the university is over-stated, and the role of university administrators is neglected entirely. The availability of federal patronage and the existence of some faculty members willing to accept it did not alone provoke the changes within the university. Rather, the changes both preceded and accompanied the availability of new sources of patronage and were made precisely in order to attract this patronage. The role of university administrators in effecting the transformation of their institutions was significant. At the end of World War II, just as during the depression, administrators were watching closely the changes in the research economy while seeking to chart the future course of their institutions. Having made the commit-ment to draw on new sources of patronage—industrial as well as fed-eral—after the war, they were interested in ensuring that faculty mem-bers were able to attract the desired patronage. When traditional roles and relationships appeared to stand in the way of this development, university administrators made the necessary changes.

The way in which traditions within the university began to change and the connection between these changes and administrators' interest in developing patronage are particularly clear in the case of Stanford University. There, administrators were blunt about their aims, perhaps because they, unlike administrators at other major research universities, not only were focused on developing resources for their university but also harbored ambitions for achieving national acclaim for Stanford. Faculty members were equally clear about their reaction to the adminis-tration's plans, some embracing them eagerly and others choosing to resist. The agonizing conflicts that resulted centered not so much on the development of new forms of patronage as on the challenge posed by administrators to university tradition, particularly to the authority and autonomy of the academic department.

Planning a Transformation

Plans to revitalize Stanford emerged in late 1941 at the prompting of trustee president Donald Tresidder. As general man-ager and president of the dominant concession in Yosemite National Park, Tresidder had transformed the park from a wilderness area into a ski resort and vacation retreat for the well-to-do. Concerned over

Stanford's flagging reputation and shaky finances, Tresidder believed that he could effect a similarly dramatic transformation of his alma mater. With that in mind, in December 1941 he invited a few professors—including Frederick Terman and his father, Lewis Terman, some wealthy alumni, and Stanford's general secretary, Paul Davis—to a weekend retreat at his Ahwahnee Hotel in Yosemite Valley to discuss Stanford's future. Money, Tresidder's informal advisors agreed, was the key to reforming Stanford. The university needed funds to allow it to raise salaries, to hire noted scholars and scientists, and to provide them with opportunities for research. In 1941 Tresidder was not yet willing to consider federal patronage; the group agreed that the university's best hope for a new source of funds was private industry.[4]

News of the attack on Pearl Harbor interrupted the weekend meeting, and the participants were soon scattered around the country by their wartime assignments. By mid-1942, however, the group was again conferring about Stanford's future. Especially important in shaping Tresidder's thoughts were Paul Davis and Frederick Terman. Davis was a ubiquitous presence in university affairs in the 1930s and 1940s. He was a good friend of the Termans and was personally close to a number of the university's trustees, including Herbert Hoover, and to wealthy alumni. For advice on university affairs he drew on these contacts as well as on his acquaintances William Crocker, the president of Crocker First National Bank, and Charles Merrill, an advisor to Crocker and a regent of the University of California. Many years later, Davis recalled that in his efforts in the 1930s and 1940s to reform Stanford, he had always sought advice from people he felt were "great and astute"; they would "help me and guide me."[5]

By late 1942 Davis had collected the ideas of his informal advisors and reported his recommendations for transforming Stanford to Tresidder. Stanford must be reorganized to operate more efficiently and economically, he urged. Administrators also needed to mount a public relations campaign which stressed that Stanford was not only an eminent research institution but that it was also a university of "High Service in all forms." Service, in Davis's conception, meant assistance to private industry and to local and national governments with the expectation that the university would receive financial support in return.[6]

Davis's suggestion that Stanford could be run more efficiently and economically echoed the suggestions that Hoover had made as early as the mid-1910s to President Wilbur. Influenced by scientific management practices and willing to look upon the university as a business enterprise, Hoover had urged Wilbur to centralize the university's operations and reduce the power of department chairpersons. By the 1930s the notion that universities should be run according to good business principles was being promoted eagerly by some university administrators as a partial solution to universities' financial troubles; for example, Robert G. Sproul, president of the University of California, was a consistent advocate of achieving economies by eliminating small classes and the elective curriculum.[7]

Davis's recommendations for reorganizing university operations were drawn chiefly from the ideas of Lewis Terman, a Stanford psychologist and contemporary of Hoover who had devoted most of his professional life to developing tests to quantify personality traits and intelligence. The Stanford-Binet I.Q. tests had been used in the First World War to identify those considered unfit for military service. After the war, Terman had encouraged businesses to adopt testing as a way to sort and channel employees. To Terman, who also advocated the use of testing to determine admissions to Stanford, the university might best be thought of as a factory. As did a factory, the university dealt with "raw materials and with processes" and produced "something that is bought and paid for by the consuming public." But unlike a factory or business enterprise, universities were poorly organized and managed.[8] Davis agreed, explaining to Tresidder that Lewis Terman had suggested to him "the analogy of a business factory for a university."[9]

Davis thus urged Tresidder to consider eliminating all small classes, which, however conducive to learning, represented an inefficient use of Stanford's buildings. "Surely no commercial business would tolerate the luxury of such low load factors," Davis objected. He also advocated eliminating those university programs and departments that were insufficiently attractive to students and to patrons or that were not contributing to making Stanford appear as a "pacemaker in education." Thus, the journalism and the history departments might go, he offered, and the economics department could be placed within the business school, where its professors might properly focus on issues of concern to industry. This would both save the university money and also increase Stanford's attractiveness to potential patrons. Additionally, Davis encouraged Tresidder to reduce drastically the authority of the department chairs. The president should instead rely on deans, to whom he should allocate money according to the eminence and productivity of the faculty members under their supervision. "To put the university funds into departments or fields at a more or less regular pace is a common University fault," Davis advised Tresidder.[10]

Lastly, Davis suggested that Stanford should move into new fields, all of which might attract attention from industrial concerns. Wholly new institutes might be added, as well, such as a division for microwave research, which would build upon the commercially oriented work that Stanford's physicists had begun in the 1930s with the support of the Sperry Gyroscope Company. He also suggested creating a school of public administration. Such innovations, Davis hoped, would encourage faculty members to increase the effort they devoted to "applied knowledge" in fields of interest to state and local governments and to business; this increased participation in "the affairs of the region," he believed, would "greatly increase the sales opportunities" to business.[11]

Davis was advocating the explicit abandonment of the idea of the university as an institution remote from society and from commerce. The view of the university as such a haven had been important in the past, although it certainly had not gone unchallenged. Conceptions of a university engaged in some way with society had also gained adherents. In the 1930s progressive educators and leaders of public universities had stressed the responsibility of institutions of higher education to assist both local communities and the nation in contending with the disastrous economic situation and to study ways to prevent another economic collapse. It was a position with which the leaders of some private universities, including those of Yale and Princeton, had been uncomfortable. President Wilbur, hostile to the Roosevelt administration, had seen virtue in the argument put forth in the 1930s that universities, particularly private ones, must not allow themselves to become instruments of the federal government and, by extension, of political interests. During the war, however, Davis, as well as administrators at other universities, had eagerly sought to bring their universities to the service of the nation, and Davis had recognized early on that such service conferred institutional prestige. He wanted Stanford to continue to play the role of a service institution after the war. In his mind, industry still seemed to be the most likely patron of academic research after the war, and he urged Tresidder to make plans to attract industrial patronage.

Tresidder, who was soon to be named president of Stanford, took seriously Davis's suggestions. They confirmed his own inclinations and complemented the advice that he was receiving from other quarters. For example, Harley Notter, a Stanford alumnus who was working closely with Cordell Hull as executive secretary to the State Department's Advisory Committee on Postwar Foreign Policy, encouraged Tresidder to abandon the German concept of the university: it was time to realize that universities were "coming to occupy a new position domestically in the nation," Notter argued, and to recognize that those in the West were especially well positioned to take advantage of wartime political and economic changes.[12]

Frederick Terman also believed that changes occurring in the nation's political economy, especially in the West, boded well for Stanford's future, provided that the university acted to take advantage of them. "The years after the war are going to be very important and also *very critical ones* for Stanford," Terman wrote from the RRL to Paul Davis in 1943. Stanford had a chance to achieve "a position in the West somewhat analogous to that of Harvard in the East," but Stanford was also likely to sink to "a level somewhat similar to that of Dartmouth," Terman warned, if university administrators failed to make much needed changes in Stanford's operations and outlook. Terman agreed with Davis that Stanford needed to emphasize applied science. He also viewed the university's departmental organization as archaic and wanted to see new institutional forms created to unite academic experts, not according to disciplinary training, but on the basis of practical problems to be solved. Terman agreed with Davis that developing industrial patronage was important, as was the training of large numbers of students in subjects of direct interest to industrial concerns.[13]

Terman's interest in industrial patronage was well developed before World War II, as was his interest in improving Stanford's academic reputation. But the war, or, more precisely, Terman's view of the impact that the war would have on the West and on industrial development, gave added meaning to his earlier inclinations and raised considerably his expectations for Stanford. Terman knew that technological developments during the First World War had contributed to the growth of a postwar chemical industry; he hoped that the wartime work of scientists and engineers such as himself would lay the foundation for the development after World War II of a large and varied electronics industry. Thus, he expressed evident delight when Harvard president and former chemist James Conant opined that Terman's work in radio communications "now had a degree of importance that was greater than chemistry by at least one power of ten (and Conant is a chemist!)."[14] If there were to be a postwar blossoming of businesses involved in radio communication, telephony, television, and airplane navigation, Terman wanted Stanford to be prepared. "War research which [is] now secret will be [the] basis [of a] postwar industrial expansion in electronics," he predicted to a Stanford administrator in a telegram in which he sought permission to bring electrical engineer Karl Spangenberg to the RRL. Without access to information about wartime scientific and engineering developments, Spangenberg's academic career and his ability to provide advice and attract patronage from industry would be handicapped.[15]

When Terman left Stanford for Harvard in 1942, the San Francisco Bay Area had only a nascent electronics industry, which had provided little in the way of either research funds or employment opportunities for his students. But Terman realized that the wartime spending by the federal government had significantly changed the economy of the western United States. The West now had a booming industrial sector that included airplane and ship manufacturing, both of which would depend on the electronics industry for key components of their products and so ensure its expansion. Terman was also aware that the war had revived the West's oil industry; he advised Davis that, after the war, Stanford should be sure to "be good in all fields [oil] is tied to." With the West quickly becoming an industrially advanced region, it would be able to support, and would likely need the services of, a major research university. Stanford, Terman hoped, would dominate the region.[16]

Agreeing that after the war Stanford should emphasize service to regional industry, Terman, Tresidder, and Davis also discussed how the university might be reorganized to better serve industry. As did Davis, Terman believed that university administrators should set goals for academic departments and hire faculty members accordingly. Using Stanford's physics department as an example, he urged Tresidder not to allow the department's members to fill a vacancy in their department. Instead, the administration needed to decide first "what direction it is desired for the Physics Department to go, and particularly on what it should concentrate." Only then should the vacancy be filled, and with "the best man available" in the entire country, not simply someone deemed satisfactory to the department's members.[17]

While Terman's suggestions for reorganizing the university were clearly influenced by his father's ideas, Terman would later credit Harvard's administrators with teaching him about the proper management of a university. In Cambridge Terman lived across the street from William Claflin, Harvard's treasurer, and near Charles Coolidge, a member of the Harvard Corporation. Terman was particularly close to Claflin, who, in numerous informal conversations, had shared with Terman information about how Harvard handled its finances and academic affairs. If Terman did not already know about President Conant's policy with respect to faculty promotions, he surely learned about it while at Harvard, where the challenge to departmental autonomy had begun as early as the mid-1930s. Such matters as the appointment and tenuring of faculty members "cannot be delegated to deans of faculties or departmental chairmen," Conant had written in 1934. According to Harvard's president, a university's professors determined the reputation of that university; the president thus needed to exercise strict control to ensure that only the "best" faculty members gained permanent positions within the university. The resulting policy, referred to as "up-or-out," expanded the role of the university's top administrators in determining a department's makeup and set a precedent for administrators at other universities, such as Stanford, who looked to Harvard as a model and a guide.[18]

Terman greatly admired Harvard's administrators. They were "a bunch of hardheaded Yankees" who were "organizationally minded" and knew "how to build for the future," he wrote approvingly to his father in 1943. In early 1944 Terman convinced Tresidder to visit him in Cambridge and arranged for him to meet with Claflin, Coolidge, and several Harvard deans as well as with James Conant. Tresidder "made a fine impression" at Harvard, Terman reported to his father. While Tresidder was justifiably worried about Stanford's financial problems, after talking to Claflin and others, he appeared "to appreciate . . . that internal organization needs as much attention" as did the raising of funds.[19]

Implementing the Reforms

Shortly after returning from his visit to Harvard, Tresidder began to implement the reforms that he and others had been discussing over the past few years. Between 1944 and 1946 he attempted to elaborate an administrative structure, to create institutes and other organizations to attract industrial patronage, and to reorient particular university departments to serve better the interests of regional industry, particularly the aeronautics, electronics, and oil companies. While his ideas were already well formulated, Tresidder could not have succeeded in making these changes without the assistance of a few faculty members who, for various reasons, were also highly desirous of change. They supported the premise underlying Tresidder's proposed reforms: that the tradition of departmental autonomy and disciplinary distinctions should be undermined.

Tresidder's first act was to create a new administrative post, that of vice president for academic affairs, in early 1944. Prior to this, there had been no administrative position intermediate between the deans and the university's president. Tresidder chose for the new position Alvin Eurich, an assistant professor of education who had attended the prewar meeting in Yosemite and, during the war, had been in charge of administering the navy's testing program. The choice momentarily disappointed Lewis Terman, who wrote dismissively to his son, "I think his [Eurich's] I.Q. is about 120 or 125. . . . However, he seems to function a little above his I.Q. level."[20] But Eurich and Tresidder shared Terman's interest in improving the efficiency of the university. They were soon promulgating rules intended both to rationalize university operations and to govern faculty members' use of their time. Faculty members were required to notify the administration and fill out a form if they planned to be absent from the campus; department chairpersons were required to use preprinted forms, rather than letters, to communicate with the administration.[21]

Eurich and Tresidder also began considering ways to reorganize research within the university and to develop industrial patronage. While acting as an advisor to the navy during the war, Eurich had met the president of the Illinois Institute of Technology, Henry T. Heald. The institute's professors conducted a large amount of research that was sponsored by industry through the institute-affiliated Armour Research Foundation. At Eurich's encouragement, Tresidder visited Heald and came away impressed. Armour, he learned, had $1.6 million in industry-financed projects in 1944 and a total of $2.5 million worth of research projects, all financed outside the Illinois Institute's budget. Stanford, in contrast, had a research fund of $835 in 1944; the total expenditure for research in the 1943–44 academic year, including research sponsored by the government and industry, was a mere $333,558. To Tresidder, creating a research institute similar to Armour offered a way to meet several of his administration's goals—expanding research opportunities, resolving Stanford's financial problems, and providing service to industry. An institute would "pay for itself many times over," Tresidder believed, "because it's easier to sell to industry, and is more efficient" than a university.[22]

A similar plan for creating an industrial research institute had been proposed in the late 1930s at Stanford by chemistry chair Robert Swain, and Tresidder soon involved Swain and Philip Leighton, another chemist, as well as wealthy alumni and regional businessmen, in the planning of the institute. Particularly influential was Atholl McBean, a wealthy industrialist and member of the board of Standard Oil of California. He promised to raise funds to create the institute provided that Tresidder appoint his friend William Talbot, the technical director of the Sun Chemical Corporation, as the institute's director. McBean also wanted Stanford's board of trustees to provide a low-interest loan of $1 million to get the institute started. The creation of the Stanford Research Institute was approved in February 1946 by Stanford's board of trustees. Tresidder envisioned the new institution as a division of the university that would devote itself to industrial research and turn over to Stanford a portion of its profits as well as provide research opportunities for Stanford faculty members.[23]

At the same time that Tresidder began exploring ways to organize industry-sponsored research, he also began to encourage some departments in the university to develop contacts with industry, asking the heads of departments to produce specific plans for soliciting industrial support. The initial results disappointed Tresidder. As he complained to trustee Paul Edwards in the spring of 1944, a large number of faculty members were not interested in industrial patronage; those that were had produced plans that were "so hazy as to be almost valueless."[24]

Tresidder was particularly concerned about the plans of Stanford's aeronautical engineers. The airplane manufacturing industry had expanded tremendously during the war as a result of federal investment and military demand, and as William Durand, a Stanford engineer who had worked for the NACA during the war, had pointed out, most travel would be done by air after the war. Tresidder initially suggested that Stanford's aeronautical engineers should develop further their connections with the NACA, proposing that the department seek use of the NACA's Ames Laboratory, located in the nearby town of Sunnyvale. But Durand strongly opposed the suggestion, pointing out that the Ames Laboratory did research for the military and private industry and insisting that the research and facilities of the aeronautical engineers should remain "under the immediate and sole control of the Department" at Stanford.[25]

The aeronautical engineers wanted unrestricted funds to expand their department's research facilities and support research of their own choosing. They thus proposed soliciting five major aircraft companies for donations of $100,000 each. The department planned to use the money to modernize its wind tunnel and provide fellowships for students; in turn, the aircraft companies would gain a pool of well-trained engineers as potential employees. To Elliott Reid, the author of the proposal, drawing on industrial support in this way was preferable to doing commercial testing for fees, as the engineers had been doing since 1940. Even so, the proposal, which promised the aircraft companies first use of the department's facilities, signified to him that the engineers were being "sold into bondage." [26]

To Tresidder, who agreed that the department should turn to industry for financial support, the engineers' proposal was "immature and inadequate." It represented the same mistaken idea that had been embodied in Hoover's National Research Fund in the 1920s—that industrial firms would provide money for research on the faith that research was the basis of industrial advancement, rather than with the guarantee that they would receive something for their money. Only by promising to undertake research of specific interest to aircraft companies and presenting them with estimated costs and clear objectives could the engineers hope to attract financial support from the industry, Tresidder insisted. Although the engineers stressed to Tresidder that they preferred to work on general questions related to airplane structures rather than on problems specified by industrial patrons, they agreed to modify their proposal to include a list of proposed projects with the specified costs attached. [27]

Tresidder, Davis, Terman, and others had also determined that Stanford should enhance its contacts with the oil industry and develop strengths in all fields related to the industry's interests. With this in mind, Tresidder turned his attention in late 1944 to Stanford's geology department. Headed by Eliot Blackwelder, the department had downplayed the practical applications of geological knowledge and developed instead a strong tradition of geological research and training that the oil industry considered purely "academic and impractical." [28] In the fall of 1944 Blackwelder had indicated an interest in retiring; to Tresidder, this was an opportunity to reorient the department's interests.

Tresidder made it immediately clear to Blackwelder that he hoped the department would choose a professor of petroleum geology as its next chairperson. Blackwelder, who had studied and published widely on the origin and evolution of landforms in the United States and China, assured the president that he had no opposition to appointing a petroleum geologist. He did point out, however, that if the department appointed a petroleum geologist, a field previously unrepresented, Blackwelder's own field of geomorphology would be neglected. Such a decision was an important one—it would influence the complexion of the department for many years. For the sake of department morale, the decision should be made only after discussions with all of the department's members, Blackwelder stressed to Tresidder. And since so many of them were away on war assignments, Blackwelder urged Tresidder to postpone selection of a new chairperson until after the war.[29] Blackwelder was interested in maintaining a departmental tradition of consulting the faculty about decisions affecting the fate of the department. But Tresidder, like Davis, was eager to make changes at Stanford while many of the university's faculty members were away. As Davis had shrewdly noted, at the end of the war there would be a "tendency to revert to the old status"; if the university were to be transformed, the war was "the ideal time" to act.[30]

Moreover, Tresidder already knew whom he wanted as head of the department—Arville Levorsen. Levorsen was not an academic geologist and had never taught before; he was the chief geologist for the Tidewater Oil Company in Tulsa, Oklahoma, and an independent oil operator who was known for his work in the science of finding oil. His name had been suggested to Tresidder by one of Stanford's geologists, Aaron C. Waters, who was working for the U.S. Geological Survey during the war. Extremely ambitious, Waters hoped that after the war he and Levorsen could build a strong program in petroleum geology at Stanford. Levorsen would attract money from the oil industry; Waters hoped to interest the State Department in funding a program to teach petroleum geology to South American students. Waters warned Tresidder that because of Levorsen's interests and his lack of teaching experience, the geology department might be "undersold" on having him as department chairperson. But he encouraged Tresidder not to be dissuaded by opposition. Members of the oil industry had "been sniping at [Stanford's] department and criticizing it" for years because the department was "truly deficient in the one field of most interest to these men, namely petroleum geology," Waters complained. Hiring Levorsen would correct this deficiency. Moreover, there would be a direct "payoff": Levorsen was well known to the oil industry and Stanford could expect industrial patronage.[31]

To make certain that this would indeed be the result, Tresidder contacted Stanford alumni in the oil industry. According to Harold Hoots of Richfield Oil, they were "highly enthusiastic" about Levorsen. Hoots, a friend of Levorsen, arranged a meeting between Levorsen and representatives of the oil industry in California to assure him that they wanted him to take the job at Stanford. Levorsen accepted Tresidder's offer. To ensure further the development of good relations between the department and the oil industry, Tresidder advised Levorsen to outline a program for Stanford's geology department and send it to members of the oil industry for comments. "If you folks think best, it might be well to revise [the program] or change it," Levorsen wrote accommodatingly to California oilman L. L. Aubert.[32] Upon hearing of Levorsen's appointment, Waters, who was more interested in his own career than in the procedural details of the proposed appointment, was elated. Before Tresidder became president, "I would have labelled this program 'castles in the air,' " he wrote, but the new administration was proving admirably decisive.[33]

Frederick Terman was also pleased by the appointment of Levorsen. It was, in his view, "a real start toward solving one of our major problems." Terman had just accepted Tresidder's offer of the deanship of Stanford's school of engineering, succeeding Samuel Morris, who had resigned from the position in late 1944 to assume the directorship of the Los Angeles Municipal Water and Power Company. Ambitious and full of plans, Terman now had an opportunity both to advance his career at Stanford and to implement the reforms that he, Davis, and Tresidder had discussed.[34]

Terman's appointment was not received with unanimous enthusiasm by Stanford's engineers, who met to discuss the appointment and then offered Tresidder their reservations. Terman, they warned, was difficult to get along with and was "impatient of others' opinions, and set in his own," according to the acting chairperson of the civil engineering department, who reported the group's opinion. More important, many of the faculty members believed that Terman was too narrow in his interests to be an effective dean. His expertise was in a subfield of electrical engineering; a dean, they argued, needed to be familiar with several engineering fields if he were to guide the school and play an important role in appointments and promotions.[35] But it was, in part, this narrowness that made Terman an appealing candidate for the deanship. Tresidder knew well that Terman was interested in building a strong program at Stanford in communications and radio engineering that would have close ties to the electronics industry, and Tresidder wanted him as dean precisely for this reason. The members of the engineering school, however, worried that Terman was interested only in developing a particular facet of engineering and was dismissive of other engineering traditions. Some feared that the school's tradition of breadth of coverage would be lost with Terman as dean.

Their concern was apt. Terman was soon making clear to the acting chair of the electrical engineering department, Hugh Skilling, the particular focus his administration of the engineering school would have. Terman was planning to hire the former director of research for Caterpillar Tractor to fill a new position with responsibility for developing and managing the engineering school's contacts with industry. The job would involve developing industrial patronage as well as "steering our younger people . . . into fields which are going to have a big rather than a small future," he explained.[36] The interests of industry were, of course, playing a large role in determining what fields would have a "big" rather than a "small" future.

Fields that were "big," in Terman's mind, were those that were of interest to expanding industries and that were perceived as having contributed significantly to the development of war technologies. Electronics was one such field; it would be "big" after the war primarily because the electronics industry would rapidly exploit for commercial purposes the technologies that had been developed during the war. One field with a "small" future, Terman had already made clear, was illumination. This was an area of "rather limited opportunities," Terman had indicated in early 1941 to President Wilbur, recommending that two professors in his department be let go. Firing them would be "disagreeable, messy, and not entirely in accord with usual traditions of academic tenure," Terman admitted, but he rationalized that the university could get "more for its money" with other professors.[37] Wilbur did not take Terman's advice, but some in the school of engineering may well have feared that with Terman as dean, similar attempts would be made to give preference to some engineering work and to deemphasize or even eliminate other kinds.

By early 1945, then, Tresidder had placed new people at the head of two divisions within the university in the belief that they would draw engineering and geology firmly toward cooperation with industrial concerns interested in sponsoring academic research. He also hoped that the university's aeronautical engineers would develop strong ties to the aeronautics industry. In addition, Tresidder wanted to effect changes in Stanford's physics department. Terman and Davis had convinced him that research related to microwaves was a field that, like its allied field, electronics, was sure to have a "big" future after the war. The physicists involved in work on the klystron had succeeded in attracting substantial industrial patronage in the late 1930s; Tresidder was eager to renew the department's ties to industry after the war.

So were some, but not all, of Stanford's physicists. The suggestion that Stanford create a microwave laboratory and solicit support from industrial patrons stirred considerable controversy among the physicists and between some physicists and the Tresidder administration. The physicists debated not only whether industry was an appropriate patron but also how patronage and new institutional forms might affect the role of the academic scientist and alter academic traditions. These concerns were not singular to the physics department but were very much related to the broader transformation being wrought at Stanford and other universities at the end of World War II. In the disputes over the microwave laboratory, it is possible to see clearly what was being lost and what others hoped to gain by establishing new institutions, eroding the tradition of departmental autonomy, and developing new forms of patronage.

The Microwave Laboratory

In late 1942 Ray Lyman Wilbur, soon to cede the leadership of Stanford to Donald Tresidder, called into his office the two senior physicists still on campus—Paul Kirkpatrick, acting chair of the physics department, and Felix Bloch. He informed them that he was allocating to their department all of the royalties that Stanford had collected to date from the Sperry Gyroscope Company.[38] Wilbur himself was less interested in how the money was spent than in making sure that the physicists were the ones to make the decision. He was aware that Davis, Tresidder, and others on the board of trustees were strongly interested in reforming the university, possibly eliminating some departments and exercising more control over others. About the same time, Tresidder confessed unhappily to Paul Edwards, head of the trustee committee planning Stanford's future, that he had erred seriously: he had shared with Wilbur the details of Davis's ideas for reforming the university, and Wilbur had reacted quite badly. According to Tresidder, Wilbur was "vehemently of the opinion that [Paul Davis's plan for reform] would be a mistake both for Stanford and for Paul." Thus, in allocating the klystron royalties to the physicists and urging them to spend the money promptly, it seems that Wilbur, who had granted departments considerable autonomy during his presidency, was trying to ensure that the physicists, rather than the trustees or the university's next administration, determined the future of Stanford's physics department.[39] The result was that the physicists, unlike their colleagues in other departments that Tresidder sought to transform, became engaged in lengthy, often heated debates about their department, about its proper relation to industrial patrons, and about the role of an academic scientist.

Felix Bloch and William Hansen hoped to use the proffered funds to create a laboratory for research on microwaves, which would be funded in part by industry. Bloch had suggested the idea, arguing that this was the "natural use" of money derived from research on microwave devices, but it was an unusual suggestion from the physicist who before the war had criticized his department's involvement with Sperry. The war, however, had changed Bloch's views about the proper domain of academic physics. The federally sponsored research program, which put academic scientists to work designing weapons of war, had impressed him. He now regarded his prewar devotion to the concept of "*l'art pour l'art*" as both "snobbish" and untenable.[40]

While wartime developments justified the establishment of a new tradition in the physics department, according to Bloch, they did not motivate his proposal for the laboratory. As he admitted to Hansen, the lab was intended as "a kind of bait" to lure the talented young experimentalist back to Stanford after the war.[41] Hansen had been unhappy at Stanford before the war, believing that Webster, head of the department, was dictatorial and that Webster and Stanford's administration did not properly appreciate his inventiveness. For example, in 1940 Hansen had sought both early promotion to full professor and a substantial raise, using as leverage an offer from Westinghouse to join the company's laboratory at $6,000 per year (a salary well above that of a full professor at Stanford). Webster had responded by encouraging Hansen to take the new position.[42] Bloch, however, had a highly favorable view of Hansen's talents and wanted him to return to Stanford.

Coloring Bloch's estimation of Hansen were his own research interests and his ambitions for Stanford. The microwave laboratory, Bloch hoped, would draw attention to Stanford and make it competitive with Berkeley and Caltech. Unlike Stanford, those universities had moved into "big science," establishing laboratories that provided their physicists with advanced scientific equipment and that attracted substantial patronage, large numbers of students, and, occasionally, attention from the popular press. Moreover, Bloch, a theorist, had begun to do experimental work in nuclear physics in the 1940s and realized that to pursue his research interests further he needed the support of an experimentalist. It was during the war that Bloch conceived the idea for measuring the magnetic moment of the neutron, work for which he would win the Nobel Prize in 1952. "I needed somebody [with knowledge of radio techniques] and Bill Hansen was a great expert," he would later recall. (Hansen and Bloch developed the technique and patented it after the war.) By midwar, then, Bloch had decided that, other than himself, Hansen was the most valuable member of Stanford's department. Cajoling Hansen, he suggested that if they were together at Stanford after the war, the two physicists "would be strong enough to get an awfully nice physics department."[43]

As Bloch had hoped, Hansen, deeply flattered, embraced the laboratory proposal with enthusiasm. Although by the late 1930s Hansen himself had found working under Sperry's sponsorship frustrating, he did not generalize from the experience and hoped to develop new alliances between the physics department and industry after the war. The war, in fact, reinforced Hansen's interest in applied physics and in working with industrial concerns. Since 1940 his expertise had been in great demand; he traveled continuously between Sperry's Long Island lab, where he worked on applications of the klystron, and MIT's Radiation Laboratory, the locus of work on radar, and he took out seventy patents in his name over the course of the war. Although he worked unceasingly, permanently impairing his health (Hansen would die a few years after the war at the age of 39), Hansen found the experience exhilarating. It convinced him both of the value of his particular talents and interests and of the possibility of successfully bridging the worlds of industrialists and academicians, to the mutual benefit of both.[44]

Confirming and shaping his views was Frederick Terman, with whom Hansen conferred about the proposed laboratory. The lab, they agreed, would foster further cooperation between the electrical engineering and physics departments. In the late 1930s, Terman, who believed that a knowledge of physics was becoming crucial to his own discipline of electrical engineering, had assigned two of his graduate students to work in the physics department and help Hansen with engineering problems related to the klystron. The microwave laboratory, which would be located between the physics and engineering departments, would both institutionalize their interdepartmental interests and provide a means for attracting industrial patronage. "We have something to sell that Sperry and/or others will want," Hansen proposed in a letter to Tresidder, using language that no doubt resonated with Stanford's president. The laboratory's "products" might include research, expert advice, and access to students (potential employees), Hansen wrote, but not "our souls."[45] Hansen and Terman were convinced that through careful attention to institutional arrangements, the physicists would be able to control the relationship with industry, as they had failed to do before the war.

Others in the physics department were wary, however. Webster, in particular, was extremely skeptical of the proposal to renew microwave research with industrial sponsorship. His experience with Sperry had confirmed his earlier views that industrial patronage and academic physics were inherently incompatible because the basic interests of each were fundamentally different. In Webster's view, industry sought profits, and academic physicists sought truths about the physical world. Any interaction with industry inevitably, if not immediately, warped the physicists' research because industry, as the patron, ultimately controlled the relationship and twisted it to its own purposes. If the physicists again took money from Sperry, Webster warned, the company would no doubt "gently hint that if only we direct the royalty-fed researches into more useful lines, and if only we would not publish yet— 'will you come into my parlor?' said the spider to the fly." No institutional arrangement could correct for this basic inequality in power. If Hansen and Bloch insisted on pursuing industrial rather than pure physics after the war, they should establish the laboratory in the engineering school, Webster advised.[46]

The department's other senior physicists—Paul Kirkpatrick and Norris Bradbury, who worked on the Manhattan Project during the war and became the first postwar director of the Los Alamos Laboratory— also expressed concern that the proposed laboratory might open their department to undesirable pressures from industrial concerns. Like all of the department's physicists, they regarded the windfall from the klystron as an opportunity to improve their department, but for them, creating a laboratory was neither the only nor the best way to do so. They agreed with Webster that at least a portion of the royalties should be used to create fellowships for gifted students. Unlike Webster, however, they were unwilling to regard microwave research as outside the domain of physics. As Kirkpatrick pointed out, Hansen believed he was doing physics, and that alone should satisfy the department.[47]

After a flurry of debate over the laboratory, the physicists had reached an impasse, and Webster agreed to Bradbury's suggestion that the decision about how to use the klystron royalties be postponed until after the war, when the physicists would all be back at Stanford and could thoroughly discuss the matter.[48] But the postponement, Bloch and Hansen believed, spelled the end of the laboratory idea. A majority of the department's members opposed, or at least were wary of, the microwave laboratory, and Webster, as chairperson, would influence significantly the final decision. Eager to act before Webster returned from his wartime duty with the army, the proponents of the laboratory decided to appeal directly to the university's administration. Rather than take their case to Wilbur, then in the final months of his presidency, they went to Tresidder, Wilbur's designated successor and known to them to be friendly with Frederick Terman. They were, in effect, seeking to circumvent the tradition of departmental autonomy, which Wilbur, in proffering the klystron royalties to the department, had been hoping to reinforce.[49]

Tresidder, already deeply involved in planning with Terman and Davis to exercise administrative control over the direction and future of academic departments and to develop industrial patronage, enthusiastically endorsed the proposed microwave laboratory. "We were lucky in the choice of our new president," Bloch wrote to Hansen. Tresidder was "more on the practical than the scholarly side and it may well be that history, classics, etc. may not fare too well under his influence . . . but I am not the least afraid for physics."[50] This "serves Webster right," Bloch gloated to Hansen. Indeed, Tresidder, once president, not only approved the creation of the microwave laboratory, he also fired Webster from his position as chairperson, regarding him as an impediment to the plans to transform the physics department and, more broadly, the university.[51]

The demotion of Webster did not suppress the controversies over the laboratory, however. They were, instead, immediately raised again with respect to staff for the laboratory. Problems arose in early 1945 when Hansen, with Tresidder's approval, began looking for an assistant director for the laboratory, who was also to have a position in the physics department. Hansen soon selected Edward Ginzton, an electrical engineer who had received his doctorate at Stanford working under Frederick Terman and had been one of the students assigned to work with Hansen on the klystron. Ginzton had never held an academic job, having gone to work for Sperry immediately after graduating from Stanford. In fact, it was his position as Sperry's capable and respected director of research that made him an especially attractive candidate to Hansen. (Ginzton would soon play a major role in convincing Sperry to renew its sponsorship of microwave research at Stanford.)

The proposed appointment troubled Webster and Kirkpatrick, who had replaced Webster as department chair. Not only had Ginzton not been trained as a physicist, but his research interests were also highly specialized. If the excitement over research on microwaves should spend itself and industry should lose interest, what would the department do with Ginzton, who was unfamiliar with most areas of physics? To Webster this was one of the dangers of specializing in a field strongly tied to commercial interests. But Ginzton's narrow training also raised questions about his ability to teach. Department members traditionally shared the responsibility for teaching the undergraduate physics courses, a practice emanating from Webster's belief that an academic physicist should be committed to teaching as well as research. It was such a commitment, in fact, that had strongly influenced Webster's decision to come to Stanford in 1920. At that time, he had also entertained a generous offer from General Electric, which promised him virtually unrestricted funds to develop an x-ray laboratory. "Without any doubt I am passing up the chance of a lifetime in research," he had written then. But as he explained his decision to Irving Langmuir of G.E., "The problem of teaching physics . . . is one that appeals to me strongly. It is not well done in most places."[52] Thus, Webster was troubled by the appointment of Ginzton, who, as an engineer, would be ill prepared to teach basic physics courses. Further, although Ginzton would have few, if any, teaching responsibilities, he was being promised a salary of $4,000, an extraordinary figure at that time for an assistant professor at Stanford. (Assistant professors earned between $1,500 to $2,000 annually in the mid-1940s.) Although Hansen pointed out that the amount was justified to lure Ginzton from a well-paid job in industry, it signified to Webster and Kirkpatrick a devaluation of teaching.

The choice of Ginzton threatened more than the department's traditional commitments to teaching. With Tresidder's approval, Hansen had selected a new member of the department without consulting the other members of the department or the chairperson, thereby challenging both the authority of the department chairperson and the departmental tradition of discussing collectively such matters as faculty appointments. Unlike Webster, who could be belligerent, Kirkpatrick usually avoided controversy. But Kirkpatrick was also committed to maintaining his own authority as chair and to the idea of a department as a collection of scientists who together determined the course of their department. He thus attempted to open the proposed appointment of Ginzton to consideration by the entire department. The effort was futile. With the exception of Webster, who had already been alienated from both the department and the Tresidder administration, no one else in the department was willing to challenge Hansen's newly conferred authority or, by extension, the authority of the administration. The appointment was made. To mollify Webster, Ginzton's title was modified: he would be an assistant professor of "applied physics."[53]

Kirkpatrick's stubborn insistence that the physics department act as a collective in making decisions about appointments irritated both Bloch and Hansen, and eventually Stanford's administration asked for Kirkpatrick's resignation. Kirkpatrick put up no opposition. As he later wrote, he was not the right sort of person for the head of a physics department after the war. What was needed was "a skilled and enthusiastic promoter of supportive contacts and contracts," someone not overly concerned with what kind of research these contracts supported, with whether the department's members were committed to teaching as well as research, or with the way the department made decisions about its future. Kirkpatrick was acknowledging, in effect, that he represented older values and modes of operation; he preferred to resign rather than embrace the new.[54]

Who Controls the University?

A new set of values and relations were being institutionalized in the university at the close of World War II to enable the university to take better advantage of an expected outpouring of patronage after the war. Stanford's administration was making clear that in the sciences and engineering, research was now more highly valued than teaching, and research likely to have a big future and to attract industrial patronage was more highly esteemed than research deemed impractical, or purely academic. The idea of the university as a haven from the world of commerce and, more broadly, from society had never been uncontested. But at the end of the war, those professors who still held this view found themselves in an inhospitable environment as university administrators, along with some faculty members, rejected the concept of the ivory tower as obsolete. University administrators envisioned the university as an efficiently run, businesslike enterprise, an idea that also had roots in the past, beginning with Hoover's interest as a trustee in the 1920s in reorganizing and rationalizing the university's operations. Now, administrators and some professors were explicitly describing research and trained students as salable products and welcoming interested buyers, leading Webster to wonder how Stanford "stays tax-free when it functions partly as an industrial laboratory."[55]

Impelling the administration to transform Stanford and challenge the older academic tradition of the university were a need for money and a belief that financial needs could best be met by equating the administration of a university with the management of a business. President Tresidder, who was in contact with other university presidents and an active participant in the Association of American Universities, also believed he was moving Stanford in the direction most likely to confer prestige upon the institution. The developments in Stanford's science and engineering departments signaled the university's determination to foster work of relevance to certain groups in society and to discourage and downgrade work designated merely academic in nature.

The tradition of departmental autonomy was an obstacle to this set of values and concerns. To older professors like Blackwelder and Webster, departments provided insulation from interference in academic affairs and disciplinary developments by administrators, who were suspect because of their responsibilities for fund-raising and their connections to the university's board of trustees. To some younger professors, such as Hansen, however, departmental autonomy was an obstacle to career aspirations; these professors, who did not see the academic and industrial worlds as diametrically opposed, eagerly joined forces with Stanford's administrators to thwart departmental traditions. Together with the university administrators, they created and celebrated a new academic type—a professor devoted to research and strongly connected to the world outside the university, an entrepreneur in search of research funds upon which his career, and the university's financial well-being and reputation, depended.

The rejection of one tradition and the concerted effort to establish a new one occurred within a short time at Stanford and provoked considerable dismay and some opposition from the university's faculty. To the watchful faculty members on campus during the war, Tresidder's first significant act as president—the creation of the position of vice president—was the first signal that Tresidder intended to reorganize the university and centralize control over faculty affairs. As one biology professor reported at the time, "[T]here was a boiling and burbling and quite some sputtering among a good many of the faculty members of the whole darned University" in response to Tresidder's action. When challenged by a committee of senior professors, Tresidder had upset them further by bluntly warning them that the president, not the faculty, ran the university and that the president's authority derived from the board of trustees, who "ARE the University as far as policies and administration is concerned."[56]

Stanford's administrators were not alone in their efforts to make clear to faculty members that they controlled the university. Some professors at the University of California at Berkeley had also become distressed that the true purpose of the American university—free and independent inquiry—was being "jeopardized by the accession to power in the educational world of men who have no adequate appreciation of the significance of scholarly pursuits. . . . They regard administration as the master of scholarship instead of its servant."[57] These Berkeley professors drafted "An Affirmation of Purpose of the American University," a petition that was soon circulating on the Stanford campus and attracting the endorsements of Blackwelder, Webster, and senior professors in Stanford's departments of chemistry, biology, history, mathematics, romance languages, and medicine.

Some of these professors had clashed with Tresidder over the appointment of a vice president, others over appointments in their own departments. Some had been upset to discover that professors working in fields established during the war, such as microwave research and area studies, were receiving higher salaries than professors with longer service and heavy teaching duties. As one senior professor wrote plaintively in 1944, "*Why* is it that I do not receive a similar salary to that paid scores of others here with no more, and usually less, experience and reputation? . . . How many years must a person slave before he is accorded what others (in the same and other departments) have long received?"[58]

The suspicion that Tresidder, in addition to challenging departmental autonomy, was intent on forcing those professors interested in research to seek support from outside the university budget, particularly from industrial patrons, swelled the ranks of disgruntled faculty members at Stanford. Tresidder's support for Hansen and Bloch in the physics department and for Levorsen and Waters in geology might alone have created this suspicion. But in early 1946, shortly after the administration announced the creation of the Stanford Research Institute, Tresidder informed the faculty that he was abolishing the university's own research fund. Created by President Wilbur after World War I, the fund had been intended to provide those faculty members interested in research with support free of any constraints. Other universities had similar, although much larger, funds; Stanford's, at its largest, was only a few thousand dollars, evidence of the university's perpetual financial difficulties. Faculty members appreciated the money that was available, however, as it made possible research trips and small-scale experiments. By eliminating the fund, Tresidder appeared to be compelling faculty members who were interested in research to conduct research relevant to industry through the new institute. He also seemed to be demonstrating a lack of appreciation for research of modest proportions as opposed to large-scale, expensive projects such as those being proposed by Hansen and Bloch in the physics department.[59]

Tresidder's announcement confirmed for Blackwelder and other senior and emeritus professors that Stanford's administration was hostile to the tradition of free and unfettered scholarly and scientific research and, further, that the president was determined to reduce the faculty to the status of mere employees. Tresidder's action had "shaken the faculty to its fdn [foundation]," Blackwelder fumed. "Is U. [university] to be run like a business—Bd. [Board of Trustees] decides, employees execute!"[60] Some of the youngest members of Stanford's faculty were also upset. Without established reputations, they stood little chance of attracting patronage; the university's research fund was for them a significant source of research support, and its elimination was especially troubling.

At Blackwelder's instigation, a meeting of the faculty was called to discuss the actions of Stanford's administrators. About sixty faculty members attended, half of them senior or emeritus, the other half very young members of the faculty; they agreed, according to a "spy" who recounted the gist of the meeting to Tresidder, that Stanford administrators were the "worst gang of blackguards that ever came down the pike" and that it was time for faculty members to "assert their rights."[61] Within days, they had arranged a meeting with Tresidder, who, under pressure, promised to restore the university's research fund.[62] The restoration of the university's fund for faculty research was a gesture of conciliation by Tresidder, but a small one; the fund remained tiny and would never provide an alternative to outside patronage for those faculty members with extensive research plans. Tresidder was not indicating a change in his plans for Stanford; by April 1946, when the faculty staged its protest, most of Tresidder's plans for reform had already been put in place.

The members of the faculty did not again organize and protest the actions of the Tresidder administration, and the profound anger expressed by Blackwelder and a few others did not spread to a larger body of the faculty. Clearly, a significant number of Stanford's faculty members either had no opinion about the changes occurring within the university or, like Bloch and Hansen in physics and Waters in geology, they approved of the administration's goals and rejoiced in the weakening of departmental authority.[63] Most of those who disagreed vehemently with Tresidder were either emeritus professors or senior professors near retirement; their expression of outrage was, in effect, a last protest before leaving the scene. The younger professors who were unhappy with the administration had other concerns as well—such as obtaining tenure—that militated against prolonged expressions of dissatisfaction.

But larger forces were also at work that may have discouraged faculty members at Stanford, and at other universities as well, from expressing dissatisfaction with the university's new relationships with society and from challenging openly the authority of university administrators. By early 1947 the Red Scare was underway, as the House Un-American Activities Committee (HUAC) launched investigations into alleged communist infiltration of federal agencies, labor unions, Hollywood, and educational institutions and President Truman established the Federal Employee Loyalty Program. The impact of the Red Scare on college campuses has been well documented: professors fired for their political views or affiliations or for invoking the Fifth Amendment, university faculty and employees required to take loyalty oaths, university administrators secretly cooperating with the FBI or with representatives of HUAC and its counterparts at the state level.[64]

The resulting atmosphere of fear and suspicion no doubt had a chilling effect on those at Stanford and elsewhere who might under other circumstances have voiced their opinions about political matters. The climate of conformity may also have discouraged dissent that lacked direct political import, such as criticism of universities and their administrators. It is possible that, at Stanford, the accusations that one participant in the April 1946 meeting—Thomas Addis—was a political subversive may have split the ranks of disgruntled faculty members, some of whom were conservative and vocal anticommunists. Although Addis's accusers did not cite his complaints about Stanford's administration as evidence that he was a subversive, the attack on him may well have given pause to others who had up to that point felt free to state their views.[65]

The Red Scare, as played out at Stanford and other universities, leaves no doubt that university administrators ultimately controlled affairs within their institutions and that faculty members, however skilled in subverting departmental authority, did not. This fact was made painfully clear to Hansen and Bloch beginning in 1947. Having won Tresidder's approval to select a new chairperson for the physics department, the two physicists had settled on Edward U. Condon, the newly appointed head of the National Bureau of Standards and a highly respected physicist. While the offer was privately conveyed to Condon, it was never made officially. Seeking validation for the physicists' choice, President Tresidder in mid-1947 had turned to Vannevar Bush, who was aware of Tresidder's aspirations for Stanford and was well positioned as both advisor to the government and head of a research institution to judge the proposed appointment. Although Condon had not yet been labeled by HUAC as "one of the weakest links in our atomic security," Bush no doubt knew of Condon's wartime conflicts with Gen. Leslie Groves over security regulations at Los Alamos, as well as of his vocal opposition after the war to proposed governmental restrictions on scientific research and the exchange of information. Bush advised Tresidder of the "limitations" of the appointment. He supported instead the appointment of the head of the Atomic Energy Commission's (AEC) Los Alamos Laboratory, Norris Bradbury, and suggested that Tresidder seek the AEC's opinion.[66]

Unaware of Tresidder's decision, Bloch and Hansen continued to expect Condon's appointment and to express "complete confidence" in Stanford's administration. It was not until early 1948, after Condon had been charged publicly with disloyalty by HUAC, that Bloch and Hansen understood that the appointment would not be made.[67] Alvin Eurich, who had become the acting president of Stanford upon Tresidder's death in January 1948, suggested that Condon, according to Hansen, was "unstable" and that too many people were "sore" at him; Eurich proposed instead that Bradbury be appointed chair.[68]

The incident stunned Bloch, who seemed to have been convinced that Stanford's administration had granted him, but not other professors, complete freedom of action. In a series of letters to Hansen, Bloch asked repeatedly why the administration had dropped Condon, although the answer was clear.[69] He then attacked "His Eurichship" for interfering in the selection of the department chair.[70] Bloch did not, however, voice his opinions to Eurich, nor did he seek to forge with other faculty members a united opposition to the administration's active involvement in what had once been defined as strictly departmental matters. That Stanford's administrators ultimately controlled the internal affairs of the university was undeniable, something that those professors who had sought to uphold the tradition of departmental autonomy had well understood.

Clearly, the activities of university administrators were themselves responsive to forces outside the university and constrained both by the developing political climate and by institutional financial needs. The sensitivity of university administrators to attacks on professors as "disloyal" was in large measure related to their concerns that such attacks damaged their university's reputation and hence its ability to attract patronage. But while the era known as McCarthyism was clearly unique, it is important to recognize that the efforts of academic administrators to shape departments and to channel intellectual efforts were not specific to the Red Scare. In the decades following World War II, Stanford administrators would continue to reshape their university with the aim of developing patronage and institutional prestige.

4

"Exploiting a Wonderful Opportunity"

By the end of World War II a virtual consensus existed throughout the country—in policy circles, in Congress, among the leaders of the scientific community and the universities—that the federal government had an important role to play in the support of postwar academic science. Scientists, it was claimed, had become essential for waging war. The proposed United Nations might succeed in preventing future conflicts, but military preparedness could not be neglected, particularly in light of the technological developments of World War II. Air power and guided missiles had changed the nature of global warfare, rendering insignificant the vast distances between the United States and potential enemies. The atomic bombing of Japan reinforced the views that war could now begin and end instantaneously and that a nation's science, not its soldiers, ultimately determined the outcome of any conflict. Preparedness was thus essential, and a crucial component of this preparedness was a well-funded scientific community, producing the research and the next generation of scientists upon which the next war's technology would depend.

This was the context in which federal support for academic science became available, and the views of the nation's academic leaders and most of its scientists fit squarely within it. A few scientists did decry the military origins of most postwar federal support, but most did not. Even these objections, however, were focused on the possible constraints that a military sponsor might place on academic research, not on the ultimate uses to which civilian science might be put. Postwar military patrons successfully met these concerns. The Office of Naval

Research (ONR), the principal military patron in the years immediately following the war, was not only extraordinarily generous by prewar standards but also placed few restrictions on the scientists receiving research support.[1]

But if federal patronage was widely accepted after the war, university administrators initially differed in their thinking about the kind of relationship their institutions would form with federal sponsors. The relationship was, within certain limits, malleable, and ideology and institutional needs influenced the way academic administrators approached federal patronage in the late 1940s. James Conant of Harvard, for example, ruled out contracts with the military for applied or classified research as being in conflict with the traditions of the university and of science. Administrators at Brown University, by contrast, argued that universities might justifiably reject patronage from industry for applied or secret research but that they were obliged to undertake research for the military, regardless of whether the research was strictly in keeping with academic tradition. After all, the government was not, like industrial patrons, in search of profits; it was concerned with "matters of public moment."[2]

Karl Compton of MIT, whose institution did not have recourse, as did Harvard, to a large endowment, had still a different viewpoint. He urged university administrators to accept contracts for applied and classified work but to demand generous recompense for bending academic tradition to assist the military. At the annual meeting of the AAU in 1946, Compton encouraged administrators to ask for overhead payments from the government in excess of their institutions' indirect costs. "I don't like to speak of it as profit," Compton insisted. But whether he spoke openly or merely thought privately about profit, Compton's message was clear: universities had a duty to assist the federal government, but that duty need not involve sacrifice. If handled properly, in fact, the relationship with the federal government might enrich America's universities.[3]

Concerned about institutional finances and reputation, Stanford's administrators generally shared Compton's perspective. Government-sponsored research, as Frederick Terman was quick to point out to President Tresidder, offered the university "a wonderful opportunity if we are prepared to exploit it."[4] But while Tresidder encouraged Terman's interest in using federal patronage to Stanford's advantage, he and Terman disagreed over the mode of exploitation and the degree to which the university should become dependent on federal patronage. At the heart of their disagreement were different views of the postwar research economy and of the proper relationship between the university and the federal government.

Tresidder, still taking seriously the distinctions between the public and the private spheres, was wary of federal patronage. The university should not become dependent on such support, he believed; cultivating industrial patronage was essential, in part, to provide a balance to military-sponsored research. Terman, in contrast, was eager to blur the boundaries between the federal government and the university. Not troubled by the prospect of the university becoming dependent on federal support, he in fact encouraged this development, anticipating a postwar research economy characterized by generous and stable military patronage. Believing that the university could depend on federal patronage, Terman began reconceptualizing the university's alliance with industry, seeing it not as separate from and a necessary balance to the university's relationship to the federal government but rather as an integral part of a triangular relationship.

Developments in the late 1940s favored Terman's inclinations and outlook. At the time, private industry showed little interest in supporting academic research, whereas federal support for academic research grew and then stabilized, reaching approximately $140 million in 1949.[5] The dominance of federal monies in the research economy concerned some university administrators, but to Terman the proper response to this development was to take advantage of it and forge extensive links between Stanford's School of Engineering and military patrons. Terman's overriding goal was to make Stanford into a nationally significant institution, which, by the late 1940s, meant an institution involved in and shaped by the cold war.

Envisioning the Federal-University Relationship

Stanford administrators expressed interest in postwar federal patronage even before the end of World War II, proposing in late 1944 that Stanford maintain its office in Washington, D.C., after the end of hostilities. The office was to function much as it had in wartime, providing the university with "a base of operations" for "making and maintaining contacts with the federal government." The eagerness of Stanford administrators to obtain research support from the federal government after the war reflected institutional concerns. President Tresidder clearly expected that, just as close association with the OSRD had conferred status, so postwar contracts with the federal government would be an indicator of a university's prestige. That Stanford had largely been left out of the wartime research program made participation in a federally sponsored program of research after the war especially important to Stanford's administrators, who had no intention of allowing their university to be again left out of an important development. Moreover, Tresidder, a strong anticommunist, had no doubt about the importance of military preparedness, warning as early as 1945 of the "ominous implications of the present differences among the Allies" and condemning the "endemic disease known as collectivism."[6]

Like Tresidder, Terman believed that federal patronage was crucial to Stanford's postwar development. He was also entirely supportive of the purported aim of federally sponsored research—improving the defense of the nation. The idea that the work of scientists and engineers was essential to national defense confirmed Terman's firm belief in the importance of experts to modern society, a belief that had been shaped by his father as well as by his graduate advisor, Vannevar Bush.

Terman also had a deep faith in the abilities of engineers like himself to solve the nation's problems. In contemplating the postwar world, he doubted both that political and diplomatic efforts would succeed in thwarting an arms race and that the United Nations would be effective in preventing future conflicts. "It is entirely conceivable that the world may have to go through one atomic war before the lesson is learned," he wrote to the physicist James Van Vleck, who objected strongly to Terman's ideas. Terman believed that his own wartime expertise, directing the development of techniques to counter the war technologies of the nation's enemies, would be of particular value to the nation's postwar defense. "Countermeasures can not of course provide full protection against an atomic bomb," he admitted; still, they would "make the difference between the destruction and survival of the nation in the event an atomic war broke out." Believing in the significance of electronics to the nation's defense, Terman was eager for Stanford to contribute.[7]

Terman and Tresidder agreed that Stanford should not wait for federal agencies to offer research support. Instead, as during World War II, a representative of Stanford should go directly to those offering the research contracts and convince them of Stanford's interest. Terman, who had made many useful contacts during the war with those who were responsible after the war for letting research contracts to academic scientists and engineers, was happy to act "as initial man for the university."[8] On one of a number of trips to the East Coast, Terman met separately with seven different representatives of the ONR, as well as with representatives of the navy's Bureaus of Ships and Aeronautics, the NACA, the Army Air Force, and the Army Signal Corps to ascertain their interests and offer Stanford's assistance. This aggressive pursuit of patronage paid off. A year after the war, Stanford had over $500,000 worth of research contracts with military agencies. The amount was small compared to contract support at other universities such as MIT, Caltech, Berkeley, and Johns Hopkins, but it represented almost twice what Stanford had obtained over the course of the war from the OSRD. A few faculty members, acting on their own, had obtained research support from the federal government; Terman, acting on behalf of the departments of chemistry, physics, aeronautical engineering, electrical engineering, and mathematics, brought $380,000 worth of contracts to Stanford in the first year after the war.[9]

While Stanford's administrators agreed that federal patronage was desirable and should be pursued aggressively, they disagreed over the nature of the relationships between the federal government and the university and between federal and industrial patronage. These disagreements were rooted in different philosophies about the relationship between public and private institutions, in different expectations for the postwar political economy, and in different ideas about the role of academic experts in society. Tresidder, who at the end of the war had begun reshaping Stanford to attract industrial patronage, continued to regard industry as the preferred patron and the one on which Stanford should rely most heavily after the war. Unlike government patronage, to which he had objected before 1941, Tresidder never had reservations about industrial support. He regarded the private university and private industry as natural partners, reinforcing and supporting each other's interests and needs. The possibility that Stanford might become heavily dependent on industrial support did not trouble Tresidder; in fact, it suited him and he looked forward to developing a cooperative relationship with industrial patrons. The clearest expression of his interest in and hopes for industrial patronage was the establishment, with a large loan from Stanford, of the Stanford Research Institute (SRI).

Tresidder's expectations for industrial support were not unique. Between 1944 and 1947 seventy institutions of higher education established institutes for industry-sponsored research or made organizational changes to facilitate industrial patronage, believing that the wartime developments of the atomic bomb and radar had finally made clear to private industry the crucial link between scientific research and technological innovation and the importance of funding academic research. As Karl Compton explained in early 1946, "Many people who had been skeptical of the power of research . . . are now aware of what it can accomplish. The problem now is not to sell the idea of research so much as to find ways and means whereby small companies can get the benefits." While Tresidder expected industry to be interested in supporting academic research after the war, he and other university administrators were also ready to compromise should industry again show reluctance to provide patronage without promise of a clear return on its investment as it had in the 1920s, when the National Research Fund failed to attract sponsors. The purpose of university-affiliated institutes such as SRI was to offer a locus on campus for research of direct interest to industrial patrons.[10]

The kinds of industrial enterprises solicited by SRI and the kinds of industries Tresidder assumed would support university-based research reveal his expectations for the postwar economy. Institute representatives and some Stanford professors sought patronage from the airline industry, the oil industry, agricultural companies, utilities, and the food-processing and forestry-related industries. Absent from Tresidder's field of vision were the electronics industry and other businesses that had benefited directly from the wartime governmental research program and would continue after the war to produce defense-related products.[11] Tresidder expected the postwar economy to be a healthy version of the prewar economy; he certainly did not anticipate a militarized postwar economy.

Thus, in Tresidder's view, the relationship developing between Stanford and its military patrons was distinct from and unrelated to the university's industrial research program. Unlike industry, the military (and more broadly, the federal government) was not looked upon by Stanford's president as a potential partner or collaborator of the university. The federal agencies offering contracts for research were, after all, funded with public money; Stanford, conversely, was a private institution. This distinction between the public and the private still mattered to Tresidder and was reflected in his strong reluctance to allow Stanford to participate in the G.I. bill.[12] While Tresidder was willing for Stanford to do research under contract to federal agencies, he did not want Stanford to become dependent on federal funds, the source of which he regarded as undependable and subject to the vagaries of politics. Industry would be Stanford's main postwar patron, Tresidder expected, and industrial support would ensure that the university maintained its independence from the public sphere.

And yet, Tresidder readily approved of military patronage for Stanford, in part because he believed, as did Dean R.D.G. Richardson of Brown University, that accepting military contracts, including those for applied or classified research, was an obligation incumbent upon all postwar universities. But he also viewed military patronage from the perspective of Stanford's institutional needs and was open to "exploiting" governmental patronage. Tresidder's ideas about the institutional value of federal patronage were shaped by his understanding of the wartime relationship between the OSRD and universities. Contracts with the federal government seemed to offer two things. First, they provided good publicity for the university involved, making clear to the public that the university was eminent enough to attract federal patronage and that it was contributing to the nation's well-being. Second, federal contracts provided overhead payments, which Tresidder had used since the war as unrestricted funds.

Tresidder's views about the university's relationship to military patrons was illustrated by his opinions of two contracts offered to Stanford soon after the war. One was a contract with the Chemical Warfare Service that had been offered to Philip Leighton, chairperson of the chemistry department and wartime director of the Chemical Warfare Service's research on gases and incendiary bombs. The research was classified and unrelated to the academic interests of the chemistry department, and most of the contract funds were used to hire researchers who worked on month-to-month contracts and did not have faculty appointments. These features bothered Leighton, who had accepted the contract with Tresidder's approval but had intended to turn it over to the SRI as soon as it was established.[13] But the contract was wholly in keeping with Tresidder's thinking about the postwar relations between Stanford and military sponsors of research. Given his concern that the university not become dependent on federal patronage, the month-to-month contracts, which bothered Leighton, seemed sensible to Tresidder. He did not believe that government contracts would be renewed indefinitely and so preferred that the university have no commitment to the researchers involved. Tresidder, himself a postwar advisor to the Chemical Warfare Service, accepted restrictions on the exchange of information as both necessary to the nation's defense and the prerogative of the patron: "The hand which holds the purse strings sways the throne," Tresidder reminded his colleagues in the AAU in 1947. The axiom was, to Tresidder, incontrovertible; he did not urge his fellow administrators to challenge the right of federal patrons to dictate the terms of the federal-university relationship. Instead, Tresidder warned them that they must not allow their institutions to become dependent on federal patronage and must seek industrial patronage as well.[14] Partly because Tresidder was committed to developing industrial patronage and envisioned SRI as the primary link between the university and industry, he rejected Leighton's suggestion that the Chemical Warfare contract be transferred to SRI. Tresidder also wanted the contract to remain on campus because it was reimbursing the university for its indirect expenses at the rate of 30 percent of direct costs. Although less than Stanford had received during the war, the overhead funds were highly valued by the budget-conscious president.[15]

Tresidder also enthusiastically embraced the suggestion of the navy's Bureau of Aeronautics that Stanford accept a contract for managing the bureau's landing-aids facility in Arcata, California. As with the Chemical Warfare contract, Stanford's management of this facility would not contribute in any way to the university's academic program. To Tresidder, this was neither important nor especially desirable; moreover, he expected that Stanford would be amply rewarded by the navy for its efforts. Additionally, Tresidder may well have believed that managing a military facility would draw favorable attention to Stanford by both linking Stanford in the public mind with national defense and making clear that Stanford was a university of the same rank as its two rivals on the West Coast—the University of California (which was managing the AEC's Los Alamos Laboratory) and Caltech (which was managing the Jet Propulsion Laboratory for the Army Air Force).[16]

To Terman, Tresidder's thinking about federal patronage was misguided. Grafting a program of sponsored research onto faculty members' other duties in return for publicity and overhead payments showed both a misunderstanding of the basis of a university's prestige and a lack of respect for the expertise of Stanford's faculty members. Moreover, Tresidder was overly negative about the dependability of federal patronage. Terman wanted Stanford to "exploit" thoroughly governmental patronage in order to improve both Stanford's reputation and its financial situation. The best way to do this, he believed, was to blur the boundaries between the university and the federal government, integrating the government-sponsored research program fully into the university's academic program.

A Competing Vision

A university's reputation and influence were established not through a public relations campaign but through the production of experts and expert knowledge. These were quantifiable factors, measured by the number of students awarded graduate degrees each year and by the number of research papers published annually by faculty members. To increase the production of both students and research, the university needed patronage. Terman had drawn these conclusions in the late 1930s after studying other, more prestigious engineering schools and noting that they, unlike Stanford, provided generous graduate student stipends and enjoyed considerable research support. Then and during the war, he had expressed interest in developing industrial patronage, but by the end of the war, he believed that the newly available governmental patronage would work just as well. Unlike Tresidder, Terman did not see federal and industrial patronage as qualitatively different; either might be used to improve the university.[17]

Developing industrial or governmental patronage did not automatically improve the academic quality of a university, however. Administrators had to establish patronage relationships that worked to their institution's benefit, which in Stanford's case meant approving only those research contracts that would contribute directly to increasing the university's production of experts and expert knowledge. Thus, Terman believed that Stanford's administrators should not accept government contracts, such as the one with the Chemical Warfare Service, that bore little relation to the university's academic program and thus could not contribute to the education of students or to the development of its faculty members' reputations. For similar reasons, Terman did not want Stanford to manage a laboratory for the government, and he encouraged Tresidder to turn down the offer from the navy's Bureau of Aeronautics. The landing-aids facility was already staffed; it would provide no research opportunities for faculty members or graduate students and would not enrich the academic program. It would thus place Stanford in the position of a mere "paymaster" to the federal government. Clearly, Terman's opposition to managing a government laboratory and to programmatic research was not rooted in lofty ideals about academic science and free inquiry. In suggesting that the university select only those governmental contracts compatible with the university's academic program, Terman was guided mainly by practical considerations.

Improving the university's academic reputation was one such consideration.[18]

Improving the university's financial situation was another. Federal contract funds, if related to the university's academic program, could be used in place of fellowships (of which Stanford was in short supply) to support graduate students. Equally important, contract funds could be used to pay a portion of the salaries of those faculty members involved in the sponsored research program. The instructional funds thus freed could be used to hire new faculty members, preferably those who would attract patronage and, thus, whose salaries could also be split. Salary-splitting, as it was called, could allow Stanford to expand its faculty at no cost to itself and thereby increase its capacity for both research and the training of students.[19]

Terman, like Tresidder, regarded overhead payments as one of the desirable features of contracts with the federal government. But while Tresidder relied on overhead to cover shortfalls in the university's operating budget (a practice begun in World War II), Terman wanted to use overhead funds to benefit the university's academic program and enhance its capacity to attract more federal patronage. He urged that at least half of the overhead funds received should be made available to those departments whose faculty members had governmental contracts. This money might then be used by departments to buy the research equipment necessary to conduct sponsored research or to attract additional research contracts. The funds could also be used to inflate the salary offers made to professors who might otherwise not be lured to Stanford. In other words, overhead funds were to be used to help ensure that federal support for research at Stanford continued and expanded. Terman also wanted the university to receive the highest possible overhead rate available from military patrons. To this end, he began collecting information on the overhead rates that other universities were receiving from their government contracts.[20]

Few of Terman's suggestions for exploiting governmental patronage were original; to a large extent, he was recommending the extension into peacetime of practices begun during the war, such as the use of contract funds to pay faculty members' salaries. MIT's administrators were among the first to employ salary-splitting after the war. By the academic year 1947–48, $1 million of MIT's $3.8 million instructional budget was being charged to governmental contracts. Some universities continued, as they had during the war, to collect overhead payments in a discretionary fund; for example, the University of California at Berkeley established such a fund, to which departments generating contract revenue were given special access. By 1954 that fund totaled $13.5 million. And Karl Compton, of course, had been pressing federal patrons since the early 1940s for more generous overhead payments to universities.[21]

Terman was particularly impressed with MIT's administration. Once a great admirer of Harvard's administrators, by the end of the war Terman had begun to see them as stodgy and overly reluctant to recognize the possibilities presented by federal patronage. An incident at the end of the war involving the final reports of the OSRD laboratories highlighted for Terman the difference between Harvard's and MIT's views of university-federal relations. All OSRD-sponsored laboratories were required to provide reports summarizing their wartime work and presenting their achievements. Administrators at MIT had, with the approval of Vannevar Bush, engaged a for-profit publisher for the final report of the Radiation Laboratory, and Terman began making similar arrangements for the report of the RRL. But Harvard administrators stopped him. "No, no, no," Harvard treasurer William Claflin adamantly told Terman. "[Harvard's] job is to render a report to Washington. Our job is not to spend government money making a book." President Conant sided with Claflin. A private corporation should not seek to profit from work conducted for the government with public funds, Conant believed; the report of the RRL would be published by the Government Printing Office.[22]

Conant's unwillingness to "exploit" OSRD funds was, to Terman, evidence of snobbery rather than probity, and he privately complained that Conant had "put on his Harvard cap" and made a pronouncement.[23] Terman came to this conclusion easily; after all, he did not have to look far to find respected university and government administrators, like Compton and Bush, who were providing sanction for his own inclinations. Conant's concern that researchers supported by the federal government spend their time solely on matters relevant to the government was probably unusual, just as had been his concerns during the war about overhead payments. To Terman and others, Conant's attitudes were outmoded. Harvard would clearly continue to be regarded as the preeminent American university in the postwar years, but it would no longer be the primary institution to which academic administrators would look for guidance. MIT was legitimizing for Terman the blurring of the boundaries between the government and private institutions.[24]

If in MIT Terman found support for his views on exploiting governmental patronage, he found affirmation for his plans to integrate the government-sponsored research with the university's academic program from the ONR, Stanford's main patron in the late 1940s. Believing that national security depended upon science, the military was interested in sponsoring scientific research at a reasonable cost and in enlarging the nation's pool of scientists and engineers, upon whom the military would rely in the event of another war. This dictated involving university students—a cheap source of labor and, at the same time, the next generation of scientists—in government-sponsored research. As Emmanuel Piore, assistant chief of research for the ONR, noted at a meeting of the Research and Development Board, an advisory body to the Pentagon, "Graduate students working part time are slave labor."[25] Terman understood the interests of military patrons. As he assured Piore, he had found "it a simple matter to integrate the ONR sponsored research activities directly into the program of advanced training" in the School of Engineering. "As a result, we are now training more students, and training them to *higher levels of scientific competence,* than ever before."[26]

Despite the approval of the ONR, Terman's ideas about governmental patronage got mixed reviews from Stanford's president. Concerned about university finances and prestige, Tresidder clearly appreciated Terman's suggestion that governmental patronage might save the university money. But Tresidder doubted the assumption at the heart of Terman's plan to integrate federal patronage with the university's academic program: that federal patronage was reliable and therefore that it was safe for Stanford's academic program to become dependent on it. When Terman suggested in 1946 that funds from an ONR contract be used to hire to Stanford two statisticians, Tressider applauded the idea. But Tresidder also assumed that the contract represented a finite commitment, and he warned Terman that when the contract expired, Stanford would have no further obligation to the statisticians. Terman, by contrast, believed that federal patronage would continue indefinitely, especially if Stanford worked to perpetuate it. As he explained with respect to the contract for statistical research, it was unlikely that Stanford would find itself stuck with faculty members that it could not support: "The likelihood of further statistical work is large—the NACA . . . and the Air Corps . . . have already expressed an interest."[27]

Tresidder was never won over to Terman's sanguine view of the dependability of federal patronage. He did, however, accede to Terman's suggestions for exploiting federal patronage, although largely out of expediency. During the same years that Terman was pressing him to permit the integration of the government-sponsored research with Stanford's academic program, Tresidder was plagued with worries about Stanford's financial situation and its reputation, both of which appeared to be as shaky as they had been during the depths of the depression. As early as 1944, *School and Society* had warned university administrators that the immediate postwar years might well be "the most devastating for our higher institutions, rivaled only perhaps by another world depression." The journal predicted persistently low interest rates and high postwar inflation, a particularly disastrous combination for private universities. Facing similar financial problems during the depression, university presidents had cut salaries and postponed improvements to research facilities. After the war, with scientists and engineers in great demand and being offered large salaries by both government and industry, universities would find it difficult to compete.[28]

Stanford's administrators were aware that their salary scale was not competitive with that of industry or leading research universities. In 1945–46 the average minimum salary for a full professor at Stanford was $4,500, compared to $10,000 to $12,000 being offered by the nation's wealthiest private universities and by industry. The average salary for a full professor at the University of California at Berkeley was considerably lower but at $6,000 was still well above what Stanford could offer. Salary scales were not the only indicator of the financial disparity between Stanford and neighboring Berkeley. In contrast to the dire warnings in *School and Society,* the University of California and many other public universities were faring quite well after the war, benefiting from an outpouring of support from state governments, whose coffers had been swelled by wartime tax revenues, and from the G.I. bill, which paid out-of-state tuition rates for all veterans.[29]

Tresidder also realized that in terms of research facilities, Stanford was not competitive with its neighbor. A survey of Stanford's facilities in early 1945 had made plain the results of earlier neglect: "We find attic and basement space utilized for important research, containing extremely valuable equipment; with no means of adequate exit; with poorly laid out and erected high tension wires; with an accumulation of dirt and dust. . . . Highly trained, valuable men in underdeveloped departments seem to have given up completely any hope of remedying the conditions" which were, in short, "very demoralizing."[30]

Despite their awareness of Stanford's drawbacks, Stanford administrators were unprepared for the loss, immediately after the war, of George Beadle, a prominent biogeneticist (who would later win the

Nobel Prize), who had accepted a position at Caltech. The departure of Beadle, whom the dean of biology likened in significance to "Halley's comet or the atom bomb," was a severe blow to administrators and faculty alike.[31] It was read both as evidence that Stanford could not compete with other universities and as an ominous indicator of other losses sure to follow. The departments of chemistry, biology, physics, and engineering began pressing Tresidder for larger budgets and improved research facilities. As one discouraged dean wrote, Stanford was becoming widely known for "losing her good men and replacing them with cheap punks."[32]

Tresidder was troubled by this evidence that Stanford's academic reputation was worsening rather than improving after the war. Moreover, his hopes that private industry would assist the university with patronage were not being realized. All of the leading aircraft manufacturing companies had turned down the request of Stanford's aeronautical engineers in 1945 for donations to support their postwar research program. The proposal came "about a year too late," Lockheed's chief of research engineering had responded; with the end of the war in sight, the company had become "greatly concerned" about its financial situation. Indeed, the federal government, which had been responsible for the industry's wartime boom, canceled over $21 billion in aircraft contracts in 1945, and by 1946 the twelve major aircraft companies had lost an aggregate of $35 million. The Lockheed engineer concluded his letter with the suggestion that Stanford seek the support it needed from the federal government.[33]

Tresidder's hopes that the Stanford Research Institute would attract large amounts of industrial patronage were also disappointed. The institute, in fact, was proving to be a drain on scarce university funds. Stanford's trustees had agreed to underwrite the initial costs of SRI upon the assurance of Standard Oil's Atholl McBean that he would quickly raise $500,000 to repay the university, but by July 1946 McBean had failed to raise any of the promised funds. At McBean's suggestion, Stanford's trustees had reluctantly agreed to loan the nascent institute $1 million in the expectation that McBean would raise $300,000 over the next three years. Still, McBean did not succeed in raising the funds, and by mid-1947 the director of SRI inaugurated a new plan to raise a minimum of $855,000 from fifty companies. When the industries approached expressed no interest, the plan was quickly abandoned. Within two years after the war, Tresidder and Stanford's trustees had thus become skeptical about SRI's chances for success. The university had invested over $1 million in the enterprise, which was running a $50,000 deficit.[34]

As Tresidder faced severe pressures on the university's budget and industry's reluctance to support research at Stanford, he was persistently pressed by Terman to recognize the value of his ideas for "exploiting" governmental patronage. Terman was not subtle, addressing bluntly Tresidder's worries about the university's finances and its reputation. "Sponsored research *saves the University money*," he emphasized in one of many letters to Stanford's president. Terman also warned Tresidder that to postpone a decision about the use of governmental funds was a mistake; delay itself might prove damaging to Stanford just as it had during the Second World War. "We failed to take advantage of a similar opportunity presented by the research activities of the war," Terman reminded Tresidder, who was sensitive to this criticism. "We are fortunate to have a second chance to retrieve our position," he continued, adding darkly, "It is doubtful if there will ever be a third opportunity."[35]

Predicting dire consequences if Tresidder failed to follow his advice while promising a way out of Stanford's dilemmas if he did, Terman succeeded in gaining Tresidder's approval for his plans to exploit governmental patronage.

Exploiting Military Patronage

Terman's goal in developing governmental patronage and rebuilding Stanford's engineering school after the war was to make Stanford into the best school for engineering west of the Mississippi. Those who have recounted Terman's efforts, including Terman himself, have focused on his goal of improving the university's reputation and have suggested that the patronage which flowed into the university after the war resulted naturally from Terman's successes in improving the quality of Stanford's engineering program. As one historian has written of Terman's postwar efforts to improve Stanford's reputation, Terman first identified "important scientific and engineering niches"; he then assembled "top notch" faculty, students and researchers in these fields. Then he proceeded to develop "military and corporate sponsors" for the engineering program.[36]

The process of rebuilding the engineering school and developing patronage did not always conform to this particular sequence of events.

At times, offers of governmental patronage preceded the hiring of "top notch" faculty and shaped decisions about appointments. Moreover, Terman's views of what fields of engineering were "important" and which faculty members were "top notch" were not universal ones but were historically and culturally situated, formed within a context shaped by the needs of military patrons and by Terman's strong interest in attracting this patronage to Stanford. That Terman and others used such terms unreflectively, as if they represented universally valid judgments, suggests that, in seeking federal patronage for Stanford, Terman was not merely engaging in opportunism or "academic entrepreneurship" but that he also embraced the values and concerns of the nation's postwar military and scientific advisors and policymakers. Decisions about hiring and about which fields of research to emphasize, then, implicitly included estimations of their significance to federal patrons.

Further, the integration of the government-sponsored research program with Stanford's academic program did not simply involve obtaining government contracts that happened to mesh with the interests of faculty members and rejecting those contracts that did not. Although Terman appointed faculty and researchers to the engineering school partly on the basis of his expectation that they would attract patronage, he also encouraged professors to tailor their research proposals to meet the needs of potential patrons. To attract governmental patronage, Terman recognized that he might need to reshape whole departments and encourage faculty members to alter their research plans to reflect better the concerns of military patrons and their scientific advisors. According to their judgments, with which Terman agreed, two fields that would have a "big rather than a small future" after the war were countermeasures and microwave electronics.[37] Stanford's electrical engineers and physicists had begun work in the field of microwaves before the war; during the war, Terman had directed the research on countermeasures. It would be relatively easy to build on this expertise and develop a program of governmental support, Terman realized; he thus began assembling at Stanford former members of the RRL whose work promised military applications. By the end of the decade, Terman had lured at least eleven former members of the RRL to Stanford, including Joseph Pettit, who had directed the work on receivers at RRL, and Robert Buss, head of the RRL's section on airborne receivers. Terman did not have to pressure these new faculty members to obtain federal research support. They were hired in the first place with the knowledge that they were receptive to doing work in which military patrons had an interest and that military patrons were familiar with their wartime work and interested in providing them with postwar support. According to Emmanuel Piore, the head of the ONR's electronics section, he assigned a contract to Stanford in 1946 with the explicit understanding that the funds would support "those whom [Terman] took home with him from RRL" to continue work begun during the war on communications and countermeasures.[38] Terman also succeeded in appointing to Stanford's faculty Lester Field, who had obtained his doctorate at Stanford and had developed a novel vacuum tube, the traveling wave tube, at Bell Labs during the war. In Terman's estimation, the traveling wave tube was "far more significant" to the future of countermeasures and radar than was the klystron; Field would clearly have no trouble obtaining military support. Indeed, shortly after his appointment to Stanford, Field received a contract from the ONR worth $76,000 annually.[39] In appointing engineers like Field, Terman was often blunt about his intentions and expectations. For example, in recommending the appointment of Arthur Dorne, a former leader of one of the RRL's antenna groups, Terman explained that with Dorne at Stanford, it would be "relatively simple to bring to Stanford research work in this field [antennas] with Army, Navy, or industrial sponsorship." Terman also predicted that within six months of Dorne's arrival at Stanford, he would be "self-sustaining financially."[40] His appointment, then, would bring patronage to Stanford and save the university money.

In addition to bringing to Stanford young engineers who he was sure would easily obtain governmental contracts, Terman encouraged faculty members already at Stanford to shift their research plans to correlate with the needs of potential sponsors. For example, in early 1946, Terman sent Alfred Niles to the army's Wright Field to explore the possibility of research support for aeronautical engineering. When the army representative made clear that he was not interested in the two lines of research that Niles had proposed, Niles, as instructed by Terman, "immediately shifted discussion" to a topic in which the army *was* interested. Terman was pleased, as Niles no doubt knew he would be. Wright Field was sure to award Stanford a contract, Terman informed Stanford's president; after all, the research proposal had been "in considerable measure, worked out by the man on whose desk the proposal will land." Stanford soon received a contract worth $51,000 for research on airplane structures.[41]

Terman's willingness to work closely with governmental sponsors of research in order to improve Stanford's chances of receiving contracts went beyond allowing the military patron to shape a research proposal. Terman was also willing to let a potential patron play a role in the selection of Stanford's faculty members. On one of Terman's visits to the East Coast, he had talked with Mina Rees, the head of the ONR's mathematics division, and learned that the ONR was planning to let a contract for statistical sampling work. To Terman this was a clear indication that mathematical statistics was an "important" field, and he was eager for Stanford to obtain the contract which he believed would "serve as a nucleus around which to build further statistical work of high caliber." Stanford, however, did not have any mathematical statisticians on its faculty and no money to hire any. But, as Terman was quick to realize, if Stanford could obtain the ONR contract, it could use the contract funds to cover a portion of the salaries of any statisticians the university might hire; the university's portion of the salaries would be paid with overhead funds accumulated from governmental contracts. The appointments, in other words, would cost the university nothing. The university might even make money, Terman speculated. As he suggested to Tresidder, Stanford's "maximum risk would be that it might clear only a little financially" but "the probability of this set of events is small" since the statisticians were likely to attract additional patronage.[42]

Terman's plan to hire "top notch" statisticians using contract funds from the ONR clearly required the cooperation of the ONR. Terman went directly to Rees with his plan and asked her for the names of the best available statisticians in the country. She suggested Albert Bowker, a graduate student at Columbia University who, during the war, had done probability studies of strategic bombing as a member, along with Rees, of the OSRD's applied mathematics division at Columbia. Bowker was hired by Stanford; shortly afterwards, the university received from the ONR the statistical sampling contract.[43]

Terman's decisions about appointments were clearly influenced by his interest in patronage. This does not mean that Terman was not appointing gifted researchers to the faculty. But merit was clearly not the sole criterion in Terman's decisions about appointments, just as it had not been the only concern when Tresidder had selected Levorsen to head the university's geology department and when he had sanctioned the appointment of Ginzton to the physics department. In selecting new members for Stanford's faculty, Terman was seeking to emphasize certain fields—statistical probability, electronic countermeasures, microwaves, for example—that he deemed "important." He valued these fields not because they were new and he was striving to keep Stanford's engineering program up to date. Judgments about what was important were being shaped in large measure by powerful elements outside the university with whom Terman agreed and from whom Terman wanted financial support for Stanford. Terman wanted to "exploit" governmental patronage to meet institutional goals; he was able to engage in this kind of opportunism so easily primarily because he believed that in reshaping whole departments or individual research plans to reflect the interest of patrons, he was both acting in the nation's interest as well as truly improving the quality of Stanford's engineering program.

The Stanford Research Institute

Terman's assumption that federal patronage would persist indefinitely and that it was thus safe to make Stanford's engineering school dependent upon it allowed him to rethink Stanford's relationship to industry. Before the war, industry had played an important role in his plans for Stanford's electrical engineering program; he had sought from the business world research support and fellowships as well as employment opportunities for Stanford graduates. The absence of job opportunities on the West Coast had particularly aggravated Terman. During the war, he had described the ideal university-industry relationship to Paul Davis: "The idea is to get lots of good Stanford people well placed in industry . . . and then as time goes on and they begin to work up to responsibility, see that they hire good Stanford men . . . and so on ad infinitum."[44] After the war, with governmental patronage easily available, industrial patronage became less important to Terman. Instead, he was interested in developing a relationship between Stanford and private industry that would satisfy his ideas about the proper role of academic experts as well as his need for employment opportunities for Stanford graduates. Terman's thinking about industry-university relations differed markedly from Tresidder's, as may be seen from their contesting conceptions of SRI.

The Stanford Research Institute as envisioned by Tresidder embodied two approaches to industrial research. First, the institute contracted with industry to conduct research on particular problems defined by the industrial patrons. This relationship between the patron and academic experts was reminiscent of the prewar one between Stanford's physicists and the Sperry Gyroscope Company in the late 1930s. At the time, faculty members had disliked the relationship, believing that experts, not patrons, should set the research agenda; for the same reason, Terman and many Stanford faculty members disliked SRI. Although Tresidder had planned for the institute to rely on Stanford professors and to do no hiring of its own, only a few members of the faculty were willing to conduct research for the institute.[45] The institute also solicited large grants from individual companies, making the old claim that undirected scientific research would strengthen the industrial sector since basic research provided the groundwork essential to technological innovation and development. Terman recognized that this appeal yielded little; it also failed to establish a close, mutually beneficial relationship between the university and regional industry.

Terman had a model for his idea of university-industry interaction in the university's relationship with Varian Associates. The company had been founded after World War II by Russell and Sigurd Varian, informal colleagues of Stanford's physicists, who located their business near the Stanford campus to renew and facilitate interaction between the company and Stanford's faculty. The relationship, as it developed, was close: the company was tied to Stanford faculty members not only by long-standing friendships and geographical proximity, but also by financial and legal bonds. Three of Stanford's physicists sat on Varian Associates' board of directors, and a number of Stanford's professors held stock in the fledgling company. That the company did not initially sponsor research at Stanford was no impediment to the relationship. The Office of Naval Research was sponsoring research at Stanford on microwave tubes; Stanford faculty members involved in this research consulted for Varian, and Varian in turn employed Stanford graduates. By the end of the 1940s, Varian had become an important producer of microwave tubes developed at Stanford; the main consumer of Varian's products was the military. Stanford's relationship with Varian was premised on the federal government providing both patronage to the university and a market for the company.

Envisioning close ties between the university's academic departments and local industry, Terman questioned the need for an institute like SRI, which was devoted to industry-sponsored research. To Tresidder, who divided research into two categories—that sponsored by government and that sponsored by industry—the organizational division made sense. But to Terman, who based distinctions not on the source of the patronage but on the nature (basic or applied) of the research being supported, SRI was better conceived as an institution for applied research, an organization intermediate between the university and industry.

Terman's distinctions between basic and applied research were similar to those made by Vannevar Bush in *Science, The Endless Frontier*, which Terman had read and urged Tresidder to read.[46] Bush posited stages of research, beginning with "basic" research (that research "performed without thought of practical ends"), "applied" research (research emanating from the discoveries of basic research and with a practical end in mind), and industrial development.[47] Bush was presenting an argument to justify governmental patronage of academic science, which he equated with basic research. In his formulation, basic research was the fundamental activity from which all others, including industrial and military innovation, derived. He thus placed the university and its scientists and engineers at the foundation of the research and development process, a designation fitting Terman's own views of the place of academic experts in relation to both government and industry.

In deciding how best to exploit governmental patronage, Terman had determined after the war that the university should turn down contracts for applied research, as this research could not be made part of the basic training of engineering students. But because he was concerned with maintaining cordial, even close, relations with the university's military patrons, he disliked rejecting flatly contracts proffered by these patrons for applied research. By making SRI the locus for these contracts, the university could satisfy its patrons' needs while maintaining its preference for conducting only basic research on campus. There was thus an opportunistic element to Terman's suggestion that SRI undertake applied research sponsored by the federal government.

But there was also an ideological basis to Terman's conception of SRI. Terman embraced the outline provided in *Endless Frontier* for how technological development and industrial innovation occurred, and he was intent on institutionalizing the formulation. Thus, in addition to conducting research rejected by the university, Stanford Research Institute ought to embark on a program of applied research sponsored by the military and complementary to the program of military-sponsored research in electronics and communications underway in the engineering school. Ideally, the applied research would build directly on the school's basic research, and Stanford's engineers, by consulting for SRI, could ensure that the application of their research proceeded smoothly. The applications of this research would then be transferred to local industry, which would begin taking an interest in SRI once it inaugurated a research program in electronics and microwave technologies, Terman believed. This seems to have been the thinking that lay behind Terman's urging that SRI hire Ralph Krause, who had acted during the war as a liaison between the navy and the OSRD laboratories, including Harvard's RRL, and had at the end of the war helped establish the Office of Naval Research.[48]

Terman thus envisioned a postwar regional economy of sustained military expenditures for the research and development of electronics devices, with a burgeoning electronics industry feeding off of this research, employing Stanford-trained students, and eventually providing patronage for Stanford's engineering program, which, according to this vision, was doing the research essential to regional prosperity. This vision clashed with that of Tresidder, who continued to see SRI as the key to the university's relationship with industry, a relationship that he saw as necessary for maintaining Stanford's independence from the federal government.

Tresidder was becoming increasingly concerned about both SRI's lack of success in attracting industrial patronage and the university's heavy dependence on military support. In late 1947, at the annual meeting of the AAU, he expressed his concerns. Noting that the standard solution to universities' need for funds was to turn to the federal government, he insisted on the importance of considering alternatives. Careful not to say that federal support per se was objectionable, Tresidder explained, "I am saying, however, that we should exercise all the imagination and ingenuity we have to tap private sources of funds. . . . We must exercise such imagination if we are to keep our universities free."[49] Others shared Tresidder's concerns, worrying particularly about the fate of private universities, which continued through the late 1940s to struggle with inflation and a lack of capital. In late 1947, the Rockefeller Foundation invited administrators from Harvard, Princeton, the University of Michigan, and elsewhere to study the financing of higher education and research and to consider, among other things, why private industry was not providing more support for higher education.[50]

Tresidder himself focused on the director of SRI, William Talbot, as part of Stanford's problem. Talbot, he believed, was insufficiently tenacious in seeking industrial patronage and too willing to hire researchers rather than rely on the expertise of Stanford's faculty. Tresidder's frustration with Talbot peaked in September 1947 when Talbot began negotiating a $200,000-per-year contract with the navy's Bureau of Aeronautics to manage its landing-aids facility. This was the contract that Terman had earlier convinced Tresidder to reject; Terman had then recommended to the navy that it contact SRI. This would not have been SRI's first military contract. In fact, by late 1947, 70 percent of SRI's revenue was derived from contracts with the federal government, a figure that displeased Tresidder. The landing-aids contract, if accepted, would have reduced SRI's industrial support to a tiny percentage of the institute's total revenues and would have meant, essentially, an abandonment of Tresidder's plans for SRI. When Talbot refused to halt negotiations with the navy, Tresidder asked for his resignation. Two months later, on a trip to the East Coast to interview a replacement for Talbot, Tresidder died of a heart attack.[51]

Had Tresidder remained president of Stanford, it is unlikely that the course the university was on would have changed. Committed to making Stanford into a leading research university, Tresidder needed to develop substantial patronage. He had not refused support from the federal government; he had even approved Terman's use of contract funds to support part of the university's instructional program. Tresidder had never demonstrated any intention of curtailing the university's program of government-sponsored research; he had only insisted on finding additional sources of support as well. Moreover, SRI's inability to attract industrial patronage had little to do with Talbot, who had tried to attract industrial patronage, but with industry's own lack of interest. Even had industry been willing to sponsor research at SRI, Tresidder would still have faced difficulties. Stanford's faculty members were suspicious of SRI and generally reluctant to conduct research for industry.

In early 1948 Alvin Eurich became acting president of Stanford, and Jesse Hobson, an electrical engineer and former head of the Armour Institute, upon which SRI had been modeled, was appointed director of SRI. Neither Hobson nor Eurich was averse to governmental patronage and both got along well with Terman. Hobson took Terman's advice and hired the ONR's Ralph Krause, who moved SRI not only more deeply into government-sponsored research but also into a program of military-sponsored research in microwaves, countermeasures, and communications that was complementary to the one Terman had developed in Stanford's engineering school. Hobson himself began stressing to SRI's board of directors the importance of undertaking a large program of military-sponsored research, both to increase the institute's attractiveness to defense-related industries, and to ensure that in the case of another war, SRI would not be overlooked by wartime research sponsors.[52] The board of directors of SRI was not entirely swayed by Hobson, however, determining that SRI would continue to make service to industry its primary goal and that government-sponsored research must contribute to that goal. At the encouragement of Stanford trustee Charles Blyth, who had arranged a much-needed loan to the institute in early 1949, SRI again solicited contributions from private industry. By January 1950 the institute had gathered a meager $35,000 in contributions.[53]

In comparison, military support for research in the sciences and engineering had become a mainstay of the research programs in the engineering school and the physics department by the end of the decade. As early as mid-1947 the engineering school was receiving more money from military contracts than from the university's own operating budget. A year later, the school had approximately $500,000 in military contracts. By the end of the decade, the electrical engineering department's contracts for research on microwave tubes, radio propagation, and other radar and countermeasures devices totaled over $500,000 and provided support for thirty doctoral students. The physics department was similarly receiving ample research support, primarily for the development of microwave technology for use as a research tool in nuclear physics. At the end of 1948 support from the ONR and the AEC totaled about $500,000, an amount that outstripped the university's contribution to the physics department by about $375,000. The microwave laboratory, the locus of most of the sponsored research, had twice as many staff members as the physics department by 1949.[54]

Throughout the engineering school, Terman was splitting salaries and using the instructional funds thus freed to hire additional faculty members (who also brought in government contracts and whose salaries were then also split) and to raise salaries. As a result, the engineering school's faculty had expanded from thirty-two in the late 1930s to forty-one ten years later, enabling the school to train more graduate students and to become the second largest producer of electrical engineering Ph.D.s in the country by the end of the decade. While Stanford's program of sponsored research was smaller than those of MIT and Caltech, by the late 1940s Stanford was being recognized as a nationally significant institution for research and training in engineering, especially in the fields of radio propagation and microwave tubes.[55]

There is no evidence that Eurich was troubled by these developments. However, his tenure at Stanford was short. The board of trustees considered naming him president, but Paul Davis, soon to retire to a Vermont farm next door to Vannevar Bush's, warned Herbert Hoover, who was a member of the trustee committee to select a new president, that Eurich had been an ardent New Dealer. Hoover, who as early as 1943 had begun trying to rid the university of those he considered politically incorrect, assured Davis that Eurich would not be appointed president of Stanford.[56] The trustees settled on J. E. Wallace Sterling, the director of the Huntington Library and, before that, a popular radio announcer in California and a teacher at Caltech. Sterling had attended Stanford both as an undergraduate and a graduate student, receiving his Ph.D. in history in 1938. He had also worked in the Hoover library and was well liked by friends of Hoover. A Republican with little interest in politics, Sterling was conventionally minded and good-natured and would be known in later years among his friends for his zealous participation in the Bohemian Grove's yearly "Cremation of Care" and "High Jinks" rituals. Sterling seemed likely to be a good fund-raiser and, upon questioning by a trustee, had proven sufficiently anticommunist and anti-Roosevelt to please Hoover.[57]

When Sterling assumed the presidency of Stanford in 1949, cold war tensions were heightening, both at home and abroad. In the summer of that year, State Department officials conceded that the communists were the victors in China's long civil war; in the fall of that year, the Soviet Union demonstrated that it possessed nuclear capabilities. In response, Truman called for a reassessment of U.S. foreign and defense policies. The April 1950 report, NSC 68, urged a bold and massive weapons buildup and a quadrupling of the military budget. By June 1950 fighting had broken out in Korea, and the United States was, fewer than five years after the end of one war, engaged in another, which, like World War II, would affect significantly America's leading research universities. This time, Stanford University would already have a framework in place for assisting the federal government and for taking advantage of governmental research contracts to enhance Stanford's reputation and expand its influence on national affairs.

5

A "Win-Win-Win" Relationship

The Korean War deepened the relationship between universities and their military patrons. Military budgets, which had hovered around $13 billion annually in the late 1940s, skyrocketed with the outbreak of war. The Defense Department's budget for research and development, just over $500 million for fiscal year 1950 and slated for reduction the following year, nearly tripled during the first year of the war, rising to $1.5 billion for fiscal year 1951 and $1.6 billion for 1952. After the war's conclusion, total military expenditures remained high, a key feature of what one economist called America's "permanent war economy."

The development of the cold war political economy affected significantly America's research universities. Military support for research in electronics at MIT doubled almost overnight, leading to the creation of the Lincoln Laboratory for research and development of air defense and early warning systems for the air force. The budget for the Jet Propulsion Laboratory at Caltech, the locus of the army's work on guided missiles, doubled to $11 million between 1950 and 1953.[1] Military support for research in electronics at Stanford tripled between 1950 and 1952. The Stanford Research Institute, which had been slow to embrace government-sponsored research, changed its priorities with the Korean War, accepting a large electronics contract from the navy. By late 1950 military-sponsored research in electronics accounted for 25 percent of the institute's contract revenue, compared to a mere 4 percent in 1949.[2]

The Korean War marked more than a quantitative change in the relationship between universities and military sponsors, however. The increase in military funding predominantly supported research of an applied or highly programmatic nature. For the academic scientists and engineers involved, this signified not so much a change in the ultimate uses to which their research was to be put (those who had conducted basic research under military sponsorship before 1950 had understood the implications of their work for military technology) but rather changes in the work environment. The applied research programs were subject to more direction from military sponsors than was the basic research and to the imposition of production schedules. They often required secrecy, which in its most extreme form involved the posting of armed guards at the entrance to laboratories. The applied research was thus not easily incorporated into universities' academic programs. Further, the scale of the sponsored research programs required the hiring and supervising of large numbers of researchers who were not members of the faculty. The effect was to make those segments of the university that were involved in military-sponsored research resemble industrial enterprises more than they did the academic institutions of which they were a part.

These changes were not reversed after the war's end. While scientists and academic administrators would continue to stress their earlier preferences, they would also begin to normalize the new arrangements. Clark Kerr, chancellor of the University of California at Berkeley, pointed to the large laboratories staffed with myriad nonfaculty researchers and to the professors engaged in "managing contracts and projects, guiding teams and assistants, bossing crews of technicians" as distinguishing features of the multiversity.[3] By the late 1950s a Stanford engineering professor responsible for directing a large applied research project could boast unreflectively, "my annual 'sales' are $700,000. I haven't made any profit, but I haven't had a loss, either. I have a crew of over fifty people. . . . My engineers and physicists are loyal, cooperative and well motivated."[4]

Not only did some portions of the university begin to look like industry and some of its professors to use the language of industrialists, research universities also began forming close ties to industrial concerns. The military's demand for the quick development and production of new war technologies fostered interaction between its industrial and academic contractors. For universities, such as Stanford, that had long been interested in forming ties to regional industry, this development provided a "great opportunity." Frederick Terman would seize this opportunity to promote and shape relationships between Stanford and regional industry to meet institutional needs and to conform to his idea about the proper role of academic experts.[5]

By the early 1960s Terman was writing of the "extensive interactions" between universities and private industry, pointing to alliances between industry and universities such as MIT, Caltech, Arizona State, and the University of California at San Diego and declaring approvingly, "[O]ur educational institutions today are no ivory towers." Indeed, by the early 1960s they had become an integral part of a military-industrial complex.[6]

Defining the University-Industry Relationship

Shortly after the outbreak of war in Korea, the Office of Naval Research contacted Terman, offering Stanford a $1 million contract for accelerated research and development of microwave tubes and countermeasures. The contract was twice the size of all of the engineering school's other contracts. By early 1952 military support for research in electronics at Stanford had grown to over $1.9 million. Of that amount, less than $250,000 supported basic research. Although this development represented a departure from Terman's stated preference for sponsored research that could be integrated with the academic program of the engineering school, the expansion into applied research occurred in the context of war and was accepted by Stanford's administrators and approved by Stanford's board of trustees without hesitation. Harvard seems to have been the only university that rejected a proffered contract for applied research.[7]

Terman was quick to look beyond the immediate needs of the military and to perceive in the new program of applied research particular benefits for Stanford University. In fact, to him the applied research program was the "payoff" of the government-sponsored research program that he had been building at Stanford since shortly after World War II. Coolly contemplating the possibility that the localized war in Korea might become a global conflict, Terman recognized that "in the event of all-out war," Stanford would become "one of the great electronic research centers" just as MIT and Harvard had been during the Second World War. This, by Terman's standards, was a clear indication that he had succeeded in guiding Stanford's electrical engineering department into the ranks of the nation's best.[8]

Even without a third world war, the applied research program prom-

ised to benefit Stanford. As in World War II, the armed services would
be interested in close cooperation between industrial contractors and
academic experts to ensure the quick refinement and production of the
technology that was being developed in the applied research program.
Here was the opportunity for Stanford's engineers to forge close ties to
Bay Area companies and to make relationships such as that with Varian
Associates the rule rather than the exception. As Terman pointed out to
Stanford's president, the navy's proposed contract for the development
of microwave tubes correlated "almost ideally with the industrial activities" in the area. Conducting applied research at Stanford would
strengthen companies like Litton Industries, Eitel-McCullough, Heinz
and Kaufman, and Varian, and "likewise, the presence of these industrial
concerns . . . would contribute in an important way to the effectiveness"
of Stanford's research program.[9]

While Terman looked forward to extensive interaction between Stanford and industry, it was not a relationship that simply fell into place.
Terman shaped the university's interaction with industry to benefit
Stanford's electronics program and to conform to his ideas about the
role of academic experts and about the relationship between research
and technological development. The prewar relationship between Stanford's physicists and Sperry, which had given Sperry control, was not
to be replicated; Stanford's microwave experts, not industry, would
control the relationship after the war. This was possible because, as Terman recognized, the university-industry relationship was, in fact, part
of a triangular relationship that included military patrons. Stanford's
electronics experts did not need industrial patronage; they were well
subsidized by the military. Industry, however, did need the expertise of
Stanford's electrical engineering department as well as a steady supply
of well-trained employees to fulfill their own military contracts. It was
this need that Terman took advantage of to establish what he regarded
as a mutually beneficial relationship between Stanford and regional industry.

In April 1951, a few months after the establishment of an applied
research program in the engineering department and the groundbreak-
ing for a laboratory—the Electronics Research Laboratory (ERL)—to
house the basic and applied research programs, the director of General
Electric's research laboratory, R. W. Larson, contacted Terman. During
the Second World War, G.E. had designed and produced vacuum tubes
under contract to the Army Signal Corps, and Larson was acquainted
with Terman. General Electric had just received an air force contract to

develop antiradar countermeasures equipment using klystrons, Larson explained, and the company wanted to arrange a subcontract with Stanford for the design and construction of several prototype anti-radar guns.

Here was an opportunity for Stanford's engineers to work closely and collaboratively with industry. But Terman was quick to turn down G.E.'s offer. As he explained, the proposed subcontract would mean that ERL "would be merely supplying some of our limited manpower to do something which could be done almost as easily and quickly at G.E. as at Stanford." Instead, Terman proposed that Stanford's electronic experts act as informal consultants to G.E. "This could be done *gratis*," Terman offered, "similarly to the conversations which have already been held with some G.E. people in New York and at Stanford."[10]

Terman's correspondence with General Electric in this matter says much about his views of the proper relationship between Stanford's electronics experts and industry. While Terman, along with other ERL members, believed that the lab should function in part as "a service organization," they did not intend to let service to industry become the defining objective of the ERL. More important, in Terman's mind, was to ensure that Stanford's electronics laboratory would "achieve prominence such that [it] will be recognized as first" among other laboratories doing electronics research under military contract.[11] If collaboration with industry would enhance this status, so much the better, but Terman did not want it to threaten his goals for the laboratory.

The ERL would not achieve preeminence if it became simply the supplier of technical products to particular industries with military contracts. Such a relationship, if formalized by a subcontract, would lock Stanford's engineers into sharing their expertise with a particular industrial contractor and, for proprietary reasons, would likely place limits on their interactions with other industrial concerns similarly interested in Stanford's assistance. The problems of working under contract for particular companies were well known to Stanford's engineers. Karl Spangenberg, who had worked simultaneously on projects sponsored by both Sperry and ITT in the early 1940s, explained the difficulties of his situation to Terman. "I have already been for some time in the position of not letting my left hand (I.T.& T.) know what my right hand (Sperry) was doing," he complained.[12] As a result of this and other experiences, Terman had come to prefer informal consulting relationships with industry. These would permit the engineers to disseminate their research widely throughout the electronics industry and so enhance their reputations in the field of electronics. As an administrator of Stanford's electronics laboratory noted, "consulting represents one of the best means for promoting our program."[13] Terman also objected to accepting subcontracts from industry because doing so would give industry, rather than Stanford's engineers, ultimate control over both the research and the university-industry collaboration. As subcontractors, the engineers would be required to work according to the specifications of the company involved, rendering them mere technical assistants. Again, the physicists' experience with the Sperry company illustrated the hazards incumbent in such a situation.

But Terman knew from his wartime experience directing the RRL that industry's close supervision of the scientists and engineers was not a necessary concomitant of a university-industry relationship. Scientists at the RRL had given rather than taken directions from industrial concerns, guiding and supervising the transfer of ideas and techniques from the RRL through the application and production stages in industrial laboratories. Industry had depended on the expertise of the laboratory; the laboratory, however, was dependent for patronage not on industry but on the federal government's Office of Scientific Research and Development. The RRL and other OSRD laboratories had, of course, depended on industry to put successfully into production the ideas and designs they had generated; this was the reason for developing systematic liaisons between the laboratory and industry. Terman wanted to establish the same kind of relationship between Stanford's electronics laboratory and regional industry during the Korean War.[14] Providing consulting services, even at no expense to industry, as Terman suggested to General Electric, put Stanford's engineers firmly in control of the interaction with industry, giving them a role in accordance with Terman's view of them as independent experts.[15]

Refusing to become a subcontractor to G.E. signified yet another aspect of Terman's view of the university's relationship to industry. Although he believed that ERL should help industry fulfill its defense contracts, Terman also noted in a meeting of the ERL's staff that the laboratory was "in commercial competition with industry."[16] The Defense Department was letting research contracts to both, a situation of potential concern to Terman. In Terman's view, the university and industry should not be in competition because each institution had a specific function to fill. The university, the home of scientific and engineering expertise, should be responsible for research; industry should be the locus of development and production of devices and techniques emanating from the academic research program. Thus, to accept subcontracts from industry was, in effect, to invert the relationship between research and technological development. As consultants to industry, Stanford's engineers would establish the appropriate relationship between university expertise and technological development, acting as transmitters of essential knowledge from the university to industry.

Terman's ideas about university-industry collaboration were thus shaped both by his aspirations for Stanford's engineering program and by particular ideas about the role of experts in society and the course of technological development. Terman was able to gain for the ERL considerable authority in relationship to individual industrial contractors as well as significant influence over the development of the regional electronics industry, in part because Stanford's military contractors provided Terman with essential leverage in his interactions with industry. For example, the Maxson Corporation, like G.E., had a contract with the armed services—in this case, with the navy's Bureau of Aeronautics—to produce technology—a rapid-scan intercept receiver—which was being developed under the ERL's applied research program. In mid-1951 the company contacted Stanford and arranged to visit ERL to discuss receiving technical assistance. At an ERL senior staff meeting prior to Maxson's visit, Stanford's engineers agreed that they had no interest in developing or manufacturing either tubes or receivers for Maxson and thus would not accept a subcontract from the company. The engineers did have a vested interest in seeing Maxson successfully fulfill its contract obligations, however, because the receiver had been developed at Stanford. They were determined that "insofar as possible, we should have an opportunity to guide the program [to produce the receiver] in order to assure its success."[17]

Thus, the engineers agreed that they would be "prepared to offer consulting assistance, and to make tests on any tubes or receivers produced" by Maxson. The consulting work would be done at no cost to the company; the ERL would, with the navy's acquiescence, charge its services to its own navy contract.[18] Maxson would clearly need assistance in developing the microwave tubes necessary to the intercept receiver, but rather than undertake this work themselves, Stanford engineers proposed to assist the company in selecting a suitable tube manufacturer. This arrangement suited Maxson well. Donald Harris, associate director of the ERL, noted after the meeting with Maxson representatives that the company had "generally agreed that the advantages of an association of this kind with Stanford were considerable" and that it was eager for a "high standard of cooperation."[19]

Of particular importance to Maxson was that Stanford's engineers had close contacts with the planning level of the armed services. A month before Maxson contacted Stanford, Terman had established a program of "systematic liaison" with agencies—both military and industrial—that might be interested in applications of ERL's rapid-scan intercept receiver. Designated ERL researchers regularly visited military agencies, manufacturers, and other universities to compile information regarding their research interests and needs with regard to technology, like the intercept receiver, that Stanford had developed.[20] Thus Stanford, with the approval of its military patrons, was acting as a mediator between the military and companies like Maxson, transmitting the needs of the armed services to industrial concerns to assist them not only in fulfilling their contractual obligations but perhaps also in obtaining further military contracts.

If Maxson stood to benefit from its collaboration with the ERL, so did Stanford's engineers. The consulting arrangement afforded the engineers the freedom over their own work that they desired as well as some control over the work undertaken by Maxson. Unlike Sperry had before the war, Maxson was not determining the direction of research at Stanford. The ERL, however, was influencing Maxson's development program. For example, Terman noted in late 1952 that the lab had "sold Maxson on the desirability of a one-watt backward-wave oscillator," a Stanford-developed device, for an airborne jamming system that the company was developing under subcontract with Sperry.[21]

The control that ERL's engineers wielded in their relationship with Maxson and other companies helped ensure the reputation of the ERL's research program within the engineering profession and among its military funders. It allowed Stanford's engineers to guide the development of a Stanford-originated device to ensure its success as well as to disseminate widely selective information about the device to other companies that might show an interest in putting it into production. As an ERL administrator noted, ERL's "direct value to the military depends to a considerable extent on applications made outside the laboratory. It is therefore a primary concern of the Electronics Research Laboratory . . . to secure the widest possible dissemination of the information growing out of the [applied research] program and to encourage the use of this information by others."[22] Equally important, the agreement with Maxson ensured the ERL's indispensability to industry. Not only was Stanford's cooperation in providing technical advice and guidance necessary to Maxson, but also Stanford's favor was important to the electronics industry as a whole, since the ERL planned to assist Maxson in the selection of subcontractors. And in the arrangement with Maxson, Terman had placed the ERL firmly at the center of the military's relationship with industry, assuming the responsibility for liaison between the two.

Stanford's military contractors clearly approved of the role that Terman carefully carved out for Stanford's electronics laboratory. When requested by the navy in late 1951 to provide models of the rapid-scan intercept receiver and traveling-wave tubes, the ERL indicated a preference for subcontracting directly with industry for assistance. This was a departure from procedure, and ONR's contract director initially questioned the legitimacy of a university offering federal funds, through subcontracts, to companies operating on a profit basis. The objections were withdrawn, however, once Stanford assured the ONR that it would solicit competitive bids.[23]

Thus, by late 1951 the ERL had, with ONR's acquiescence, attained considerable influence in dealing with industry, as both a consultant and a contractor. Although Terman did not comment on the significance of this for the laboratory, he was quick to take advantage of this leverage to strengthen ties between the university and industry according to his view of a mutually beneficial relationship. For example, Maxson was encouraged to subcontract to Bay Area tube manufacturers, which was Terman's preference, but not necessarily Maxson's, for strengthening the electronics industry in the Stanford vicinity.[24] This practice would help ensure employment opportunities for Stanford engineering graduates; a number of strong electronics companies in proximity to Stanford would also facilitate collaboration between the university and industry.

The companies selected as subcontractors by Stanford and by the industrial concerns under the ERL's advisement were generally those already linked in some way to the university. Companies such as Litton Industries and Eitel-McCullough were staffed—and, in the latter case, owned—by Stanford engineering alumni. Varian, as already noted, had close ties to Stanford; the director of Stanford's microwave laboratory, for example, was one of Varian's founding shareholders and a member of its board of directors. Thus, these companies already had intimate knowledge of the work ongoing at Stanford. As Sigurd Varian noted in a letter proposing that his company assist Stanford's microwave laboratory in the design, development, and production of L-band klystrons,

"It is felt that Varian Associates is in a unique position to cooperate with the Microwave Laboratory to the fullest possible degree, since many of the engineers involved have at one time or another been on the Microwave staff and are personally familiar with its facilities."[25]

That the ERL's selection of subcontractors gave it considerable power over the electronics industry is suggested by a memo to Terman from one of the ERL's administrators responsible for "systematic liaison." A new tube manufacturing company, Penta Labs, had been founded by five men from Eitel-McCullough. The administrator suggested that Stanford should "encourage the development of this concern," with the expectation that Penta would eventually be a "principal supplier" of prototypes of Stanford-originated microwave tubes.[26] Indeed, Penta was soon chosen as a subcontractor by Stanford for the development of low frequency tubes necessary for prototypes of the rapid-scan receiver.[27]

By the summer of 1953 the ERL was collaborating extensively with the electronics industry, providing consulting services to companies with military contracts, among them Maxson, Philco, Varian, Litton, General Electric, Sperry, RCA, and Hewlett-Packard, and subcontracting with several of them for work related to its own applied research contracts. Terman was quite pleased, noting that "the penetration of Stanford ideas and principles into industry is really quite far-reaching."[28] This was important since the value and impact of the ERL's research program depended "almost entirely on the practical applications which are now being made extensively by others."[29]

Terman had succeeded in inverting the prewar relationship between Stanford and industry, gaining for Stanford the dominant position in the relationship. Because of the ERL's privileged relationship to the military and its expertise in research and technology bearing on military needs, industrial defense contractors needed Stanford's good will; a microwave tube manufacturer dissatisfied with its relationship to the ERL, for example, would have had few institutions to which to turn instead. Members of the ERL, by contrast, had the freedom to reject a company's request for collaboration if it did not meet their own needs; they could choose instead to work with another industrial concern or even to form their own companies. By the end of the Korean War, Terman was taking advantage of this leverage to initiate more lasting relationships between industry and the university.

Formalizing the Relationship

In the early 1950s, companies cooperating with the ERL had begun to make significant contributions to the laboratory in the form of grants and fellowships. In late 1952, for example, both Hewlett-Packard and Eitel-McCullough made grants of $10,000 to the ERL for basic research on traveling-wave tubes, klystrons, and backward-wave oscillators. The research, it was understood, was to assist the companies in fulfilling their government contracts. But by providing grants, rather than offering subcontracts, the companies were recognizing Terman's preference. Grants, as Terman explained to a representative of General Electric, afforded the ERL "greater flexibility."[30]

While it is not clear whether the idea of the grants originated with Terman or with the individual companies, by mid-1953 Terman had begun to exploit industry's need for Stanford's electronics expertise to create more systematic and permanent links between the university and industry. In 1953 he established an Honors Cooperative Program, which permitted nearby electronics companies to select employees to study part-time toward master's degrees at Stanford. The first participants were Sylvania, Hewlett-Packard, and the Stanford Research Institute, which together sponsored sixteen students. The arrangement provided the participating companies with formalized access to research at Stanford as well as with a device for attracting employees who might otherwise have chosen to continue their education full-time.

The engineering school benefited as well. In addition to tuition, companies paid a fee for each participating student, which in 1953 was approximately $10,000. As the program's popularity with local companies grew (by 1963, four hundred employees were enrolled), Terman was also able to set quotas on the number of employees each company could send to Stanford, using as one criterion the support that company was willing to provide to strengthen Stanford's graduate program in electrical engineering. The Honors Cooperative Program also furthered industry's reliance on Stanford, now for the education of its employees as well as for technical and strategic advice in its contractual relationship to the military.[31]

In yet another effort to take advantage of industry's growing reliance on Stanford's engineers in a more structured way, Terman supported the plan of John Linvill—a Stanford professor and expert in solid-state electronics—and David Packard—a former Terman student, a co-owner of Hewlett-Packard, and a Stanford trustee—to set up an Industrial Affiliates Program in solid-state electronics in the late 1950s.[32] Rather than make arrangements on an ad hoc basis to supply industry with technical advice on contracts already underway, under this program Stanford would offer companies formalized, prepublication access to the scientific and technical results of its military-sponsored solid-state research program in advance of any specific need. In return, participating companies would each give $5,000 per year for five years to Stanford.[33] This program, like the Honors Cooperative Program, was designed to benefit both industry and Stanford. It provided the participating companies with privileged and early access to technical information in a field of increasing interest to the military (and hence to large defense contractors like Hewlett-Packard) after the Soviet launching of the Sputnik satellite.[34] Stanford, for its part, obtained a regular source of research support, which though earmarked for solid-state research, otherwise carried no restrictions. Terman, in fact, was eager to develop a strong program in solid-state electronics, a field that he recognized had "national importance." He thus planned to use a portion of the grant money to hire more experts in solid-state research, both to attract more government sponsorship as well as to accommodate more students in this field.[35]

The Industrial Affiliates and Honors Cooperative Programs represented Terman's efforts to foster close and enduring ties between Stanford and industry on the basis of the electronics companies' need for access to information and potential employees. The likelihood of developing such ties would be enhanced, Terman realized, if these companies were in close proximity to Stanford. Thus, Terman began encouraging companies interested in the ERL's assistance to move their enterprises onto Stanford-owned land. In early 1950 Stanford's trustees and administrators had agreed to lease some of the university's vast acreage to light industry, commercial concerns, and residential developers. Ever concerned with increasing the university's financial stability, the trustees hoped to turn land that was taxable but producing little income into a moneymaking enterprise.[36] Terman was not involved in the initial planning stages of Stanford's land development program or what became known as the industrial park. In fact, the first company to locate on Stanford land—Varian—did so on its own initiative, and not at Terman's suggestion. But although Terman did not conceive the idea for the industrial park, he took advantage of the university's desire to lease some of its land to industry and of industry's interest in obtaining

Stanford's cooperation in meeting contractual obligations to the military to forge lasting ties between Stanford and electronics companies.[37]

For example, when General Electric contacted the ERL in May 1953 to offer another subcontract for a "collaborative project" on microwave tubes, Terman took the opportunity to propose a more enduring form of collaboration.[38] It was clear, he wrote to the engineering manager of G.E.'s electronics division, that the ERL's staff members "possess a number of skills . . . which might be brought to bear on problems of interest to your company." While cooperation between Stanford and G.E. was thus desirable, Terman suggested that the contractual relationship as proposed by G.E. would limit the benefits to be derived from university-industry interaction. As he explained, "Some . . . contractual activities of a research character are difficult to handle when the cooperating parties are widely separated geographically. This would of course not be the case if the Electronics Division of G.E. found it feasible to establish a research laboratory of its own close to Stanford."[39]

To Terman, here was "a way by which G.E. could take full advantage of Stanford's prestige among the universities in electronics, and simultaneously further strengthen electronics at Stanford." If G.E. located near Stanford, it could participate in the Honors Cooperative Program, and Stanford would benefit from the tuition income from these part-time students. Furthermore, Stanford doctoral candidates might conduct their research at General Electric under the direction of "selected G.E. people."[40] This would enhance G.E.'s chances of securing students as employees upon their graduation, and it would mesh with Terman's goal, formulated years earlier, "to get lots of good Stanford people well placed in industry."[41]

General Electric agreed with Terman that his proposal promised enormous benefits to the company. Already familiar with close university-industry cooperation, having established an advanced electronics center at Cornell, G.E., as the head of the company's electronics division noted, was "confident that other centers of a like nature should be extremely valuable."[42] Stanford had the advantage over Cornell of being a leader in the development of electronic countermeasures devices and systems, a field which was, as a company representative acknowledged, "extremely 'hot'" with the military, especially the air force. Thus, to G.E., locating near Stanford conveyed important benefits beyond access to potential employees: "We believe that the GE/Stanford alliance will have a terrific sales appeal to the military," a G.E. manager wrote, "and Tube Department Sales is confident that no difficulty will be encountered in obtaining continued [military] support."[43]

General Electric was right about the appeal to the air force of the "G.E./Stanford alliance." William Rambo, an associate director of the applied research program who, at Terman's behest, regularly traveled around the country visiting university research groups and government laboratories to glean information about their activities and interests, reported in 1955 that the air force was "very pleased" with the "great influx of electronics [companies] to the Palo Alto area" and hoped that these companies would form relationships with Stanford.[44] Thus, G.E.'s expectations were quickly borne out. Located next to the university, the company easily attracted into its employ Stanford electrical engineering graduates, many of whom had worked on government contracts at Stanford and thus had valuable connections to military patrons. Within a year of its relocation to Stanford, General Electric was crediting Stanford graduates working for the company with attracting military contracts totaling $280,000. Recognizing the significance of G.E.'s links to Stanford, a corporate representative wrote to Terman, "[W]e owe Stanford University more than we can every repay."[45]

Stanford was also benefiting from the proximity of General Electric and the other electronics companies that quickly began to fill up the two hundred acres allotted for the industrial park. To accommodate demand, the park was expanded in the early 1960s to seven hundred acres. By 1963 it was home to forty-two companies employing a total of twelve thousand people.[46] "The moving in of such nationally known companies as General Electric attracts attention to what is going on" in engineering at Stanford, L. Farrell McGhie, assistant dean of engineering, wrote to a university administrator in mid-1955. The companies were not only enhancing the "prestige of electronics" at Stanford and pleasing Stanford's patrons. They were also making generous financial contributions to the university. Both G.E. and Hewlett-Packard, which moved into the park shortly after G.E., had joined the Honors Cooperative Program and were also providing yearly grants of almost $10,000 each for a five-year period. Hewlett-Packard, Varian, and Preformed Line Products had also begun sponsoring research through unrestricted grants at the ERL, the microwave laboratory, and the Ryan High Voltage Laboratory. Additionally, Stanford's engineers and students now had numerous consulting and employment opportunities. "This leads to a very friendly and close working relationship" between industry and Stanford, McGhie wrote, "that will endure over the years."[47]

Stanford's relationship with industry was not close merely in the geographical sense; by the mid-1950s the university and some industrial concerns were also merging institutionally and intellectually. Lockheed's Space and Missile Division, which decided to locate in Stanford's industrial park in 1956, suggested that Terman let the company offer an appointment at Stanford to one of the nation's leading aeronautical engineers, Nicholas Hoff, whom the company believed it would be unable to hire without this incentive. Hoff, head of aeronautical engineering at Brooklyn Polytechnic Institute, had received his degree from Stanford in the early 1940s and after the war had begun research on supersonic aircraft and missiles with the support of substantial military contracts. To Terman, Lockheed's proposal was yet another way to link firmly the engineering school and industry and, at no cost to Stanford, to improve the aeronautical engineering program, which had been languishing for lack of funds since World War II. Lockheed would cover half of Hoff's salary and the other half, Terman expected, "could be charged to contract research," which Hoff would no doubt bring to Stanford. Lockheed also arranged for the head of its gas dynamics division, Daniel Bershader, to teach part-time at Stanford; he soon received a permanent appointment.[48] As a result of Lockheed's selection of Hoff and Bershader, Stanford's aeronautical engineering program shifted decisively from research on commercial airplane structures to research related to guided missiles and space vehicles. To Terman, the relationship with Lockheed was not an intellectual compromise necessitated by financial need but rather a tremendous boon to Stanford's engineering program. The program was moving almost overnight into an area of "national importance," and Lockheed and the armed services, rather than the university, were footing the bill.[49]

This blurring of the boundaries between industry and Stanford was also encouraged by Terman's support of those Stanford engineers who chose to go into business for themselves. For example, in 1957 Dean Watkins, an expert on traveling-wave tubes and director of Stanford's microwave tube development program, decided to start a company whose main product would be, not surprisingly, microwave tubes. Terman not only released Watkins from some of his university responsibilities but also helped him arrange the necessary financing. (Terman was to be one of the directors of the new company.)[50] Terman no doubt recognized that if Watkins's venture succeeded, it would contribute financially to the university as well as enhance the university's prestige by developing products based on Stanford's research program. Watkins himself stressed his close connection to Stanford University. He planned to continue working part-time at Stanford, he informed prospective financiers, to "keep alive the contacts" he had there and to enable him "to transfer easily and quickly the new ideas and techniques originated at Stanford to the new company."[51]

The relationship between the university and local industry seems not to have bothered Stanford's professors, administrators, or military patrons. Terman was aware, however, that the electrical engineering department's close cooperation with particular electronics concerns might excite accusations from competing companies that Stanford was giving some companies preferential treatment. As Terman counseled Watkins, "It is important that these older companies with whom we have had relations over a period of time, understand that [Watkins's] corporation will not be given a preferred position in obtaining information before it is available to others." Watkins must take care that there not "even be an opportunity for suspicion to develop that Stanford is being used to work on things that the new corporation would like to have accomplished, but cannot afford to do itself." If this could not be achieved in actuality, at least this should be "the impression that is given to others."[52]

But aside from this concern over accusations of conflict of interest, the development of close university-industry ties went unquestioned. What was happening at Stanford was happening elsewhere, most notably at MIT, and attracting favorable publicity and press attention. That public monies in the form of military patronage were supporting research from which particular individuals and companies were profiting drew no criticism. The growth and prosperity of particular companies and industries was described in terms of "national" economic growth and prosperity. Furthermore, cold war rhetoric linked economic prosperity and military might as the two pillars of America's defense against the Soviet threat. Framed in this way, with the emphasis on the "national good," the fact that private companies were profiting from the expenditure of public funds could go unremarked.

At Stanford, the relationship between the university and regional industry was seen as a tremendous success. As shaped by Terman, it was financially rewarding, and it was also completely acceptable to the Stanford professors involved. Industry was not interfering with their work; moreover, some engineers were finding the relationship to be financially lucrative. The relationship, as Terman stressed, was mutually beneficial. The electrical engineering department was indispensable to companies working under military contract as a source of technical information, advice, and employees. And the department needed close cooperation with industry to provide employment opportunities for students and to put into production the techniques and devices arising from its basic and applied research programs.

Terman's efforts to construct and shape Stanford's relationship with regional industry reflected his commitment to gaining national prominence for Stanford's engineering program. He was opportunistic, but he was also guided by firmly held beliefs about the proper role of engineers and about the relationship between technological innovation and economic development. Terman believed that scientific and engineering experts—working within the university—were the key to industrial growth and prosperity; they did the work upon which technological developments (and in turn, economic prosperity) were based. This belief, similar to that articulated by Vannevar Bush in *Science, the Endless Frontier* and earlier by Hoover, Hale, and other proponents of the National Research Fund, was part of a larger vision of an economy and society guided and shaped by experts, a vision similar to that of some early-twentieth-century progressives.

While for some of those progressives the vision of an intellectual elite guiding the nation was inseparable from the development of a state-dominated economy, Terman embraced Hoover's version of progressivism, endorsing capitalism and limited state involvement in the economy.[53] According to Terman, scientifically trained experts working within the framework of free market capitalism would solve the nation's problems and bring economic prosperity to the country. Engineers, as independent experts, were assisting industry, providing it with essential knowledge and well-trained employees. These experts, together with the entrepreneurs, Terman asserted, had brought economic growth to the San Francisco Bay Area and to other regions of the country, such as Route 128 near MIT and Harvard. At his most hyperbolic, he declared that engineers at Stanford and other universities were responsible for eliminating poverty in America.[54]

Terman did acknowledge that the federal government had played a part in fostering the economic growth and prosperity to which he pointed, but he accorded the state a strictly limited role. The federal government, according to Terman, had simply provided the seed money in the form of support for university research. This research inevitably generated new technologies, which were then rapidly exploited by industry, which in turn were responsible for economic growth. Direct government involvement in the economy was not only unnecessary, but also, Terman implied, potentially ineffectual as well as disruptive. As he explained to an audience of engineers in 1956, "While the idealists, the social planners, the do-gooders, the socialists and others of their ilk . . . called for a better distribution of wealth," the nation's engineers, working with "our system of free enterprise, solved the basic problem by making possible the creation of so much new wealth" that redistribution was unnecessary.[55]

Terman, like others, conflated the economic prosperity of certain groups and institutions with national prosperity. He also underplayed the involvement of the federal government, and specifically the military, in bringing prosperity to particular industries and to certain universities. By the late 1950s, after all, federal funds were supporting over 60 percent of the research budget of leading universities. Moreover, the growth of companies like Varian Associates, Hewlett-Packard, Lockheed, and others was based on steady military demand for war technologies. Terman also overstated the autonomy of the academic engineers. Federal funds, Terman claimed, supported the academic research which, when transferred to industry, fed the development of new technologies. But the funds, primarily from military sources, were not simply offered to the university and then put to whatever uses the university's engineers saw fit. Beginning with the Korean War, the military's support of research at Stanford involved explicit direction of the research agenda.

Because military support was crucial to Stanford, providing the funds that fostered the university's collaboration with industry, Terman was not in a position to dictate the terms of the university-military relationship. Terman and Stanford's engineers thus found themselves accommodating the military even when the interests of the military were clearly at odds with academic traditions or their own preferences. Rather than admit that there was a contradiction and that the engineers were not, in fact, the autonomous experts they claimed to be, the engineers settled for creating the illusion for others, and perhaps for themselves as well, that their collaboration with the military gave them autonomy and control over their work.

Accommodating the Military

The engineers' initial involvement in military-sponsored research after World War II had posed no problems for them. They had not questioned the appropriateness of undertaking such research; few in the national scientific and engineering communities had. Frederick Terman had been eager for military support, recognizing the usefulness of this funding for meeting his own goal of enhancing the reputation of Stanford's electronics program. Stanford's main patron in the late 1940s, the ONR, had exercised no direct control over the research agenda and had placed few if any restrictions on the dissemination of research results.

The fact that support from the ONR proved so satisfactory to the researchers involved and to academic administrators does not mean, of course, that military support was not shaping, at least subtly, intellectual production at Stanford. To attract support in the first place, Terman had sought to hire faculty members whose interests were consonant with those of military patrons. The effect was to minimize the potential for conflict between faculty and sponsors over control of the research agenda. The engineers hired by Terman perceived themselves as freely pursuing the work that interested them; that it also interested the military appeared to be serendipitous.

The inauguration of an applied research program at the outset of the Korean War changed the engineers' relationship to their military patrons. Terman recognized not only that the program of applied research could not be integrated into the university's academic program but also that it would require the employment of a full-time staff working at a "nonacademic" tempo and accepting secrecy restrictions. Moreover, the applied work would be subject to overt direction by the military. It would have "well-defined objectives," Terman noted, which "would be chosen in accordance with military needs, and priorities would be determined by military urgency."[56]

The issue of secrecy provoked no debate among Stanford's engineers, although Stanford's physicists seem to have felt some unease, arranging for the classified research to be conducted in the Electronics Research Laboratory rather than in the physics department.[57] One electrical engineer did fear that the program of applied research would have a deleterious effect on the academic environment: "Many of us are here in a university atmosphere for the purpose of doing scientific work, invention, analysis and experiment in a cool, unhurried and scientifically provocative atmosphere," noted Lester Field, who had left a position at Bell Labs to come to Stanford. With the inauguration of a large program of applied research, "problems of administration, personnel, reports, materials, scheduling, all of seemingly highest priority, [would] become the first order of business," he predicted, "while scientific productivity [would be] left for odd moments or for remote underlings to take care of." The result would be damage to "the mental health and productivity" of Stanford's engineers, Field feared.[58]

If Field's concerns were shared by others, they did not express them. They certainly were not shared by Terman, whose earlier preference for basic research contracts had primarily represented practical institutional considerations rather than strongly held beliefs about the nature of academic research. After World War II, he had sought contracts for basic research—that is, for research that was undirected and unclassified— because they were compatible with the electrical engineering department's academic program and could thus be integrated with the educational program to save the university money. He did not believe research that was directed or classified was necessarily inappropriate to a university. However, he did believe that if basic research were to be done, it should be conducted in a university by academic experts. But as long as basic research remained a part of Stanford's electronics program, Terman easily accommodated a program of applied research, particularly when it promised to benefit the university and regional industry.

Unlike Field, Terman did not contrast the academic and industrial work environments but instead looked at the university and industry as having different functional roles in the larger enterprise of creating and producing military hardware. With the applied program at Stanford, Terman wrote in late 1950, the Bay Area would have a "completely integrated set of tube facilities," which would include "basic research, advanced development, engineering of new tubes and model shop, pilot and quality production."[59] Terman thus regarded the applied research as an extension of the engineers' basic research and as an opportunity to apply concepts arising from the basic research in forms directly useful to industry and the military. Rather than seeing the applied program as polluting the academic atmosphere, Terman emphasized that it would be distinct from the basic research program while providing a rationale for strengthening it.

To Terman, developing a program of applied research did not mean abandoning basic research, which was still preferred by Stanford electronics experts such as Lester Field and Karl Spangenberg. Terman continued to regard it as necessary for laying the groundwork for the applications of interest to the military as well as important financially for the engineering school's academic program. Thus, the ERL's administrators stressed the distinctions between basic and applied research to their military patrons and emphasized the indispensability of the former to the latter in applications to the ONR for the renewal of the basic research contract. "The principle [sic] purpose of Task 7 [the basic research contract]," one administrator explained, "is the advancement of knowledge and the practical applications come as a byproduct of this new knowledge."[60]

In practice, however, the engineers found that the basic and applied research programs could not be strictly segregated and that at times it was difficult to distinguish clearly between the two types of research. Although the navy, which oversaw Stanford's joint military contracts, maintained separate contracts for applied research (known as Task 32) and basic research (Task 7), the ERL's administrators allocated contract funds within the laboratory according to militarily defined goals. In late 1951, for example, Terman earmarked 24 percent of all military support (basic and applied) for the search receiver program, 24 percent for traveling-wave tubes, and 42 percent for work on high-power pulsed microwave tubes.[61] The engineers might claim that the basic and applied research were separate and that basic research, unlike applied research, did not have defined military objectives. But Terman understood that his military sponsors had defined goals, and he, in fact, regarded the basic and applied research as part of one integrated program, which he divided into categories determined by topics of military interest.

The distinction between the applied program and the academic one, with which the basic research was identified, also became blurred. Both research programs relied on the same faculty members. Perhaps for this reason, Terman, who before 1950 had seen applied research contracts as incompatible with the university's academic program, began using contract funds from the applied research program to cover part of those professors' salaries. He also used applied, as well as basic research funds, to support graduate students, and on occasion students working on classified research projects produced dissertations that were classified.[62] This was a practice at odds with the tradition of doctoral work, but Terman seems to have regarded it as a way of preventing the restrictions inherent in the applied, classified program from limiting the usefulness of the contract funds to the university. Academic traditions were bent to accommodate changed military needs.

By the mid-1950s the claims that the programs of basic and applied research were entirely distinct and that the applied research program was not affecting the academic program were largely rhetorical. As one engineer in a moment of candor asked Terman, "Why must we make this distinction [between applied and basic research]? We have students working on our [applied electronics] contracts. We have (or have had) research associates . . . working on Task 7 [the basic research contract]. We do 'exploration into new areas' in the [applied electronics] contracts and we work toward 'specific goals' on Task 7. There is no clear distinction so why talk about it?"[63] Similar conclusions were drawn at MIT. As the administrator of contract research at MIT wrote to MIT's president, "There is in fact no measurable difference between fundamental and applied research with respect either to Government objective, the national interest, or the relation to the normal business of education."[64]

While administrators of contract research were finding it difficult, or undesirable, to maintain distinctions between the basic and applied research programs, the ONR, concerned about security, was concluding that the differences between basic and applied research had been overdrawn. Instead of classifying research reports according to the security specifications of the contract that supported the work, the ONR decided in mid-1953 to require the submission of all reports, including those emanating from the basic research programs, in draft form to the ONR; classification would be determined there. Stanford's engineers were not happy with the proposed arrangement, and Terman warned the navy that its efforts to impose secrecy restrictions on basic research reports were "contrary to our understanding" that research at Stanford should, whenever possible, remain free of secrecy restrictions.[65] But despite the voiced opposition of the engineers, the navy's position in the matter triumphed, and Stanford's engineers made the necessary adjustments.

By late 1953 another accommodation was necessary. After discussions with the ONR, ERL administrator Donald Harris reported that some in the navy were pressing for the classification of all ONR-sponsored research, basic and applied. In an effort to ward off this possibility, David Bacon, assistant director of the ERL, promised the ONR that Stanford would "reduce mingling of cleared and uncleared personnel" by transferring all classified work to a separate, restricted facility. Student participation would be minimized; the building, which would be called the Applied Electronics Laboratory, would be placed under twenty-four-hour armed guard and would be inaccessible to all but authorized personnel. Other universities made similar arrangements. Thus, Stanford's engineers once again accommodated the interests of the military, now dividing their research program not along the lines of basic and applied research, which Bacon admitted would be impossible, but according to military requirements for secrecy.[66]

The change was necessary to maintain good relations with the navy and protect at least some of the engineers' work from secrecy restrictions. At least one engineer was pleased with the separation of the research program into separate buildings. Karl Spangenberg, one of the only engineers whose affiliation with Stanford dated back to the 1930s, believed that establishing separate facilities would help maintain the distinction between basic research and applied research and thus "avoid conflict between academic and industrial patterns."[67] But others objected. Some of those who were moved to the new applied electronics laboratory did not believe that their work threatened the academic nature of the basic research program. They saw their own research as suitably "academic" and resented being relegated to a separate facility that isolated them from the rest of the academic community.[68]

Moving the classified projects to a separate, restricted facility had the effect of highlighting, for these engineers as well as for the larger university community, the fact that the electrical engineering department was engaged in an extensive classified research program. Expressions of concern about the challenge that classified research posed to the academic tradition of free and open inquiry prompted one engineer in the mid-1950s to complain that "many stones are thrown at us for doing 'applied' work." He recommended that the engineers abandon the use of the labels "basic" and "applied," terms that were leading "to misunderstanding and trouble both inside the university and out," and rename the two electronics laboratories "Building One" and "Building Two." The engineer did not believe that Stanford's engineers should not participate in applied or classified work, but rather that they should simply cease stating that they were.[69] Recognizing that the military's interests, as well as those of many of Stanford's engineers, did not accord with the traditional values of the university community, this engineer was willing to settle for creating the illusion that they did.

Terman agreed that the separation of the classified and unclassified work posed administrative and public relations problems. When the navy dropped its support of the applied research program in 1955, canceling the joint services contract and allowing Stanford to contract directly with the air force and the Army Signal Corps, Terman took the opportunity to reorganize the electronics research program, combining the AEL and the ERL into the Stanford Electronics Research Laboratories (SERL). While the classified and unclassified work would remain physically separate, the administration of the research would be established according to specific technical programs with designated directors. With this arrangement, Terman was recognizing that "an organizational split along lines of applied work vs. basic work, or classified work vs. unclassified work . . . is not always realistic."[70]

Terman had begun revising his ideas about acceptable government-sponsored research better to reflect actual practices. Whereas in the late 1940s he had regarded basic research and applied research as distinct categories of research, with the latter being incompatible with a university's educational program, by 1958 Terman proposed that the terms "applied" and "basic" be jettisoned because their use caused "confusion in semantics." He suggested instead the categories of "learning work" and "applying work." "Learning work" involved the acquisition of knowledge; "applying work" was divided into two categories—"creative work," which involved innovation and invention, and "design and development work." Academic research, Terman declared, embraced both learning work and innovation work. The two, in fact, were essentially inseparable; they required the same knowledge, training, and creativity and thus both belonged in the university in close association with the university's educational program.[71]

Terman was not only reconstructing the relationship between basic and applied research and minimizing the difference between them. He also began to shape an argument, based on the tradition of academic freedom, to support the conduct of classified and applied research on campus. In the late 1940s Terman's stated goal was to ensure that military patronage supported, rather than interfered with, the university's educational mission and the tradition of free and undirected inquiry. By the mid-1950s he was concerned with making sure that generous military patronage continued to flow to the engineering school and that no one impeded those engineers deeply involved in military-sponsored research. Thus, when laboratory administrator David Bacon suggested to Terman in early 1956 that the military's proposed doubling of funds for applied microwave tube and systems work should be accepted only "under conditions consistent with our operation in a University atmosphere," Terman responded pointedly. Whether the proposed research would be undertaken was not up to the university's administrators, but, in keeping with the tradition of academic freedom, was "up to [Dean] Watkins [director of microwave tube research] and [William] Rambo [director of systems research]."[72] Stanford's engineers, Terman was insisting, should be free to pursue research of interest to them under conditions acceptable to them. The freedom of the individual researcher was to supersede any university tradition of free and open inquiry.

A similar argument was turned against those outside the engineering school who expressed unease over the university's deep involvement in applied, classified research. Those concerned about whether research was classified or unclassified were "worried about a mere form of words," William Rambo declared. What was important was not whether the work was classified or unclassified, Terman agreed, but whether Stanford's engineers were able to do work that interested them. In Terman's estimation, to prevent the engineers from conducting classified research was tantamount to an infringement on their academic freedom. After all, the engineers had freely chosen to do the research they were doing; "it just happens," he explained, "that some of this work is also of importance to the defense of the nation" and so was subject to secrecy restrictions.[73]

The interests of Stanford's electrical engineers did, in fact, correspond closely to those of their military patrons, primarily because Terman, in hiring them in the late 1940s, had selected engineers for their likely ability to attract military patronage. But the claim that the engineers were doing precisely the research that they would have done in the absence of military patronage was clearly specious. Ideally, the engineers, as autonomous experts, were free to conduct the research of interest to them. But, in actuality, their interests were not always compatible with those of their military sponsors, and given the engineering program's dependency on military support, the engineers found it difficult to gain control over the research agenda. As with Stanford's physicists in their prewar relationship with Sperry, the patron, not the academic experts, was in control.

But whereas Stanford's physicists had engaged in ceaseless battles with Sperry's representatives, pointedly objecting to the company's attempt to direct their research, the engineers did not challenge their military patrons. Instead, they settled for achieving some input into the research agenda while continuing to claim that they, not the military, were in fact in control. As Lester Field wrote, Stanford's electronics experts, working under air force sponsorship, needed to be "left free to demonstrate new types of jamming systems *at almost our own* choice of frequency and power levels, *at least on a first approach*" (emphasis added). Field clearly had low expectations about the extent to which Stanford's engineers would be able to control or shape the research agenda. The military had determined that they would work on jamming systems in the first place, and Field was clearly conceding to his patron the right to establish certain parameters for his work and to set specific goals over the course of the research. Field did hope to provide the military with a "list of things we would like to do and that we should pretty much be able to pursue these things on our own terms." This list suggests the extent to which Field had already taken specific military needs into account, raising the question of whether Stanford's engineers were really controlling the research agenda, even when they claimed they were. Item Three on Field's list, for example, reflected a clear military objective: "anti-gun control radar short delay repeaters working against range gate characteristics of gun control radars."[74] Only by adopting the military's objectives as his own and then by seeking some input in the shaping of the specific objectives could Field claim that the navy was not controlling the research agenda.

William Rambo, director of systems research, encountered the same dilemmas as did Field. He resolved them similarly, seeking a minimum of input and consciously adopting the interests of military patrons. Both the army and the air force exhibited "natural tendancies [sic] toward 'job specifications,'" Rambo recognized. Hoping to "forestall" this tendency, he proposed to the Army Signal Corps that Stanford's engineers "should continue to originate projects on the basis of our knowledge of the Signal Corps plans." However, the Signal Corps "should retain the privilege of reorienting or halting work which gets out of line." The Signal Corps, of course, "should originate projects," Rambo continued, while granting Stanford's engineers "the privilege of *some* selection here" (emphasis added).[75] This proposal, which was acceptable to the Signal Corps, gave the engineers the opportunity at least to suggest projects to their sponsors. While this seemingly afforded them some control over the research agenda, that control could only be exercised if they anticipated the needs of military sponsors and proposed projects to these sponsors that the engineers knew they would want to see pursued. As Rambo noted privately, the air force and the Army Signal Corps might "give us trouble on technical programs unless we *feed them acceptable ideas* on what we want to do before they decide what we ought to do" (emphasis added).[76] Thus, having the right to propose projects to the military gave the engineers illusory rather than real control over the research agenda; acceptance of a proposal, as Rambo well understood, depended on the engineers' successfully anticipating the interests of the military and adopting them as their own.[77]

If by the mid-1950s, the relationship between the engineers and the military was satisfying to both the military and to Stanford's engineers, it was so because the engineers had redefined their own interests to accommodate the needs of the military. Although in the late 1940s Terman had stated his aversion to a relationship with the military that placed the university in the position of running an industrial-style laboratory that produced technology for specific military needs, by the mid-1950s, that is precisely what the university was doing, despite the denials of Terman and other engineers. They might claim that a significant portion of the research program remained "basic," or free of direction and secrecy restrictions, but in fact much of the basic program was intimately integrated with the needs of the more overtly guided applied research such that the engineers, in practice, did not distinguish between the two. And while the engineers might be proposing projects to the military, rather than taking orders directly, they were doing so with an understanding that what they wanted to do had to correlate with the interests of their sponsors. Desirous of continued military support, the engineers adapted to and merged their interests with the needs of their sponsors.

The SERL was dependent on military support not only for research support but also for maintaining its relations with industrial sponsors. The triangular relationship was, in Terman's view, a "win-win-win" situation, although it clearly was not always a "win" situation for the engineers involved. To those who did not share Terman's commitment to the cold war or his political views, it was not a "win" situation for the university.[78] That the military was the linchpin in Stanford's relationship to industry never seems to have concerned Terman. He counted on the military to "exploit Stanford to max degree," and he intended to exploit the military in return.[79] To keep military funds flowing into the engineering school might require accommodations on the part of Stanford's engineers; these, to Terman and the other engineers, were minor compromises that could be justified through a variety of semantic circumlocutions, if not some self-deception as well. While the engineers might, in isolated moments of candor, recognize that they did not enjoy the control over their work that as professionals they desired, the situation to them may have seemed the perennial problem of the engineer rather than a specific dilemma prompted by Terman's determination to depend heavily on external sponsorship.

But the "very happy internal situation" in the engineering school, which made it "remarkably free of personal stresses and strains," in Terman's words, did not prevail throughout the rest of the university, which in these same years was also becoming, to varying degrees, dependent upon external sources of support.[80]

6

Building Steeples
of Excellence

In his farewell address to the nation in January 1961, President Eisenhower defended the "huge industrial and military machinery of defense" that had been created in the preceding decade as vital to the nation's security and to world peace. But he also warned of the threats that this development posed to the nation. There was a danger that a "military-industrial complex," immune from political scrutiny, might exercise a distorting influence over government officials and public policies. Further, the federal government's reliance on science and technology and its large expenditures on academic research and development threatened to overwhelm both the "free university, historically the fountainhead of free ideas and scientific discoveries," and the scientists within it. "The prospect of the domination of the nation's scholars by Federal employment, project allocations, and the power of money is ever present—and is gravely to be regarded," Eisenhower intoned.[1]

Eisenhower's admonitions were late. In the eight years of his presidency, the government had spent over $350 billion on defense, allocating seventy-seven cents of every budget dollar for military-related purposes. Over the course of the 1950s, federal expenditures for academic research and development more than tripled; by 1960 the federal government was spending close to $1 billion for academic research and university-affiliated research centers, 79 percent of which went to just twenty universities, including Stanford, Berkeley, Caltech, MIT, Harvard, and the University of Michigan. These universities, and particularly their science and engineering programs, had become heavily dependent on federal patronage, which in 1960 accounted for well over half of their total research budgets and for between 15 and 80 percent of their operating budgets. At Stanford, 39 percent of the operating budget derived from federal support; research in engineering and physics garnered over 80 percent of the federal patronage flowing into the university.[2]

If Eisenhower's warning was belated, the image he painted of the individual scientist and university as overwhelmed by the federal behemoth was likewise out of date. While such an image retained political salience with antistatist conservatives, it no longer resonated with academic administrators as it had in the 1930s. By the early 1960s, leading university administrators—conservatives and liberals alike—viewed federal patronage not as a threat but as a necessity. As Clark Kerr, chancellor of the University of California at Berkeley, told a Harvard audience in 1963, "Federal research aid to universities has helped greatly in meeting national needs. It has greatly assisted the universities themselves. The nation is stronger. The leading universities are stronger." This was the unanimous view of the presidents of America's research universities, according to Kerr.[3]

Kerr did admit to "problems" created by extensive federal patronage of academic science, primarily the development of "imbalances" within and between universities: between those universities with enormous governmental support and those with little or none, between the well-funded sciences and the underfunded humanities, between resources for research and attention to undergraduate education, between "big science" and "little science," between the importance attached to academic fields of "national importance," such as nuclear engineering and electronics, and seemingly impractical fields, such as medieval literature.

But to Kerr, the perceived imbalance, if viewed from a different angle, revealed a new and highly "productive" balance: between the university's capacity to produce students and to innovate and society's needs for experts and for new knowledge. Because the federal government's needs were not static but shifted with the world political situation, with economic developments, and with demographic change, so too must the university's emphases and interests shift. "Balance," then, in the sense of equal attention and resources to all academic disciplines and to teaching as well as research, was no longer desirable. "The essence of balance" in the "federal grant university," Kerr explained, "is to match support with the intellectual creativity of subject fields; with the need for skills of the highest level; with the kinds of expert service that society currently most requires. None of these measures is constant. Balance requires, therefore, a shifting set of judgments." In other words, the cold war university could not be bound by old notions of balance; it must instead be flexible and ever-changing in response to national needs.[4] Stanford's administrators had reached the same conclusion, agreeing with Kerr that the terms "excellence" and "balance" should be decoupled and creating a new concept, "steeples of excellence." A "steeple" was an academic field deemed of national importance and for which ample patronage was available. This was where the university would put its resources; fields seemingly irrelevant to national interests and with few opportunities for external support would be purposefully neglected. Peaks and valleys, rather than an even plateau, was the academic landscape favored by Stanford's administrators.

Not everyone was enthusiastic about steeples of excellence, however. Not long after Kerr's defense of imbalance, critics began calling into question both national priorities and the universities' almost exclusive attention to them. Departments of biology, for example, had adopted a reductionist approach, focusing on the cellular and molecular level. What had happened, Barry Commoner wondered in his 1966 book, *Science and Society,* to those approaches to biological study that took account of the whole organism and the connections between the organism and its complex environment? Looking at the university as a whole, others expressed concern over the disproportionate emphasis on science and technology and the neglect of the liberal arts, disciplines which, it was argued, encouraged ethical and valuative inquiry. In his 1964 article "A Plea to Save the Liberal Arts," critic David Boroff voiced this worry, warning that the nation's universities were in danger of "producing a generation of mindless technicians, specialized boors or even sinister Dr. Strangeloves."[5]

Well before the public airing of such concerns, however, some academic scientists and scholars were criticizing the developing imbalances between academic departments and between fields within particular disciplines. Critics within academe were not necessarily those in fields for which governmental support was unavailable or those who had tried but failed to obtain governmental support. At Stanford, for example, many of the university's physicists, most of whom had plentiful external research support, were prominent supporters of the concept of balance. Proponents of balance were not necessarily on the political left; at Stanford, many were, in fact, politically moderate or conservative.

Those with a vision of the university as a balanced institution rather than a replica of the interests of federal patrons clashed not with federal patrons but with administrators at Stanford. Contrary to Eisenhower's imagery, federal patronage contributed to, but did not inevitably lead to, imbalance in the nation's leading universities. Imbalance was created by administrators who, for institutional reasons, were eager to see their universities adopt the nation's cold war agenda. The following two chapters explore these conflicts between administrators and some—but not all—faculty members in Stanford's science and humanities departments. Because the funding for social sciences was derived primarily from private foundations and because issues of "balance" became entangled with questions about the political beliefs of particular professors, the reshaping of the social sciences is discussed in a separate chapter.

Creating Departmental Imbalances

When Wallace Sterling became president of Stanford in late 1949, Stanford was once again facing financial dilemmas. The wave of veterans that had inundated the campuses after World War II, virtually doubling enrollments, was waning by the end of the decade, as was income from tuition. In the 1946–47 academic year, the peak year of veteran enrollment, income from tuition accounted for almost 60 percent of Stanford's income. By 1952, despite the university having raised tuition, the figure had fallen to 47 percent. At the same time, real income from endowment was declining, the result of low interest rates and persistent inflation. Between 1940 and 1950 income from endowment fell from 29 percent to 16 percent of the total income for private universities; the figures for Stanford were similar.[6]

Sterling shared none of the reservations about federal patronage that had been expressed by his administrative predecessors when faced with similar concerns about finances. The benefits of federal contracts were being clearly demonstrated by Frederick Terman, to whom Sterling extended "enthusiastic praise" and encouragement. By the end of the Korean War, Stanford's engineering school had well over $1.5 million in government contracts and was bringing into the university more than the university was expending from its own funds on the school. In addition to being self-supporting, the engineering program was by the early 1950s clearly recognized as one of the best in the country.[7]

A few other segments of the university were similarly prosperous and well regarded. The physics department had developed extensive federal patronage, largely through its microwave laboratory, which in

1953 had over $500,000 in governmental (primarily military) research contracts. A significant fraction of these funds supported the development and use of a large linear accelerator—an "atom smasher"—based on the physics department's own prewar invention, the klystron. In the early 1950s the department had hired two highly regarded experimental physicists—Wolfgang Panofsky and Robert Hofstadter—to make use of the accelerator, thus giving the department the beginnings of a steeple of excellence in high-energy physics, the area of physics attracting the most patronage and public attention in the 1950s.[8]

Stanford's department of statistics also had an impressive amount of governmental patronage. By 1949 the department was producing more for the university in the form of contract overhead than it was receiving from general university funds. Albert Bowker, the department chair, had expanded the department through salary-splitting, hiring former colleagues from the OSRD-sponsored statistical group at Columbia, who, like himself, were well known to the ONR. (The link to the ONR was strengthened when the statistician Herbert Solomon left Stanford in 1948 for a four-year post in the ONR's division of mathematics; a year later, Stanford electrical engineer Karl Spangenberg took the same route, although his appointment at ONR lasted only one year.)[9] Bowker had looked with favor on the opportunities provided by the Korean War to expand his department's government-sponsored research activities. In the spring of 1951 the department established a separate laboratory of applied mathematics and statistics and began work on three large contracts for the ONR, portions of which were classified. By early 1953 the laboratory was spending approximately $350,000 on federally funded research and receiving $87,000 in overhead payments, making Stanford, in Bowker's estimate, the university with the most "outside money in the mathematical sciences of any . . . university." Like the physics and electrical engineering departments, the statistics department was also well regarded nationally, suggesting a correlation between a department's close relationship with military patrons and determinations of a department's status.[10]

The psychology department, headed by Ernest Hilgard, had also moved quickly after World War II to develop federal patronage, establishing a special division of project research in the late 1940s. While the amount of external support was modest in comparison with that of the physics and statistics departments, the availability of government contracts, mainly from the U.S. Public Health Service, had enabled the department to expand its staff from seven psychologists before the war to fourteen by the end of the 1940s. Most of the new professors were clinical psychologists, a field not well represented at Stanford or other universities before World War II but which had become of interest to governmental agencies responsible for dealing with veterans' psychological problems and with helping veterans readjust to civilian life. The department also took advantage of the ONR's interest in understanding the relationship between soldiers and the increasingly complicated technology that they were expected to operate. By 1953 the department had $30,000 worth of contracts with the ONR for research on problem solving and decision making as they related to personality characteristics.[11]

Even Stanford's philosophy department, under the leadership of John Goheen, had taken advantage of the military's interest in the process of decision making, negotiating contracts with the ONR and with Army Ordnance for similar work. The department had also expanded the size of its staff by making appointments jointly with the statistics department and using "soft" money to cover salaries. With the new appointments, the department was able to add courses in advanced logic, mathematical logic, and the foundations of set theory—subjects related to the department's sponsored research—to its traditional curriculum of ethics, moral philosophy, and history of philosophy.[12]

But these departments were the exceptions. Most departments in both the School of Humanities and Sciences and the School of Mineral Sciences had little in the way of research patronage and were not regarded as nationally significant. The absence of patronage in departments like literature or classics was understandable; federal patrons were not providing support for these disciplines. But even departments for which external support was available—economics, geology, and biology, for example—had little in the way of patronage. Moreover, neither these departments nor the well-funded department of physics were following the example of the statistics and electrical engineering departments and engaging in salary-splitting. By hiring faculty members on soft money, the latter departments had expanded their staffs in fields deemed nationally important at no cost to Stanford. With more faculty members, all on governmental contracts, these departments were able to fund and instruct more graduate students and thus increase the number of doctorates awarded annually, one measure of a department's influence.[13]

Other departments were not ignorant of the path that the departments of engineering and statistics had taken. Rather, they objected to that path and had determined not to follow it. This does not mean that the members of these departments were united in opposition to governmental patronage. Almost every member of the physics department, for example, was conducting research with governmental support. But, in contrast to the engineering school, where there was a general consensus in favor of federal patronage, there was a diversity of views about federal support among the faculty members in other departments.

A few scientists—such as Charles Stein, a statistician, and Paul Kirkpatrick, a physicist—objected to accepting military patronage of their research for moral or political reasons.[14] More typical, however, were concerns that patronage might be incompatible with maintaining control over one's own work and pursuing research of one's own choosing. A number of social scientists at Stanford expressed concerns about federal and other forms of patronage for these reasons. "There is much worthwhile research that is not likely to obtain foundation or government support," noted the members of a special committee on research in the behavioral sciences, adding that "one of the peculiar functions of a private university is to foster this type of completely free investigation." The committee perceived "a further hazard to the University in permitting too large a share of research activities, and of the faculty's personal income, to be dependent on sources over which it has no control."[15]

Similar concerns lay behind the decisions of some natural scientists not to seek governmental patronage or to accept only modest support. Biologist Lawrence Blinks, for example, feared that research requiring large amounts of governmental patronage inevitably meant involvement in administrative matters and a change in the style and pace of his research; these were changes he and others were disinclined to make. Others preferred teaching to research or had only modest research plans that did not require large amounts of support and so they saw no need to obtain federal contracts. Thus, most scientists at Stanford did not view federal, or even military, support as morally tainted; a significant number did, however, believe that dependence on patronage might compromise their research interests and academic pursuits.[16]

If certain scientists preferred not to obtain governmental patronage, certain departments, which included faculty members who were conducting research under contract to the federal government, were united in opposition to salary-splitting. Some made the case that salary-splitting made their departments, and indeed the entire university, unacceptably dependent upon the federal government. Should the patronage be curtailed suddenly, the university would find itself with myriad professors whom it was unable to support. Or, should the terms of the support at some time become unacceptable to the scientists involved, those dependent upon that support for their livelihoods would find it difficult to disengage from the relationship with the patron.[17]

Added to these concerns were worries that salary-splitting posed a threat to departmental and professional autonomy. This worry differed from that which had been expressed by David Locke Webster, chair of the physics department, and other faculty members in the early 1940s in response to the administration's effort to pressure departments to seek industrial patronage. Then, Webster and others had argued that industrial patronage inevitably distorted academic research and was inappropriate to a university. Webster had taken the most extreme position, insisting that his department could not accommodate those physicists who were conducting industry-sponsored research without compromising and distorting the entire department and, by extension, the discipline of physics. Webster, and the view of departmental purity that he had tried to uphold, had lost the battle not only with Stanford's administration but with other members of his department as well. While a number of the department's physicists themselves had had no interest in industrial patronage, they believed that the department could accommodate those who did without compromising itself.

It was this position that became the generally accepted one among the physicists and the other scientists at Stanford who had followed closely the developments in that department. Those with and those without external support found common ground in the position that those who wanted to rely on external patronage—governmental or industrial—should be free to do so and that no other member of the department should attempt to prevent them. And they agreed that, conversely, those who chose not to seek patronage, for whatever reasons, should be free not to. By emphasizing the scientist's freedom in relation to others in the department, the question that Webster had raised—whether patronage necessarily or inevitably distorted the work of academic researchers—no longer had to be debated by the entire department. Those who answered in the affirmative could simply eschew patronage.

The ethos of tolerance represented, in effect, an accommodation to the availability of patronage and to the interest of some faculty members and of Stanford's administration in obtaining it. But concomitant with the emphasis on tolerance was a commitment to maintaining a balance within a department among methods and fields of research. Thus, while scientists were to be free to pursue patronage if they so chose, to shape their work to the interests of a patron or risk a patron's interference in their research, departments as units would not allow the availability of patronage itself to distort the department as a whole. A department would accommodate the interests of those whose work was heavily subsidized by patrons, even if, as in the case of the physics department, this meant adding a new field of study (microwaves) and a new laboratory (the microwave laboratory) to traditional interests and facilities. The interests of those with patronage would not, however, be permitted to overwhelm the department, disturb the work of others, or supersede other departmental interests.

This commitment to a balanced department was at the root of the opposition to salary-splitting. Salary-splitting could be deliberately implemented only if a department hired professors who were known to have federal contracts. This not only meant that the department would have to add patronage to the factors traditionally used in judging a candidate for appointment, a situation that came close to violating the ethos of tolerance. It also meant that the department would be unable to hire those whose research interests had traditionally been represented by the department but who might not have access to external support. For a department like statistics, which had essentially been created by military patrons, salary-splitting presented no difficulties. For the members of other departments, however, following the path taken by the statistics department and the engineering school meant permitting their departments' interests to be skewed by the interests of patrons; it meant, essentially, surrendering control over the shape of their departments.

Whether Stanford's administration understood the reasons why many departments chose not to emulate the engineering school is unclear. It is clear, however, that President Sterling wished them to follow the engineering school's path. To impress upon them the university's budgetary constraints, and perhaps to prod them to obtain external support, he declared a "financial emergency" in 1951 and asked all departments to cut their budgets by 5 percent.[18] The response was mixed. Bowker reminded Sterling that his department was not only paying for itself but also bringing to the university, in the form of overhead, almost twice what the university was providing the department from its general funds. Rather than cutting his budget, he thus requested an increase to enable him to raise faculty salaries. John Goheen, whose philosophy department was not self-supporting, informed Sterling that he had cut his department's budget but only by one-quarter of what the president had requested. At the same time, he reminded Sterling of his department's contract with the ONR. If the department were not damaged by further budget cuts, the contract would certainly be renewed, and the university would thus realize savings in the form of salary expenses that would be paid by the contract.[19]

The response from the economics department, which for several years was pressed to reduce its budget, was more typical. Unlike Goheen and Bowker, the department chair, Edward Shaw, did not indicate a willingness to obtain federal contracts to prevent or limit cuts to his budget. Instead, he explained to Sterling that he had cut his budget as requested by eliminating several positions for teaching assistants. This was an unfortunate development for the department's graduate program, according to Shaw, and he warned the president that further budget reductions would seriously damage the department. Shaw was, in effect, pointedly reminding Sterling of his previously stated opposition to the administration's suggestion that, in place of fellowships and teaching positions, the economics department support graduate students as research assistants on government contracts. To do so, Shaw believed, would lead to a distortion of Stanford's graduate program in economics and to an inappropriate channeling of a student's interests.[20]

If responses varied, the overall message to the administration was clear. Those departments and professors willing to obtain governmental contracts and to use federal patronage to cover expenses, such as salaries, that had traditionally been paid with university funds saw themselves as assets to the administration, and because they were also bringing to the university substantial income in the form of contract overhead, their objections to budgetary cuts were difficult to challenge. But the others who were not interested in developing and becoming dependent on federal support would need more than subtle encouragement and small budget cuts to push them into the desired pattern of behavior. So in 1954 President Sterling selected Frederick Terman to be Stanford's provost and encouraged him to restructure the departments in the School of Humanities and Sciences and the School of Mineral Sciences according to the model of those in the engineering school.

The choice of Terman for provost was a shrewd one. Terman had extensive contacts with federal patrons that would be useful in obtaining contracts for Stanford's science departments: by the mid-1950s he was a member of both the Naval Research Advisory Committee and of the Army Signal Corps Research and Development Advisory Council and a consultant to the National Science Foundation (NSF) and the Institute for Defense Analysis. Terman was also deeply loyal to Stanford and dedicated to making it into a widely respected institution. These commitments had kept him at Stanford despite his being passed over for the presidency of Stanford in 1949 and a generous offer from Northwestern in 1953 to become dean of engineering.

Terman's personality, which may have militated against his selection as president of Stanford, also suited Sterling's purposes. Terman was unwavering in his own convictions, uncomfortable with subtleties, and impatient with those who disagreed with him. He was also relentless and willing to be ruthless in pursuit of his goals. Recognizing that reshaping departments might create tension and even provoke conflict, Sterling needed as provost someone who would be undeterred by the protests of dissenting faculty members. At the same time, Terman might become the focus of faculty unhappiness, thus deflecting criticism from the president himself. It was Terman who was regarded by many professors as tactless, narrow-minded, excessively utilitarian, and eminently unlikable. Sterling, by contrast, was widely loved, his main contact with Stanford's faculty members occurring at intimate cocktail parties held at his home every Friday afternoon.

Imposing the Engineering Model on the University

Terman brought to the position of provost the energy and determination of a person who believed deeply in the validity and necessity of the changes that he was expected to effect. He began immediately to collect data on every department and on individual professors to determine their yearly research output, the number of doctorates produced yearly, the number and size of undergraduate courses, and the amount of money expended per student. Such information, Terman believed, would help him determine which professors and which departments were, according to his standards, producing too few students, drawing too heavily on university resources, and neglecting to take advantage of available patronage. In Terman's ideal university, every department and even every professor was self-supporting; every faculty member produced at a minimum one doctoral student per year.

Financial concerns were partly responsible for Terman's attention to output and external support. A desire to see Stanford produce large numbers of Ph.D.s and to build steeples in particular fields of national importance also reflected his commitment to increasing Stanford's influence and prestige. To these concerns Terman brought a particular interest in efficiency and a faith in statistical measures of merit, both of which would have pleased his father, who had dedicated his professional life to the dubious goal of quantifying intelligence and had regarded the university as a business enterprise, albeit an inexcusably inefficient one.

If Terman was carrying into the postwar period the interests of some prewar corporate progressives, he was also representing (although perhaps in extreme fashion) the enthusiasms of the cold war decades. The early postwar years were marked by a general faith in objective measures of merit and the widespread use of intelligence, achievement, and personality tests at all levels of the educational system. The application of standards of efficiency and productivity to the university was also in keeping with the interests of the period. By the mid-1950s, educators, administrators, and policymakers were anticipating a significant increase in demand for higher education in the next decade, when the "baby boomers" would reach college age. The nation's universities were not producing enough college teachers to meet the expected demand, and one solution was to increase the efficiency and productivity of the universities. Increasing the number of doctorates in science and engineering also became an explicit national goal after the launching of Sputnik triggered fears that Americans were falling behind the Russians in scientific and technological developments. These concerns—for increasing production and improving efficiency in institutions of higher education—were reflected in the 1958 National Defense Education Act (NDEA), which, among other things, provided loans and fellowships for undergraduate and graduate students. They were also embodied in a multiple-year grant to Terman, beginning in September 1956, from the Ford Foundation's Fund for the Advancement of Education (headed by former Stanford administrator Alvin Eurich) for a study of university productivity, based on data from Stanford. Aiding Terman with his study were Albert Bowker and R. V. Oakford, a Stanford industrial engineer.[21]

Shortly after becoming provost, Terman held meetings with those departments in the university that were falling short of his standards. In his opinion, departments that had little in the way of external support and no clear opportunities for developing any were a drain on the university's funds. The very fact that they lacked patronage opportunities was evidence of their low value; it also meant that they could not develop large graduate programs (funded with federal patronage), which Terman viewed as a measure of a department's influence. These departments, the provost determined, would be service departments; they would support themselves by teaching large numbers of undergraduates while their graduate programs would remain small or be discontinued. The classics department presented the extreme example of an impractical discipline lacking access to external support, and Terman was quick to address what he regarded as the department's drain on university resources. He informed the department that he was eliminating the two positions that had remained unfilled since the retirement of two professors in the early 1950s and suggested that the department manage with fewer professors by offering fewer courses (to larger numbers of students) and eliminating courses for advanced students.[22]

The plaintive objection of Stanford's classicists that to remain a good department they had to be able to train graduate students led the provost to agree to talk to the "dissodents [sic]." The strongest objections were voiced by the department's senior member, Hazel Hansen, whose views Terman privately dismissed as those of a "single woman—lonely—frustrated." While displaying more sympathy for other members of the department, Terman wasted little time pondering the merits of their arguments.[23] He was not interested in departments such as classics that had no opportunities to develop patronage and were of no apparent practical value. It was departments that did have opportunities to develop patronage but were failing to take full advantage of them that drew the provost's energies.

These departments—like biology, chemistry, geology, and economics—had the potential to become prestigious departments but were instead, in Terman's view, perpetuating their own "weakness." The provost chastised these departments, suggesting that their chairpersons had been insufficiently aggressive in pursuing governmental patronage and telling them that they needed to increase the number of doctorates they awarded annually. The economics department, which awarded no more than a few doctorates per year, was told that it compared unfavorably to Harvard's and that it needed to produce eight to ten Ph.D.s per year. The geology department was simply told to increase graduate enrollment by 25 to 50 percent, which, the provost pointed out, would greatly please potential university patrons. To accommodate the larger numbers of graduate students, Terman suggested that the departments teach larger classes and that they obtain governmental contracts (which would provide support for students in the form of research assistantships). Even the statistics department, the department operating closest to Terman's ideal, did not escape Terman's scrutiny. One member of the department—Charles Stein—was discovered to have no federal research support.[24]

Shortly after Terman's round of departmental meetings, Albert Bowker met privately with Stein, told him that his lack of government support "looked bad," and requested that he obtain a government contract. Bowker, who was close to Terman and would soon be named dean of graduate studies, may have meant that given Terman's ideal of a department in which every professor was self-supporting, Stein's lack of outside support was an embarrassing deviation. Or Bowker may have meant Stein to infer that given his political history—Stein had been a fellow traveler in the 1930s and had resigned from Berkeley during the loyalty-oath controversy—Stein should do nothing to draw unwanted attention to himself, including refusing to obtain a government contract. Whichever the case, Stein heeded Bowker's warning. He had no trouble arranging a contract with the ONR; he was widely regarded as a brilliant statistician and was well known to those at the ONR, having been a member of the wartime statistical research group at Columbia.[25]

Others, faced with similar pressure from their departmental chairs, may have acted as did Stein. Certainly those faculty members not yet tenured, or those like Stein with leftist political sympathies, may have feared that to act otherwise was to put their academic careers at risk. But while it is unclear how many other faculty members responded to administrative pressure as did Stein, a number of departmental chairs who were less closely aligned with Terman than Bowker was expressed unhappiness, and even anger, with the provost. They rejected all or part of his request for larger course enrollments, heavier reliance on external support, and increased production of doctoral students and in some cases challenged his imputation that a reluctance, or an inability, to follow this course reflected on the academic quality of the work of their department.

Victor Twitty, who was the head of the biology department, a member of the National Academy of Sciences, and Terman's next-door neighbor, offered mild resistance. In a letter to President Sterling, he noted that the biology department in fact had substantial external patronage, but it came from private foundations, not the federal government. He also insisted that while some members of his department produced little in the way of research or graduate students and had virtually no external support, they were the "most useful" to the department in terms of undergraduate instruction. Stanford's biologists should be judged not individually but as a departmental unit, Twitty suggested, and he judged the department, overall, to be a strong one.[26]

Kenneth Arrow, who had replaced Shaw as chair of the economics department, was blunter in his objections to Terman's evaluation and proposals. The problem with obtaining federal patronage, he pointed out, was that support was available only for particular fields. For example, the ONR was supporting mathematical economics but not other fields of interest to the department, such as resource conservation, social security, and comparative economic systems. In a letter to President Sterling, Arrow, whose own work was supported by the ONR, concluded that it would be a "mistake to channel all research into the particular lines for which outside support is available and into relatively large projects. . . . The Individual Scholar, working in a field which may or may not be currently fashionable plays a very vital role in economics."[27]

The most hostility to Terman's plans was expressed by Charles Park, a geologist and the dean of the School of Mineral Sciences. (The school, created at Terman's urging in 1947, combined the engineering school's departments of mining and metallurgy with the geology department, which was headed by Levorsen.) Along with other geologists in the school, Park complained about the provost's lack of appreciation for the qualitative, as opposed to the quantitative, aspects of education and, particularly, about his desire to set standards of production for each member of the school and his insistence that courses that enrolled few students should be eliminated. As one field geologist pointed out, the engineering-school model simply did not work for all disciplines within the university. For example, the reliance on lectures and unsupervised laboratory courses, while satisfactory for the training of engineers, would be disastrous for geologists, whose "laboratory" was the natural world. "A would-be geologist must learn to sort relevant facts from a multitude of sense-impressions; to formulate as many pertinent hypotheses as possible . . . to juggle all these hypotheses impartially in his mind, mentally testing each one against his accumulating observational data. . . . In short, a geologist more than other scientists must learn to cultivate judgment," he wrote. And judgment was best fostered in small seminars where students were able to interact with their professors.[28]

But Park and others objected to more than Terman's interest in efficiency and production. They disliked the provost's insistence that the school was not taking full advantage of available external support. (In

1953 governmental support for the entire school was about $46,000.) Park, a specialist in the location of ores, was not averse to governmental patronage; he had several governmental contracts, including one with the AEC. But he opposed Terman's suggestion that the school use governmental funds to pay faculty salaries and support graduate students. Doing so would make the school dependent on governmental support, and the result, he feared, would be that the school would lose sight of its own objectives as its members, out of necessity, focused on the interests of their patrons.[29]

To Park, Terman, and not any specific patron, was the real threat to the interests of the School of Mineral Sciences. Besides suggesting that it depend on external patronage, Terman was clearly interested in directing the school's interests into particular fields and away from others. He wanted to see the school strengthen its work in physical metallurgy, as MIT was doing. As he knew from conversations with friends in the electronics industry, research in the properties of materials was of great interest to companies developing products for the military, which depended on new materials like semiconductors and heat-resistant metals.[30]

While Park seems not to have objected to the idea of strengthening the school's work in physical metallurgy, he may well have suspected that the provost expected this to occur at the expense of other fields traditionally represented. In his meeting with Park, Terman had suggested that he eliminate the field of mining (Park's own field), which Terman judged to be "dying." Terman's insistence that small classes be eliminated may also have been seen by Park as a challenge to the tradition of fieldwork and an attempt to push the department toward mathematical and physical approaches to geological exploration. While there is no evidence to suggest that Park was hostile to these newer approaches, which reified nature, Park was a nature lover with conservationist (but not preservationist) leanings and an internationally recognized gift for fieldwork. Finally, Park may also have doubted (although incorrectly) Terman's commitment to petroleum geology. Shortly after becoming provost, Terman had rejected Park's appointment of an assistant professor of petroleum geology to the school, citing the geologist's disappointing undergraduate transcript. This was a highly unusual reason for denying an appointment, and Park no doubt regarded it as insufficient explanation for the provost's action. In early 1956, in protest over Terman's interference in the school and questioning of his authority, Park submitted his resignation as dean.[31]

The reaction to his agenda for the university caught Terman off guard. Momentarily stricken with self-doubt, the provost admitted to President Sterling that his approach had "misfired" and asked, "What did I do wrong?" Sterling's reply ("Nothing.") restored Terman's confidence.[32] Over the next ten years, the provost would continue to pressure departments to build steeples of excellence and obtain external support and would give weight to this pressure by freezing the budgets of recalcitrant departments and aggressively intervening in departmental searches. He would also continue to meet sporadic opposition to his plans, notably from the biology and physics departments and from the deans of the Schools of Mineral Sciences and Humanities and Sciences, resistance he overcame either by maneuvering around the recalcitrants or, when that was not possible, labeling them troublemakers and arranging for their removal from positions of authority. Although not always successful by his own standards, Terman played an important role in making departments at Stanford dependent on external funds, making entrepreneurship a necessary behavior of faculty members, and institutionalizing within departments, if not the particular interests of cold war patrons, then, at minimum, the understanding that academic programs and departmental interests needed to be justified in terms of national importance and access to patronage.

Steeple-Building and Salary-Splitting

To Terman, Park was an obstacle to his plans for the School of Mineral Sciences, and his resignation was therefore welcome. But President Sterling was unwilling to see Park resign. The mineralogist was not only respected and liked by Stanford's other geologists, who were reportedly demoralized by his resignation. More important, he was an excellent fund-raiser and had succeeded in building strong links between the School of Mineral Sciences and the oil and extractive industries, realizing Tresidder's earlier hopes for the mining and geology departments. Stanford's administration did not want to disturb this relationship between the school and powerful patrons. Administrators wanted Park to remain dean, but they also wanted the School of Mineral Sciences to began serving more fully the interests of the military-industrial complex.[33]

Thus, President Sterling intervened, massaging egos while at the same time expressing full agreement with Terman that the school needed to eliminate small seminars, enroll more graduate students, and recognize the university's financial difficulties by developing more governmental patronage and by splitting salaries.[34] Park retracted his resignation and agreed with the administration's decision to divide the school into four departments—geology, petroleum engineering, mineral engineering, and metallurgical engineering—each of which would enjoy considerable autonomy. Pressure on Park to push Stanford's geology department into a mode of operation similar to that of the engineering school eased as Terman concentrated on encouraging the metallurgical engineering department to develop a steeple of excellence in materials science. Useful to Terman in this endeavor was the entrepreneurial Robert Huggins, an MIT-trained metallurgist who had joined the Stanford faculty in 1954. Unlike Park, Huggins had no reservations about salary-splitting. Within five years he had expanded his department by three professors, overseen an increase in federal support from approximately $60,000 to over $200,000, and raised graduate student enrollment from a mere handful to twenty-five.[35]

Huggins was taking advantage of the need of the AEC and the armed services for research on materials problems, a need which, after Sputnik, was declared by the President's Science Advisory Committee to be urgent. Federal support, provided chiefly through the Defense Department's Advanced Research Projects Agency (ARPA), skyrocketed at the end of the decade; Huggins and Terman were able to take advantage of this heightened interest, and in 1961 Stanford was one of five universities to receive multimillion-dollar support for the establishment of a center for materials science. By the end of the decade, the center had 59 faculty members, 79 research associates, almost three hundred graduate students, and about $1.4 million annually in government contracts.[36]

Shortly before appealing to ARPA for funding, Terman had transferred Huggins's metallurgy department from the School of Mineral Sciences to the engineering school. President Sterling had learned from Carl Borgmann, the director of science and engineering programs for the Ford Foundation, that such a move would increase the department's attractiveness to potential patrons, including the Ford Foundation.[37] Removing the metallurgy department from the School of Mineral Sciences (which was then renamed the School of Earth Sciences) highlighted the small amount of governmental patronage that the school had developed since Terman's first confrontation with Park in late 1955. From approximately $40,000 at that time, the figure had risen to approximately $64,000 by the 1960–61 academic year. In 1960 the provost informed Park that the school could no longer expect the university to cover expenses for research, for secretarial assistance, or for publishing. In other words, the school, which had received immunity from the provost's pressure for a few years by agreeing to accommodate the department of metallurgy, was now being told it must depend on federal patronage. Terman's renewed pressure on Park also corresponded to an apparent increase in patronage opportunities for geophysicists. In 1959 the NSF had recommended that Congress provide $651 million over a ten-year period for the study of the oceans, which would include explorations of the geophysics of the sea floor. The NSF proposal built upon the popularity of oceanography in the wake of the 1957 International Geophysical Year (IGY), a coordinated international exploration of the oceans and the atmosphere, and on the military's interest in obtaining information useful to undersea warfare and submarine detection.

Terman's effort to force the School of Earth Sciences to seek more governmental support was effectively ignored, and in 1962, the provost, while approving the school's budget, again warned Park that the geology department must begin attracting more government support. In a departmental meeting, the geologists discussed the provost's warning and acknowledged that hundreds of millions of dollars were available from the federal government. But it was the very amount and ease of acquiring contracts that caused them concern. Noting that a "dangerously large fraction" of faculty members at some schools were supported by funds from federal contracts, the geologists agreed that while they would seek governmental support, they must not become dependent upon it. The renewed pressure from the provost apparently disheartened Park, however. At a subsequent departmental meeting, he asked to go on record as opposed to using governmental patronage to support the teaching staff, clerical assistants, students, or technicians. He then informed Stanford's administration of his plans to resign his deanship and take early retirement from the university.[38]

This time, the administration did not urge Park to reconsider. As Terman explained to President Sterling, Park's resignation was an opportunity; the next dean should be someone who would really "exploit the possibilities" of sponsored research and make the School of Earth Sciences "hum."[39] The administration settled on Richard H. Jahns, dean of earth sciences at Penn State University and before that a professor of geology at Caltech. An economic geologist like Park, Jahns was acceptable to Stanford's industrial patrons. But Jahns was also familiar with and supportive of geophysical approaches to geological exploration and, unlike Park, comfortable with relying on support from the federal government. Within a few months of coming to Stanford, Jahns was congratulated by the administration; governmental contract support for the school of earth sciences had increased by 132 percent since his arrival.[40]

During the same years that Terman struggled with Park over the direction of the School of Mineral Sciences and its reliance on governmental patronage, the provost also came into conflict with members of the biology department. In Terman's view, that department, like geology, was unproductive and "weak"; it turned out fewer than one doctorate per professor per year, had obtained little in the way of governmental support, and was refusing to split salaries. The department, moreover, had ranked only thirteenth in a 1957 nationwide survey of biology departments. To gain national prominence for the department and to gain access to large amounts of external patronage, Terman purposely set out to create imbalances in the department, to build steeples in oceanography, biomedicine, and biochemistry—fields deemed "nationally significant" and for which substantial patronage was available. As in the case of the geologists, Stanford's biologists were for the most part committed to the concept of a balanced department and thus came into significant conflict with the provost.

In early 1959 Terman sent the dean of graduate studies, Albert Bowker, to visit the department's Hopkins Marine Station in Monterey to assess the possibility of turning the quiet seaside facility into a leading oceanographic center.[41] According to Bowker's impressions of his meeting with the biologists, the "last thing they wanted was for a member of the Stanford administration to spur them into a pattern of operation different from the present one." Stanford's four marine-station biologists, two of whom were members of the prestigious National Academy of Sciences, were, in Bowker's words, "devoted scholars" who enjoyed working at the relatively isolated and biologically rich, eleven-acre site on the Monterey Peninsula, exploring the biological world both as experimentalists and naturalists. Although one of them had a small governmental contract, the biologists had no interest in obtaining a large governmental contract and little interest in deep water biology. Moreover, they believed that it was not possible to undertake a large, externally funded program of oceanography without destroying their ability to continue doing tidal biology in the quiet atmosphere that they desired. To Bowker, they "repeatedly commented on how terrible it was at Scripps [Institute of Oceanography], where there were hundreds of people . . . that all kinds of people have government projects and employ lots of assistants." The University of California's Scripps Institute, located on the San Diego coast, had once been a quiet biology-oriented marine station but had emerged from World War II as one of the leading centers of military-sponsored oceanographic research and of graduate education in oceanography. Stanford's biologists, it was clear, did not want to take this path.[42]

Terman would likely have faced resistance from Lawrence Blinks, the head of the station, had not the University of California at Berkeley indicated its interest in obtaining NSF funds and establishing its own marine station near Monterey. News of Berkeley's plans upset Blinks, who described the University of California as the "General Motors of Universities." With two universities working on the peninsula, there was a *"real* danger of over-collecting," Blinks wrote with alarm to Terman, pointing out that his ecology students had found several species severely diminished in numbers in the last few years. "What will happen to these and other species when subjected to systematic hunting by a large group of students is gruesome to contemplate." To avoid the depletion of the area's marine life, which he believed would inevitably result from the location of a Berkeley-operated marine station on the peninsula, Blinks agreed that Stanford should pursue the NSF support and expand the marine station in order to keep the University of California off the peninsula. Blinks still hesitated to forge a close relationship with the NSF, preferring that the marine station invite cooperation from the state and national fish and wildlife bureaus. (They would be "GOOD neighbors," he wrote, "noncompetitive, not depleting the shore collecting . . . and fitting nicely into Stanford's traditional fisheries interest.")[43] In mid-1960, in response to a proposal from Blinks, the NSF awarded Stanford almost one-quarter of a million dollars for the construction and renovation of the marine station's laboratory facilities. Blinks's pleasure at receiving the requested funds was blunted by irrepressible worries about the effect that the expansion of the marine station would have on his own work. "[I] should be more joyful over all this," he lamented, "did I not fear that it will take two good years out of my scientific career to do an engineering job for which I am not trained and have no bent at all."[44]

But Terman was buoyed by the ease with which Stanford had obtained NSF support, correctly read it as evidence of the NSF's confidence in the marine station, and began pressing Blinks to seek funds from the NSF for the operation of an oceanographic vessel. John Wilson at the NSF had informed Terman that his agency hoped to develop on the West Coast a facility comparable to Woods Hole in Massachusetts and that the agency saw "tremendous potential" in a location at Stanford.[45] With funding from the NSF, Stanford's scientists would be able to participate in the Indian Ocean expedition, an extension of the IGY; such participation would signal to other universities, as well as to the NSF, that Stanford was committed to a program of oceanography. The obstacles to participating in the Indian Ocean expedition were significant, however. In addition to a lack of interest among the marine biologists, the university did not have an oceanographic vessel, thus making it difficult to apply for funding from the NSF for participation in the IGY expedition. And Blinks had begun again to voice reservations about involvement in a large-scale, government-funded research program. He was "worried," he admitted to Terman, "that most of us would cease being scientists and become only logistical background for the Indian Ocean and later expeditions." Involvement in a "big science" program, he feared, would make impossible the continuation of the marine station's "little science" approach.[46]

Countering the biologists' lack of enthusiasm was Wilson, who continued to encourage Stanford to acquire a vessel and apply for NSF support, at one point offering that, although technically the university could not include overhead in its estimated contract costs (because the vessel would be operated off-campus), it was the NSF's "preference" that Stanford "charge the normal overhead rate" and use the overhead "to strengthen the academic operation at the Hopkins Marine Station." In addition to promising, in effect, to provide special funds to bolster Stanford's work in oceanography, Wilson also advised Terman in his dealings with the university's reluctant marine biologists, suggesting initially that Blinks and the others at the station "will need some help and some pushing." When Blinks's intransigence became clear, Wilson and Terman agreed that while Blinks would remain nominal head of the marine station, they would find a more pliable biologist to direct the oceanographic program.

When informed by Terman that he need not concern himself with the oceanographic program, Blinks was grateful. Disinclined by personality to do battle with the administration and no doubt realizing as well that, despite his views, the fate of the marine station was largely out of his control, Blinks opted for preserving his own freedom from entanglements with federal patrons and disruptions to his research by bowing out of the project.[47] Rolph Bolin, the assistant director of the marine station, replaced Blinks in the negotiations with the NSF. While Stanford succeeded in acquiring a vessel in time to participate in the Indian Ocean expedition, difficulty in hiring an eminent oceanographer to direct the program and the NSF's view that more promising programs were developing elsewhere limited the success of Terman's steeple-building in this instance.

Blinks's opposition to Terman's steeple-building had been rooted in his objection to becoming involved in a program of "big science" that would, by its very nature, overwhelm the marine station and prevent the biologists from pursuing their traditional interests. The substantial resistance of the members of the regular biology department to developing a steeple of excellence in biochemistry and biomedicine was rooted in the department's explicit commitment to the concept of balance. Department chair Victor Twitty had cooperated with Terman in negotiating governmental support for the marine station, but he had done so believing that adding oceanography to the department's offerings would not upset his commitment to "maintain[ing] a balanced representation" of biological fields as well as to according equal importance to teaching and to research.[48]

Twitty had indicated his commitment to a strong teaching as well as a strong research program in his objections to the administration's involvement in setting departmental salaries, an involvement that, as Twitty recognized, enabled the administration to reward those professors with successful, externally supported research programs and effectively to penalize those whose main effort was devoted to undergraduate teaching. "When the salary of an assistant professor during his second year . . . exceeds that of associate professors several years his senior and with a dozen years of service on the faculty, our salary structure becomes pretty difficult to defend on any grounds," he protested to the dean of humanities and sciences.[49]

Twitty further demonstrated his belief in the importance of a balanced department by defending the request of George Myers, director of the department's natural history museum, for permission to fill a slot opened by the death of the museum's zoological curator. Terman had judged the museum, which embodied the department's traditional interest in descriptive and naturalist biology, to be of little value to the university and hoped that it might eventually be disbanded. The provost had thus ignored Myers's request until Myers sent a "letter of protest" threatening to close the museum if he were not given the necessary administrative support. In Twitty's view, Myers's request was legitimate. While admitting that Myers could be temperamental, he reminded Terman that he was also one of the country's, and perhaps the world's, most renowned ichthyologists, a scientist with "monumental knowledge" who continued to attract large numbers of graduate students (eighteen in 1955) and who had obtained a research grant from the NSF.[50]

To Terman, Myers's work was out of date and unlikely ever to attract significant external support. (The provost's evaluation was reflected in departmental salaries: in the 1958–59 academic year, Myers received $9,500, Twitty $14,500, and Clifford Grobstein, a prominent molecular biologist who had just joined the faculty, $12,000.) Terman's judgment was clearly not a universal one, however. Myers's work, for example, was not outdated in the views of those students who flocked to Stanford to work with him or in the opinion of Donald McKernan of the Interior Department's Fish and Wildlife Bureau. In 1962 McKernan informed Terman that his bureau was interested in expanding research in the systematics of marine life and because of Myers's preeminence in this field, was eager to work closely with Stanford.[51] But to Terman and President Sterling, it was biochemistry and biomedicine, not naturalist biology, that promised to be "exciting and significant"; it was thus "important that Stanford have a leading position in them."[52]

What made these fields seem exciting and significant to Stanford's administrators was, in large measure, the fact that important patrons found them to be exciting and significant. The biochemistry department, which was part of the medical school and had been created in the late 1950s when a group of talented biochemists was lured from Washington University to Stanford, was clearly demonstrating the advantages of developing a steeple in this field. By the early 1960s the department had $400,000 in external support (primarily from the National Institutes of Health), an amount more than four times what the department was receiving from the university's general funds. By the early 1960s, the private foundations were also expressing an interest in supporting work in the field. In late 1962 Paul Pearson of the Ford Foundation visited Stanford and implied that the foundation would provide support for Stanford's biology department if the university encouraged collaboration between the biologists and the medical school, produced more Ph.D.s, and eliminated its work in descriptive biology and systematics. The involvement of the biology department was essential, in the view of the foundation, since it was the university department that provided instruction to undergraduates and graduate students and thus transferred to the next generation the skills and knowledge valued by patrons. Pearson's concerns complemented those of Stanford's administration, which had transferred the university's medical school from San Francisco to Stanford in 1959 to promote interaction with the university's academic departments partly in the expectation that external support enjoyed by the medical school could contribute to the support of the biology department's academic program.[53]

As chair, Twitty had ensured that the reductionist approach was represented in the biology department. Yet his often expressed belief in balance made clear that he explicitly rejected the administration's steeple-building plans. It is likely that Terman was glad to see Twitty retire in 1962. He was replaced by Grobstein, who was supportive of the administration's plans to move the department away from the fields of morphology, descriptive ecology, and systematics. But Grobstein soon left Stanford for a position at the fledgling branch of the University of California at San Diego; Donald Kennedy, a gifted teacher with a reputation for reasonableness and the ability to work well with people of different viewpoints, became acting chair and initiated a search for a permanent replacement.[54]

Aware of the administration's preference, Kennedy and the members of his search committee unanimously selected Howard Bern, an outstanding neuroendocrinologist from Berkeley. Bern was also regarded as an excellent teacher of both graduate and undergraduate students. Moreover, Bern had expressed an "enthusiastic commitment to the ideal of a broad department," noted Kennedy, one in which all fields of biology were valued equally.[55] The selection of Bern was thus ideal from the department's perspective: he shared the commitment to balance that had persisted despite Twitty's departure while, at the same time, seemed sure to appeal to administrators eager to emphasize biomedicine.

Terman, however, was "flabbergasted" and infuriated by the selection, which he would later recall as "illustrative of the problems that I had at Stanford in attempting to upgrade . . . our academic operations." Not only had the department chosen a chairperson and made an unofficial offer without consulting the provost, an action acceptable in earlier times but rarely braved during Sterling's and Terman's tenures. The department had also made a poor choice, in Terman's opinion, because Bern was not "a builder." His very commitment to a balanced department was evidence to Terman that Bern could not make Stanford's biology department into a great department, as this valuation depended on the department's becoming focused exclusively on the biomedical and biochemical fields. Terman's concerns were soon echoed by two Stanford biologists whom the administration valued highly: Joshua Lederberg, a geneticist with appointments in the medical school and biology department who had received the Nobel Prize in 1958, and Arthur Kornberg, a biochemist in the medical school who had been awarded the Nobel Prize in 1959. "Lederberg really chewed me out," Robert Sears, the dean of humanities and sciences, reported to Terman. "We'll probably have some bitching" to deal with, he predicted, unless the administration acted to prevent Bern's appointment.[56]

Although the selection of Bern had become known to biologists outside the Stanford community, Stanford's administrators refused to accept the choice as a fait accompli of the department. Instead, President Sterling announced the appointment of an ad hoc committee to study the biology department and make recommendations as to its future. Included on the committee were Kornberg, Lederberg, Stanford chemist Carl Djerassi, and a handful of biologists from the department, including Kennedy. To head the committee, Sterling selected a biologist from outside the university: William McElroy, a biochemist from Johns Hopkins, where administrators had already committed themselves to an exclusive focus on cellular and molecular biology and microbiology. Given its composition, the committee not surprisingly endorsed Terman's vision of the department's future, encouraging the elimination of the department's work in systematics and naturalist biology and suggesting Paul Berg, a biochemist in Stanford's medical school, for department chair. Reflecting on the work of the committee, Terman noted with satisfaction that the department had had its "collective wrist slapped" for trying to circumvent both his authority and the concept of steeple-building.[57]

Stanford's biologists, however, believed that they had received more than a wrist slapping. "I have never before witnessed such high feeling and unanimity among the regular members of the Department in opposition to an administrative action," Myers wrote to President Sterling, complaining that the administration "has ridden roughshod" over the department. It was not so much the administration's interference in the department's search that upset the biologists. The biologists knew that such interference had become commonplace, and they had simply tried to avert it. Rather, it was Terman's insistence that the department's interest in balance was evidence of the department's weakness and his determination that the department must develop steeples that upset a number of Stanford's biologists. However, only Myers vented his anger directly to the administration. His affiliation with Stanford had begun as a student in 1926; thus, he had observed the way the university had changed since the prewar period. His seniority, moreover, gave him license to speak, he believed, whereas others in the department, including nontenured faculty, felt they could not take such a "risk."[58]

Myers did not dispute the importance of biochemistry and biomedicine, but he did insist that they were not more valuable than other fields of biology: "That biomedical and biochemical fields—like so many now-eclipsed biological specialties of the past—have shown a meteoric rise in honors and public acclaim, has tended to dazzle and warp the judgment not only of the biologists engaged in them but also of administrators seeking prestige for their institutions." The fact that external support was available in abundance for medically oriented biology and not for other fields, Myers contended, was "still further warping" the judgment of administrators, whom he judged to be more interested in "garnering kudos" for Stanford than in "advancing biology broadly."

The danger of focusing on fields that attracted money and prestige was that other fields, which attracted neither, were being neglected. But some of these fields—such as taxonomy and ecology—were, however unglamorous, essential to addressing some of the "most insidious and imminent" problems facing humankind. "The destruction and poisoning of man's complex biological and physical environment by man himself" was one such problem, along with overpopulation and the shortage of natural resources. In Myers's view, scientists "who operate in muddy boots instead of lab coats" were the ones who understood the natural world and its interdependencies; they and not biochemists were the ones best prepared to address these problems.[59]

Stanford's administrators decided to ignore Myers's letter. Terman, who had difficulty appreciating viewpoints other than his own, reassured Sterling that Myers was someone who "easily gets all worked up about an issue and is therefore at times a difficult personality"; he dismissed him as "a hard working but not particularly bright biologist in the Jordan tradition who specializes in fish." Because Myers was the only biologist who felt free to speak up, Terman, both by inclination and as a strategy, could easily pass such a judgment. Objections to steeple-building, in Terman's opinion, could only be raised by a marginal biologist of limited ability, and thus he felt under no obligation to engage in open discussion with the department as a whole about its future.[60]

Terman's goals for the biology department were not entirely realized. Berg made his acceptance of the offer conditional upon the creation of nine new positions in the department, permission to make a total of thirteen appointments, construction of new laboratory at the cost of over $1 million, and the commitment of several thousands of dollars for use at his discretion. Whether Terman, who on becoming provost had begun setting aside a percentage of overhead monies in a "fighting fund" to be drawn on to meet the demands of "star" appointments, would have met Berg's demands is unclear, but even by Terman's standards, Berg's request was extravagant. The issue became moot when Berg withdrew his name from consideration.[61] Kennedy, who had proved skillful in dealing with the various personalities involved, was named chair. He acceded to pressure to close the natural history museum, eliminated the field of systematics, and strengthened the department's work in the biomedical and biochemical fields. He did, however, manage to prevent a complete emphasis on reductionist biology and to develop the department's strength in population biology, his own field and one for which external support was available, particularly from the private foundations. This represented the limited extent to which steeple-building could be resisted; retaining representation in fields other than those of specific interest to the administration had to be justified in the administration's own terms—national importance and access to external support from prestigious patrons.

The objections to steeple-building and the preferences for balance expressed by members of the biology department were, in the early 1960s, being voiced as well by Stanford's dean of humanities and sciences. Rhinelander was not opposed to creating new programs or departments in expectation of generous patronage, nor was he opposed to institutionalizing a dependency on federal support through salary-splitting. But he was concerned that Terman was imposing his concept of imbalance on the university as a whole, devoting an excessive amount of the university's scarce resources to the sciences and engineering and purposefully neglecting the humanities. In the opinion of Rhinelander, who before coming to Stanford had been a professor of classical philosophy at Harvard, "[N]o university has ever achieved greatness without distinction in the humanities disciplines."[62]

Rhinelander was not alone in thinking that the humanities were underappreciated at Stanford. On their own initiative, a group of faculty members including economist Kenneth Arrow, physicists Felix Bloch and Leonard Schiff, creative writing professor Wallace Stegner, and representatives from the philosophy and history departments had begun meeting in the late 1950s to discuss the state of the humanities and sciences at Stanford. This group, along with Dean Rhinelander, urged President Sterling to devote more university funds to the school as a whole as well as to the departments of humanities.[63]

President Sterling, an historian by training, was sympathetic to their concerns, and between 1956 and 1959 the allocation for the School of Humanities and Sciences rose from $431 per student to $567 per student, a 31 percent increase. While Rhinelander appreciated the change, he regarded it as only a gesture toward improving his school, the humanities in particular. In these same years, the allocation for the engineering school had grown from $686 per student to $919 per student, a 34 percent increase. In relation to the engineering school, the School of Humanities and Sciences had actually lost ground. While the budget for the 1960–61 school year provided a 15 percent increase in expenditures per student in the humanities and sciences and an increase of only 9 percent to the engineering school, the humanities and sciences remained impoverished in comparison to engineering. The difference in each school's expenditure per pupil was larger than ever, having grown to $372 in 1961 from only $255 in 1956.[64]

Rhinelander's detailed study and criticism of the university's budget and his advocacy of decentralizing the university's budgeting process disturbed Terman. In requesting more funds for the School of Humanities and Sciences, the dean was challenging the provost's desire to make "each tub stand on its own bottom." Moreover, in suggesting that support for the humanities and sciences should increase relative to support for engineering, Rhinelander made clear that he did not share the provost's judgment that some divisions of the university were more valuable, and thus deserving of more support, than others.[65] Terman and Rhinelander had also begun to disagree over the allocation of funds within the School of Humanities and Sciences. Terman wanted departments to be ranked in terms of their national importance and budget allocations to be made on this basis; Rhinelander, while willing to expand departments deemed significant to national interests, was unwilling to penalize other departments in the process.

Their disagreement peaked in 1961 when Terman asked Rhinelander to list his priorities for new appointments to the School of Humanities and Sciences. Terman himself was eager to add two professors to the Department of Asian Languages, which had been created in 1958 and quickly attracted NDEA funds from the Office of Education. Stanford had an "opportunity to achieve national leadership in the East Asian field," which the provost predicted would become a field of "central importance" to the nation as the decade wore on. It was also a field likely to attract further governmental and foundation support.[66] But Rhinelander, in response to the provost's request that he establish priorities, had ranked the appointment of two professors in East Asian studies as seventh in importance, behind allowing the English, journalism, and anthropology departments to hire replacements for retiring professors. As dean, he could not take funds away from these departments simply because Terman saw opportunities in another field, Rhinelander explained. Pressed by the provost to admit that some fields were more important than others, the dean refused. As Terman noted to himself, Rhinelander insisted that it was not possible to say, for example, that a "man in ant[hropology] more or less important than man in history." Rhinelander also rejected Terman's suggestion that he eliminate the geography department in order to finance appointments to the Department of Asian Languages. The dean was willing to make the appointments desired by the provost but only if he need not do so at the expense of other departments.[67]

This dispute, one of many between the two men, convinced Terman not just that Rhinelander's vision of the university differed from his own but that Rhinelander was unwilling to sacrifice his own vision to Terman's, perhaps because he knew that his vision had the support of a number of senior faculty members. Thus, in a private meeting with the president in the summer of 1961, Terman reported that Rhinelander was not "well in that emotionally he cannot stand administrative stress" and predicted that he was "likely to have break down." As evidence for his estimation of Rhinelander's psychological state, Terman explained that the dean was "afraid to make difficult decisions," "unwilling to list priorities," and "difficult to communicate with." Terman also accused Rhinelander of believing that "his own ego more important than inst[itution]" and of working "to align faculty against adm[inistration] to cover up own shortcomings." Whether Sterling accepted Terman's psychological profile of Rhinelander is unclear. Shortly afterward, however, Rhinelander submitted his resignation and Terman was thus saved, in his words, from a "major hassle" over budget allocations for the coming year.[68]

Learning of Rhinelander's resignation, Leonard Schiff, chair of the physics department, drafted a long memo to President Sterling. Schiff did not ask that Rhinelander be reinstated but instead declared his agreement with the dean that "Humanities and Sciences is the core of the university" and as such needed to be accorded adequate funds and facilities, as well as autonomy from the provost. President Sterling, of course, had no intention of granting autonomy either to the school or to individual departments. The centralization of authority, which had begun during Tresidder's presidency and had culminated in the granting of extraordinary authority to the provost, was seen as necessary to bring both national attention and extensive external support to the university.[69]

That the School of Humanities and Sciences and the departments within it would not be granted autonomy from the provost soon became clear to Schiff as his own department became engaged in a bitter struggle with Terman over salary-splitting. The physics department—which enjoyed national prestige (it was ranked sixth in the nation in a 1957 survey and had two Nobel laureates on its staff), received considerable governmental support, and produced doctoral students in sufficient numbers to please the provost—was one of the few departments outside the engineering school that had been largely immune from Terman's criticism and from interference in departmental matters. But when the department decided to pursue funding from the AEC for the construction and operation of a two-mile linear accelerator, Stanford's administration viewed it as an opportunity to expand the physics department and its production of doctoral students and to attract national, even international, attention to Stanford. The resulting strife among the physicists and between the physicists and Stanford's administration was perhaps the bitterest of the conflicts that arose as the administration set out purposefully to create imbalanced departments and to make Stanford's academic program dependent upon external support.

The Stanford Linear Accelerator

The idea for the accelerator had originated not with Terman but with a group of Stanford physicists. Interested in supporting the "peaceful atom" and not just the production of nuclear weapons, the AEC had indicated that it would be funding, at the rate of one machine per year, the construction of particle accelerators capable of reaching multibillion-electron-volt energies. Stanford's high-energy physicists, Robert Hofstadter and Wolfgang Panofsky, were eager to seize this opportunity to obtain a new machine that would allow them to explore higher energy ranges than did the physics department's one-million-volt electronic accelerator, the Mark III, which had been designed by Stanford physicists and built and operated with support from the ONR.[70]

While Schiff supported the physicists, the senior member of the department, Felix Bloch, raised a number of objections. As the director in late 1954 of the European Center for Nuclear Research (CERN), an internationally organized laboratory for high-energy physics, Bloch had become convinced that it was not possible to "do physics on a large scale yet in 'University style.'" Should the physics department receive funding for the proposed facility, Bloch warned Hofstadter, it would be overrun with "administrators, personnel managers, foremen, auditors, navy contact men, prolonged sojourns in Washington . . . in short, a fantastic burocratic [sic] and political rigamarole" that would unavoidably disrupt their research. Bloch, who had been unhappy with the navy's effort to impose security restrictions on the department's microwave lab in the late 1940s, also warned Hofstadter that it would be impossible to prevent a government-sponsored laboratory of the size proposed from becoming "security-hunted." Finally, the very magnitude of the project would necessarily imbalance the department. Acquiring such an expensive facility would essentially force the physicists into making "nothing short of an ironclad commitment to use [the accelerator]—or better be used by it."[71]

Bloch's concerns, as Panofsky and Hofstadter knew, were not without foundation. Before coming to Stanford, Panofsky had worked at the University of California's Berkeley Radiation and Livermore Laboratories. He had disliked the Radiation Laboratory's security measures, among them the requirement that anyone seeking entry to the lab present an identification badge. These and other governmental regulations, he thought, created an undesirable atmosphere for the conduct of academic physics. But unlike Bloch, Panofsky and the other physicists believed that they could develop a satisfactory relationship with the AEC.[72] The "problems having to do with bigness" could also be dealt with; bureaucratic matters, Hofstadter suggested, could be left to administrators, and the physicists would deal only with physics.[73]

Bloch made no further attempt to dissuade the physicists and they proceeded to seek the approval of Stanford's administrators. Although the Mark III had only recently been completed, a new machine was needed if Stanford's physicists hoped to keep up with the competition from "aggressive physicists" at MIT, Harvard, and Brookhaven, who were already planning to build multi-BeV accelerators. If Stanford did not "throw our hat into the ring now" and obtain funds for a large machine, Hofstadter wrote to Bloch, the physicists would soon lose their position on the "front-line" of developments in the field of high-energy physics.[74]

The argument no doubt appealed strongly to the administration, which supported the physicists' application for AEC support. But the physicists soon discovered that, as Bloch had warned, the very magnitude of the proposed facility meant that it could not, as they had seemed to expect, be treated as had the Mark III, as simply "another research tool" that would not significantly disrupt the department's traditional structure or the style of research to which the high-energy physicists were accustomed.[75] While the AEC, which was eager to deemphasize government-run laboratories and to support private initiatives, looked with favor upon the Stanford proposal, the Joint Committee on Atomic Energy (JCAE)—the congressional committee charged with overseeing the AEC—questioned whether public funds of such magnitude could justifiably be allocated to a private university. By 1957 the AEC commissioners and their advisors agreed that the accelerator might indeed be built at Stanford, but on the condition that the facility be designated a national laboratory, open to physicists from around the country and governed by a committee chosen from among the nation's physicists.[76]

To Hofstadter, the AEC's suggestion was unacceptable. Like Bloch a few years earlier, Hofstadter was writing from CERN, where he, too, had become disillusioned with big science. The atmosphere at CERN was "more like that of an industrial laboratory" than an academic one, Hofstadter wrote to Schiff. Scientists' access to the machine (or beam time) was limited, encouraging them to work in large teams and thus, in Hofstadter's opinion, robbing them of "the joyous feeling of individual accomplishment." Moreover, the scientists had to justify their requests to use the machine to a committee; to Hofstadter, this was an unacceptable restriction of the freedom he associated with academic physics: the freedom to do whatever research he wanted, whenever he wanted.[77]

The Mark III, the machine with which Hofstadter had made the discoveries that had brought him the Nobel Prize, was a government-funded machine, yet it was completely controlled by Stanford's physicists. Administrative staff was negligible, and Hofstadter and Panofsky each had been guaranteed 40 percent of the machine's beam time, ensuring little competition for access. Hofstadter had assumed that the large accelerator, although expected to be about one hundred times more costly, would be operated in the same way. Realizing now that this was not likely, Hofstadter decided to have nothing to do with "the gadget (M)," as the physicists called it. To do physics in a laboratory not controlled by the physicists themselves would not be "fun . . . but a means of developing ulcers."[78] Hofstadter, like Lawrence Blinks, had decided that the costs of big science exceeded the benefits. But while Blinks could disengage himself from the administration's plans to develop a program in oceanography, Hofstadter faced a dilemma. As a high-energy physicist, his research depended on his access to particle accelerators. Rejecting the available facilities meant, effectively, leaving the field that he had been trained in. But Hofstadter's objection to "the gadget (M)" was so serious that he was willing to consider that option; he confided to Bloch in early 1959 that he was searching for "some other branch of physics that will take me away from big machine physics."[79]

Panofsky, however, was not deterred by the AEC's decision that the accelerator would be a national facility. By the late 1950s he was more concerned that the AEC would provide no support for the linear accelerator, whether a national facility or not. The AEC had become more selective about funding new accelerators and more attentive to their regional distribution. California's Bay Area was already the site of several high-energy machines, and Stanford was competing for funding with the Midwestern Universities Research Association (MURA), a coalition of universities bidding for an accelerator in an area where there was none.[80] Concerns over how to allocate resources and post-Sputnik worries that the United States might lose its lead over the Soviet Union in the construction of massive particle accelerators, symbols of the nation's scientific strength, prompted Eisenhower's science advisor, James R. Killian, to convene a panel of scientific experts to establish guidelines for the funding of high-energy facilities. The panel, appointed by the President's Science Advisory Committee (of which Panofsky was a member), joined with the AEC's General Advisory Committee in recommending immediate support for the Stanford proposal. In the spring of 1959 President Eisenhower announced his support for the Stanford Linear Accelerator Center (SLAC).[81] The proposed accelerator, a larger version of the Mark III, would pose no unforeseen technical problems that might delay its construction. It would also be based on advanced microwave technology, which had made Stanford's proposal "of particular relevance to the interests of the DOD [Department of Defense]." Finally, Panofsky's familiarity with the nation's leading science advisors had also worked in Stanford's favor.[82]

The way was not yet clear for the project, however. The AEC intended to take full responsibility for the design and construction of the facility to ensure that the $100 million project did not run over budget as had most of the multi-BeV accelerators the agency had funded. Additionally, SLAC would be expected to conform to all AEC security regulations.[83] To Hofstadter, the AEC's decision might have been proof of the error of accepting SLAC's designation as a national facility. But he had already renounced participation in the project, and Panofsky, adept at the politics of science and skilled at negotiating around administrative obstacles, sought a compromise with the AEC. With the aid of President Sterling and the chair of the board of trustees, David Packard, the physicists reached an agreement with the AEC. They would take responsibility for the design and construction of SLAC on a "trial-run basis."[84] And the AEC, "in connection with its applied mission," might "from time to time request the University to include certain additional programs in [SLAC's research] schedule."[85] Having chosen to pursue research at ever higher energy levels requiring more powerful and more expensive machines that only the federal government could afford to fund, Stanford's physicists accepted the constraints involved. Those who had declined to participate in SLAC could at least be certain that the facility, as much as they disliked it, would not interfere with their own work or with their department.

This assumption, it soon turned out, was naive. Panofsky, the designated director of SLAC, began seeking staff for the facility shortly after receiving word that it had been awarded federal support. To attract eminent scientists to SLAC, Panofsky believed that he must offer them positions in the physics department as well. The best scientists, he argued, preferred university appointments and the opportunity to work with graduate students to research appointments in government-administered laboratories. Stanford's administration agreed. The new facility was to be the basis of a steeple in high-energy physics, and the administration wanted to be sure that it was a steeple that attracted international attention and respect. Further, the administration recognized that by giving SLAC's federally funded researchers full academic privileges, the department's faculty would be greatly expanded, as would the production of graduate students, all at no cost to Stanford.[86]

Many in the physics department opposed the suggested joint appointments, including Bloch and Hofstadter, but so did Schiff and others who had supported Panofsky's pursuit of funding for SLAC, believing that, in doing so, they had supported the interests of the high-energy physicists but had not necessarily undermined their own interests. Any formal relationship with SLAC, these physicists feared, would crush their eighteen-member department, overrunning it with dozens of high-energy physicists and making it impossible to maintain a balance between the various fields of physics.

This very commitment to balance had led the department's members to oppose salary-splitting despite constant pressure from the provost and even though the decision had meant that their department had remained small. Thus to accept joint appointments with SLAC was not only to risk upsetting the department's balance; it might also be seen by the provost as an opening to pressure all of the department's members to split their salaries. The department had taken such a risk in 1959 when, short of teachers, the physicists had reluctantly agreed to grant to a research associate in the microwave laboratory a one-year appointment as an acting assistant professor. The onetime use of salary-splitting had bothered the physicists. "I am not the only one who feels rather bad about the 'mixed' appointment," Bloch wrote at the time to Schiff. Like Schiff, he, too, expressed concern "lest it [the appointment] will be considered by the administration as a breach in our wall of principles through which Terman can hope to see his fond dreams of unprincipled opportunism come closer to fulfillment."[87]

The physicists' belief that, in suggesting that SLAC researchers be given appointments in their department, the administration was trying to force them to accept salary-splitting was not unwarranted. At the same time that the dean of graduate studies, Albert Bowker, suggested that the department make two appointments jointly with SLAC, the dean of humanities and sciences, Philip Rhinelander, informed the physicists that he was freezing their department's budget, thus restricting them from hiring new faculty members with university funds.

The physicists rejected the suggested joint appointments, and Dean Bowker decided, on Terman's advice, not to argue with the physicists.[88] Instead, he took the matter to the university's advisory board, a group of seven tenured, full professors who were elected by the Academic Council to advise the president on, among other things, faculty appointments. After explaining to the board the necessity of ensuring that SLAC become a prestigious institution and not a mere "service station" for scientists from other universities, Bowker asked the board to approve the appointment to SLAC of two physicists who would also be accorded tenured faculty positions. These appointments, Bowker regretted, would be research appointments only, although the physicists in question would be permitted to advise graduate students.[89]

Bowker's action relieved Panofsky and Sidney Drell, a young theoretical physicist who had been lured from MIT to Stanford in 1956 and who would later become associate director of SLAC as well as a member of the President's Science Advisory Committee. Others in the physics department, however, were alarmed by the administration's bypassing of their department. On becoming department chair in 1950, Schiff had renewed the practice initiated by Kirkpatrick of opening all matters relevant to the physics department to full discussion by the department's members; the practice had brought Schiff wide respect within his department and throughout the university. Schiff thus initiated a series of discussions among the physicists about the relationship between the department and SLAC. The majority of the physicists agreed that while the relationship might be a close one, it must remain informal. There would be no joint appointments. Teaching privileges were to be reserved for the physics department, although a member of SLAC's staff might, if given special permission by the department, direct a graduate student's doctoral work, but only in conjunction with a full member of the department. The decision, in effect, conceded to SLAC as much as possible without breaching the department's opposition to salary-splitting.[90]

To the supporters of SLAC, however, the department was clearly bent on making SLAC's staff "second-class citizens" of the university. The opposition to joint appointments was, to Drell, tiresome and pointless. While he understood the basis of the opposition, he believed, as he wrote to Panofsky, that "we have to admit at a certain time that we have lost, we are powerless against Terman and we are just hurting ourselves." It was time for the physicists to "accept the facts of Stanford's financial life" and stop "hamstring[ing] ourselves by refusing to split salaries," he argued. Determined that SLAC's researchers should be accorded privileges equal to those enjoyed by the physics department's faculty, Drell and Panofsky appealed to Terman asking that the administration grant SLAC the status of a department, giving it the right to admit and train its own students. "Then let the PD [physics department] worry who are the second class citizens!" Drell fumed.[91]

While Panofsky and Drell's proposal received the full support of Terman and Bowker, the suggestion upset a number of the department's physicists. If the department's budget remained frozen while at the same time the administration created at SLAC a separate physics faculty with authority to grant doctorates, the physics department might slowly be degraded to a service department for undergraduate instruction. Clearly, the administration's proposal to grant SLAC departmental status was intended as a threat, a "club being held over [the department's] autonomy," in Bloch's words, in the expectation that the department would capitulate and allow joint appointments.[92]

Recognizing the futility of trying to reason with the provost, the physicists in late 1962 decided to place their views before the university's advisory board, as the administration had done earlier.[93] But Terman, learning of the physicists' intention, told Bowker to inform the chairperson of the advisory board that he should ignore their request for a hearing. If the board did not heed Bowker's advice, he would ask Stanford's president to ignore the board's opinion and to take the matter directly to the board of trustees. Any involvement of the board of trustees in the matter would clearly lead to a "worsening" of the university's "internal relations," Bowker admitted to Sterling. But "at least SLAC [would be] off to a good start." Bowker's preemptive action was effective, and the physicists received no support from the advisory board.[94]

The administration was clearly fully supporting the interests of Panofsky and Drell. Both, however, had become concerned that their struggles with the other physicists were becoming known outside of Stanford and would damage their effort to recruit scientists to SLAC. Thus, in early 1963 they resigned from the physics department and were given appointments at SLAC. In arranging their transfer, the administration committed itself not to making SLAC a separate, degree-granting institution but to granting SLAC's staff both the status of faculty members and the right to train graduate students. In June 1963 President Sterling met with the members of the physics department and announced his decision. A policy of "parity" was being established, he explained. SLAC would be permitted to make academic appointments equal to the number of tenured faculty members in the physics department. Doctoral students in the physics department would be permitted to work with the faculty at SLAC, but their theses would be signed by a member of the physics department as well.[95]

Sterling's announcement eased worries that the department would be pressured again to make joint appointments and thus be faced with the prospect of becoming overrun with high-energy physicists. But the physicists continued to fear that the glamour and enormous federal support for high-energy physics would result in SLAC's staff attracting a disproportionate number of the department's graduate students. While the department itself might not become imbalanced, the next generation of physicists might if most students chose to work with faculty at SLAC instead of the physics department, which might then find itself acting mainly as a department of undergraduate instruction. Thus, a few months after meeting with Sterling, the physicists agreed to set a limit on the number of graduate students whose theses could be supervised by staff at SLAC: 10 percent of the second-year physics students would be permitted to work with physicists outside the department. The figure was not arbitrary but rather was based on the average number of students yearly who had had advisors outside the physics department since the creation of the microwave laboratory in 1946.[96]

The quota upset Panofsky. As few as six or eight students a year might be permitted to do thesis work outside the department, Panofsky calculated, and an even smaller number might come to SLAC. But SLAC could easily accommodate five times as many students, Panofsky estimated. And, as he pointed out to Stanford's administration, it was in the national interest to expand, not limit, the opportunities for students interested in graduate work in physics. In light of Panofsky's reaction, Schiff diplomatically proposed that the SLAC and physics department staffs meet and discuss their disagreement.

But Panofsky had tired of wrangling with the physics department and was by this time confident that Stanford's administrators shared his views. Terman, always interested in increasing Stanford's production of graduate students, agreed with Panofsky that the quota was "arbitrary and unreasonable" and would unduly limit the advantages to Stanford of the $114 million facility. Panofsky also wrote directly to President Sterling, warning that should the AEC learn of the problems at Stanford—the quota as well as the physics department's unwillingness to allow a member of SLAC's staff to teach a course in the department—it would likely seek to impose more control over SLAC.[97] Panofsky's klaxon had the desired effect. As Sterling's assistant warned him, "[W]e are headed for a major blow-up" if an important member of SLAC should resign over the issue of teaching privileges. The AEC would no doubt order a complete review of SLAC's operations and possibly suggest that SLAC be disassociated from Stanford. Funding for SLAC would be "seriously jeopardized" as a result, and this, in turn, might tarnish Stanford's relationship with its other federal patrons.[98]

Facing the possibility of embarrassment to Stanford and damage to Stanford's relations with the patrons upon which it had become so dependent, President Sterling decided to take the steps necessary to ensure that SLAC's needs were met. And yet, unlike the administration's dealings with other faculty members who had voiced complaints about administrative interference or expressed opposition to salary-splitting, Sterling took care not to "ride roughshod" over the physicists. Some were scientists of considerable eminence; moreover, the conflict had attracted the attention of others at Stanford, and the mathematics faculty, as well as eminent members of the chemistry department, had expressed to Sterling their support of the physics department's position. Sterling thus requested, rather than demanded, that the department's quota be lifted and that the SLAC member in question be permitted to teach a course in the department.[99]

When Leonard Schiff refused, explaining that the conflict had reached the stage at which it had become "psychologically impossible" for the physicists to change their minds, Sterling asked the new dean of graduate studies, English professor Virgil Whitaker, a seemingly neutral party to the conflict, to reassess the conflict between the physics department and SLAC. The physicists agreed to accept Whitaker's recommendations. In an expression of misdirected sympathy with the physics department, Whitaker confessed that "Panofsky can be irritatingly persistent" and suggested to Sterling that the department be promised protection from him. The physicists, however, had not been unhappy with Panofsky but with the administration's decision to grant SLAC faculty all the privileges of physics department faculty while freeing the former of undergraduate teaching responsibilities and imposing a budget freeze on the latter. Whitaker, however, did not take their side in this matter, agreeing with Panofsky that the department's insistence on limiting the number of graduate students trained at SLAC was "intolerable" and that its refusal to permit SLAC faculty to teach in the department demonstrated "bad faith."[100]

The physics department had lost. Sterling, acting on Whitaker's recommendations, ordered them to lift the quota and permit one of SLAC's members to teach in the department.

In contesting salary-splitting, Terman's budgeting preferences, and his goal of making every department and every professor self-supporting, members of the geology, biology, physics, and other departments were seeking to retain some autonomy for themselves and their disciplines as practiced within the university and transmitted to their students. Dissenting faculty members were not insisting that their entire department had to reject external patronage in order to maintain this autonomy. By the 1950s they had taken the weaker position, rooted in a notion of tolerance: departments agreed that professors interested in conducting sponsored research should be permitted to do so unimpeded while at the same time recognizing both the right of professors to choose not to conduct sponsored research and the value of particular areas of work for which external support might not be available. It was the administration, not the faculty, that had adopted an extreme position—stressing that every department, and ideally, every member of the department, depend upon external patronage and thus become significantly shaped by it—and it was this position that some faculty members were rejecting.

As provost, Terman did not succeed in realizing his goal of every professor in every department becoming self-supporting. Nor did all of Terman's steeple-building plans succeed according to his own terms. The biology department's Hopkins Marine Station, for example, did not develop a nationally significant program of oceanographic research. But Terman's inability to achieve his aims in each instance should not be interpreted as evidence of the success of faculty members in resisting his plans. The failure to develop a steeple of excellence in oceanography, for example, bore no relation to the biologists' initial reluctance to participate in Terman's scheme, a reluctance that Terman contrived to maneuver around in any case. Rather, that Terman did not achieve all of his aims should be a reminder of how extremely ambitious these aims were; to use Terman's own measure of success might mistakenly lead us to underrate the tremendous influence he had on Stanford during the early cold war.

It is also important, however, not to overestimate Terman's significance for Stanford and, as did many Stanford faculty members, see him as an independent actor responsible for the changes being wrought at Stanford in the 1950s and early 1960s. Terman's success as provost depended on the steady support of Stanford's president. And the concerns of Sterling and Terman—for institutional prestige and external support—represented, although perhaps in exaggerated form, the concerns of administrators of other institutions of higher education in this period.

Like their administrative counterparts at other universities, Terman and Sterling were completing the reorientation of their university that had begun during World War II. It was in the 1940s that universities were reoriented toward service, with those departments in the university deemed ivory tower-ish forced to justify their existence in instrumental terms or face budget and staff reductions. During the 1950s and 1960s, academic departments, and Stanford as a whole, became financially dependent on those whom they served—primarily military patrons, but also other federal patrons as well as private foundations and some industrial concerns. As money from federal patrons was woven into a department's budgetary structure through mechanisms such as salary-splitting, so also were the intellectual interests of these patrons embedded in a department. In the instances where steeple-building succeeded, these interests existed not alongside other interests but rather to the exclusion of all others.

Not all faculty members were troubled by the administration's goals and the implications for their departments and the shape of their disciplines. For those whose work was highly valued by powerful patrons and deemed nationally significant, the administration was valued not only for negotiating on their behalf with patrons and for extending them institutional resources and privileges but also for throwing the weight of administrative authority to their side in disagreements with departmental colleagues. Thus, while professors like Huggins and Panofsky clearly exercised initiative, they were ultimately dependent on administrators, like Terman, who both made it possible for them to act entrepreneurially and also rewarded them for it. The relationships between Stanford's high-energy physicists and the AEC, between the biologists and the NSF, and between the material science experts and their sponsor cannot be understood fully without also understanding the role played by university administrators.

There were faculty members who did not benefit from the administration's preferences and who actively disliked Terman but who still embraced the administration's viewpoint and priorities. For example, chemist Eric Hutchinson retained a visceral dislike for Terman many years after his retirement from Stanford and was able to recall specific interactions with the provost that had convinced him that Terman was unmannerly, of limited imagination, incapable of enjoying a work of literature or art, and thus unsuited to guiding a great university. Terman, for his part, had decided that Hutchinson lacked "greatness" as a chemist and had pressed upon Hutchinson numerous administrative and teaching duties, including assistance in hiring to Stanford "great" chemists. While Hutchinson recalled with some bitterness the extraordinary salaries offered to some of the department's chemists, among them William Johnson and Carl Djerassi, the inventor of the birth control pill, as well as other privileges extended to them, such as exemption from administrative tasks and from normal teaching responsibilities, Hutchinson also invalidated his own complaints by agreeing that these men were of Nobel Prize caliber whereas he, one of the world's experts in soaps and detergents, was not. Hutchinson's field was not, as Terman would have put it, of national significance; this both diminished considerably Terman's interest in Hutchinson and led Terman to evaluate negatively Hutchinson's talents as a chemist. In contrast to biologist George Myers, Hutchinson internalized this evaluation, and he chose, despite his dislike for Terman, to play an important role, as acting chair of the chemistry department, in rebuilding the department to reflect Terman's values and concerns.[101]

This example points to another accomplishment of Terman and other administrators like him. The provost succeeded in linking the administration's preferences (which, as Terman's conversations with John Wilson of the NSF suggest, were themselves related to, if not created by, the preferences of powerful patrons) with valuative terms such as "excellence" and "important." In this way, Terman also successfully devalued those fields and those scholars whose work was not of national importance and was of little interest to patrons. In Terman's scheme of things, for example, George Myers was a hack, a marginally talented biologist, and Philip Rhinelander was an hysterical philosophy professor whose mind was unsuited to budgetary analysis. These judgments were likely shared by some others—by biologists working in the fields of biochemistry and biomedicine, in the case of Myers, for example. But Terman's judgment was not a universal one. Again, in Myers's case, the fish and wildlife bureau was impressed by him, as were students and a significant number of his colleagues.

But administrators such as Terman succeeded in using their authority and power to render their judgments as if they were universal ones. And most members of the university, but by no means all of them, accepted these judgments, in some cases because they shared them or benefited from them, but often even if they reflected badly on themselves. To reject such judgments required strength of conviction in one's own abilities but also a sense of independence from administrative authority and from the authority that the administration's judgments derived from—those of patrons and more broadly, the nation's opinion makers. Myers, a senior member of the department close to retirement, possessed both these qualities. So did Felix Bloch, whose sense of his own rightness was traceable not to a marginal position, as in Myers's case, but to his elevated position, as Stanford's first Nobel laureate. Most did not possess these traits, however, and Hutchinson's response—absorbing rather than challenging the administration's message—was certainly more typical.

Terman's definitions of excellence and significance corresponded with those of military and other powerful federal patrons. This was as it should be, according to Clark Kerr, for in the cold war university excellence correlated with successfully meeting the needs of those outside the university. To be sure, this resulted in the privileging of certain scholars and certain fields of study: naturalist biology had to give way to biomedicine; classical studies to technical and scientific ones. While many professors preferred to embrace the new without sacrificing the old and to define, with their colleagues, the intellectual contours of their departments, in the cold war university the concept of balance, along with that of departmental autonomy, had been rendered obsolete.

7

Private Foundations and
the "Behavioral Revolution"

In the fifteen years following World War II, as the physical sciences and engineering at leading universities were shaping and becoming shaped by the military-industrial complex, the social sciences were also undergoing change. New programs, fields, and departments—among them international relations, Soviet studies, East Asian studies, cultural anthropology, communications, and statistics—were institutionalized in leading universities after the war, and a new emphasis was placed on interdisciplinary and team research. The intellectual landscape of extant social science disciplines was also resculpted. Scientism—a stance of political and value neutrality and an emphasis on description, explanation, and verification—became dominant after the war, accompanied by the privileging of particular methodologies—survey research and quantification—and of inquiries focusing on individual behavior as the fundamental unit upon which knowledge of society and politics should be based. At the same time, ethical and philosophical inquiry was relegated to the margins of the social science disciplines, as were normative approaches to the study of society and explorations focused on categories of class, race, and the social impact of technological change. The tacit goals of social science in the early cold war were prediction, not prescription; social adjustment, not social change.[1]

This shift in emphasis and aims, often referred to as the "behavioral revolution," has attracted less systematic study than have the changes occurring during and after World War II in the engineering and physical sciences. Those who have explored the history of the social sciences have tended to treat it as distinctly different from that of the natural sciences. For example, in seeking to understand changes in the social science disciplines after the war, patronage, which is generally considered significant in understanding change in the physical sciences, has assumed less importance than have the motives of the social scientists themselves as they were shaped either by the postwar climate of political conformity and repression or by the acclaim and even adulation enjoyed by America's physicists—creators of the atomic bomb—after the war.

The most commonly asserted (but undocumented) explanation for the popularity of the scientistic approach after World War II points to the status anxiety of social scientists. In debates after the war over the formation of the NSF, the consensus was that the social sciences were insufficiently scientific to be included in the proposed funding program. This was a blow to the social scientists' self-esteem, as this story is told. The enormous prestige, influence, and patronage enjoyed by their colleagues in the physical sciences after the war was another unhappy reminder of the relative lack of status of the social scientists' own disciplines. The turn toward scientism thus represented a widespread and genuine desire among American social scientists to improve the reputation of their disciplines.[2] Others, more critical of the turn toward scientism, have speculated that the ascendancy of behavioralism after the war is best explained not by social scientists' desire for status but by their fears that a normative or prescriptive approach to the study of society might invite criticism in conformist times or, worse, attacks from the McCarthyist forces at work in the 1950s. Ellen Schrecker, in her carefully documented study of the political purges of America's universities in the 1940s and 1950s, suggests that the dominance in the 1950s of behavioralism and consensus history might represent the "intellectual fallout" of McCarthyism.[3]

These explanations are not mutually exclusive; given the cultural and political climate of the early cold war, both are plausible explanations of individual behavior and deserve exploration. But while particular individuals may be shown to have been motivated either by fear or by desire for status, it is less clear that the discovered motives of one or more individuals can reasonably be ascribed to a collectivity of individuals, such as an entire discipline.[4] Moreover, there is no reason to believe that vast numbers of social scientists converted to behavioralism after World War II, as these explanations imply. Rather, the dominance of behavioralism might more plausibly suggest that the behavioral approach, which had coexisted before World War II with a number of other approaches to the study of society and politics (but was dominant at a few institutions such as the University of Chicago), was privileged after the war. The privileging of one disciplinary trend over another did not mean that a great majority within the discipline decisively chose to employ one method instead of another. Rather, it meant that institutions and patrons began to prefer that trend and to give those social scientists identified with that trend prominence and preference in granting patronage and seeking advice (in the case of patrons) and in hiring and granting (or not granting) tenure (in the case of university administrators). Thus, in seeking to understand the turn toward scientism, not just within the work of particular social scientists but also within entire scholarly disciplines, those same factors important to understanding change in the natural sciences and engineering—institutional context and patronage relationships—need to be taken into account.

Postwar patronage of the hard sciences was provided chiefly by the military; some historians of science have thus begun looking for a similar patronage relationship between social scientists and the cold war state. Allan Needell, for example, has brought to light the involvement of prominent social scientists in advising the State Department at the beginning of the Korean War on how successfully to wage political and psychological warfare.[5] But in looking for similarities in the histories of the social and natural sciences, there is no reason to assume that the history of the social sciences simply recapitulates the history of the natural sciences. For example, one historian of science, surveying the postwar history of the social sciences and the rise of behavioralism, has written that, as the cold war heated up at the end of the 1940s, "the purposes of the government . . . impinged on the work of many social scientists, especially because the government had taken over from the private foundations the funding of research."[6] This, of course, sounds very much like the history of the physical sciences, which before the war, and particularly before the Great Depression, enjoyed significant support from the major private foundations but after World War II, and especially by 1950, were relying almost exclusively on the federal government, primarily the military, for research support. This is not an accurate description of the postwar history of the patronage of the social sciences, however.

In the first fifteen years after World War II, private foundations provided substantial support for social science research, particularly research of a behavioral and scientistic bent. The end of the 1940s marks not the end of foundation support for the social sciences but rather the beginning of the Ford Foundation's massive program of patronage of the social sciences and, specifically, of the behavioral sciences. Although the exact amount of money expended in support of the academic social sciences by the federal government and by the major private foundations—Carnegie, Rockefeller, Ford—is unclear, estimates suggest that support from the private foundations at least matched and may have exceeded the support available from the federal government in the early cold war. Moreover, at many universities, foundations were the dominant source of support for the social sciences. In the first twelve years after World War II, the Ford Foundation alone provided Harvard University with almost $14 million, the University of Chicago with almost $10 million, and Stanford University with over $3 million, an amount many times larger than what Stanford was receiving from its few federal contracts for social science research.[7]

Clearly, the development of the social sciences during the early cold war cannot be understood fully without considering the role of patronage and, specifically, of foundation support. The following discussion focuses on one foundation—the Ford Foundation—and the ascendancy at Stanford of the "behavioral persuasion" after World War II. This chapter explores the forces shaping the Ford Foundation's interest in promoting the behavioral sciences and the relationships among the Ford Foundation, Stanford's administrators, and Stanford's social scientists, paying special attention to Stanford's political science department. Like their colleagues in other departments at Stanford, the university's political scientists were committed to the concept of balance; their department, they believed, should represent a variety of methodologies and areas of study. They clashed with university administrators committed to developing a steeple of excellence in behavioral science, a commitment shaped by the desire for external support and national prestige.

The Ford Foundation and the National Security State

In 1936 Henry Ford took advantage of a loophole in the New Deal Revenue Act, which raised taxes on inherited wealth but exempted bequests to charitable foundations: he created the Ford Foundation and willed it over 90 percent of his family's stock holdings in the Ford Motor Company. By the late 1940s both Ford and his son, Edsel, had died, leaving the foundation considerably enriched. Henry

Ford II, chair of the board of trustees, determined that the foundation should shed its parochial interests and join the other major private foundations—the Carnegie Corporation and the Rockefeller Foundation—in seeking solutions to important social, economic, and political problems facing the postwar world. Part of this search for solutions involved providing generous support for research in the social sciences.[8]

The basis of the major foundations' interest in supporting the academic social sciences has been a subject of debate. The generally accepted view during the early cold war (and a view still dominant in scholarly studies) held that foundation support represented strategic benevolence. With the federal government supporting the physical and medical sciences at levels that the private foundations could not match, foundation officials realized that if they were to make a recognized contribution to academic research, they would need to support fields for which patronage was not at that time available. The social sciences were the obvious choice, both because they lacked external support but also because, as human-centered disciplines, they needed support to ensure that technical knowledge did not outstrip knowledge of people and society. Moreover, in supporting the social sciences, the foundations were seeking to do good. In his well-known 1956 profile of the Ford Foundation, Dwight Macdonald portrayed the foundation as essentially what its officers said it was—a disinterested benefactor—and not a front for corporate capitalists, as Macdonald feared some European intellectuals might assume. Those who saw the foundations as basically benevolent have also assumed a correspondence of interests between the foundations and academic social scientists. Thus, the foundations did not impose an agenda on the social scientists; they provided funds in response to the social scientists' own needs and interests. The foundations, in other words, appear to have been ideal patrons.[9]

This depiction of foundation patronage implied a contrast with federal patronage and an attachment to the distinction between "private" and "public" patronage. According to this dichotomy, state support, derived from taxpayers' dollars and thus subject to political considerations, was restrictive and potentially coercive. Foundations, by contrast, provided an independent source of funds, unrestricted and untainted by politics. Foundation support was not only preferable to federal support; it was a necessary alternative to it.

It was an attachment to this dichotomy that led Vannevar Bush and other leaders of the scientific community to oppose the inclusion of the social sciences in his proposal for the NSF after World War II. In describing the social sciences as insufficiently scientific, Bush was primarily concerned that, unlike the hard sciences, the social sciences were not reliably objective or value-free (and, particularly, free of liberal biases). Thus, it would not be possible to guarantee that governmental funds, which emanated from a political body, would not influence the content and outcome of the sponsored social scientific research.[10] Bush did see value in the social sciences and recognized their potential usefulness, however. In omitting the social sciences from the proposed NSF, Bush, a trustee of the Carnegie Corporation, no doubt realized that the social sciences would not go unfunded, but would receive support from a source—private foundations—of which he and others of his outlook approved. To Bush, an elitist and, like his friend Herbert Hoover, strongly inclined to accept his own perceptions as true, the private foundations may well have appeared free of political motivations not only because they were not controlled by the federal government but also because he assumed that the interests represented by the foundations were similar to his own.

If some, like Bush, were predisposed to see the foundations as apolitical, the McCarthyite attacks on the big three foundations by some congressmen in the early 1950s reinforced this view and created sympathy with some, like Macdonald, who in another time might have been more critical. To Macdonald and, no doubt, to the foundation officials themselves, the Ford Foundation, if not above politics, was at least enlightened, being allied with intellectual effort and internationalism, in contrast to the anti-intellectual, provincial McCarthyites and the public that supported them.[11]

But the major foundations, while certainly not hotbeds of communistic activity, were hardly free of political interests. The Ford Foundation's funding program, laid out in the foundation's 1949 study report, was based in part on concerns that rapid change brought on by industrialization and war might produce "dislocations and breakdowns" in societies around the world and might lead to the questioning of "basic political and moral principles." Foundation officials believed that studies of human behavior and motivation would provide information useful for averting such questioning, for preventing social unrest, and for helping individuals to "adjust" to change. This was the aim of the so-called Program V, which supported research in the behavioral sciences, and of the foundation's other programs, such as the "strengthening of democracy," the "establishment of peace," and the "strengthening of the economy" (presumably capitalist rather than socialist). Such goals certainly cannot be described as apolitical, regardless of whether that was how the foundation's officials described them or whether one agrees with their aims. According to Peter Seybold's study of the Ford Foundation, these aims, if not shaped by, were at least thoroughly compatible with, corporate capitalism.[12]

Thus, to Seybold and other sociologists writing in the late 1960s and 1970s, the foundations, like military and other state patrons, were not, as was generally believed, simply benevolently dispensing largess; they had an agenda. And, like military patrons, they influenced the shape and content of the academic disciplines for which they provided support. In addition to minimizing the differences between foundation and federal patronage, some sociologists have also argued that the distinction between private and public patronage has been overdrawn. They have pointed to the overlaps in the membership of those guiding the major foundations, leading corporations, universities, and agencies of the federal government and suggested that the interests of a "ruling elite" influenced or determined the goals and agendas of all of these purportedly distinct organizations and entities.[13] Vannevar Bush, for example, was at various times (and sometimes simultaneously) president of the Carnegie Institute of Washington (a research institution), a trustee of the Carnegie Corporation (a private foundation), head of the OSRD (a wartime agency of the federal government directly responsible to the president), and member of the Research and Development Board (which advised the Defense Department).

Taking into account the dual or multiple roles played by particular individuals does not require embracing a theory about a conspiratorial elite in control of all major institutions. It may, however, deepen our understanding of how the foundations interacted with other institutions, what factors shaped or contributed to the definition of a foundation's funding program, and who received funding and who did not. The multiple roles played by the Ford Foundation's social science advisors is particularly significant for understanding the shape of the Ford Foundation's program of support for the behavioral sciences.

When Henry Ford II indicated an interest in establishing a committee to rethink the Ford Foundation's place in the philanthropic world, Karl Compton, a trustee of the Ford Foundation recommended his friend, H. Rowan Gaither to head the committee. Compton, who, in addition to serving as a trustee for the foundation was also president of MIT and head of the Defense Department's Research and Development

Board, had met and become close to Gaither during World War II, when Gaither was the assistant director of the OSRD-funded Radiation Laboratory at MIT. In that position, Gaither had acted as liaison between the military and the laboratory's scientists. In the late 1940s he was playing a similar role as the head of RAND Corporation, which had been created after World War II as a think tank for the air force and was established in 1948 as a nominally independent corporation that conducted research sponsored by the air force. In 1948 the Ford Foundation's trustees expressed their confidence in Gaither, as well as in the aims of RAND, by granting $1 million in working capital to the new corporation and by appointing Gaither to head the Ford Foundation's Study Committee.[14]

After heading the Study Committee, Gaither was then appointed to formulate and implement one of the programs recommended by the Study Committee—Program V—which was explicitly dedicated to promoting the behavioral sciences. (Other program areas provided substantial support for the behavioral sciences, but under the rubric of specific aims. For example, through Program I, "The Establishment of Peace," substantial aid went to international studies programs, communications research, and studies of political behavior.)[15] In 1953 Gaither was named president of the foundation to replace the moderate Republican Paul Hoffman, an administrator of the Marshall Plan and a supporter of Eisenhower's presidential bid. Hoffman's outspoken internationalism had provided fodder for McCarthyite attacks on the foundation and had made him, in the trustees' view, a liability. Gaither, a "cool professional" who had "a mind like an IBM machine" and no discernible personality, according to some observers, personified the nonideological organization man.[16]

The origins of Gaither's commitment to making the social science disciplines more scientific—that is, free of bias and useful for making predictions—are unclear, but according to one Ford Foundation administrator Gaither's interest in the social sciences began when he joined RAND.[17] Certainly, the interest of Gaither, Compton, and others in promoting the so-called behavioral sciences was encouraged by their contacts with, and engagement in problems of interest to, the military. The postwar military was not only interested in the development of hardware for waging war. It was also concerned with the human element of warfare, including the behavior and morale of soldiers and what was referred to as the "man-machine relationship," a relationship that began to assume more importance to the military as technological systems became increasingly complex. The Defense Department (as well as the State Department) also realized that to wage war—hot or cold—successfully required an understanding of the behavior and culture (referred to as "human factors" and "human systems") of potential enemies in order to predict how individuals—leaders as well as the public at large—would respond to military attack, military threats, and propaganda. The military and state agencies, both during World War II and after, were not interested in ideological or philosophical discussion or in challenges to their own goals. They expected the social scientists from whom they sought advice to adopt the rhetoric of objectivity and to conduct research which had predictive and practical value.[18] That the general needs of the military and state agencies were important in the foundation's formulation of its support for the behavioral sciences is suggested by the Ford Foundation's own description of its behavioral science division. According to a memo explaining the division's purpose, the behavioral sciences "received a considerable impetus during World War II by virtue of the heavy demands made by governmental offices." Since the war, there had been a "rapid expansion" in the interest in the "scientific study of human behavior," represented by the "increased pressures" placed on universities by both the federal government and industry seeking research assistance. One of the goals of the foundation's behavioral science division was thus to help universities meet this demand for assistance by providing funds to foster research in the behavioral sciences.[19]

To help him plan Program V in 1951, Gaither, who was trained as a lawyer and not as a social scientist, relied heavily on two consultants who were deeply committed to making the social sciences more "scientific": sociologist Hans Speier and social psychologist Donald Marquis. Both Speier and Marquis had put their social science expertise to work during World War II. Speier, already interested in studies of "mass behavior" when he emigrated from Germany to the United States in 1933, analyzed German propaganda during the war, first as a member of the Foreign Broadcast Intelligence Service of the Federal Communication Commission (FCC) and then as a member of the Office of War Information. Marquis, a behavioral psychologist who before the war conducted research on the behavior of occipitally decorticated dogs, refocused his interests on military psychology and the attitudes of soldiers during the war, working first as director of the NRC's Office of Psychological Personnel and then as an aid to the OSRD. After the war, Marquis continued to pursue his new interest in social psychology as chairperson of the psychology department at the University of Michigan. Speier, after a stint as acting chief of the Division for Occupied Areas for the State Department and the publication of a book on psychological warfare, became the head of the division of social sciences at RAND.[20]

After the war, Speier's and Marquis's interest in the behavioral sciences continued to be appreciated, if not influenced, by the military as well as the State Department. Marquis, who had been a member of the original Ford Foundation Study Committee under Gaither, was in the late 1940s the chairperson of the Committee on Human Resources, a group of social scientists and scientists interested in behavioral studies that was formed by the Defense Department's Research and Development Board to suggest social scientific research of use to the military. Speier served as a consultant to Marquis's Human Resources Committee. Speier and Marquis had also participated in a 1947 conference sponsored by the air force to outline RAND's social science program. And both men had been members of the 1950 State Department–sponsored, top-secret Project Troy, which had been established in collaboration with MIT and Harvard administrators to provide guidance in the conduct of psychological and political warfare.[21]

To help them in outlining Program V, Speier and Marquis relied, according to Gaither, on leading social scientists in the United States. But those to whom Speier and Marquis turned were not simply the "best" social scientists in the country; they were, rather, the leading experts in the behavioral method of studying politics and society. For example, Speier and Marquis sought out the opinion of leaders in the study of political behavior (Paul Lazarsfeld, David Truman, Ithiel de Sola Pool) but not political philosophy, in the study of values (Robert Merton) but not political ideology, and in psychoanalysis and organizational analysis (Herbert Simon, Lawrence Kubie, Nathan Leites) but not the analysis of class or race, for example. A number of these social scientists had, like Speier and Marquis, been active in World War II in bringing their expertise to bear on problems defined by wartime agencies; after the war, many acted as consultants to the military. Leites and Truman, for example, had worked during the war for the FCC's Foreign Intelligence Broadcast Service, as had Speier; after the war, Leites joined Speier's social science division at RAND. Samuel Stouffer, who provided advice on behavioral science methodology to the Ford Foundation, had headed the research branch of the War Department's Information and Education Division and after the war was a member of

Marquis's Human Resources Committee as well as a participant in the 1947 air force–RAND conference. Bernard Berelson, who was appointed at Speier's suggestion to head the Ford Foundation's Program V, had worked with Speier during the war at the FCC; he had also attended the air force–RAND conference.[22]

In providing advice to the Ford Foundation and to various military or military-related agencies and in pursuing their academic work, it seems doubtful that these social scientists strictly separated the interests and needs of the individual groups and agencies to which they offered advice. There appears, for example, to be an overlap between the advice provided to the State Department by social scientists involved in Project Troy and the advice provided by Marquis and Speier in planning Program V. The social scientists advising the State Department in late 1950 concluded that more research was needed on "target populations" (those populations—the Soviet Union, China, Europe, and Soviet-bloc defectors—at which U.S. propaganda was aimed) and on American public opinion regarding U.S. foreign policy. An addendum to the Troy Report, to which Marquis contributed, recommended that more researchers be trained in the behavioral sciences and that a research institute be established on a university campus to conduct government-sponsored research related to political warfare. (A follow-up study to Project Troy was then initiated to explore further certain recommendations made in the report; MIT acted as the contractor and Richard Bissell, an advisor to the Ford Foundation as well as an administrator of the Marshall Plan, was appointed to head the study.)[23]

Marquis and Speier's plans for Program V, which they began drafting a few months after the completion of Project Troy, recommended support for research on totalitarian governments, with attention to the factors creating stability or instability. They also recommended supporting communications research related to the image of foreign policy and research on psychological and political problems related to the cold war and Western Europe. They also endorsed the creation of an institute for the advanced training of behavioral scientists (which was established with $3.5 million at Stanford in 1953 as the Center for Advanced Study in the Behavioral Sciences) and the establishment of a center for the study of international communications for conducting research on target audiences, economic development, and political stability in foreign countries.[24]

While the general recommendations for Program V and for Project Troy were strikingly similar, it is clear that Speier's proposal for the creation of a center for international communications was the direct result of his contact with those who had been involved in Project Troy. In developing the proposal in late 1951, Speier consulted Edward W. Barrett, assistant secretary of state for public affairs, head of the department's information and educational exchange program, veteran of the Office of War Information, and the initiator of Project Troy. Speier also sought the advice of Gordon Gray, director of the Psychological Strategy Board, president of the University of North Carolina, and former secretary of the army. And Speier talked to the MIT administrators involved in planning the Center for International Studies, the university-based center for government-sponsored research on political warfare that had been recommended by Project Troy's social scientists. The Ford Foundation's program of support for international communications research, it was agreed, would be located at MIT's Center for International Studies (CENIS) and would be advised by a committee headed by Hans Speier. According to an internal Ford Foundation memo, the Ford Foundation was "intimately involved" in outlining the research conducted with foundation support at CENIS and in selecting the personnel. The communications project was initiated with a grant of over $500,000 in 1952, and in 1953 the Ford Foundation's administrators selected Ithiel de Sola Pool, a political behavioralist at the Hoover Institute and one of the social scientists consulted by Speier in the planning of Program V, to direct the project. The first director of CENIS was Max Millikan, an economist who had participated in the 1950 Project Troy study and then spent a year with the CIA; among those on the center's board of directors was Julius Stratton, MIT provost and Karl Compton's replacement on the Ford Foundation's board of trustees.[25]

Clearly, then, the shape of postwar academic programs in the social sciences was not being determined solely by the interests of the scholars involved. Patrons who funded the programs and even established them in the first place favored certain approaches to the study of society and politics and thus favored certain scholars over others. This was true of the private foundations as well as state patrons. It may, in fact, be misleading to assume that the private and state patrons were both distinctly different and completely separate. The production of knowledge in the social sciences was influenced by postwar patrons of the social sciences, who determined which kinds of work would receive funding. It was also affected by the institutions—universities—where most academic social scientists worked. The concerns of university administrators—for institutional prestige and external support—were also important in determining the kinds of knowledge produced and taught.

The Behavioral Sciences at Stanford

Stanford University was among the top seven recipients of Ford Foundation support, along with Harvard, the University of Chicago, Columbia University, MIT, Yale, and the University of California at Berkeley.[26] In the same years that Stanford received several millions dollars of support from the Ford Foundation, the social sciences at Stanford underwent reorganization and change. In the 1950s, for example, the university created an Institute for Communications Research; this eventually became part of the Department of Communications, which replaced the older Institute for Journalistic Studies. The university expanded its work in cultural anthropology in anticipation of a continuation of interest by the federal government (the university had hired its first anthropologist in 1943 to enable it to fulfill its contract with the army to train soldiers in language and area studies) and the expectation of attracting support from private foundations. The Department of Political Science moved gradually toward an emphasis on political behavior. The university also created a center for the study of child behavior and a survey research facility to assist social scientists in conducting opinion polls and in collecting and processing data.

These developments—reflecting an interest in quantification, human behavior and culture, and mass communications—were related, directly or indirectly, to patronage provided by foundations, primarily the Ford Foundation. But it was not simply the case that these changes were initiated by Stanford social scientists who, for whatever reasons, became interested after World War II in new methods and ideas and then sought external funding to support their research. Rather, as in the case of changes in the science and engineering departments at Stanford, the university's administrators were involved in seeking patronage and in encouraging, and even pressuring, departments to focus on research areas of interest to patrons. Stanford's social scientists themselves were divided over the desirability of foundation support and of the behavioral approach to the study of politics and society. Only a few of them were eager to attract foundation patronage and to make the university a leading center for research in the behavioral sciences. It was these social scientists who would be the recipients of foundation grants, who would be favored by the university administration, and who would be given opportunities and the means to develop new programs and departments.

Information about the Ford Foundation's interests was conveyed first not to Stanford's social scientists but privately, to Stanford's president (just as the foundation's support for MIT's Center for International Studies was privately negotiated with MIT's administrators). During a retreat at the exclusive Bohemian Grove at the beginning of 1950, H. Rowan Gaither, at the time the head of the Ford Foundation's Study Committee, discussed with Sterling the foundation's programs and provided Sterling with a copy of the Study Committee's report. In January 1950 Sterling wrote to Gaither that he shared "those basic beliefs which the Committee asserts"—the promotion of democracy, capitalism, and peace—while making clear that he did not believe that war should be avoided at any cost. He thus urged the foundation to support extensive studies of the USSR and the "world communist movement," writing, "I cannot stress too much my feeling that the need for such study of the external danger is great and urgent." Although in commenting on the foundation's Program V Sterling noted that "here, there is not much competence in me," the Ford Foundation soon contacted him to encourage Stanford to apply for support for research in the behavioral sciences. In mid-1950 Sterling received a note from William McPeak, one of the associate directors of the Ford Foundation, informing him that Stanford had been awarded $100,000 for research in the behavioral sciences and advising him that the foundation "gave Stanford a much higher rating in the behavioral sciences because of you and their expectations of you."[27] Indeed, Stanford was not particularly strong in the behavioral sciences in 1950, but with the promise of more patronage from the Ford Foundation, Sterling began to seek to improve Stanford's reputation in this area.

In response to the grant, Sterling created the Committee for Research in the Social Sciences (CRISS), drawing together social scientists from a variety of departments as well as from the Food Research Institute, the business school, and the Hoover Institute. Among those involved in CRISS was Ithiel de Sola Pool of the Hoover Institute, who was participating in Carnegie Corporation–funded studies of the impact of revolution on international relations since 1890, a project under the general editorship of Harold Lasswell of Yale. Working with Pool on his studies of communication and symbols was Daniel Lerner, who held a joint appointment at the Hoover Institute and in the Department of Sociology and Anthropology. The first director of CRISS was Albert Bowker, who was succeeded by the developmental psychologist Ernest Hilgard, a close colleague of Donald Marquis (before the war, the two had worked together on the study of canine behavior) and dean of graduate studies at Stanford. Marxist economist Paul Baran, who was interested in the economies of Third World countries, was also involved in CRISS, as was Claude Buss, an historian of the Philippines and Far East, and Chilton Bush, a journalism professor who studied public opinion.[28]

The social scientists involved in CRISS were distinguished from their departmental colleagues not only by their specific interest in the study of human behavior, communications, or the quantification of social and economic phenomena; many of them had also served in governmental agencies during World War II or in some way applied their expertise to assisting the government to prosecute the war. Baran had served in the OSS as a specialist on USSR and Polish economics; economist Moses Abramovitz had worked for the War Production Board and the OSS; Bowker had been a member of the OSRD-sponsored Statistical Research Group at Columbia; Daniel Lerner had worked in the intelligence section of the army's psychological warfare division; Hilgard had administered civilian surveys in Washington; and Buss had served with the U.S. high command in Manila in 1940 and later in the Office of War Information.

The wartime experiences of these social scientists are not sufficient to explain their research interests in the postwar period. While Daniel Lerner's experience during the war was clearly significant in shaping his intellectual pursuits afterward (he received his Ph.D. in social psychology after the war, choosing as his dissertation topic an analysis of the psychological warfare division in which he had participated), the interests of others seem to have been formed prior to the war.[29] Chilton Bush's interest in survey research and public opinion, for example, dated to the post–World War I period. But the wartime experiences of these social scientists may have been significant in creating among them a desire to continue providing advice, indirectly if not directly, to the federal government. One of the articulated goals of CRISS, for example, was to foster studies that would contribute to the formation of "enlightened foreign policy."[30]

The Ford Foundation grant was expended by CRISS to develop ongoing research programs in the behavioral sciences. On the recommendation of CRISS, the university created in early 1952 a committee on communications, with Lerner as its first chairperson. This committee introduced courses in communications into the university curriculum. It also sought governmental support for research, receiving two contracts for psychological warfare studies worth over $100,000 from the

Human Resources Research Office (an office funded by the Defense Department and administered by George Washington University). On CRISS's recommendation and with Ford Foundation money, the university also established its survey research facility. Finally, CRISS dispensed the Ford Foundation support, mainly among its own members, for research on cultural and social change in Latin America and Eastern Europe, on decisionmaking, public attitudes, and political behavior.[31]

The initiation of the Ford Foundation's patronage and of Stanford administrators' enthusiasm for the behavioral sciences coincided with the height of anticommunist hysteria and witch-hunting in the United States. The widespread anxiety about communism was fomented by the end-of-the-decade triumph of the communists in China's long civil war and the Soviet Union's successful development of an atomic bomb; it was manipulated and fed by Senator Joseph McCarthy and others who attributed these American "losses" in the cold war to communist subversion at home. Among those institutions attacked during the Red Scare for supposedly harboring disloyal Americans were the nation's universities.[32]

Even before McCarthy appeared on the scene, Stanford's administrators, like their counterparts at some other universities, had been vigilant in seeking to keep left-wing teachers off the faculty. For example, in 1940 President Wilbur sent a private note to William Hansen inquiring about the physics department's appointment as a teaching assistant of Robert Oppenheimer's brother, Frank, whom Wilbur described as having a "rather definite relation to communistic activities." Oppenheimer was not reappointed. A few years later, Stanford's administrators denied reappointment to Holland Roberts, an untenured professor in the School of Education, because of his "radical left-wing activities." Roberts, whose political views were left of center (after leaving Stanford in 1944, he began teaching at the California Labor School) had stirred administrators' wrath when he attempted to organize a Teachers' Union at Stanford.[33]

University administrators preferred this self-policing to the public attacks on their institutions leveled in the late 1940s and early 1950s by legislative committees at the state and national level and by right-wing university benefactors and alumni.[34] In response to such attacks, President Sterling, like most university presidents, did not choose to take a strong public stand in favor of academic freedom, despite the urging of several prominent Stanford faculty members. Instead, Sterling declared his opposition to allowing members of the Communist Party to teach at Stanford and began cooperating quietly with California's aggressive Un-American Activities Committee, led by state senator Hugh Burns.[35]

There is no evidence to suggest that any of Stanford's faculty members who came under attack as potential subversives were or had been members of the Communist Party. Those on the political far right in California took broad aim, easily including among their targets New Deal liberals, Keynesian economists, supporters of labor's right to organize, and critics of the Chinese Nationalists. In such a political climate, "admiration of Sweden's middle way" could be misconstrued and misused by red-baiters, as Bernard Haley, a political scientist at Stanford, pointed out; it is thus quite possible that some academic social scientists sought refuge in the nominally objective, apolitical rhetoric and methods of the behavioral sciences. At least, according to Haley, by 1953 a "feeling of insecurity within the faculty" had "already had some effect in curtailing discussion of highly controversial issues in the classroom."[36]

At Stanford, however, many of those who were attacked for their political views were members of CRISS who had already adopted the stance of value-neutrality and were already deeply interested in the study of human behavior and in the quantification of economic and social phenomena, particularly in relation to studies of international affairs. Among those CRISS members accused of holding politically suspect beliefs—by the organized right wing in California, by benefactors of the Hoover Library such as ardent pro–Chinese Nationalist Alfred Kohlberg, or by Herbert Hoover himself in the late 1940s and early 1950s—were Ernest Hilgard, Paul Hanna, Paul Baran, and Daniel Lerner. Others accused of improper beliefs who were not members of CRISS but were involved in international studies, held Ford Foundation grants, and employed the rhetoric of dispassionate analysis in their work were Robert North, a political scientist; H. H. Fisher, an historian and the chair and director of the Hoover Library; C. E. Rothwell, Fisher's assistant; and Carl Spaeth, the dean of the law school.[37]

Hoover, who had begun a battle with Stanford's administration in 1944 to wrest control of the Hoover Library from the university, primarily to ensure that library scholars were unequivocally anticommunist, was fed information about the political views of scholars affiliated with the library in the late 1940s and early 1950s by a right-wing Polish émigré working at the library. He was also made aware of the studies by Lasswell, Lerner, and Pool of the impact of world revolution on international relations, which were funded by the Carnegie Corporation and published under the imprint of the Hoover Institution, and was upset by what he believed to be their leftist viewpoint.[38] Hoover's hostility toward particular teachers and researchers at Stanford reflected not only his suspicions about their political views but also his dislike for the scientistic approach and the stance of value-neutrality—"squirrel-cage scholasticism," in his words.[39] Hoover did not want value-neutrality from researchers associated with the Hoover Library; he wanted the hortatory rhetoric of anticommunism. At Stanford, then, the adoption of a behavioral approach was no security against political attack.

The precise way in which accusations of improper political beliefs were handled by Stanford's administration is unclear, just as it remains obscure how many scholars at Stanford came under attack. Of the social scientists upon whom suspicions of un-Americanism were cast, only Lerner left Stanford. Pool, who seems not to have been suspected of undesirable political beliefs, left Stanford as well, to become the director of MIT's Ford Foundation–funded Center for International Communications in 1953. (Lerner became a research associate at the center.)[40] In the case of the other social scientists who came under attack, Stanford's president seems to have worked behind the scenes, mainly with the aim of preventing a public relations disaster. For example, when in response to charges of un-Americanism for publicly criticizing Chiang Kai-shek and Senator McCarthy, H. H. Fisher offered his resignation as chair and director of the Hoover Library, President Sterling became concerned lest the resignation be regarded by the public as evidence of Stanford's failure to support academic freedom. The problem was largely resolved by allowing Fisher to retain the title of chairperson while ceding directorship of the library to his assistant.[41] In the case of Paul Baran, President Sterling may have worked with the Burns Committee to discourage efforts to subpoena the economist. While the administration was not overly fond of Baran ("Baran, being in the Econ. Dept., may give us real trouble one day," Fred Glover, secretary to the president, warned Sterling in the early 1950s), he had tenure, which, in this instance, protected him from being dismissed merely for his political views. University administrators did not become seriously unhappy with Baran until several years later, when he began to speak out in support of the Cuban revolution. Although pressed by benefactors of the university to dismiss Baran, Stanford's administration chose instead to encourage Baran to leave Stanford by keeping his salary considerably lower than that of his colleagues in the economics department.[42]

The departures of Pool and Lerner in 1953 were a blow to Stanford's effort to build its research programs in political behavior and communications. This effort was again impeded when Stanford's administration decided in 1955 not to grant tenure to Alfred de Grazia, a political scientist deeply committed to scientizing his discipline and promoting studies of political behavior. De Grazia had been hired in 1952 with Ford Foundation support to be executive director of CRISS. Precisely why he was not given a permanent position at Stanford is unclear. In 1955 he accepted a grant from the Relm Foundation for a study of "the origins and present restrictions on the political activities of workers." In preparing notes for a meeting of Stanford's board of trustees, Fred Glover flagged the grant and de Grazia's name. Two months later, Provost Terman informed de Grazia that he would not be given tenure. He did not get along well with his colleagues, Terman explained, and had been overeager in pressing his views.[43]

Despite these setbacks—largely self-induced—in the development of the behavioral sciences at Stanford, in 1953 the university was offered the opportunity by the Ford Foundation to participate in a self-survey of its behavioral science capabilities and facilities. The invitation was correctly regarded as an opportunity to make institutional changes that would attract further foundation support. Awarded approximately $50,000, Stanford embarked on its survey, which required assessments by each social science department of its strengths and weaknesses, interviews with individual faculty members, and appraisals of each department by a visiting committee chosen by the Ford Foundation.[44]

Most of the departments expressed an interest in increasing their staff and their resources in the behavioral sciences. The psychology department, for example, reported that it was interested in "pushing the behavioral sciences forward . . . both theoretical and empirical." The statistics department also called for an increase in staff and resources to enable it better to serve researchers in the behavioral sciences. And the sociology and anthropology department, the "very heart and core" of the behavioral sciences, according to the Ford Foundation visiting committee, needed additional staff in social anthropology.[45]

But beneath the surface of these commitments to strengthening the behavioral sciences were expressions of concern by some faculty members. A compilation of interviews with Stanford's social scientists revealed that some had misgivings both about the behavioral approach and the large amounts of external support available for research in the behavioral sciences. Rather than believing that the behavioral sciences needed increased support, some faculty members believed that "the total flow of money for research in the behavioral sciences may in fact be too large." According to the unnamed interviewer, a number of faculty members thought that "too many projects are invented for their possible appeal to a foundation's fancy," that the emphasis on research led to a neglect of teaching, and that too little research support was available for individual scholars to "move in whatever directions [their] intellectual curiosity may lead." The proposal by CRISS to create an institute of the behavioral sciences at Stanford aroused "little enthusiasm," according to the interviewer.[46]

Some social scientists also expressed ambivalence for the behavioral science approach. Both the Department of Statistics and the Department of Sociology and Anthropology had been created after the war; an interest in the behavioral sciences had thus been built into these departments. The Department of Economics had been rebuilt after the war; it thus had "a 'planned staff' " interested in mathematical and statistical approaches and in cooperating with members of other departments whose members were also interested in these approaches.[47] But some in the history and political science departments and in the Institute for Journalistic Studies, while open to the behavioral approach, did not view it as superior to other methods or approaches. As the Ford Foundation's director of the self-surveys commented, referring not just to Stanford but to all the universities surveyed, there remained a "deep cleavage" between those social scientists committed to the humanistic, philosophical approach to studying politics and society and those adherents of the "scientific, empirical" approach. According to one Stanford administrator, the conflict between "choosing a descriptive and hortatory approach or an analytical and behavioral approach" was particularly pronounced in Stanford's political science department.[48]

In the view of the members of the political science department, however, there was no conflict over choosing an approach to the study of politics. In its self-evaluation, the department made clear that it had no hostility toward the behavioral approach (at that time, one member of its faculty—de Grazia—was explicitly committed to behavioral study). It did, however, question whether empirical and statistical analysis should become the only approach to the study of politics. According to the majority of the department's members, there was no escaping normative issues; the department thus did not intend to abandon the approach that had produced "such classic works by such as Veblen, Beard, Tocqueville, etc." In making appointments to the staff, the department announced, "coverage and balance," both in terms of fields of research and in terms of competence in teaching as well as research, would be the main criteria.[49]

Stanford's administration, however, was not interested in coverage and balance but in building steeples that would draw national attention and patronage to Stanford University. After completing the self-survey, the dean of graduate studies, Ernest Hilgard, submitted a request to the Ford Foundation for several thousand dollars to expand research at Stanford in the behavioral sciences. The Ford Foundation, which had concluded that Stanford's representation in the behavioral sciences was "spotty" and thus in need of improvement, responded with a grant of over $400,000, half of which was to be used to appoint to Stanford professors in the fields of communications, social psychology, sociology, and mathematical applications to the behavioral sciences. Within a year Stanford had added Wilbur Schramm, a communications professor, Leon Festinger, a social psychologist, and Samuel Karlin, a mathematician, to its faculty. While Hilgard discussed these choices with the Ford Foundation, it is not clear whether the Ford Foundation played a role in the selection of these faculty members.[50]

The appointment of Schramm was crucial in firmly establishing communications as a discipline at Stanford, for he was a leading figure in the nascent discipline. Trained in literature, Schramm had become education director of the Office of War Information in 1941 and, after the war, had created one of the first communications programs in the country at the University of Illinois. He also acted as a consultant to the National Security Council, State Department, U.S. Information Agency, and the air force and had directed research sponsored by these agencies. As Chilton Bush, the head of the Institute for Journalistic Studies, correctly anticipated, "Dr. Schramm would be very successful in assisting us to procure grants and contracts in support of the research work of the Institute."[51] In fact, soon after Schramm's appointment, the Ford Foundation provided him with $75,000 for work on the practical utilization of the behavioral sciences. In 1956 the institute's name was changed to the Department of Communications and Journalism; in the early 1960s the name was changed, again, to the Department of Communications, and the journalism program was all but eliminated. Schramm had moved into the new field of international communications with support from the federal government and the Ford Foundation, embarking on studies of the perceptions in Third World countries, such as India and Colombia, of the United States and the Soviet Union and of how communications technology and propaganda might be used to speed economic development in these countries.[52]

These changes were not greeted with enthusiasm by all members of the communications department. While none seemed to have complained about the work undertaken by Schramm, those professors associated with the journalism program were not eager to see it eliminated. Even Bush, who had been Schramm's advocate initially, had become disgruntled by 1960. In welcoming the development of a communications program at Stanford, he had not intended that the training of journalists be eliminated. Such training, Bush believed, was important for providing would-be journalists with an understanding of the media and a "set of values" in the conduct of their profession.[53] To Schramm, however, journalism courses should be left to the "San Jose States of the world." Stanford's administration decided to "support the policy of backing Wilbur [Schramm] in the quantitative direction," allowing him two new appointments at the same time that it proposed to eliminate instruction in journalism. By 1963 the department had over $1.1 million in foundation grants and government contracts, thanks largely to Schramm; university support for the department was a mere $108,000.[54] While the development of the communications department elicited some complaints from the faculty, this aspect of the administration's larger plan to strengthen the behavioral sciences at Stanford proceeded smoothly in comparison with the administration's efforts to reorient the Department of Political Science toward an emphasis on organizational and political behavior.

The Political Science Department

The conflict between Stanford's administration and the political science department began as a disagreement over the direction and focus of the department, an issue raised when a position in the department was opened in 1957 by the death of the department's political theorist, Arnaud Leavelle. The ten-member department, headed at the time by James T. Watkins, a specialist in international law and organizations and, politically, a cold war Democrat, regarded instruction in political theory as an essential component of its graduate and undergraduate programs and he was thus eager to replace Leavelle with another theorist. The department, which placed a high value on good teaching, also wanted Leavelle's replacement to be a gifted teacher as well as scholar.[55]

But Stanford's administration had other plans for Leavelle's slot. The administration agreed with the Ford Foundation's 1953 visiting committee that the university's political science department identified itself too closely with history and law, neglecting the newer approaches that emphasized the links to statistics and the behavioral sciences. Terman, moreover, had little appreciation for traditional political theory, which he viewed as unscientific; in his view, the department's insistence on the importance of political theory was greatly exaggerated. He wanted the department's slot for a theorist to be filled by a prominent behavioralist, such as Ithiel de Sola Pool or David Truman.[56] Such an appointment would do much to improve the national reputation of the department, which was ranked thirteenth in the nation in 1957. A prominent behavioralist would no doubt also attract external support to Stanford. In the mid-1950s the political science department had virtually no outside support, a situation that irked the provost, who was committed to the policy of "each tub on its own bottom." Despite Terman's antipathy, the department found an ally in the dean of humanities and sciences, Philip Rhinelander, a philosopher by training; it was agreed that the department would hire a theorist as a temporary replacement for Leavelle.

The department chose Mulford Q. Sibley, a professor of political theory at the University of Minnesota interested in the history of political ideas, including utopian thought. Sibley was well known as a scholar (he received the American Political Science Association prize in 1952 for his book *Conscription of Conscience: The American State and Conscientious Objectors*) and as a remarkable teacher. Sibley thus fit the department's requirements of a traditional theorist deeply committed to teaching as well as to scholarship. Once at Stanford, Sibley further impressed Stanford's political scientists. He was a friendly, energetic, and stimulating colleague, and he quickly demonstrated his gifts as a teacher, attracting twice as many students as usual to the introductory course in political theory. Early in 1958 the department voted unanimously to offer him a permanent position.[57]

Perhaps because he was aware of the administration's lack of support for the hiring of a theorist, Watkins forwarded his recommendation of Sibley along with the recommendation that the department hire Heinz Eulau, a political behavioralist. Rhinelander endorsed the Eulau recommendation, but not the appointment of Sibley. Without informing the department, the administration had already initiated its own search for a theorist, and Terman had fixed upon political scientist David Easton as the ideal candidate.[58] In contrast to a traditional political theorist, such as Sibley, Easton was interested in developing a systematic, empirical political theory. This concept of theory, which was borrowed from the natural sciences, assumed the ability and desirability of separating "facts" from "values" or ethical inquiry. General theories about politics were to be based on observed facts alone, thus providing a value-free guide to understanding political behavior. This scientistic approach to theory impressed Terman. It was the antithesis of Sibley's approach, which the political science department preferred and which required consideration of ethical issues and of the relationship between what "is" and what "ought" to be.

The disagreement over the value of traditional political theory versus empirical theory was not singular to Stanford but was being echoed in the larger political science community and becoming the subject of debate and of numerous essays in these same years.[59] Opinions solicited by Stanford's administrators and political scientists as to the desirability of hiring Sibley or Easton reflected this division in the larger community. Thus, the suggestion of Easton for a position in political theory at Stanford elicited scorn from Jerome Kerwin and Leo Strauss, traditional political theorists at the University of Chicago. Political theory was fundamentally a moral science and as such was not reducible to "merely a process of political techniques," Kerwin wrote. "The description of processes, the use of statistical techniques, the various sociological approaches, and the attention to methodology may have fruitful application in certain fields of Political Science, notably in politics, but the very important question of 'why?' the behaviorist by his method can not give an answer." He continued, "It does no good to know how Hitler came to power if we as Political Scientists can pass no rational judgment upon him and his activities." For similar reasons, Francis G. Wilson, a political scientist at the University of Illinois, endorsed Sibley's appointment in glowing terms. "Sibley is a person of great learning. . . . He loves ideas . . . he is humanistic and philosophical." Moreover, Sibley had "none of the narrowness so characteristic of those who are the current enemies of philosophy," such as the "behaviorists, the logical positivists, the quantifiers," and "those who believe that the digital computer will be to the social sciences what the microscope has been to the biological sciences."[60] But these overwhelmingly positive judgments were countered by others, whose opinions were more highly valued by Terman. For example, Ithiel Pool judged Sibley to be an outdated political theorist whose appointment would neither harm nor help Stanford's reputation.[61]

Deeply upset over the administration's rejection of the political science department's unanimous recommendation of Sibley, Watkins confronted Dean Rhinelander, who agreed not to veto the appointment but to pass the department's recommendation on to Terman.[62] Rhinelander and Terman then met privately and decided to remove Watkins as head of the department. They replaced him with Robert Walker, a professor of public administration who was receptive to the behavioral approach and whom the administration believed to be pliable. But to the surprise of Rhinelander and Terman, one of Walker's first acts as chairperson was to press the administration in March 1958 to grant Sibley a permanent appointment.[63]

By that time, however, a decision in favor of Sibley was out of the question. In seeking opinions of Sibley, Stanford's administrators turned up information about Sibley that had little to do with his merits as a scholar or teacher. Sibley was a pacifist, a "tactless radical," an "ultra AAUP type," and a "screwball," according to Terman's notes of conversations with sources at the University of Minnesota.[64] Sibley's political views were already known to the members of Stanford's political science department. In his letter of application, which Hubert Marshall, a member of the department, recalled as "truly extraordinary" in its frankness, Sibley had described himself as a Christian socialist, an anarchist, and a pacifist who had been a conscientious objector in World War II. Knowledge of Sibley's political views had not dissuaded the department, whose members ranged, politically, from conservative Republicans to liberal Democrats; the department, in fact, had found Sibley's openness about his politics "appealing," in Marshall's words. The department clearly did not believe that Sibley's politics unfitted him for teaching at Stanford.[65]

But information about Sibley's politics made him anything but appealing to Terman. Despite evidence of Sibley's gifts as a teacher and the assertion of a former colleague of Sibley's that "many students will follow him and have their intelligence and their imagination stirred by his conduct of the class room," Albert Bowker, an advisor to Terman, now opined that Sibley "could not be a very popular lecturer as he has extreme views on pacifism." Terman, whose comments about Sibley's merits had previously been limited to concerns that Sibley was not an eminent behavioralist, now noted not only that Sibley did not appreciate quantitative work, but also that Sibley published in "off-beat journals" and that his personal values made his teaching "controversial." Although Sibley had, in fact, published in such mainstream academic journals as *American Quarterly, American Political Science Review,* and *The Journal of Politics,* and no student seems ever to have charged Sibley with propagandizing for his own viewpoint in the classroom, Sibley's political views marginalized him in the opinions of Bowker and Terman.[66]

If Sibley's views meant that he would not bring national acclaim to Stanford's political science department, they also meant that it was unlikely that Sibley would become a self-supporting professor. A traditional political theorist (in contrast to a behavioralist) was in any case unlikely to attract external support. If Stanford were to hire a traditional theorist, Terman wanted to support the professor with funds that had been provided by William Robertson Coe, a generous benefactor who had supported the creation of programs in American studies at leading universities in the 1950s. But Coe, a right-wing businessman, had placed restrictions on his patronage; his money was to be used to meet "the threat of Communism, Socialism, collectivism, Totalitarianism and other ideologies opposed to the preservation of our System of Free Enterprise."[67] Thus Coe's patronage could not be used to pay Sibley's salary. Coe funds might, however, be used to support one of the conservative members of the political science department, thus freeing university funds to hire Sibley. This was Rhinelander's suggestion after Walker, the new department chair, warned him that the political scientists felt so strongly about Sibley that several of them had threatened to resign if he were not appointed.[68]

Terman refused to consider this option, however. By the spring of 1958 Terman had also learned from John Darley, an associate dean of the University of Minnesota, that Sibley had "been a constant thorn in the side of the administration" at Minnesota. Sibley had, for example, protested the university's requirement that students state their religion on their admissions applications. He had also objected to the tradition of opening the annual graduation ceremony with an invocation. While Darley assured Stanford administrators that Sibley would be "a remarkable figure for your faculty," he also warned that Sibley was "naive." "He belongs in the academic atmosphere and environment of a much simpler time when the forces of society were pleasantly remote and when the academic life was a truly contemplative life."[69]

Of course, the "forces of society" were not remote from Stanford University in the 1950s. By the late 1950s, Stanford was conducting millions of dollars worth of research for the Department of Defense and was beginning to forge close ties with a variety of industrial enterprises which themselves were under contract to the Defense Department. Terman had encouraged this merging of Stanford with the outside world.

And by April 1958, when the issue of Sibley's tenure was again before the administration, Sibley had begun raising challenges to the forces upon which Stanford had become so dependent.

In the wake of Sputnik, and with concerns growing about the dangers of radioactive fallout from nuclear tests, groups in England and America had formed to protest the nuclear arms race and nuclear testing. Sibley added his voice to the calls to "ban the bomb" and, in the spring of 1958, began speaking in support of a test ban at meetings in the local community and on the Stanford campus. Perhaps more disturbing than Sibley's activism was evidence that a significant number of Stanford students shared Sibley's views and may have been emboldened by him. In mid-April, as the administration was reconsidering the political science department's appeal that Sibley be given tenure, the lead editorial of the student paper, the *Stanford Daily,* made a passionate plea for an end to the arms race and a halt to nuclear testing "before we are forever committed to this carnage, this destruction, this appalling waste of money, energy and human life." On 17 April a large group of students staged a silent protest on campus; more than 350 students signed a petition addressed to President Eisenhower calling for an end to nuclear testing. In early May Terman announced that Sibley would not be granted tenure.[70]

The administration's decision quickly reached the local newspapers, the San Francisco *Examiner* and the San Francisco *Chronicle,* which ran articles with headlines "Stanford Drops H-Bomb Test Foe" and "Stanford Firm—No Job for Socialist Despite Protest." A number of alumni and members of the surrounding community also viewed the administration's decision as a political one and wrote letters of protest to Stanford's president. Students similarly believed that the administration had denied Sibley tenure because of his politics and because of his strong commitment to undergraduate education, which students believed the administration did not value. More than three hundred students signed a petition requesting that President Sterling reconsider the Sibley decision. Student unhappiness over the decision was so great, in fact, that the resident assistant of one student dormitory felt compelled to warn the administration that "the student temper is . . . dangerous." A "movement" was afoot, involving Stanford's most "responsible students," to stage a large demonstration and to hang Terman in effigy.[71]

The furor over the Sibley decision and, especially, the accusations that Sibley had been denied tenure because of his political views stung Terman, who insisted that his decision had been based on an evaluation of Sibley's scholarship, not his politics.[72] Terman, of course, had indicated reservations about Sibley before he knew of Sibley's political views. But Sibley's politics had mattered, and particularly, his activism, as Terman's notes regarding possible replacements for Sibley suggest. Terman first considered Max Lerner, a noted journalist and liberal political scientist at Williams College. His appointment, Terman noted, "would dispel any feeling that Stanford blackballs all liberals; at the same time presumably wouldn't be a campus crusader." Rhinelander agreed, assuring President Sterling that he did not believe Lerner to be "sufficiently 'left wing' to cause any legitimate concern; at the same time he seems sufficiently so to offset any implication that political views were a factor in the Sibley case."[73] Further inquiries about Lerner, however, turned up the opinion that while Lerner had never "been a fellow-traveler or a communist," he was "well to left of center," and that view may have been a factor in the administration's decision not to pursue Lerner. The administration instead selected Yale professor Wilmoore Kendall, a vocal anticommunist and mentor to William F. Buckley, Jr. While Terman worried that the contrast between Kendall and Sibley might reinforce the view that the administration's decision regarding Sibley had been a political one, this concern was outweighed by the fact that Kendall's salary could be paid with Coe funds. The political science department could thus have a theorist at no cost to the university, and the slot originally opened by Leavelle's death could still be filled by a behavioralist.[74]

That Sibley's activism was directed at the arms race and nuclear weapons testing may have been especially troubling for Stanford's administrators is suggested by the controversy a few years later over the administration's decision to deny tenure to another political scientist, John Bunzel. As in the case of Sibley, the administration had doubts about the initial decision to hire Bunzel, whom Terman and Bowker (who was by this time the dean of graduate studies), agreed was not firmly within the behavioralist camp and showed more interest in teaching than in research.[75] But Bunzel's chances of changing the administration's assessment of him were dashed in 1962, when Bunzel revealed his antinuclear sentiments while attending a speech on the Stanford campus by Southern California congressman John Rousselot, a favorite of the John Birch Society. News that Bunzel had apparently laughed and perhaps ridiculed the congressman was quickly conveyed to Stanford's board of trustees by Thomas Barclay, an emeritus professor of political science and a member of the Winds of Freedom Foundation, an organization of right-wing emeritus Stanford faculty members. Also on the board of trustees was David Packard, a member of the board of directors of SRI and co-owner of Hewlett-Packard, a successful company located in Stanford's industrial park that manufactured electronics measurement and test equipment for the army, navy, and air force. He called President Sterling for information on Bunzel's politics, according to Fred Glover, and was told that Bunzel was "anti-nuclear." Packard then requested that President Sterling "flag" Bunzel's name if he did not yet have tenure. A few weeks later, Thomas P. Pike, another Stanford trustee who was also on Hewlett-Packard's board of directors (as was Terman), wrote to Glover, asking "Does Bunzel have tenure?" Despite the unanimous support of the political science department, Bunzel was denied tenure.[76]

A Question of Judgment

Although the politics of both Bunzel and Sibley clearly played a role in the decision of Stanford's administration to deny them tenure, the political science department never joined the chorus of voices—students, alumni, and press—accusing the administration of political bias. Convinced of Sibley's merits as a scholar and teacher, the political scientists focused instead on the issues of departmental and professional autonomy, insisting that the members of Stanford's political science department, not university administrators, were best qualified to judge Sibley and to decide who merited appointment to their department.

While Stanford administrators might have had a difficult time responding honestly to accusations of political bias, they were well prepared to become engaged with the political science department over the issues of autonomy and control. This issue had already arisen in relation to the Department of Geology and would be raised again by the Departments of Physics and Biology. Thus, in response to complaints that the administration was ignoring the unanimous judgment of Stanford's political scientists, who believed both that good teaching and traditional political theory were important to their department, President Sterling responded that his administration did rely on the judgments of its faculty members in matters of appointment and promotion, except in instances when these judgments were faulty. "It is an open secret," he offered, "that some departments are more far-sighted, diligent, meticulous and exacting than others in initiating appointment recommendations." In other words, the political science department might have enjoyed autonomy and control over appointments and promotions had the department possessed the ability to make good judgments. The president of the university, was, of course, the final arbiter of good judgment.[77]

In his calculated response to the political science department's complaints, Sterling skirted the issue of whether the department had lost a traditional prerogative of controlling its own affairs and, at the same time, played off of the insecurities of the department's members as to their professional stature and the prestige of their department. The department, after all, was ranked thirteenth in the nation; had it been ranked fifth, Sterling seemed to imply, perhaps the department would not have recommended Sibley in the first place.

While the department as a whole did not respond to Sterling and raised no more complaints about the Sibley decision, one member of the department, Cornelius Cotter, refused to accept the administration's judgment of himself and his colleagues and complained directly to President Sterling. The political science department was fully aware that it was not one of the strongest departments in the country, Cotter pointed out. But it was also not "one of those weak departments, to which you referred some six days ago, who seek to perpetuate their weakness." The political scientists were fully aware of their department's weaknesses and were "sufficiently sound in our collective judgment" to correct them, Cotter insisted. This had been amply demonstrated in the department's recommendation of Eulau in the field of politics, as well as of Sibley in the field of theory. Since the administration had never provided the political science department with evidence to suggest that the choice of Sibley was not a sound one, Cotter had drawn his own conclusions about the administration's rejection of the appointment. The administration, he had heard, did not believe that classical political theory needed to be represented at Stanford. And since the appointment might be the department's last for many years, the administration was insisting that the department "buy" a man "who will make a nation-wide 'splash.' "[78] "I will not dwell upon the appropriateness, in a learned community, of indulging in the simile of 'buying' and 'selling' persons," Cotter fumed, or on the "singular inappropriateness of treating an appointment to a professorship at Stanford University as if it were the hiring of a star, instead of the quest for a person who is substantively sound and has given evidence of scholarly achievement." To Cotter, who had given up a successful business career to become a political scientist, the academic world was supposed to operate according to different principles from those of the business world; in the academic world, he believed, one did not have "to accept the compromises of principle which, in the business world I *might* have accepted at little or no cost to my psyche and tissue."[79]

Cotter's view of university life was, of course, naive. Stanford University, like leading universities across the country, were not the ivory towers that Cotter had imagined them to be. They were places where professors with political views to the left of center had trouble finding a foothold; they were institutions run by administrators concerned about attracting national prestige and patronage from private foundations, the federal government, and the business world. Instead of internalizing the administration's assessment of his department's judgment, Cotter reminded President Sterling of the principles for which a university had traditionally stood. But the administration was not moved by Cotter's appeal, and three and a half years later, perhaps recognizing that the administration was again going to disregard his department's judgment by refusing to grant tenure to Bunzel, Cotter resigned from the university. Barclay, who had worked with the administration to ferret out politically incorrect professors, bemoaned Cotter's departure, describing him as "one of the most brilliant of the younger political scientists" and "a person of conservative point of view, a quality urgently needed to balance the presentations of the faculty 'lunatic' fringe."[80]

Cotter had correctly adduced the administration's philosophy. The administration wanted to hire a "star" to the political science department, but a star of a particular sort—one who worked in the behavioral tradition, who would attract not only attention to Stanford but also external support. In 1963 the administration finally found such a person, Gabriel Almond, who became chair of the department. The following year, Sidney Verba, an eminent political behavioralist and leader in the field of comparative politics, moved to Stanford from Princeton, thus setting the political science department on the track that the administration had long determined desirable. "The Almond appointment has paid off beyond my wildest expectations and hopes," one Stanford administrator wrote to Robert Wert, a vice-provost. In 1964 Stanford's political department was ranked seventh in the nation.[81]

Clearly, the interest of Stanford's administration in political behavior as opposed to political theory had a political dimension; those engaged in political theory were interested in discussing values and "oughts," whether from a conservative, liberal, or leftist position. While administrators were willing to tolerate an archconservative such as Kendall, their institution's ties to the Defense Department, defense contractors, and conservative trustees and alumni made it impossible to tolerate someone of Sibley's views. But a political behavioralist who rendered "value-free" judgments and produced sheets of data was preferable to a conservative theorist who lectured to students on the state of political life, because a political behavioralist was nominally apolitical and was also more likely to attract external funding.

———————

A number of forces acted to shape intellectual production during the cold war. McCarthyism narrowed scholarly and political discussions on campuses as university administrators eliminated from their faculties those believed to be or have been members of the Communist Party or fellow-travelers. University administrators (including trustees) policed their institutions, acting to ward off attacks from state and national un-American activities committees, but also to protect their own interests. Liberal internationalists, for example, did not fare well at Stanford in the early 1950s; in the late 1950s university administrators exercised their institutional power to discourage those opposed to the nuclear arms race and to nuclear-weapons tests from voicing their opinions. Academic social scientists who were openly critical of the status quo had trouble attaining positions in major universities during this period, unless they were ideological conservatives, like Wilmoore Kendall.

The politically repressive climate undoubtedly had a chilling effect on those in the university concerned with holding their jobs and receiving promotions. Political behavioralism or scientism may have been seen by some as a safe approach to studying politics, one that freed them from drawing potentially controversial conclusions. Additionally, the cultural celebration of the physical and biological sciences may have led some to reject normative approaches as unscientific and to adopt methods for studying society and politics that claimed the certitude of science. Individual scholars may have responded, even only half-consciously, to cultural and institutional pressures.

In the case of Stanford, however, the evidence indicates that the intellectual channeling that occurred there was in large measure the result of deliberate administrative policy and action. By defining research areas according to those outlined by patrons of research—in the case of the social sciences, primarily by the private foundations—by closely involving themselves in departmental matters of appointment and promotion, and, if necessary, by disciplining recalcitrant departments and individual professors, administrators worked to reconfigure the intellectual contours of the social science disciplines. This is not to say that individual social scientists did not, for their own reasons, embrace scientism. But this alone cannot account for the dominance of scientism in the early cold war. The interests of private foundations, such as the Ford Foundation, which were shared, to some extent, by the State and Defense Departments, acted to set the boundaries within which externally supported social science research would take place in this period. The institutional needs and the ideological interests of university administrators created additional constraints as administrators pressured faculty members to seek external support for their research and pushed departments to hire and promote those faculty members likely to attract external support and unlikely to excite controversy or stimulate debate.

8

The Undergraduates

Critics and champions of the cold war university could agree on one thing—the university's undergraduates were not happy. While some within the burgeoning postwar profession of psychology directed the public's attention to the stresses of adolescence, some within the university pointed to the institution itself as the source of students' anxiety and apathy. Clark Kerr, no critic of the multiversity, noted in 1963 the restlessness and unhappiness of the institution's students and admitted that undergraduates were a neglected segment of the postwar university's population.

Identifying the problem was much simpler than solving it, however. Neglect of undergraduate education had been built into the postwar university, in which faculty members were rewarded for their research output, graduate student Ph.D. production, and the procurement of external research support, but not for time devoted to undergraduate education. To restructure the institution's system of rewards would have required rethinking the patronage relationships at the heart of the institution, something university administrators were unwilling to consider. Faced with evidence of the university's failures—in the form of specific complaints from undergraduates as well as evidence of widespread anxiety among the students—university administrators turned to the counseling professions and to grade inflation to help students adjust to and accept the cold war university.

Anxiety and Apathy

"As our educational institutions become larger, their curricula become more crowded, and the amount of knowledge considered fundamental in any particular field increases, the individual student
may find his own part in the educational process somewhat confusing.
He may feel that he is insignificant . . . he may actually be destructive."
So explained Dana Farnsworth, director of Harvard University Health
Services and a leading expert on the mental health of college students,
in a series of lectures given at the Lowell Institute of Boston in 1956 and
published the following year as *Mental Health in College and University.*
Farnsworth was not alone in his concern for the emotional well-being
of college students in the 1950s and 1960s.[1] By 1956 thirty-five full-time
psychiatrists were employed in the nation's universities and colleges, a
50 percent increase since the end of World War II. The rate of growth
would have been even greater, in Farnsworth's view, but for a scarcity
of psychiatrists and the financial resources to employ them. Indeed, an
informal survey of the presidents of one hundred leading colleges and
universities in America in 1954 revealed that academic administrators
believed emotional difficulties to be the chief health problem among
students.[2]

Whether emotional problems among students were really on the rise
after World War II is unclear. The decade following the war saw a tremendous increase in the number of trained clinical psychologists, the
result, primarily, of generous support from the United States Public
Health Service and the Veterans Administration. Beginning in the 1940s
popular culture began to reflect this interest in psychology, as movies
like Alfred Hitchcock's *Spellbound* offered psychological explanations,
rather than moral or sociological ones, for the behavior of the film's
characters. But concerns about students' mental health may have represented more than a growing interest in psychological analysis, and attention to a long-standing but previously unnamed problem. In the
opinion of Farnsworth, "emotional tension" among students (and
among faculty members as well) was on the rise.[3]

Some psychologists and psychiatrists followed the lead of the prominent developmental psychologist Erik Erikson, focusing on postadolescence itself as a stressful stage productive of emotional and mental
problems. Farnsworth and others, however, believed that America's
postwar institutions of higher education were part of the problem.

Universities had become large and impersonal; students had little if any contact with their professors and no opportunities to explore and discuss their values or their emotions.[4] As a former psychiatrist at Harvard's student health service noted, "One does hear the complaint that Harvard is an impersonal, apathetic environment where no one cares what happens to the student."[5]

Farnsworth regretted the absence of caring, closeness, and community that he thought had characterized the prewar university. He also believed, however, that the changes that had occurred in the university were irreversible, reflective of larger, inevitable changes occurring in American society. And yet the message of *Mental Health in College and University* was far from gloomy. The sense of caring and community could be recreated on college and university campuses, Farnsworth assured, through the "development of the 'counseling attitude.' " If in the postwar university, professors rarely interacted with students and were responsible, at best, only for students' intellectual development, then counselors and psychiatrists should be available on campuses to help students explore their emotions, define their values, and in general, ensure that they enjoyed full mental health. "In a sense psychotherapy is a highly specialized type of education," Farnsworth explained, "with one pupil and a teacher concentrating on the problem of understanding the internal emotional complexities of the pupil or patient as well as his relations to the world around him."[6]

The intentions of those advocating the provision of mental health services to college and university students were laudable; they were encouraging treatment, rather than ignoring or stigmatizing young people facing emotional or mental difficulties. Moreover, they squarely addressed a particular problem—student suicides—that had rarely been discussed before. As James A. Paulsen, psychiatrist-in-chief of Stanford's student health services revealed in the *Atlantic Monthly* in 1964, one to two students per ten thousand per year committed suicide on the nation's campuses. At Stanford, Paulsen posited, perhaps as many as fifty students per ten thousand per year attempted suicide. While most students were not severely troubled, Paulsen estimated that 30 to 35 percent of the student body would benefit from some contact—perhaps only an hour or two—with a counselor or psychiatrist.[7]

But while encouraging the development of the "counseling attitude" represented a new sensitivity to mental health issues, it was a response to the symptoms rather than the source of the problems. By classifying student anxiety and apathy as psychological problems, whether spawned by the impersonality of postindustrial society or by the tensions experienced in postadolescence, attention was deflected from the university itself and its structural flaws. In the views of many students experiencing dissatisfaction and alienation, these flaws were clearly visible: teaching at the university was abysmally bad, and more generally, universities stifled rather than stimulated intellectual thought and the discussion of ideas.

Some students (as well as some professors) objected to large lecture courses, a postwar innovation for handling large enrollments. A survey of Stanford's senior class in 1955, designed by faculty members who had been appointed to study undergraduate education at Stanford, asked students whether they would have preferred small discussion courses instead of lectures and whether they would have liked more "personal contact" with the faculty. Over 80 percent of the seniors responding indicated that more contact with the faculty would have made their college experience more valuable; a slightly smaller percentage indicated a preference for small discussion courses.[8]

But large lecture courses were not solely the cause of student unhappiness with the instruction they received at Stanford. Students, for example, had flocked to Mulford Q. Sibley's large introductory lecture course, the size of which did not detract from Sibley's ability to instruct or from students' ability to learn. When students explained why they wanted to study with Sibley, they noted that Sibley took an interest in them and that he talked about ethics and values, challenging them intellectually by provoking thought and reflection. As one sophomore wrote to Stanford's president, Sibley brought "stimulation" and "enthusiasm" to the classroom, in marked contrast to the student's history professor, "who shows absolutely no interest in his students, who, rather, is absorbed in writing textbooks." Similar sentiments were expressed by students in a meeting with President Sterling, arranged in the wake of protest over the Sibley decision.[9] Some students, it seemed, craved not only personal attention from a faculty member but also intellectual stimulation.

The freshman year at Stanford was particularly bad, according to a group of dormitory sponsors, upper division students selected to provide guidance to younger dormitory residents. It was a year marked by an "alarming lack of challenge to the mind and spirit," by "intellectual gutlessness," and by "sterility and absence of serious discussion," they reported, adding that this was the very "opposite of the ferment and debate supposed to be excited by a first exposure to life in a great university."[10] Others felt that the instruction offered in introductory courses was so poor as to make it impossible for them to learn and pass their courses. Particularly objectionable were the introductory biology, freshman English, and Western civilization courses, in which significant numbers of students who had never received grades lower than B in high school floundered, some getting Ds or Fs. Most of the instruction in courses such as these at Stanford, as well as at other universities, was provided by graduate students rather than professors, a factor which may have in part accounted for the students' dissatisfaction with the courses. Additionally, the ratio of teaching assistants to students at Stanford was small. In freshmen chemistry courses, one graduate student instructed an average of twenty-three students in the laboratory section of the course, and was responsible for grading an average of sixty-six students. In contrast, at Harvard, each teaching assistant graded and instructed an average of eighteen students; the ratio of teaching assistants to students at Caltech was one to ten.[11] The difficulties that students experienced with introductory science courses were conveyed by one student, who complained about his introductory biology class to a Stanford administrator despite feeling guilty for doing so. The professor stood before the class and read his notes, the student reported; he assumed prior knowledge of chemistry and biology and provided no textbook for those who had been unable to follow the lecture. Worse than a distant professor, however, was no professor at all. The laboratory portion of the course was run by graduate students, who were rarely available to answer questions and provided written, but no oral, explanation of the assignment.[12]

If courses were badly taught and the subject matter sterile, students found no space outside the classroom for intellectual stimulation in the 1950s. Stanford, like other campuses, reflected the social conformity and political repressiveness of the decade. The university barred political speakers and religious activity from campus. And those students rejected by, or choosing not to belong to, the fraternities, which dominated the social life of the campus in the 1950s, were relegated to dormitories tightly controlled by parietal rules. Wilbur and Stern Halls, two large, graceless dormitories for men, were the worst of the student accommodations. According to a faculty member, their very design conveyed to students the idea that "you are here to be processed, your individual freedom is on probation, and therefore you are afforded the comforts . . . of a well-appointed prison."[13]

Finally, students, especially freshmen, expressed considerable anxiety about grades. A survey of freshmen in 1962 revealed that over 60 percent worried about their grades and over 80 percent believed that competition for grades at Stanford was "severe." Parents of Stanford students complained to university administrators that their children, when home during quarter breaks, seemed obsessed about their grades and about Stanford's policy of grading on the curve. In response to the concerns of friends whose son attended Stanford, history professor William Bark visited Wilbur Hall, where he discovered that one student had had a nervous breakdown on the eve of his "Western civ" exam and that the others seemed to be "suffering from a pretty bad state of 'nerves.' "[14]

Worries about grades were not unique to Stanford students. In the late 1950s the provost of Cornell wrote to his counterparts at Stanford, Yale, Harvard, and Princeton, commenting on students' anxiety about grades and suggesting that their concerns might be relieved by eliminating the standard practice of grading on a curve. Stanford was the only university unreceptive to the suggestion. According to Terman, grading on the curve had been introduced at Stanford in the 1920s at the suggestion of his father; the idea had been to standardize grading throughout the university as well as to use the grading curve to separate and rank students according to their abilities.[15] While there may have been some merit to this idea during the years when entrance to the university was determined as much, if not more, by wealth and family background than by ability and avidity for education, by the mid-1950s the rationale for grading on the curve no longer existed, according to Cornell's provost.

Indeed, by the mid-1950s the undergraduate class at Stanford and at other elite universities was, as a whole, markedly different from those of prewar years, and even of those just five years previously. As a group, the first-year students had scored higher on standardized admissions tests, like the SAT, and had received better high school grades than had previous entering classes. This reflected changes in admissions procedures. After World War II, Stanford and other universities had removed their limitations on the enrollment of Jewish students, and in the early 1950s Stanford stopped automatically admitting the children of alumni (although standards for athletes and for the children of alumni and university patrons remained somewhat lower than for other applicants). The university also reduced the weight given in admissions decisions to extracurricular activities. Increased competition and redefined admissions standards meant that, over the course of the 1950s, it had also become more difficult to gain admission to Stanford and other elite universities. At Stanford in 1957, for example, the ratio of applicants to admitted students was 4.2 to 1, in contrast to 1.7 to 1 in 1950.[16]

The increased selectivity went hand-in-hand with the increased demand for higher education after World War II; both reflected the ascendancy of the idea of meritocracy in postwar America. The public embraced this idea, which to many seemed to be embodied in the G.I. bill, believing that those with ability, regardless of class background or religious identity, could, with the proper education, attain status and material comfort, if not wealth. Administrators of elite universities, leery of the leveling implications of the G.I. bill, determined strictly to limit enrollments at their institutions; the elite institutions would focus more on merit and less on family connections or wealth than had been the case in the past, but they would admit only the "best and brightest" of the college-bound students. These universities in the postwar years, largely by their own design, came to be regarded as the training ground for the next generation of American leaders upon whose shoulders the outcome of the cold war, and the fate of the "free" world, might rest.[17] Thus, for students in the postwar university, parental and societal expectations were high.

Students' responses to these expectations varied. Some, of course, met the goals laid out for them, performing as expected and never questioning or complaining about the instruction they received. Others undoubtedly ignored expectations entirely, pursuing their own interests, intellectual and otherwise.[18] Still others found that, given the poor instruction available in the university and the stultifying nature of campus life, they could not meet parental and societal expectations. A few articulate students complained to university administrators or professors and a few, less confident and perhaps experiencing other problems as well, became self-destructive.

Addressing the Symptoms

As early as 1954, university administrators had recognized that something was seriously wrong with undergraduate education at Stanford. That year, the Ford Foundation's Fund for the Advancement of Education awarded Stanford University a grant to study and recommend improvements in its undergraduate program. The committee of faculty members chosen by President Sterling to conduct the study easily concluded that Stanford's focus on research and graduate education resulted in the neglect of the undergraduate. As a senior professor explained the behavior of younger faculty members to the committee, "teaching is slighted because felt to be unrewarding; again and again I have seen young men abandon their idealistic position in relation to students because, as they frankly stated, they could not afford to maintain it." But the committee provided no clear suggestions as to how this situation might be improved, agreeing that a change in the university's system of rewards required the action of the president and his administrative assistants, not the faculty.[19] Stanford's top administrators were not about to change the system of rewards, however. The 1950s was the decade during which university administrators had put this system firmly into place, emphasizing to faculty members the necessity of publishing and obtaining research grants. A serious commitment to undergraduate teaching would have required a rethinking not only of the basis of faculty tenure and promotions, but also of the postwar goals of Stanford, the university's finances, and its relationship to its patrons.

The issue of the adequacy of undergraduate instruction and campus life was raised again in the late 1950s as tension among undergraduates appeared to be increasing. In 1957 the dean of humanities and sciences, Philip Rhinelander, warned President Sterling that "increasing numbers of undergraduates are expressing, both in public and privately, a serious dissatisfaction with the kind of instruction they are currently receiving at Stanford."[20] Rhinelander believed that the "progressively higher level of intelligence" of Stanford undergraduates explained their restiveness: the more intelligent students demanded courses that were well-taught and challenging. History professor William Bark agreed that it was indeed these "new 'best ever' students" who seemed to be unhappy, although he was less sympathetic to their complaints. Noting that in earlier years, Stanford students had been "less highly intellectualized" but, in his view, better adjusted, Bark wondered, "Could we have somehow overshot the mark a little?" The "strain, frustration" experienced by first-year students at Stanford and elsewhere was also commented upon by Terman, who believed it to be an indirect response to Sputnik: concern that the United States was lagging the USSR in the development of scientific and engineering talent had placed enormous pressures on students throughout the educational system.[21]

The suicide of a Wilbur Hall student in late 1960 and the subsequent discovery that some high-school counselors had stopped recommending Stanford to their college-bound students, forced university administrators and faculty again to consider how the undergraduate experience at Stanford might be improved. While faculty committees were created on instruction in the freshman year and on undergraduate education, ultimately little effort was put toward addressing the inadequacies of undergraduate instruction.[22] Rhinelander did initiate an effort to improve instruction in freshman courses, discussing with the chairperson of the biology department, Victor Twitty, the possibility of using more faculty members in the introductory biology course. But Twitty quickly rejected the idea, reminding Rhinelander of the structural limits to educational reform. If the administration required faculty members to do more teaching, they would have less time for the research that was essential to the university, both in establishing its prestige and in attracting the patronage upon which the university depended. To hire additional faculty to perform teaching duties would be "prohibitively expensive." "The awkward but inescapable fact," Twitty concluded, was that "at Stanford, as well as in all American universities, we are attempting to accomplish two quite different and almost incompatible things"—undergraduate instruction and research and graduate-level training.[23]

The use of graduate students in the biology laboratory courses—a practice about which undergraduates had consistently complained—was unavoidable, the two men agreed. Twitty suggested taking disciplinary steps against graduate students to force them to pay more attention to their attitude about undergraduate instruction. It was also agreed that the laboratory course would be held half as often, allowing the university to reduce by half the number of graduate students employed but to pay them more in order to improve morale. It was a solution dictated by the financial constraints and structure of the cold war university; whether undergraduates experienced an improvement in instruction is doubtful. They interacted with an instructor half as often as before, the work for each class was now intensified, and students were assigned more work outside of class.[24]

While the effort to improve instruction was limited, Stanford's administration took other measures aimed at softening the edges of an institution that all agreed was inhospitable to undergraduates. In essence, administrators followed the recommendations made by Farnsworth in *Mental Health in College and University*. Upon the recommendation of its committee on instruction in the freshman year, the administration increased the counseling staff at the student health center and hired a full-time psychiatrist. It also took the path already agreed upon by Yale, Cornell, Princeton, and Harvard and abolished the use of the grading curve.[25] And, at the recommendation of Dean

Rhinelander, the university established a "faculty residents" program, placing faculty members in student dormitories with the aims of breaking down the barriers between the classroom and student life, challenging the prevailing anti-intellectualism on campus, and providing students with mentors.

One of the first faculty residents was Allard K. Lowenstein, who accepted the invitation of Stanford's dean of students to take up residence in Stern Hall in the fall of 1961. The dean of students had invited Lowenstein because he knew him to be gifted at working with and inspiring young people. Intellectually and politically precocious and committed to carrying forward the tradition of American liberalism, Lowenstein had coordinated youth campaigns for Adlai Stevenson's presidential bids and had recruited students for the College Association of the United Nations and the National Student Association in the 1950s; he was more widely known for his book *Brutal Mandate,* a travel account and commentary on the political and social inequalities in Southwest Africa.[26]

If the university's goal was to stimulate students and replace apathy and anxiety with energy and intellectual enthusiasm, Lowenstein was an excellent choice. Indeed, Stern Hall, long rated by students as one of the worst dormitories on campus, became, during Lowenstein's tenure, a lively place and a hub of student activity, as Lowenstein encouraged students to humanize the dormitory by decorating it themselves and to challenge the social eminence of fraternities. Lowenstein also succeeded in stimulating students to think and care about world affairs, national politics, and the civil rights movement, as well as about the nature of the university itself. But if the cold war university could not accommodate a scholar such as Sibley, it could not tolerate the presence of an activist like Lowenstein. By the end of the year, Lowenstein's stint at Stanford was over.[27]

Students did not relapse into apathy on his departure, however. Lowenstein acolytes, acting as dormitory sponsors, student body presidents, or editors of the student paper, encouraged other students to think about the social and political issues to which Lowenstein had drawn their attention and concern. Students also began to articulate more fully their complaints about undergraduate education and the place of undergraduates in the multiversity.[28] When, in the late 1960s, university administrators once again addressed the issue of undergraduate life and undergraduate teaching, it was not in response to parental concerns about student anxiety and unhappiness, but rather in response to organized pressure from the undergraduates themselves who clearly stated their views about how undergraduate education and life within the university could be improved. But student activism by then was not limited to the goal of improving the lot of the undergraduate within the multiversity. In exploring the source of their own unhappiness within the university, students had also developed a critique of the structure, functions, and finances of the cold war university itself.

Epilogue

The indictment of the cold war university by student activists did not initiate the discussion of the university's structure and function, nor did it politicize that discussion. The discussion had begun decades earlier among university administrators and some faculty members; it had always had a political dimension, as men like Donald Tresidder, Vannevar Bush, and others well knew. Student activists simply insisted on making these discussions more public and broadening them by bringing to them a viewpoint shaped by their particular experiences within the multiversity and by their understanding of larger political and social forces. Whether or not one shares this viewpoint does not alter the fact that students responded to, rather than initiated, the politicization of the university.

Some critics of today's university assert that its current flaws are the responsibility of the student activists who they claim succeeded in imposing their agenda on university campuses.[29] In fact, very little of the activists' agenda was ever realized. Some students called for an end to war-related research on university campuses and a severing of the relationship between the university and the Defense Department; these calls were ignored by university administrators. Also demanded was the barring from campus of classified research, a demand met in some instances but in a way that involved cosmetic changes rather than a rethinking of the university's purpose and its relationship to its patrons. The involvement of university professors in research that some found objectionable and in violation of the university's traditional commitment to open inquiry continued; the work was simply conducted off campus by professors acting as consultants. Some of the goals of student activists were met—for example, the expansion of the curriculum to include previously neglected topics such as ethnic studies. But university administrators were willing to accommodate these demands in large part because they required no fundamental alteration of the university's financial structure and function. Student activism, significant politically and culturally, did not alter the postwar university's role in society or its relationship to the political economy. As Clark Kerr observed in the 1980s, "The Harvard of 1982 is not all that different from the Harvard of 1963, or the Berkeley of 1982 from that of 1963. . . . The big research university is particularly impervious to structural change."[30]

The decades of the 1960s, 1970s, and 1980s did see fluctuations in the amount of federal and industrial patronage provided for academic research. But the basic relationships that had been established since the Second World War, both between the university and its patrons and within the university itself, persisted. The federal government continued to provide large amounts of money for defense-related basic and applied research in major universities. Industry, with the encouragement of federal patrons, continued to feed off of the knowledge produced to develop products for the military. This triangular relationship, or in Terman's words, this "win-win-win" relationship, was broadened in the 1980s as federal policy became aimed explicitly at fostering university-industry interaction in fields such as biotechnology, which had no direct relevance to the national defense but were justified as crucial to the maintenance of America's economic competitiveness in a global economy.

This close cooperation among industry, the university, and the federal government was not an inevitable development but was shaped by particular people with particular aims in mind at a particular historical moment. In the case of the university administrators who were involved in this development, institutional needs and ideology reinforced each other. In the years before World War II, university administrators who supported the development of close ties between industry and universities did not imagine that these hoped-for ties might depend on federal patronage. But the financial straits created by the Great Depression pushed even conservative academic administrators to postpone the search for industrial support and to seek federal aid. It was the OSRD's practice of letting contracts for research during World War II, the innovation of political conservative Vannevar Bush, that formed the basis of the postwar federal-university relationship. The context of war, both hot and cold, and the use of contracts, implying payment for services rendered rather than a government subsidy, made it possible for university administrators to ignore the contradiction between their ideological opposition to federal aid and their practice of depending heavily on the federal government for both research support and overhead payments.

The genius of the postwar generation of university administrators, such as Frederick Terman, was to recognize that the university's relationship to the federal government need not be seen as an alternative to a relationship to private industry; in fact, the university's relationship to one had to be intricately bound up in the university's relationship with the other if either were to prove lucrative. Terman understood that industry would see participation in this triangular relationship as a "win"; it stood to profit from both research and the training of potential employees that was being paid for with taxpayers' money. The university "won" its long-standing aims—industrial patronage, consulting opportunities for its scientists and employment for its students.

The forging of ties to patrons—industrial and governmental—required a reorientation of the university's role in society and an explicit commitment of "service" to specific patrons. This redefinition of the university and its relation to the political economy, in turn, necessitated changes within the university, in the role of faculty members, and in the academic disciplines themselves. Of these changes, the most recognized and commented upon has been the predominance in the multiversity of academic entrepreneurs—faculty members evincing little interest in, or ability to, teach, who devote their energies to attracting patronage and building research empires, who demonstrate little sense of purpose larger than obtaining the next research grant. In the eyes of many, such behavior is hardly admirable, and it is not surprising that some critics of today's institutions of higher education point to these academic entrepreneurs as the source of the university's ills.[31]

But as this history makes clear, the academic entrepreneur was a product, not the creator, of the cold war university. To be sure, there have always been professors who have single-mindedly pursued research support and public attention to the neglect of their responsibilities to students and colleagues. But the cold war university, structured to depend on faculty members' relationships to external patrons and ability to attract their support, made academic entrepreneurship the rule rather than the exception. With salaries and even positions within the university dependent upon outside support, with promotion dependent upon research, which required external support, with no institutional rewards for energies devoted to undergraduate instruction, academic scientists and scholars not surprisingly became avid seekers of grants and contracts. A desire for fame and power may have motivated some; most, however, simply responded rationally to the university's system of rewards and penalties.

While the academic entrepreneur is largely the product of the cold war university, this creature is unlikely to disappear despite the end of the cold war. As long as the university continues to depend upon external patronage and to use figures such as the amount of research published and the number of Ph.D.s produced as indices of academic prestige, academic entrepreneurship will persist, as will the penalties for behaving otherwise.[32] Pressure on faculty members to seek patronage may well even increase as today's universities face budgetary crises as severe as any since the 1940s, perhaps even since the Great Depression. Huge cuts in state support for higher education have created financial difficulties for many universities; in addition, federal support is no longer expected to expand, and in some areas, such as the humanities and the social sciences, it has already contracted significantly. Faced with increased competition for less money, university administrators, much as their counterparts of a half-century ago, talk openly of "downsizing," of making the university more efficient, of requiring more work from faculty members without offering additional rewards, and of finding new sources of patronage. A reputable institution, Bennington College, recently abolished tenure, allowing it more easily to punish faculty members who do not satisfy the administration's aims of attracting patronage, garnering prestige, and making the college better reflect current definitions of national significance. It is likely only a matter of time before other institutions follow suit.

Treating the university as a business enterprise is certainly not new; what is new is the prevalence with which administrators speak openly of imposing the values and practices of the business world on their institutions. In 1994 the *Chronicle of Higher Education* reported that Hahnemann University had "threatened to fire anyone who doesn't attract research grants that provide between 50 and 100 per cent of his or her salary." In justifying this action, the dean of the university's School of Medicine explained, "If IBM expects [productivity] from its employees, why should we not expect it of the academic community? It's a big business."[33] That the dean intended no irony in likening the university to IBM reveals the extent to which the ideas of postwar university administrators like Frederick Terman have pervaded the academic world; it also says much about the problems at the heart of today's institutions of higher education.

When, over fifty years ago, Stanford administrators began seeking increased productivity from faculty members and pressuring academic departments to make appointments and move into research areas of interest to potential patrons, some professors objected. They were not "mere employees," they insisted, but independent scholars and scientists. These professors saw university administrators, in their efforts to restructure the university, purposely erode faculty control over the shape and content of their departments and by extension, over the academic disciplines. Indeed, in a university becoming heavily dependent on external patronage, "impractical" fields, such as classics, which were unlikely to attract funding from the Defense Department or other major cold war patrons, did not fare well in comparison to high-energy physics or nuclear engineering. Similarly, some subfields of biology and political science, which, for a variety of reasons but not because of lack of intellectual or social merit, did not attract patronage, withered during the cold war. The role of university administrators in mediating the relationship between professors and patrons and in pressing the former to meet the needs of the latter has been ignored by those critics of the university who blame federal patrons for distorting the content of and balance between academic disciplines. Changes in the academic disciplines could not have occurred without the active involvement of university administrators who pressured faculty members to make changes in their departments, and sometimes in their own research plans, to attract this patronage. These changes also could not have occurred without the eager assistance of some faculty members and the passive compliance of many others. The inability of faculty members to unite across departmental and status lines to confront the forces controlling their institutions was crucial to the creation of the cold war university.

So was the absence of open and searching discussion about the role of the university and its relationship to the political economy. The discussion that might have occurred at the end of World War II was stifled by the chilling atmosphere of the early cold war and by those university administrators who, committed to a particular course, worked to suppress the few insistent critics among faculty members. Today, with the cold war behind us, there ought to be no impediment to such discussion. Whether such a discussion, if it does occur, proves substantive will depend both on who is encouraged to participate and on whether the participants address squarely the critical questions: What is the proper role of the university in American society? And can the university truly define its role independently of the nexus of forces upon which it has become dependent?

Abbreviations Used in the Notes

AEC   Atomic Energy Commission records, U.S. Department of Energy

CAUCBO   *Central Association of University and College Business Officers*

DLW   David Locke Webster papers, Stanford University Archives

FB   Felix Bloch papers, Stanford University Archives

FET   Frederick E. Terman papers, Stanford University Archives

FF   Ford Foundation collections, Ford Foundation Archives

JAAU   *Journal of the Proceedings and Addresses of the Annual Conference of the Association of American Universities*

JCAE   Joint Committee on Atomic Energy records, National Archives

JWS   J. Wallace Sterling papers, Stanford University Archives

LMT   Lewis M. Terman papers, Stanford University Archives

LS   Leonard Schiff papers, Stanford University Archives

NACA   National Advisory Committee on Aeronautics records, Federal Records Center, Suitland, Maryland

OSRD   Office of Scientific Research and Development records, National Archives and Federal Records Center, Suitland, Maryland

PE   Paul Edwards papers, Stanford University Archives

RDB   Research and Development Board records, National Archives

RLW   Ray Lyman Wilbur papers, Stanford University Archives

SLAC   Stanford Linear Accelerator records, Stanford Linear Accelerator Center Archives

SOE   School of Engineering papers, Stanford University Archives

WWH   William W. Hansen papers, Stanford University Archives

Note: Unless otherwise stated, "Terman" refers to Frederick Terman.

Notes

Introduction

1. This brief description, a composite of the characteristics of the leading universities, cannot encompass the variations among America's universities. For example, both Clark University and Johns Hopkins University made, to a greater extent than the other universities, scientific research in the pursuit of truth their defining purpose. The public universities such as the University of Wisconsin and the University of California, along with Cornell and Stanford, placed a relatively greater stress on the idea of service, although this was variously conceived. For the classic treatment of the early university, see Veysey, *Emergence of the American University.* Some land grant universities, through their agricultural experiment stations, did serve the federal government. See Dupree, *Science in the Federal Government.*

2. Kerr, *Uses of the University,* pp. 53–55.

3. In search of the determining factors that create successful "science regions" are Kargon, Leslie, and Schoenberger in "Far beyond Big Science." Kerr's celebration of "the city of intellect," or the "new Ideopolis," may be found in *Uses of the University,* pp. 91–94; 123–26.

4. On the development of "big science," see, for example, Galison and Hevly, eds., *Big Science,* and Heilbron and Seidel, *Lawrence and His Laboratory.* On the social sciences, see, for example, Heims, *The Cybernetics Group*; Klausner and Lidz, *Nationalization of the Social Sciences*; Seidelman, *Disenchanted Realists*; and Geiger, *Research and Relevant Knowledge,* pp. 92–116.

5. Kerr, *Uses of the University,* pp. 41–45, 90. Kerr himself did not use the term *academic entrepreneur,* but referred to the "affluent professor" and the professor who had taken on "the characteristics of an entrepreneur." Others critical of academic entrepreneurs and the state of undergraduate education in the cold war university include Nisbet, *Degradation of the Academic Dogma*; Sykes, *Profscam*; and Smith, *Killing the Spirit.*

6. Nisbet, *Degradation of the Academic Dogma*; Ridgeway, *The Closed Corporation*; and Davidson, "Towards a Student Syndicalist Movement."

7. For conservative attacks on the university and a "multicultural" curriculum, see Bloom, *Closing of the American Mind*; and D'Souza, *Illiberal Education*. The standard right-wing attack on today's professoriate, purportedly dominated by former anti–Vietnam War activitists, may be found in Gingrich, *To Renew America*, pp. 217–22. On the relationship between universities, the federal government, and particular industrial enterprises, see Dickson, *The New Politics of Science*; Noble, *Forces of Production*; and Noble, "The Selling of the University." Among those stressing the economic benefits of state-supported science is Ramo, *The Business of Science*.

8. Among those idealizing the prewar university are Shils, "The University," and Nisbet, *Degradation of the Academic Dogma*. For a discussion of the university's exclusionary practices, see Synnott, *The Half-Opened Door.*

9. For criticisms of students for purportedly politicizing the universities, see Hook, *In Defense of Academic Freedom*. Subsequently, historians of the cold war university have pointed to the excesses committed by student activists, with the effect, unintended or otherwise, of drawing attention away from the content of students' criticisms. See, for example, Geiger, *Research and Relevant Knowledge*, pp. 230–42; and Leslie, *Cold War and American Science,* pp. 233–56.

10. See, for example, May, *Homeward Bound*; Boyer, *By the Bomb's Early Light*; Weart, *Nuclear Fear*; and Winkler, *Life under a Cloud.*

11. See, for example, *New York Times,* 14 March 1991, Sec. A, 23/1; *New York Times,* 23 April 1991, Sec. A, 12/4; and *New York Times,* 31 July 1991, Sec. A, 16/1. Typical of the enthusiastic literature on Silicon Valley is Everett and Larsen, *Silicon Valley Fever.* In the 1980s conservative critics of university curricula also focused on Stanford. For a typical, if unimaginative, diatribe, see D'Souza, *Illiberal Education.*

12. The most thorough and concise presentation of the literature which supports this interpretation may be found in Balogh, *Chain Reaction,* pp. 1–20. For a discussion of the social sciences, see Klausner and Lidz, *Nationalization of the Social Sciences*; Heims, *Cybernetics Group*; and Needell, " 'Truth Is Our Weapon.' "

13. Those histories depicting academic scientists taking advantage of military patronage for their own ends include Leslie, *Cold War and American Science.* For a convincing presentation of the argument that federal patrons "used" scientists and influenced the direction of their work, see Forman, "Behind Quantum Electronics."

14. Veblen, *Higher Learning in America.* Veblen was not alone in his hostility to those guiding the leading universities; see Veysey, *Emergence of the American University,* for the history of early tensions between trustees, presidents, and members of the faculty.

15. Kevles, *Physicists,* remains the most engaging general history of the American physics community in the twentieth century that also touches on changes in the funding of research, and more broadly, on developments in the academic community.

16. This point is made by Geiger, "American Foundations."

17. On the Red Scare, see Schrecker, *No Ivory Tower*; and Diamond, *Compro-*

mised Campus. For an emphasis on patrons, see Heims, *Cybernetics Group.* Somit and Tanenhaus, in *Development of Political Science,* see the postwar emphasis on quantification as emerging from a progressive impulse within the social science disciplines themselves. Ross, in *Origins of American Social Science,* sees the scientistic approach to studying society as firmly entrenched in the social science disciplines by the early twentieth century; this, however, overstates the extent to which scientism had established hegemony within the social sciences.

18. Among the best of the sociological studies that still fall prey to the above mentioned problems, are Touraine, *The Academic System*; and Ben-David, *American Higher Education.* The most thorough historical examination of the leading research universities in the twentieth century is Roger Geiger's two-volume study: *To Advance Knowledge* and *Research and Relevant Knowledge.* However, Geiger relies heavily on published sources, which reflect the views of university administrators and thus present an incomplete picture.

19. For an interesting study of the postwar social sciences and patronage by a sociologist who takes note of "direct and indirect interlocks" between scientists, universities, foundations, and government agencies, see O'Connell, "Social Structure and Science."

20. Among historians who have seen the 1930s as significant for understanding changes in the organization of physics, or in the university, see Heilbron and Seidel, *Lawrence and His Laboratory*; and Lecuyer, "The Making of a Technological University."

21. Owens, "MIT and the 'Federal Angel.'"

22. Only a handful of leading research universities became the managers of, and sites for, wartime laboratories. These included Johns Hopkins University, the University of California, MIT, Caltech, and Harvard. The medical section of the Office of Scientific Research and Development (OSRD) as well as other federal agencies sponsored small research projects at a number of different universities, including Stanford.

23. The term has been used, largely pejoratively, by critics of the multiversity, including Nisbet and most recently by Sykes in *Profscam.* Historians of science have adopted the term without necessarily implying a negative judgment.

24. For a good study of Lewis Terman, see Minton, *Lewis M. Terman.* For discussions of corporate progressivism, see Hawley, *Herbert Hoover as Secretary of Commerce*; and Hoff-Wilson, *Herbert Hoover, Forgotten Progressive.*

25. Lewis Terman, Terence Terman, Frederick Terman, Jr., and his wife, Bobbie Terman, interview by author, Stanford University, 29 May 1992.

Chapter 1.   The Thirties

1. *New York Times,* 5 March 1933, p. 1; Bauman, *Eye of the Great Depression,* pp. 3–5; Best, *Herbert Hoover,* pp. 1–7. Among the best overviews of the depression and the New Deal are Leuchtenburg, *Franklin D. Roosevelt*; and Badger, *The New Deal.*

2. For a detailed history of the founding and early years of the university, see Elliott, *Stanford*.

3. See Veysey, *Emergence of the American University*, for a history of the late-nineteenth-century transformation of higher education.

4. See Nash's study of Hoover's involvement in the affairs of Stanford University, *Herbert Hoover*, p. 32. The two trustees were J. D. Grant and Leon Sloss, both of whom were directors of the General Petroleum Company.

5. Elliott, *Stanford*, p. 296; on Stanford University's early financial problems in general, see Elliott, *Stanford*, pp. 251–308.

6. Herbert Hoover to David Starr Jordan, 9 May 1913, Series I-A, Box 89, David Starr Jordan papers, Stanford University Archives, as cited in Nash, *Herbert Hoover*, pp. 34–5.

7. See Nash, *Herbert Hoover*, pp. 41–45, and Elliott, *Stanford*, pp. 534–56.

8. Herbert Hoover to W. Mayo Newhall, president, Stanford University board of trustees, 25 October 1914, Pre-Commerce Series, Herbert Hoover Presidential Library papers, as quoted in Nash, *Herbert Hoover*, p. 50.

9. Gruber, *Mars and Minerva*, pp. 213–52.

10. See, for example, Kolko, *The Triumph of Conservatism*; and Koistinen, *The Military-Industrial Complex*. Cuff, in *The War Industries Board*, emphasizes the hesitancy and impermanence of relations between industry and the federal government during World War I; he does not examine the role of the scientific or academic communities in the war.

11. Kevles, *Physicists*, pp. 109–17, and Geiger, *To Advance Knowledge*, pp. 94–101.

12. Kevles, *Physicists*, pp. 148–54; Geiger, *To Advance Knowledge*, pp. 98–100; and Kohler, *Partners in Science*, pp. 82–87. To G.E.'s Willis Whitney, who asked, "Why should science, which is back of every one of our comforts, conveniences, and facilities today, be a matter the advancement of which, in the United States, is subject to the whims of philanthropists?" Hale responded with the query, "Do you think, for instance, that any great good would result if all of our educational institutions were run by the government and supported by tax payers?" (Goodstein, *Millikan's School*, p. 84).

13. See Hawley, "Herbert Hoover, The Commerce Secretariat"; and Hawley, *Herbert Hoover as Secretary of Commerce*.

14. Kevles, *Physicists*, pp. 185–87, and Nash, *Herbert Hoover*, p. 65.

15. Geiger, *To Advance Knowledge*, p. 125, Table 7.

16. See Geiger, *To Advance Knowledge*, pp. 123–25. Among those schools benefiting disproportionately from postwar philanthropic largess was Throop College, a tiny technical school in Pasadena, California, of which Hale was a trustee. Shortly after the war, the college became the California Institute of Technology, made Millikan its president, and began successfully cultivating enormous support from local patrons, national foundations, and private corporations.

In comparison with the private universities, the leading state universities received little in the way of private gifts and grants. They did, however, benefit from increased postwar enrollments, which boosted income from tuition, and from generous state allocations, both of which allowed them to support academic research to a greater extent than before World War I (Geiger, *To Advance Knowledge,* p. 248).

17. Nash, *Herbert Hoover,* p. 67–70, 72. Between 1924 and 1929, Stanford received a total of $750,000 from the Rockefeller Foundation's General Education Board, well behind Caltech, which received almost $3 million, but ahead of Harvard, which received $400,000 (see Geiger, *To Advance Knowledge,* p. 162).

18. Nash, *Herbert Hoover,* p. 74; Hallion, *Legacy of Flight,* pp. 45–70.

19. Herbert Hoover to Ray Lyman Wilbur, 11 November 1915, E. D. Adams Papers, Stanford University Archives, as quoted in Nash, *Herbert Hoover,* p. 54. See also pp. 38–39 and 62–64.

20. He also rejected Hoover's proposal in the late 1920s that the Hoover Library be converted into a research institute staffed with well-paid professors with no teaching duties. Creating positions that conveyed special privileges and higher salaries would damage the morale of the university's faculty, Wilbur had argued; to do so would also imply a devaluation of the university's commitment to teaching (Nash, *Herbert Hoover,* p. 83). On the university's administrative structure, see Lewis M. Terman to Guy S. Ford, 13 March 1941, LMT papers, Box 18/11; and Elliott, *Stanford,* pp. 480–94.

21. Hoover to Wilbur, [November 1924?], Box 106, Ray Lyman Wilbur Personal Papers, Stanford University Archives, as quoted in Nash, *Herbert Hoover,* p. 73.

22. Veysey, in *Emergence of the American University,* pp. 381–438, discusses the Ross case and similar incidents elsewhere in the context of the development of ideas about both academic freedom and the American university. Other historians have looked at the Ross case and other challenges to academic freedom to understand disciplinary developments within the professionalized social sciences. See, for example, Ross, *Origins of American Social Science,* pp. 180, 229–32, 250–52.

23. Geiger, *To Advance Knowledge,* pp. 36–38, 74.

24. Best, *Herbert Hoover,* p. 27; and Paul Davis, oral history, Stanford University Archives.

25. See Geiger, *To Advance Knowledge,* pp. 247–49. For the most comprehensive discussion of the depression's impact on all institutions of higher education, see Wiley, *Depression.*

26. *Report of the President of Stanford University, 1939–40,* Stanford University Archives.

27. Wilbur to Board of Trustees, Stanford University, 10 May 1933, Collection 0183, Stanford University Archives.

28. Karl T. Compton, "Income from Endowment as Affected by Conditions of the Investment Market," *Journal of the Proceedings and Addresses of the Annual Conference of the Association of American Universities* (hereinafter, *JAAU*), 38th meeting (1937), pp. 65–77; Wilbur, "Committee on Endowment Income," *JAAU,* 42rd meeting (1941), pp. 48–53; William J. S. Ritscher, Northwestern University, "Investment Policies of Universities," *Central Association of University and College Business Officers* (hereinafter, *CAUCBO*), 25th meeting (1935), pp. 62–76. For a sample of Hoover's private and public fulminations against

Roosevelt's spending and monetary policies, see Best, *Herbert Hoover*, pp. 7, 52, 64, 69–70.

29. See Mitchell, *Campaign of the Century*.

30. Roosevelt was also responding to pressure from advisors convinced that redistributive taxation would spur economic recovery. See Leuchtenburg, *Franklin D. Roosevelt*, pp. 151–53; and Badger, *The New Deal*, pp. 102–5.

31. James R. Angell, "The Reporter," *Journal of Higher Education*, 6/2 (February 1935), p. 108.

32. It also authorized industrial corporations to deduct from taxable income up to 5 percent of net profits for contributions in aid of research and education (see Kevles, *Physicists*, p. 267). See also Blakey and Blakey, *The Federal Income Tax*.

33. Thomas S. Gates, "Problems of the University in Relation to Current Economic Trends," *JAAU*, 38th meeting (1937), p. 60.

34. J. Harvey Cain, "Trends—What Financial Problems Lie Ahead?" *CAUCBO*, 28th meeting (1938), pp. 86–95; Geiger, *To Advance Knowledge*, p. 248.

35. Gates, "Problems of the University," p. 61. See also Wiley, *Depression*, pp. 30, 164–181, 367, 384–85.

36. Mirrielees, *Stanford*, p. 222.

37. David Locke Webster to President Wilbur, 4 June 1935, DLW papers, Box 10; and Webster, "Notes of the Super Voltage X-Ray Project," DLW papers, Box 1, Notebook 3. See also Peter Galison, Bruce Hevly, and Rebecca Lowen, "Controlling the Monster," in Galison and Hevly, *Big Science*, pp. 48–50. On the foundations' changing agenda during the depression, see Kohler, *Partners in Science*, pp. 233–34, 262; and Kevles, *Physicists*, pp. 247–50.

38. Robert Seidel, "The Origins of the Lawrence Berkeley Laboratory," in Galison and Hevly, *Big Science*, pp. 27–28; see also, Heilbron and Seidel, *Lawrence and His Laboratory*, p. 207.

39. David Locke Webster to Frederick Terman, 2 May 1939, FET papers, Box 2/4/15.

40. Webster, unpublished autobiography, DLW papers, Box 10; Paul Kirkpatrick, interview by author, Stanford University, 26 April 1988. For a good description of research conditions in Stanford's physics department in the 1930s, see William W. Hansen, "The Klystron," WWH papers, Box 4/35. According to Hansen, "[A]ny faculty member might count himself very lucky to have $500 to spend in one year." Because of the shortage of funds, all the physicists found themselves designing and making much of their own equipment. When the physicists needed a vacuum tank, for example, Hansen designed it, purchased the parts himself, physically moved the requisite one ton of steel himself, designed the needed welding equipment, and then did the welding himself.

41. Embree, "In Order of Their Eminence," pp. 653–66. For Stanford trustees' reaction to the *Atlantic* article, see Templeton Peck, "Paul C. Edwards: From Newsman to Trustees' President," *Sandstone and Tile*, 11/1 (Fall 1986), pp. 2–11, Stanford University Archives.

42. Fred Bush, Sinclair Prairie Oil Company, to Hubert Schenk, 16 August

1939, FET papers, Box 2/2/4; Harold Benjamin to Lewis Terman, 17 November 1939, LMT papers, Box 18/1.

43. Paul Davis to Harry B. Reynolds, 31 March 1937, FET papers, Box 2/2/14.

44. See Wilbur's comments at the annual meeting of the Association of American Universities, *JAAU,* 43rd meeting (1941), p. 51.

45. Wiley, *Depression,* pp. 375–81.

46. For figures on Stanford, see *Review of Activities of the State Relief Administration of California, 1933–1935* (Sacramento: State Printing Office, 1936), Appendix M, p. 271; and *Report of the President of Stanford University, 1933–34.* Among those schools refusing governmental assistance were elite liberal arts colleges (Haverford, Bennington, Bryn Mawr, Wheaton, Sarah Lawrence) and Catholic colleges, including Notre Dame. See Walter J. Greenleaf, "Federal Aid to College Students," *Journal of Higher Education* 6/2 (February 1935), pp. 94–97.

47. Ray Lyman Wilbur to A. E. Roth, 31 October 1933, RLW papers, Box 86, "United States." See Judd, *U.S. Office of Education,* p. 18, which notes the reluctance of some private institutions to comply with the office's requests and suggests how federal aid might be used to enforce compliance.

48. See Kargon and Hodes, "Karl Compton."

49. Harold Dodds, "Problems Arising from the Relationship of Educational Institutions to the Government," *JAAU,* 38th meeting (1937), pp. 82–85; and Dodds, "Symposium on the Relation of the Federal Government to Higher Education," *JAAU* 40th meeting (1939), pp. 80–91. See also Robert Millikan, "Symposium on Centralizing Tendencies in American Education: Governmental Funds and Controls," *JAAU* (1941), pp. 65–70.

50. See Guy Stanton Ford, president, University of Minnesota, "Symposium on the Relation of the Federal Government to Higher Education," *JAAU,* 41st meeting (1940), p. 105.

51. Charles Seymour, "The University Curriculum in its Relation to Public Service," *JAAU,* 38th meeting (1937), pp. 98–105.

52. Among the exceptions were Karl Compton and Frank P. Graham, the liberal president of the University of North Carolina. For Graham's sharp response to criticisms of federal support for higher education, see Graham, "Symposium on Centralizing Tendencies in American Education: Governmental Funds and Controls," *JAAU,* 42nd meeting (1941), pp. 72–76. James Conant suggested that the universities might act together, through the AAU, to set standards of acceptability should the federal government become a supporter of academic science (see Conant, "Future of University Research in Relation to Financial Support," *JAAU,* 38th meeting [1937], p. 79).

53. A. W. Peterson, comptroller, University of Wisconsin, "The Relation of Colleges and Universities to the Federal Government and to Federal Agencies," *CAUCBO,* 25th meeting (1935), p. 34. See also Dan T. Gray, dean, College of Agriculture, University of Arkansas, "New State and Federal Appropriations for Instruction, Research and Extension in Agriculture," *CAUCBO* 26th meeting (1936), p. 32; Fay E. Smith, secretary of the trustees of the University of Wyoming, "Relationship between Federal and State Government in the

Budgetary Control of State Institutions," *CAUCBO,* 27th meeting (1937), p. 106; and Coffman, *The State University.*

54. James B. Conant to Wilbur, 15 February 1937, DT papers, Box 22/1.

55. Conant, "Future of University Research in Relation to Financial Support," *JAAU,* 38th meeting (1937), pp. 78–81. Conant's suggestion that private industry and the private universities might be ideological allies as well as potential partners in the development and exploitation of the results of academic science was echoed by representatives of a number of industrial concerns and the U.S. Chamber of Commerce in the mid-1930s. Herbert Hoover repeated the theme in a 1939 speech asserting that unemployment could be solved by creating new industries, the source of which would be the academic scientific research that led inevitably to the inventions and applications upon which industrial innovation was based (see Kevles, *Physicists,* p. 263).

56. Servos, "The Industrial Relations of Science."

57. See Elliott G. Reid to G. W. Lewis, 12 March 1940, NACA Papers, Central Correspondence File, 1915–42, Box 54.

58. Donald Tresidder to Paul Edwards, president, Stanford board of trustees, 2 March 1944, PE papers, Box 2/2/3.

59. See Servos, "The Industrial Relations of Science."

60. See Frederick Terman to Samuel Morris, dean of engineering, 29 April 1937, FET papers, Box 2/3/9; Terman, "Information on CalTech," 10 May 1937, FET papers, Box 2/3/9; and Terman, "Comparisons of Harvard, CalTech, Stanford, and MIT," 12 May 1937, FET papers, Box 2/3/9.

61. Terman to Paul Davis, 29 October 1937, FET papers, Box 2/2/4; and Terman to Davis, 10 March 1938, FET papers, Box 2/2/4. Regarding the impulse generator, see Terman to Joseph Thompson, Pacific Electric Manufacturing Company, 13 January 1939, RLW papers, Box 101, "Electrical Engineering"; Terman to Charles V. Taylor, Gardner Manufacturing Company, 1 February 1939, FET papers, Box 2/4/7; and Al Pahl, KPF Electric Company, to Terman, 1 February 1939, FET papers, Box 2/4/8.

62. Varian, *The Inventor and the Pilot.*

63. President Wilbur to the Academic Council, 5 November 1937, DLW papers, Box 1. For information on the University of Wisconsin, see Geiger, *To Advance Research,* p. 251.

64. Agreement between the Board of Trustees of Stanford University and Sperry Gyroscope Company, 27 April 1938, DLW papers, Box 1.

65. Felix Bloch to William Hansen, 17 September 1942, WWH papers, Box 4/40.

66. Hansen, notes, [1937?], WWH papers, Box 3/33; Hansen to Webster, 30 January 1939, WWH papers, Box 1/10; and Hansen to the National Research Council, 9 May 1938, WWH papers, Box 1/9.

67. Felix Bloch to William Hansen, 26 September 1939, WWH papers, Box 2/13; Webster to Frederick Terman, 26 September 1941, FET papers, Box 2/3/6.

68. Webster, "Memo on conference with President Wilbur," 27 April 1938, DLW papers, Box 1; and Webster to Hugh Jackson, acting comptroller, Stanford University, 12 March 1938, WWH papers, Box 1/7.

69. Webster to Hugh Jackson, 13 May 1938, DLW papers, Box 1.

70. Russell Varian to Webster, 17 June 1939, Russell and Sigurd Varian papers, Box 22, Stanford University Archives.

71. Webster, memo to file, 14 June 1939, DLW papers, Addendum, Box 1; Webster to Hansen, 27 July 1939, WWH papers, Box 1/12.

72. Webster to Hansen, 30 May 1938, WWH papers, Box 1/8.

73. See Galison, Hevly, and Lowen, "Controlling the Monster," pp. 52–53.

74. Hansen to Webster, 23 October 1939, WWH papers, Box 2/4; Webster to Norris Bradbury, 10 March 1943, DLW papers, Box 10.

75. Webster, memo, 15 December 1939, DLW papers, Addendum, Box 1.

Chapter 2.   Stanford Goes to War

1. Because of the prominence of academic physicists in these projects, some have called the Second World War the "physicists' war"; see Kevles, *Physicists*, pp. 302–23. Studies of the postwar relationship between scientists and the federal government include Leslie, *Cold War and American Science*; Forman, "Behind Quantum Electronics"; Seidel, "Accelerating Science"; and Gilpin and Wright, *Scientists and National Policy-Making*.

2. See Owens, "Counterproductive Management," Appendix.

3. Most of the literature on scientists and universities during and after World War II assumes that the war produced a cataclysmic break with the past.

4. E. P. Lesley to Harry F. Guggenheim, 1 May 1939, SOE papers, Box 5/24.

5. Harry F. Guggenheim to Lesley, 9 May 1939, SOE papers, Box 5/24.

6. Minutes, Executive Committee, NACA, 10 January 1939, NACA papers, Minutes of the Executive Committee, Box 7; Vannevar Bush to Ames (draft), 28 March 1939, NACA papers, Central Correspondence Files, 1915–42, Box 55; and "Report on the Availability of Additional Funds for Contracts for Research in Educational Institutions," 19 October 1939, NACA papers, Central Correspondence Files, 1915–42, Box 55.

7. Samuel Morris to President Wilbur, 1 June 1939, RLW papers, Box 102, "School of Engineering"; Elliott Reid to G. W. Lewis, NACA, 25 August 1939, SOE papers, Box 5/24.

8. The conflicts between Stanford's aeronautical engineers and the NACA can be followed in correspondence in the SOE papers, Box 5/24, and in "Chronology of Contract Relations—NACA and Stanford University," July 1940, NACA papers, Central Correspondence Files, 1915–42, Box 61. Regarding the aeronautical engineers' views of industrial contracting, see Elliott G. Reid to G. W. Lewis, 12 March 1940, NACA papers, Central Correspondence Files, 1915–42, Box 60; and Elliott Reid to Ernest Neill, 3 December 1943, FET papers, Box 1/1/3.

9. See E. P. Lesley to G. W. Lewis, 5 December 1937, NACA papers, Central Correspondence Files, 1915–42, Box 60; and J. F. Victory to E. P. Lesley, 5 January 1937, NACA papers, Central Correspondence Files, 1915–42, Box 60. See also Roland, *Model Research*.

10. My analysis has been influenced by Owens, "MIT and the Federal

'Angel.'" Owens explains the ideological as well as practical appeal that contracts held for both university and governmental administrators.

11. See Lesley to G. W. Lewis, 22 May 1939, SOE papers, Box 5/24; Arthur Domonoske to Charles Lindbergh, (draft) 10 July 1939, SOE papers, Box 5/24; and Domonoske to Lindbergh, 14 July 1939, SOE papers, Box 5/24.

12. Erwin to Domonoske, 14 January 1941, DT papers, Box 4/1.

13. Domonoske to Lindbergh, 14 July 1939, SOE papers, Box 5/24.

14. Paul S. Johnston, "Report of the Coordinator of Research," 18 April 1940, NACA papers, Central Correspondence Files, 1915–42, Box 54.

15. Wilbur to George Zook, 19 July 1940, RLW papers, Box 112, "Stanford University National Defense Committee." See also Wilbur to Zook, 20 June 1941, RLW papers, Box 116, "Defense." Regarding salaries, see Morris to Wilbur, 16 April 1940, RLW papers, Box 107, "School of Engineering."

16. Baxter, *Scientists against Time,* p. 19.

17. See Vannevar Bush to Irvin Stewart, executive secretary, OSRD, 4 February 1942, OSRD papers, Entry 13, Box 22, "Overhead Survey," National Archives.

18. James Conant to Vannevar Bush, 30 April 1942, OSRD papers, Entry 13, Box 21, "Overhead, Salary Basis," National Archives.

19. Samuel Morris to Wilbur, 3 July 1940, RLW papers, Box 112, "Stanford University National Defense Committee." Morris was appointed committee chair because he had already begun developing a program for involving the engineering school in preparations for national defense.

20. Karl T. Compton to Vannevar Bush, 13 March 1941, OSRD papers, Entry 13, Box 21, "Overhead 1940–1942," National Archives. Regarding Stanford's contracts with the NDRC, see Wilbur to Board of Trustees, 21 October 1940, and Wilbur to the Trustees, 17 March 1941, RLW papers, Box 112, "Stanford University National Defense Committee."

21. Morris to Frank Jewett and James Conant, 18 March 1941, RLW papers, Box 112, "Stanford University National Defense Committee."

22. Baxter, *Scientists against Time,* Appendix C, p. 456.

23. See Vannevar Bush to Judge Sloss, 15 December 1941, Bush to Hoover, 4 February 1942, and Hoover to Bush, 5 February 1942, Vannevar Bush papers, Box 108/2521, Library of Congress.

24. Frank Fish Walker, Stanford financial vice-president, "Memo," 13 February 1942, and Wilbur to Colonel John N. Andrews, 10 February 1942, RLW papers, Box 120.

25. Morris to Wilbur, 12 January 1942, RLW papers, Box 117, "School of Engineering."

26. Wilbur to Dean Stouffer, University of Kansas, 8 April 1942, DT papers, Box 22/4. See also Wilbur to Stouffer, 16 June 1942, DT papers, Box 22/2.

27. John Dodds to Paul Fejos, 31 December 1942, University Services papers, Box 2, Stanford University Archives. Dodds, a professor of humanities, was expressing disappointment over the military's rejection of his offer to provide courses for "morale officers." "What hurts me is the shortsightedness of those who fail to see that the Humanities, far from being frills, have something deep and integral to contribute to those who are waging ideological warfare."

28. Paul Davis to Frederick Terman, 18 April 1942, FET papers, Box 1/1/2.

29. For information on the army's investigation, see Donald Tresidder, memo of meeting with Colonel Eden, Lt. Colonels Bruns and Hulett, and Frank Walker, 19 November 1943, DT papers, Box 28/14. For information on the various training programs undertaken at Stanford during the war, see *Report of the President of Stanford University, 1942–1946,* Stanford University Archives.

30. Paul Kirkpatrick to David Locke Webster, 10 December 1942, and Kirkpatrick to Webster, 3 April 1943, DLW papers, Box 10; Paul Kirkpatrick, interview by author, Stanford University, 26 April 1988.

31. Karl Spangenberg to Terman, 5 April 1942, FET papers, Box 1/1/8. Spangenberg quickly changed his mind, perhaps fearing criticisms or questions about his loyalty. On 8 April 1942, he wrote Terman, "I almost let myself be talked into" the idea that "effective research" could not be done at Stanford. "I feel sure that good research can be done around here." FET papers, Box 1/1/8.

32. Samuel Morris to Tresidder, 21 December 1943, RLW papers, Box 134.

33. Morris to Wilbur, 3 July 1940, RLW papers, Box 112, "SUNDC"; Stanford National Emergency Committee to Wilbur, 5 January 1942, RLW papers, Box 116, "Defense." For evidence of Wilbur's concerns about costs as they related to gift procurement efforts during the war, see Lou Roseberry to Morgan Gunst, 31 March 1941, PE papers, Box 2/2/1, and Paul Davis to Wilbur, 5 January 1942, PE papers, Box 1/1/4.

34. Paul Davis, oral history, Stanford University Archives.

35. Donald Tresidder to Herbert Hoover, 23 December 1941, DT papers, Box 38/1, Stanford University Archives.

36. Paul Davis to Donald Tresidder, 20 November 1942, RLW papers, Box 125, "Board of Trustees Planning and Development Committee"; Paul Hanna, interview by author, Stanford University, 26 March 1986.

37. Paul Davis, "Proposal to Organize Stanford Resources for Public Service," 24 August 1942, FET papers, Box 1/1/2.

38. Salary expenses were also lowered, of course, when faculty members left campus for war-related work elsewhere. By the spring of 1943, Stanford had saved almost $180,000 that would normally have been expended on salaries. See "Salary Savings, 1943," RLW papers, Box 124, "President's Office"; and Irvin Stewart, Memo to NDRC-OSRD, 31 January 1942, OSRD papers, Entry 13, Box 21, "Overhead, 1940–42," National Archives. See also Babbidge and Rosenzweig, *The Federal Interest,* pp. 13–16.

39. Davis to Wilbur, 1 January 1943, DT papers, Box 38/7. See also Paul Hanna to Wilbur, 5 January 1943, RLW papers, Box 125, "Military Government Schools."

40. Davis to Tresidder, 31 December 1941, and Davis to Wilbur, 1 January 1943, DT papers, Box 38/7.

41. Hanna to Lewis Terman, 26 January 1943, University Services papers, Box 2, Stanford University Archives; Paul Hanna, interview by author, Stanford University, 26 March 1986.

42. Paul Hanna, interview by author, Stanford University, 26 March 1986. Hanna and Davis themselves organized a luncheon at the exclusive Cosmos

Club for fourteen Stanford alumni who were well placed in Washington, whom they prodded for information about approaching the War Production Board's Research and Development division, and the State, Agriculture, and Commerce Departments.

43. See Davis to Wilbur, 4 January 1943, DT papers, Box 38/7; Hanna to Wilbur, 5 January 1943, RLW papers, Box 125, "Military Government Schools"; Hanna to Wilbur, 6 January 1943, University Services papers, Box 2, Stanford University Archives; Paul Hanna, interview by author, Stanford University, 26 March 1986.

44. W. B. Roberts to W. F. Edwards, "Overhead Examination—Stanford University Contracts," 20 June 1947, OSRD papers, Entry 15, Box 221, Federal Records Center, Suitland, Maryland. I would like to thank Larry Owens for bringing this set of records to my attention. See Owens, "Counterproductive Management," pp. 515–76. See Baxter, *Scientists against Time,* Appendix C, for a list of the total dollar value of the contracts received by the OSRD's twenty-five largest nonindustrial contractors.

45. Paul Davis to Wilbur, 4 January 1943, DT papers, Box 38/7.

46. Irvin Stewart to Vannevar Bush, 16 January 1942, and Bush to Stewart, "Memo, Contracts with Universities," 4 February 1942, OSRD papers, Entry 13, Box 22, "Overhead Survey," National Archives. See Gruber, "The Overhead System," for an account of OSRD overhead policies that is more sympathetic to university administrators.

47. Bush to Stewart, 4 February 1942, OSRD papers, Entry 13, Box 22, "Overhead Survey," National Archives.

48. Stewart to Bush, 16 January 1942, Bush to Robert Underhill, 20 January 1942, Stewart to Horace Ford, 26 January 1942, and Stewart to Floyd Morey, 27 January 1942, OSRD papers, Entry 13, Box 22, "Overhead Survey," National Archives.

49. James Conant to Vannevar Bush, 30 April 1942, OSRD papers, Entry 13, Box 21, "Overhead, Salary Basis," National Archives.

50. R. B. Stewart to Irvin Stewart, 21 April 1942; Irvin Stewart to Floyd Morey, 9 March 1942; and Morey, Stewart, Underhill, and Ford, "Proposed Plan of Allowance for Indirect Costs and Contingencies (now called Overhead) on Contracts of the OSRD with Educational Institutions," 21 March 1942, OSRD papers, Entry 13, Box 22, "Overhead Survey," National Archives.

51. Carey Cruikshank to Irvin Stewart, 5 May 1942, OSRD papers, Entry 13, Box 21, "Contracts—Overhead, 1940–42," National Archives.

52. Cruikshank to Stewart, 12 September 1942, OSRD papers, Entry 13, Box 21, "Information Sheet—Contracts," National Archives.

53. Cruikshank to Irvin Stewart, 23 November 1943, OSRD papers, Entry 13, Box 21, "Overhead, 1943," National Archives. Other universities that Cruikshank listed as having large overhead surpluses were Harvard ($238,000), and Johns Hopkins ($75,000).

54. Vannevar Bush to Irvin Stewart, 3 December 1943, OSRD papers, Entry 13, Box 21, "Contracts—Overhead, 1943," National Archives.

55. Bush to Stewart, 8 February 1944, OSRD papers, Entry 13, Box 21, "Contracts—Overhead, 1944," National Archives.

56. See Lloyd Morey, Report on visit to University of Chicago, 3 March 1942, OSRD papers, Entry 13, Box 22, "Contracts—Overhead, Survey," National Archives. For other responses to the OSRD's inquiry, see OSRD papers, Entry 13, Box 21, "Contracts—Overhead, Experience," National Archives.

57. See William Claflin to Irvin Stewart, 26 August 1942, OSRD papers, Entry 13, Box 21, "Contracts—Overhead, 1940–1942," National Archives.

58. Cruikshank to Irvin Stewart, 19 February 1946, OSRD papers, Entry 13, Box 21, "Contracts—Overhead, temporary folder, 1945," National Archives.

59. Cruikshank to Stewart, 3 February 1944, and "Office for Emergency Management: OSRD, Administrative Circular 5.23: 'Determination of Overhead Costs on OSRD Contracts with Academic Institutions,'" 10 March 1944, OSRD papers, Entry 13, Box 21, "Contracts—Overhead, 1944," National Archives.

60. Fay E. Smith, secretary of the trustees of the University of Wyoming, "Relationship between the Federal and State Government in the Budgetary Control of State Institutions," *CAUCBO*, 27th meeting, (1937), p. 106.

61. Paul H. Davis, "Will Gifts to Universities Continue?" *School and Society*, v. 61/1576 (10 March 1945), pp. 145–47.

Chapter 3.   Eroding Departmental Autonomy

1. See, for example, Thorstein Sellin, "Liberal Education after the War," in McConnell and Wiley, eds., *Higher Education and the War*, pp. 81–87.

2. Harold Stoke, "The Future of Graduate Education," *Journal of Higher Education*, v. 18/9 (December 1947), pp. 473–77. For the contrast between the views of Stoke and James Conant, see "Two University Presidents on Critical Problems of Postwar Education," *School and Society*, v. 61/1584 (5 May 1945), pp. 293–94.

3. Carl Seashore, dean emeritus, University of Iowa, "Academic Business," *School and Society*, v. 62/1603 (15 September 1945), pp. 161–64.

4. See Lewis Terman, notes, "Pick of the Crop Committee," n.d., LMT papers, Box 18.

5. Paul Davis, oral history, Stanford University Archives.

6. Davis to Donald Tresidder, 20 November 1942, RLW papers, Box 125, "Planning and Development."

7. Robert G. Sproul, "Opportunity Presented by Budgetary Limitations," *Journal of Higher Education*, 5 (January 1934), pp. 7–13. See also J. B. Speer, "The Functional Organization of the University," *Journal of Higher Education* 5 (August 1934), pp. 414–21, which advocated the application to universities of F. W. Taylor's industrial management techniques; and Seashore, "Academic Business," *School and Society*, v. 62/1603 (15 September 1945), pp. 161–64.

8. Lewis Terman, "The Gifted Student and His Academic Environment," *JAAU*, 40th meeting (November 1939), pp. 67–76. See also Minton, *Lewis M. Terman*.

9. Davis to Tresidder, 21 December 1942, RLW papers, Box 125, "Planning and Development Committee."

10. Ibid.

11. Ibid.

12. Harley Notter to Tresidder, 25 June 1942, DT papers, Box 38/5. Tresidder incorporated Notter's ideas into a speech to Stanford alumni, "Stanford Looks Ahead," 14 October 1942, DT papers, Box 38/6.

13. Terman to Davis, 29 December 1943, FET papers, Box 1/1/2.

14. Terman to Hugh Skilling, acting chairman of electrical engineering, 27 March 1942, FET papers, Box 1/1/11.

15. Terman to Alvin Eurich, Stanford vice-president, 30 October 1944, FET papers, Box 1/1/4. See also Terman to Skilling, 20 June 1944, FET papers, Box 1/1/11; and Terman to Davis, 29 December 1943, FET papers, Box 1/1/2.

16. Terman to Davis, 29 December 1943, FET papers, Box 1/1/2.

17. Terman to Davis, 9 February 1944, FET papers, Box 1/1/2.

18. James B. Conant, *Report of the President of Harvard College: 1933–34* (Cambridge: Harvard University Press, 1935), as quoted in Rodney Triplet, "Harvard Psychology, The Psychological Clinic, and Henry A. Murray: A Case Study in the Establishment of Disciplinary Boundaries," in Rossiter and Elliot, *Science at Harvard*, p. 236. Conant first applied the policy when he fired Alan Sweezy and J. R. Walsh from the economics department.

For Terman's relationship to Claflin and Coolidge, see Terman to Davis, 23 August 1943, FET papers, Box 1/1/2; and Terman to his mother, 24 March 1943; Terman to his father, 27 August 1943, and Terman to his father, 29 February 1944, all in FET papers, Box 12/3/1.

19. Terman to his father, 29 February 1944, FET papers, Box 12/3/1.

20. Lewis Terman to Frederick Terman, 28 February 1944, FET papers, Box 12/4/1.

21. The administration also began considering ways to regulate how faculty members used their sabbaticals and summer quarters and contemplated requiring professors to turn over to the university any money earned in addition to their university salaries as lecturers or consultants. See Lewis Terman to Frederick Terman, 19 October 1944, FET papers, Box 12/4/2; Hugh Skilling, interview by author, Stanford University, 6 April 1988.

22. Tresidder memo on meeting with Henry Heald, October 1944, DT papers, Box 26/6; see also *Report of the President of Stanford University, 1943–44,* Stanford University Archives.

23. See Gibson, *SRI: The Founding Years,* pp. 26, 60, and 67.

24. Tresidder to Paul Edwards, 2 March 1944, PE papers, Box 2/2/3.

25. William Durand to Samuel Morris, 27 September 1943, SOE papers, Box 4/4.

26. Elliott Reid, "Proposal: Postwar Aeronautical Engineering Program for Stanford University," 5 October 1943; and Reid to Ernest Neill, 3 December 1943, both in FET papers, Box 1/1/3.

27. Tresidder to Edwards, 2 March 1944, PE papers, Box 2/2/3; Elliott Reid and Alfred Niles to Tresidder, 17 April 1944, SOE papers, Box 4/4; and Niles to Roy A. Miller, Consolidated-Vultee, 21 April 1944, FET papers, Box 1/1/3.

28. Fred Bush, Sinclair Prairie Oil Company to Hubert Schenck, 16 August 1939, FET papers, Box 2/2/4. According to Bush, members of the oil industry

believed the best geology programs in the country were those at the Colorado School of Mines, the University of Oklahoma, and the University of Texas.

29. Eliot Blackwelder to Tresidder, 29 September 1944, DT papers, Box 24/2.

30. Davis to Terman, 9 August 1943, FET papers, Box 1/1/2.

31. Aaron Waters to Harold Hoots, Richfield Oil, n.d.; Waters to Albert Levorsen, 9 October 1943; Waters to Tresidder, 23 November 1943; and Waters to Tresidder, 2 March 1945, all in DT papers, Box 24/2.

32. Harold Hoots to Waters, 19 December 1944; and Albert Levorsen to L. L. Aubert, 9 December 1945, both in DT papers, Box 24/2.

33. Waters to Tresidder, 2 March 1945, DT papers, Box 24/2.

34. Terman to Tresidder, 26 February 1945, FET papers, Box 1/1/3; and Frederick Terman to Lewis Terman, 5 December 1944, FET papers, Box 12/3/1. For reasons that are unclear, shortly after Terman accepted the position of dean, administrators stopped discussing the idea of creating a technological institute. It is possible that the institute was proposed, in part, to lure Terman back to Stanford after the war. Extremely ambitious, Terman had advanced as far as it could at Stanford, until Morris resigned. For speculations on why Morris decided to leave Stanford, see Lewis Terman to Frederick Terman, 12 December 1944, FET papers, Box 12/4/2.

35. Leon Reynolds, acting chair, civil engineering, to Tresidder, 4 December 1944, DT papers, Box 26/6.

36. Terman to Samuel Morris, 18 June 1945, FET papers, Box 1/1/8.

37. Terman to President Wilbur, 16 March 1941, LMT papers, Box 18.

38. Felix Bloch to William Hansen, 17 September 1942, WWH papers, Box 4/40. According to Bloch, Wilbur had stressed to the physicists that "whatever we do . . . will serve as a record and a reminder for the time when Wilbur retires and a new president has to be convinced of the importance of our department."

39. Tresidder to Paul Edwards, 24 December 1942, PE papers, Box 2/2/3.

40. Bloch to Webster, 23 March 1943, RLW papers, Box 10; see also Bloch to Hansen, 17 September 1942, WWH papers, Box 40/4.

41. Bloch to Hansen, 17 September 1943, WWH papers, Box 40/4.

42. Webster, memo, 3 June 1940, DLW papers, Box 1. For samples of Hansen's complaints about Webster and his opinion of his own abilities, see Hansen, notes in preparation for request for promotion, n.d., WWH papers, Box 3/33; and Hansen, "The Klystron," a deposition written in connection with a patent dispute, n.d., WWH papers, Box 4/35.

43. Bloch to Hansen, 30 December 1942, WWH papers, Box 4/40; Bloch, oral history, American Institute of Physics.

44. See Hansen, "Proposed Micro-Wave Laboratory," 17 November 1943, FET papers, Box 1/1/8; Hansen to Tresidder (draft), 27 September 1944, WWH papers, Box 40/4; and Hansen to Eurich, 11 October 1945, WWH papers, Box 40/4. Hansen's wartime experience was not unique. See Galison, "Physics," and Etzkowitz, "Entrepreneurial University."

45. Hansen to Tresidder (draft), 27 September 1944, WWH papers, Box 41/4. See also Hansen to Bloch, 5 November 1942; Hansen to Webster, 4 February 1943; and Bloch to Hansen, 14 February 1943, all in WWH papers, Box 4/40.

46. Webster to Hansen, 13 February 1943, WWH papers, Box 40/4. See also Webster to Hansen, 17 January 1943, WWH papers, Box 40/4; and Webster to Paul Kirkpatrick, 9 January 1943, DLW papers, Box 10.

47. See Kirkpatrick to Webster, 4 January 1943; Kirkpatrick to Webster, 14 January 1943; Kirkpatrick to Webster, 18 February 1943; Kirkpatrick to Webster, 10 March 1943; Bradbury to Kirkpatrick, 3 March 1943; Bradbury to Kirkpatrick, 1 April 1943; and Webster to Kirkpatrick, 8 April 1943, all in DLW papers, Box 10.

48. Webster to Kirkpatrick, 8 April 1943, DLW papers, Box 10.

49. See Davis to Hansen, 5 April 1943; and Tresidder to Hansen, 21 December 1943, both in WWH papers, Box 40/4.

50. Bloch to Hansen, 14 February 1943, WWH papers, Box 40/4.

51. Bloch to Hansen, 24 March 1943, WWH papers, Box 40/4; Tresidder to Hansen, 16 January 1945, WWH papers, Box 41/4; and Webster to Kirkpatrick, 22 February 1945, DLW papers, Box 10. Terman made the suggestion that Tresidder fire Webster (Terman to Tresidder, 22 December 1944, FET papers, Box 1/1/13).

52. Webster to Albert W. Hull, 20 April 1920; and Webster to Irving Langmuir, 10 April 1920, DLW papers, Box 1.

53. Webster had argued that Ginzton should be appointed as a "research associate" at the microwave laboratory, but not in the physics department.

54. Paul Kirkpatrick, "Autobiography" (unpublished, 1971), Stanford University Archives. I thank Bruce Hevly for bringing this source to my attention. See also Felix Block to Alvin Eurich (confidential), 9 July 1947, WWH papers, Box 4/42.

Kirkpatrick, who was a pacifist, was also concerned that the physics department's growing involvement with industry and military patrons would influence the work the physicists undertook; he chose to do no sponsored research. Paul Kirkpatrick, interview by author, Stanford University, 26 April 1988.

55. Webster to Kirkpatrick, 16 April 1945, DLW papers, Box 10.

56. Ira Wiggins to George Myers, 10 April 1944, Ira Wiggins papers, Box 3/24, Stanford University Archives.

57. See Eliot Blackwelder to Webster, 20 June 1945, DLW papers, Box 10. Blackwelder enclosed a copy of "Affirmation of Purpose of American Universities," which had been signed by Stanford professors Eliot Blackwelder (geology), J. W. McBain (chemistry), Gabor Szego (mathematics), C. V. Taylor (biology), Thomas Addis (medicine), George Dowrie (business), M. Kirkwood (law), Fred Anderson (romance languages), and Berkeley professors Joel Hildebrand, Norm Hicks, John S. Burd, Edwin Dickinson, B. H. Lehman, and George P. Adams.

58. Thomas Barclay to Edward Cottrell, 20 August 1944, JWS papers, Box B-5. See also Maxwell Savelle to John Dodds, 21 January [1943], John W. Dodds papers, Stanford University Archives.

59. Minutes of the Academic Council, 5 April 1946, Stanford University Archives.

60. Blackwelder, notes to himself, n.d., Eliot Blackwelder papers, Box 1, Hoover Institute Archives.

61. Stephens to Tresidder, 11 April 1946, DT papers, Box 37/4. Among those attending the meeting was a large number of female faculty members; numbering around ten, they represented virtually all of the female professors on campus. In addition to the concerns they shared with others at the meeting, they may also have been disturbed by the rumor that Tresidder was planning to forbid the employment of wives of faculty members.

62. Minutes of the Academic Council, 16 April 1946, Stanford University Archives.

63. At least one professor, Hugh Skilling, thought that Tresidder's efforts to depersonalize university administration and to use preprinted forms for conducting business with departments was a vast improvement over Wilbur's informal administration; Hugh Skilling, interview by author, Stanford University, 6 April 1988.

64. See, for example, Schrecker, *No Ivory Tower,* and Diamond, *Compromised Campus.* For a general history of McCarthyism, see Caute, *Great Fear.*

65. See Andrew Copp, Jr., to Paul Edwards, 14 April 1948, PE papers, Box 1/2. Copp, a Stanford alumnus who donated regularly to the university, warned Edwards that Addis was a "stalwart of the National Federation for Constitutional Liberties," which "consistently has pursued its Communist purposes of attacking agencies that investigate Communist activity." Addis had retired by 1948 and thus was not a problem for the university, Stanford's president reassured Copp; Eurich to Copp, 25 May 1948, PE papers, Box 1/5.

66. Bush did not reply in writing to Tresidder but suggested they discuss the matter on the phone. See Samuel Callaway, secretary to Bush, to Tresidder, 12 June 1947, Vannevar Bush papers, Box 112/2670, Library of Congress. See also Bush to Donald Tresidder, 26 May 1947, and Tresidder to Bush (telegram), 6 June 1947, Vannevar Bush Papers, Box 112/2670, Library of Congress.

For a detailed discussion of the attacks on Condon, see Wang, "Science, Security and the Cold War," pp. 238–69; see also Kevles, *Physicists,* pp. 379–80.

67. Hansen to Condon, 10 January 1948, WWH papers, Box 4/42; see also Hansen, notes, 13 February 1948, WWH papers, Box 4/42.

68. Hansen notes, 12 March 1948, WWH papers, Box 4/42.

69. Bloch to Hansen, 5 March 1948; and Bloch to Hansen, 5 April 1948, both in WWH papers, Box 4/42.

70. Bloch to Hansen, 10 April 1948, WWH papers, Box 4/42.

Chapter 4. "Exploiting a Wonderful Opportunity"

1. Yergin, *Shattered Peace,* pp. 193–220; Sherry, *Preparing for the Next War;* Kevles, *Physicists,* pp. 340–41. The range of attitudes about postwar military support for science may be found in Ridenour, "Should the Scientists Resist Military Intrusion?" and "Comments" to this article by Philip Morrison, Vannevar Bush, Albert Einstein, Norbert Weiner, and others, pp. 213–25 and 353–60. Einstein and Weiner were exceptional in stating an aversion to putting science to work for the military in peacetime.

2. See comments of R. G. D. Richardson, dean, Brown University, in

JAAU 47th meeting (October 1946), p. 43. For Conant's views, see Hershberg, *James G. Conant,* pp. 397–98. Despite the prohibition on classified research contracts, Conant permitted individual faculty members to consult on classified research contracts. See Dennis, " 'First Line of Defense,' " pp. 427–55, for a discussion of the negotiated relationship between the military and two postwar laboratories.

3. Karl T. Compton, "The Relations of Government and Industry in University Research," *JAAU* 47th meeting (October 1946), pp. 38–39.

4. Frederick Terman to Donald Tresidder, 25 April 1947, DT papers, Box 27/2.

5. See Geiger, *Research and Relevant Knowledge,* pp. 29, 44.

6. Alvin Eurich, "Memorandum on a Stanford Office in Washington, D.C.," 10 August 1944, DT papers, Box 20/13; Donald B. Tresidder, "My Hands to the War," *Journal of Higher Education,* v. 16/6 (October 1945), pp. 343–50.

7. Terman to James Van Vleck, 30 March 1946, and Van Vleck to Terman, 8 March 1946, both in FET papers, Box 1/3/11.

8. Terman to Tresidder, 16 April 1946, DT papers, Box 27/1.

9. For figures on contract support, see Terman to Tresidder, 14 June 1946, DT papers, Box 27/1; and *Report of the President of Stanford University, 1946–47,* Stanford University Archives. See also Terman, "Details of Eastern Trip, 26 April through 11 May," 20 May 1947, DT papers, Box 27/2. According to Herbert Solomon, a Stanford professor of statistics who had worked for the ONR, Stanford administrators were notably aggressive in pursuit of patronage (Herbert Solomon, interview by author, Stanford University, 19 March 1990).

10. Compton to Kenneth E. Bell, chairman, research committee, New England Council, 15 May 1946, MIT President's papers, Box 235/8, MIT Archives. See also "Report of the Committee on Graduate Education," *JAAU* 48th meeting (October 1947), pp. 112–19; and Vagtborg, *American Industrial Development,* pp. 151–55.

11. Gibson, *SRI: The Founding Years,* pp. 123–25. This book, and its sequel, *SRI: The Take-Off Days,* by one of the institute's earliest staff members, are celebratory but draw on a wealth of documentary evidence. When asked for access to these documents by the author, Gibson stated that the documents had all been destroyed in the 1969 fire in President Sterling's office. Stanford Research Institute's board of directors comprised the university's board of trustees, Donald Tresidder, and Alvin Eurich.

12. On Tresidder's dislike for the G.I. Bill, see *Report of the President of Stanford University, 1945–46;* Harold Bacon, professor of mathematics, to Tresidder, DT papers, Box 24/5; and Terman to Tresidder, 8 January 1947, DT papers, Box 27/3.

13. Leighton to Eurich, 20 January 1947, DT papers, Box 23/7; and Graydon D. Essman, Colonel, Chemical Warfare Service, to Leighton, 25 May 1945, DT papers, Box 23/5.

14. Tresidder, "The Aim and Scope of the Association of American Universities," *JAAU* 48th meeting (October 1947), pp. 18–27, 32–46.

15. Fred Glover, interview by author, Stanford, California, 3 March 1987.

See also Leighton to Eurich, 20 January 1947, DT papers, Box 23/7; and Gibson, *SRI: The Founding Years,* p. 31.

16. Terman to Tresidder, 15 January 1946, DT papers, Box 27/1.

17. Terman's interest in quantifying university prestige began in the 1930s; see Terman to Samuel Morris, 29 April 1937; and Terman, "Comparisons of Harvard, CalTech, Stanford and MIT," 12 May 1937, FET papers, Box 2/3/9. The following description of Terman's ideas for "exploiting" government patronage is drawn from Terman's correspondence with Tresidder and Eurich in DT papers, Box 27.

18. Terman to Tresidder, 15 January 1946, DT papers, Box 27/1; Fred Glover, interview by author, Stanford, California, 3 March 1987.

19. See Terman to Tresidder, 8 January 1947, and Terman to Tresidder, 27 April 1947, both in DT papers, Box 27/3.

20. Terman, "Details of Eastern Trip, 26 April through 11 May," 20 May 1947, DT papers, Box 27/2. See also Terman to Tresidder, 8 January 1947, DT papers, Box 27/3; Terman to Tresidder, 25 April 1947, DT papers, Box 27/2; and Terman to Tresidder, 31 May 1947, DT papers, Box 27/1.

21. Geiger, *Research and Relevant Knowledge,* pp. 63–64 and 74–5.

22. Transcript of telephone conversation between William Claflin and Frederick Terman, 7 December 1945, FET papers, Box 1/1/4; see also Terman to Earl Cullum, 8 December 1945, FET papers, Box 1/4/4.

23. Terman to Cullum, 8 December 1945, FET papers, Box 1/4/4.

24. This has been misunderstood by other historians, who have written that Terman's stated aim of making Stanford into the "Harvard of the West" was temporarily abandoned after World War II while Terman focused on the competition with MIT for preeminence in the field of electrical engineering. (See, for example, Leslie, *Cold War and American Science.*) Clearly, MIT was for Terman a model as well as a competitor. Moreover, Terman had never sought to remake Stanford on the model of Harvard. While he did admire greatly the way in which Harvard was administered (approving, particularly, of Harvard's "ruthlessness" with respect to tenure decisions), his goal, as stated in a wartime letter to Paul Davis, was not to copy Harvard but to gain for Stanford as much "influence on national life" as Harvard enjoyed. In this letter, Terman also criticized Harvard, along with Princeton, Columbia, and Yale, for neglecting the applied sciences and focusing almost exclusively on the arts and "pure sciences." Stanford, he made clear, would not take this path. See Terman to Paul Davis, 29 December 1943, Terman papers, Box 1/1/2.

25. See Piore's comments, Minutes, Committee on Basic Physical Sciences of the Research and Development Board, 7 June 1949, RDB records, Entry 342, Committee Files, Box 9. On the interests of the Office of Naval Research, see Sapolsky, *Science and the Navy.*

26. Terman to Emmanuel Piore, 15 August 1947, DT papers, Box 27/2.

27. Terman to Tresidder, 22 May 1946, and Tresidder to Terman, 29 May 1946, DT papers, Box 27/1.

28. "What of the Present?" *School and Society,* 60/1548 (26 August 1944), pp. 139–40.

29. See Terman to Hugh Skilling, 28 September 1945, FET papers, Box 1/1/

11; and "Salary Comparisons," PE papers, Box 1/5. On the relative prosperity of public universities in comparison to the private universities, see Geiger, *Research and Relevant Knowledge,* pp. 40–47.

30. Director of Planning, "Progress Report," 28 February 1945, DT papers, Box 15/20.

31. Douglas Whitaker to Eurich, 24 April 1946, DT papers, Box 23/4; see also Whitaker to Tresidder, 19 November 1945, DT papers, Box 23/4.

32. Whitaker to Eurich, 14 May 1946, DT papers, Box 23/4. See also Charles V. Taylor to Tresidder, 27 December 1945, DT papers, Box 23/4; William Hansen, memo, 28 August 1946, WWH papers, Box 2/23; Leighton to Eurich, 13 June 1946, DT papers, Box 23/6; and Frederick Terman and Hugh Skilling to Tresidder, 1 January 1946, DT papers, Box 27/1.

33. Chief of research engineering, Lockheed, to Elliott Reid, 14 August 1944, SOE papers, Box 4/4. See also Arthur Raymond, Douglas Aircraft, to Samuel Morris, 21 August 1944; and E. C. Wells, Boeing, to Elliott Reid, 21 September 1944, both in SOE papers, Box 4/4. See also Rae, *Climbing to Greatness,* p. 173; and McDougall, *Heavens and Earth,* p. 89.

34. See Gibson, *SRI: The Founding Years,* pp. 26, 60, 67, 103–104, 109–11. Precisely why industry displayed so little interest in supporting SRI is unclear. Some, like the aircraft industries, had retrenched after the war; some preferred to do their research in-house or to rely on East Coast research establishments. Corporations may have rejected McBean's efforts to raise endowment funds for the institute for the same reasons that industry had ultimately refused to support Hoover's National Research Fund: business was primarily interested in proprietary access to the research that it funded.

35. Terman to Tresidder, 25 April 1947, DT papers, Box 27/2. Tresidder's disappointment over the fact that Stanford had largely been overlooked during the war by the OSRD may have been made more acute because he, along with Wilbur and Hoover, had maintained an isolationist position on the war up to 7 December 1941. Terman and his father, Lewis Terman, had been early proponents of intervention, and Lewis Terman had led an anti-isolationist campaign on campus in the late 1930s, earning the enmity of Hoover. See Minton, *Lewis M. Terman.*

36. See Leslie, "Playing the Education Game," p. 60. See also Terman's own account of his activities in Terman to Paul Klopsteg, 30 March 1953, JWS papers, Box 39.

37. Terman to Samuel Morris, 18 June 1945, FET papers, Box 1/1/8.

38. Emmanuel R. Piore to Alan Waterman, 17 December 1946, Naval Research Advisory Committee records, Office of Naval Research, Ballston, Virginia. See also Terman to Tresidder, 8 January 1947, DT papers, Box 27/3. For a full list of former RRL members at Stanford by 1950, see Terman, "Proposal for Expanded Electronics Countermeasures Program (Confidential)," n.d., FET papers, Box 2/14/18.

39. Terman to Tresidder, 1 January 1947, DT papers, Box 27/3; see also "Summary of Sponsored Research Projects since May 1, 1946," SOE papers, Box 1/3/3.

40. Terman to William Hansen, 7 September 1945, FET papers, Box 1/1/6.

41. See Alfred Niles to Tresidder, 27 May 1946, and Terman to Tresidder, 28 May 1946, both in DT papers, Box 4/1.

42. Terman to Tresidder, 22 May 1946, DT papers, Box 27/1.

43. Albert Bowker, interview by author, Washington, D.C., 4 April 1991.

44. Terman to Paul Davis, 29 December 1943, FET papers, Box 1/1/2.

45. By the end of 1947, only seven of Stanford's 304-member faculty were involved in research at SRI. See Gibson, *SRI: The Founding Years,* pp. 97, 141, and Gibson, *SRI: The Take-Off Days,* p. 12. See also Tresidder, memo, 19 November 1947, DT papers, Box 17/18.

46. Terman to Tresidder, 6 August 1945, FET papers, Box 1/1/3.

47. Bush, *Endless Frontier,* pp. 18–19.

48. Gibson, *SRI: The Founding Years,* p. 141, and Gibson, *SRI: The Take-Off Days,* p. 12. See also Ralph Krause to Jesse Hobson, 15 November 1948, PE papers, Box 3/7.

49. Tresidder, "The Aim and Scope of the Association of American Universities," *JAAU* 48th meeting (October 1947), pp. 18–27. Tresidder was urging the AAU to change its focus from accrediting universities to representing the views of institutions of higher education in national forums. Tresidder's criticism of the AAU, which offended many of its members, became the focus of the discussion which followed; none remarked on his comments about the dangers of overreliance on the federal government.

50. Geiger, *Research and Relevant Knowledge,* p. 42. See also the Commission on Financing Higher Education, *Nature and Needs of Higher Education*; Millet, *Financing Higher Education*; and the U.S. President's Commission on Higher Education, *Higher Education for American Democracy.*

51. Tresidder, notes, 19 November 1947, DT papers, Box 17/18; Gibson, *SRI: The Founding Years,* pp. 109–13. For SRI's contracts, see Gibson, *SRI: The Founding Years,* p. 123. According to Gibson, *SRI: The Take-Off Days,* p. 27, Talbot also preferred industrial contracts, believing that the federal government did not provide adequate reimbursement for overhead expenses.

52. See Ralph Krause to Jesse Hobson, 15 November 1948, PE papers, Box 3/7; Gibson, *SRI: The Founding Years,* p. 141, and *SRI: The Take-Off Days,* pp. 50–51.

53. Gibson, *SRI: The Take-Off Days,* pp. 6, 44–46, 34–37, 118.

54. For information about the physics department and microwave laboratory, see Fred Pindar to George Parks, 29 December 1950, JWS papers, Box 24, and Ginzton and Pindar to Sterling, 8 January 1953, JWS papers, Box 8. Regarding the engineering school, see Terman to Tresidder, 8 January 1947, SOE papers, Box 3/3/6; Terman to Eurich, 26 May 1948, SOE papers, Box 3/3/6; Terman to Tresidder, 25 April 1947, DT papers, Box 27/2; and *Report of the President of Stanford University, 1947–48* and *Report of the President of Stanford University, 1949–50,* Stanford University Archives.

55. The number of instructors and lecturers also grew, from nine in 1937–38 to twenty-seven ten years later. For evidence of salary-splitting throughout the engineering school, see Lydick Jacobson to Terman, 22 October 1948; Hugh Skilling to Terman, 15 October 1948; and Terman to Eurich, 2 October 1948, all in SOE papers, Box 3/3/6.

56. Nash, *Herbert Hoover,* p. 123.

57. Shortly after assuming the presidency of Stanford, Sterling was invited to join Hoover's Caveman Camp at the Bohemian Grove. See Nash, *Herbert Hoover,* p. 124; and Domhoff, *The Bohemian Grove,* p. 40.

Chapter 5.   A "Win-Win-Win" Relationship

1. Melman, *Permanent War Economy*; Kevles, "Korea, Science, and the State," pp. 319–21.

2. Terman to Sterling, 2 January 1952, JWS papers, Box 38; "SRI: Complete List of Government Projects, October 1946 through August 1951," PE papers, Box 3/9; and Gibson, *SRI: The Take-Off Days,* pp. 52, 93, 104.

3. Kerr, *Uses of the University,* pp. 43, 48.

4. Dean A. Watkins to Thomas Davis, Jr., 27 October 1957, FET papers, Box 3/34/6.

5. Terman to Sterling, "Proposed Project in Applied Electronics," 12 September 1950, FET papers, Box 2/13/18.

6. Terman, "Higher Education and Training in a Research Community," in *Research and the Community* (New York: Department of Commerce, 1962), pp. 11–21. (A copy of this article may also be found in FET papers, Box 10/1/71.)

7. Terman, "Memorandum on War Defense Program in Electronics," 15 August 1950, FET papers, Box 2/13/18; and "Government-sponsored Research in Electronics," 25 February 1952, FET papers, Box 2/17/19. The ONR, Signal Corps, and air force approached six institutions: Columbia, MIT, Harvard, Stanford, University of Michigan, and University of Illinois. Stanford was the first to reply positively; negotiations with Harvard broke down when the Harvard Faculty of Arts and Sciences declared its opposition to classified work. (See Karl Spangenberg to Terman, n.d., and Terman, "Notes on Applied Electronics Project," both in FET papers, Box 2/13/18.)

8. Terman to Sterling, "Proposed Project in Applied Electronics," 12 September 1950, FET papers, Box 2/13/18.

9. Terman, "Stanford University as a Facility for Research and Development in Electronics," 15 August 1950, FET papers, Box 2/13/18.

10. R. W. Larson, General Electric's Research Laboratory, to Terman, 30 April 1951, and Terman to Larson, 21 May 1951, both in FET papers, Box 2/18/8.

11. Notes of meeting of senior staff of ERL, 14 May 1951, FET papers, Box 2/17/2.

12. Spangenberg to Terman, 8 January 1943, FET papers, Box 1/1/12.

13. "AEL [Applied Electronics Laboratory] Policy on Laboratory Sponsored Advising," 28 January 1955, FET papers, Box 3/18/6.

14. On the RRL's relationship with industrial contractors, see Terman, "Administrative History of the Radio Research Laboratory," 21 March 1946, FET papers, Box 1/9/1. (The report was actually written by Oswald Villard, Jr.)

During the war, G.E. had been singled out for criticism by the OSRD's vacuum-tube development group for poor cooperation between those responsible for research and those involved in development and production. Its "very poor record" was contrasted with that of Litton Industries, which was praised for its willingness to discuss problems with both scientists at the Radiation Laboratory and its contractor, the navy. See report of H. C. Dienst, director of Vacuum Tube Development Group, 10 August 1945, FET papers, Box 1/4/14.

15. Layton, *Revolt of the Engineers,* pp. 1–6, discusses the dual roles played by engineers, who acted both as independent experts and as adjuncts to the business world. As Layton notes, "[T]he role of the engineer represents a patchwork of compromises between professional ideals and business demands" (p. 5).

16. Farrell McGhie, notes of ERL personnel committee meeting, 5 April 1951, FET papers, Box 2/17/2.

17. Notes of ERL senior staff meeting, 1 June 1951, FET papers, Box 2/17/2. As Donald Harris stated in a memo to ERL's senior staff on 6 June 1951, Stanford and Maxson shared a "common objective"—the successful production of Stanford-originated microwave tubes. See FET papers, Box 2/15/33.

18. Notes from ERL senior staff meeting, 1 June 1951, FET papers, Box 2/17/2.

19. Harris, memo on 6 June meeting with Maxson representatives, 11 June 1951, FET papers, Box 2/16/22.

20. Minutes, applied electronics senior staff meeting, 21 May 1951, FET papers, Box 2/17/2. According to William Rambo, he was the first to do routine, systematic surveys of the country's government labs and university research groups working on governmental contracts. He reported the findings of his "circle tours" to Terman. William Rambo, interview by author, Stanford, California, 18 May 1987.

21. Terman, memo, 24 November 1952, FET papers, Box 2/15/30.

22. "The Influence of the Electronics Research Laboratory Program on Other Activities in the Radar and ECM Fields," 26 August 1953, FET papers, Box 2/17/15.

23. "Proposal for Procurement of Evaluation Prototypes of the Rapid Scan Search Receiver," 28 December 1951, FET papers, Box 2/16/5; and Donald Harris, confidential memo on conversation with representatives of the navy's Evans Signal Laboratory, n.d., FET papers, Box 2/16/5. During World War II, the RRL sublet contracts to industry.

24. Donald Harris, memo, 11 June 1951, FET papers, Box 2/16/22.

25. Sigurd Varian to Edward Ginzton, 4 September 1951, Hansen Laboratories papers, Box 12/6, Stanford University Archives.

26. Donald Harris, memo, 4 January 1952, FET papers, Box 2/15/20.

27. "Proposal for Procurement of Evaluation Prototypes of the Rapid Scan Search Receiver," 28 December 1951, FET papers, Box 2/16/5.

28. Terman to H. R. Oldfield of General Electric, 8 April 1954, FET papers, Box 2/18/8.

29. "The Influence of the Electronics Research Laboratory Program on Other Activities in the Radar and ECM Fields," 26 August 1953, FET papers, Box 2/17/15.

30. Terman to Oldfield, 8 April 1954, FET papers, Box 2/18/8. See also Terman, memo, 24 November 1952, FET papers, Box 2/15/21; and Terman, memo, 24 November 1952, FET papers, Box 2/15/10.

31. See Hugh Skilling to Sterling, 18 December 1953, JWS papers, Box 38;

and Terman to William Cooley, president of Television Shares Management Corporation, 15 August 1955, FET papers, Box 5/7/6, for discussions of the program and its benefits to industry and Stanford. The fee was set at the cost of tuition.

For the criteria for selecting participants, see "Honors Cooperative Program in Electrical Engineering: 1957 Situation," 28 January 1957, FET papers, Box 3/31/6. Other criteria included the stated needs of the participating company and the scholastic performance of the company's previous Honors Cooperative students.

32. See Terman to David Bacon, 10 December 1957, Box 3/18/5, FET papers, in which Terman congratulates Linvill for conceiving the program. See also Terman to David Packard, 25 June 1958, FET papers, Box 3/18/1.

33. See Joseph Pettit to Howard Vollum, president of Tektronix, 25 July 1958; Linvill to W. H. Forster of Philco, 1 August 1958; Terman to Robert Shank of Hughes Aircraft, 9 September 1958; and Linvill, memo on "immediate benefits" to industry from industrial affiliates program, 11 September 1959, all in FET papers, Box 3/18/1.

34. One result of Sputnik was an expansion of U.S. military-sponsored research. Terman hoped to "take advantage of this opportunity" to move into areas of increasing interest to the military, among them solid-state electronics and space science. Terman to Kenneth Cuthbertson, 7 July 1958, SOE papers, Box 1/7.

35. See John Linvill to Terman, 29 April 1958; and Linvill, memo, 28 May 1958, both in FET papers, Box 3/18/1.

36. See the announcement of Stanford's land program in the *San Jose Mercury News,* 13 October 1950, Stanford Lands Scrapbook, Volume I, Stanford University Archives. For further information on the development of Stanford's land-leasing program, see DT papers, Box 3; FET papers, Box 3/58/6; and JWS papers, Boxes 30, 50, and A33.

37. See Lowood, "From Steeples of Excellence."

38. Donald Harris, memo on "Collaborative Project with General Electric Company," 1 May 1953, FET papers, Box 2/18/8.

39. Terman to I. J. Kaar, 2 July 1953, FET papers, Box 2/18/8. In writing to Kaar, Terman was taking advantage of a former contact: as Terman explained, he and Kaar had been "fellow 'hams' together back around 1917, and used to communicate with each other by spark radio" (Terman to Tom C. Rives, 5 August 1953, FET papers, Box 2/18/8).

40. Terman to Kaar, 2 July 1953, FET papers, Box 2/18/8. See also Terman to H. R. Oldfield, 8 April 1954, FET papers, Box 2/18/8.

41. Terman to Paul Davis, 29 December 1943, FET papers, Box 1/1/12.

42. Tom C. Rives to Terman, 29 July 1953, FET papers, Box 2/18/8.

43. "G.E. Proposal for G.E. Microwave Laboratory at Stanford University," 12 April 1954, FET papers, Box 2/18/8.

44. William Rambo, memo, 15 February 1956, FET papers, Box 2/16/19.

45. H. R. Oldfield to Terman, 3 January 1955, FET papers, Box 2/18/8.

46. Terman, "Stanford University," *Industrial Research* (April 1963), p. 56, a copy of which may be found in FET papers, Box 10/2/1.

47. Farrell McGhie to Kenneth Cuthbertson, 18 May 1955, JWS papers, Box 39.

48. Terman, notes on telephone conversation with Willis Hawkins, director of engineering, Lockheed, 12 July 1956, FET papers, Box 3/38/1. See also Terman, notes, 9 February 1956; Louis Ridenour, Lockheed's director of research, to Terman, 5 March 1956; Willis Hawkins to Terman, 12 July 1956; and Terman to Hawkins, 21 November 1956, all in FET papers, Box 3/38/1.

49. The relationship between Stanford's aeronautical engineering program, Lockheed, and military contractors is discussed in Leslie, *The Cold War,* pp. 110–32.

50. Terman to William Cooley, 11 December 1957, FET papers, Box 5/7/6.

51. Dean A. Watkins, notes for presentation to Kern County Land Company (KCLC), 19 October 1957, FET papers, Box 3/34/6. See also, Terman to George Montgomery of KCLC, 1 August 1957; Thomas J. Davis, Jr., vice-president of KCLC, to Terman, 9 August 1957; Watkins to Davis, 27 October 1957; and Terman to Watkins, 27 November 1957, all in FET papers, Box 3/34/6.

52. Terman to Watkins, 27 November 1957, FET papers, Box 3/34/6.

53. According to Terman's sons, Terman always admired Hoover but did not begin systematic reading of Hoover's writings until after his retirement in the mid-1960s. Lewis Terman, Terence Terman, Frederick Terman, Jr., and his wife, Bobbie, interview with author, Stanford University, 29 May 1992.

54. See Terman, "Engineering and Engineering Education in a Modern World," *Journal of Petroleum Technology* (November 1956), pp. 19–20, in FET papers, Box 10/1/55; Terman, "Higher Education and Training in a Research Community," *Research and the Community* (New York: Department of Commerce, 1962), pp. 11–21, in FET papers, Box 10/1/71; and Terman, "Stanford University," *Industrial Research* (April 1963), pp. 55–58, in FET papers, Box 10/2/1.

55. Terman, "Engineering and Engineering Education in a Modern World," *Journal of Petroleum Technology* (November 1956), pp. 19–20, in FET papers, Box 10/1/55.

56. "Proposed Program for Applied Research and Development in Electronics," [Fall 1950?], FET papers, Box 2/13/18.

57. See Felix Bloch to Emmanuel Piore, 18 May 1951, FET papers, Box 2/14/10. Bloch was proposing to the ONR a military application of his work on nuclear induction. "Because of its restricted nature, it would not seem appropriate to carry the work out in our physics department. The applied electronics laboratory under the direction of Dr. Terman would seem the logical place." Before the outbreak of war in Korea, Bloch had made clear his opposition to security restrictions. In late 1949 representatives of the ONR and three Stanford physicists had held a closed meeting in a physics department's lecture room in which classified information was discussed. As he wrote at the time, "[R]esearch requiring such restrictions belongs primarily to institutions and laboratories where the principle of free research has been openly abandoned." He did note that, given "very exceptional and compelling reasons," this principle might be compromised (Bloch, memo, 21 September 1949, LS papers, Box 17).

58. Lester Field, "Views on Stanford's Tube Program with Respect to Additional Air Force or Other Support," 17 October 1951, FET papers, Box 2/15/10; Felix Bloch to Emmanuel Piore, 18 May 1951, FET papers, Box 2/24/10.

59. Terman, "Stanford University as a Facility for Research and Development in Electronics," 15 August 1950, FET papers, Box 2/13/18.

60. "Proposal for Extension of Task 7," 30 September 1952, FET papers, Box 2/14/17.

61. Terman, notes, 1 October 1951, FET papers, Box 2/17/13.

62. William Kays, "Frederick Terman," 6 February 1992 (unpublished speech).

63. See notes by unnamed engineer on the back of Terman's "Draft of discussion of changing AEL, ERL structure," [1955?], FET papers, Box 2/17/5.

64. Quoted in Forman, "Behind Quantum Electronics," pp. 219–20.

65. Terman to Gould Hunter, 2 October 1953; and Donald Harris, memo, FET papers, Box 2/17/1.

66. David Bacon to James King, 24 December 1953, FET papers, Box 2/16/3. See also, Bacon to King, 12 January 1954, FET papers, Box 2/13/4; Terman, notes, 12 January 1954, FET papers, Box 2/13/4; and David Harris, memo, 25 November 1953, FET papers, Box 2/17/1.

67. Spangenberg to Terman, 23 November 1955, FET papers, Box 2/17/4. Spangenberg was not averse, however, to undertaking some classified work himself or to allowing students to participate in the applied program. As he explained, there was "real advantage" in letting students do "a limited amount of classified research"; this gave them "access to much important information" and to "valuable contacts" in the military (Spangenberg to Stanford's dean of graduate studies, 14 June 1957, FET papers, Box 3/18/5). And yet, Spangenberg continued to worry "lest the research tail wag the academic dog" and insisted that the electrical engineering department "should avoid operating in such a way that we effectively have a group of Research Institutes which overshadow the E.E. department" (Spangenberg to Terman, 28 January 1957, FET papers, Box 3/18/5).

68. That some stigma was attached to working in the AEL building is suggested by AEL engineer Dean Watkins's eagerness to move his work back to the ERL, claiming that three-fourths of his project involved basic research. ERL engineer Karl Spangenberg protested, explaining that Watkins's work "may be 3/4 unclassified but as I see it, it's only 1/4 basic" (Spangenberg to Terman, 23 November 1955, FET papers, Box 2/17/4).

69. Notes by unnamed engineer on the back of Terman's "Draft of discussion of changing AEL, ERL structure," [1955?], FET papers, Box 2/17/5. As this engineer believed, some were unhappy, not because the engineers were doing applied work "but because we *say* we are." Despite this engineer's clear concern about the opinion of those on and off campus, I have found no recorded expressions of unhappiness among Stanford faculty members with the classified research program in the mid-1950s.

70. Terman, "Draft of discussion of changing AEL, ERL structure," [1955?], FET papers, Box 2/17/5; see also "Proposal for Extension of Applied Electronics Program under Signal Corps Sponsorship," 18 July 1955, FET papers, Box 2/13/31.

71. Terman, "Why Do We Research?" speech to 17th Annual Stanford Business Conference, 22 July 1958, in FET papers, Box 10/1/59.

72. Bacon to Terman, 6 April 1956, FET papers, Box 3/18/5. Terman's comments were penciled in the margins.

73. Terman to Sterling, 6 May 1966, and William Rambo, memo, May 1966, both in FET papers, Box 3/10/8. See also Hugh Skilling to Executive Committee of the Academic Council, 31 May 1966, FET papers, Box 3/10/8.

74. Lester Field, "Views on Stanford's Tube Program with Respect to Additional Air Force or Other Support," 17 October 1951, FET papers, Box 2/15/10.

75. Rambo, notes, 9 April 1956, FET papers, Box 3/18/5; and Rambo to Ira Meyers, 14 May 1956, FET papers, Box 3/16/19.

76. Rambo, memo, 30 June 1955, FET papers, Box 2/16/19.

77. Historian David Noble finds this to be the dilemma of professional engineers: they "strive continuously to anticipate and meet the criteria of those in power simply so that they may be able to practice their calling." "It is no wonder," Noble continues, "that, in subtle and not so subtle ways, they tend to internalize and even consciously adopt the outlook of their patrons" (*Forces of Production,* p. 43).

78. Lewis Terman, Terence Terman, Frederick Terman, Jr., and his wife, Bobbie, interview by author, 29 May 1992, Stanford University.

79. Terman, notes on conversation with air force representatives, 15 November 1951, FET papers, Box 2/13/2.

80. Terman to Paul Klopsteg, 20 March 1953, JWS papers, Box 39.

Chapter 6.   Building Steeples of Excellence

1. Dwight D. Eisenhower, "Farewell Radio and Television Address to the American People," 17 January 1961.

2. For figures on Stanford, see "Annual Financial Statement, year ending 31 August 1960; Government Research Contracts," *Annual Financial Statement of the University,* Stanford University Archives. Figures on federal support of academic research and development are drawn from Kerr, *Uses of the University,* pp. 53–55; Kevles, *Physicists,* pp. 369, 386; and Kevles, "K1S2: Korea, Science and the State," pp. 314, 320. See also Horowitz, Carroll, and Lee, *On the Edge,* p. 326.

3. Kerr, *Uses of the University,* pp. 68–69. A similar view is expressed by J. L. Morrill, "Higher Education and the Federal Government," in Brown and Sellin, *Higher Education Under Stress,* p. 42.

4. Kerr, *Uses of the University,* pp. 113–114, 75.

5. Commoner, *Science and Survival,* pp. 44–46; David Boroff, "A Plea to Save the Liberal Arts," *New York Times Magazine,* 10 May 1964, p. 78.

6. Geiger, *Research and Relevant Knowledge,* pp. 44–45.

7. Lewis Terman to President Sterling, 13 October 1950, JWS papers, Box 6.

8. Edward Ginzton to Ernest Hilgard, 20 April 1953, WWH papers, Box 14/1. The physics department, exclusive of the lab, had about $80,000 in government research funds in 1953 (see "Instruction, Research and Libraries . . . All Sources of Funds," 31 August 1953, JWS papers, Box 49).

9. Budget for Statistics Department, 1948–49, JWS papers, Box 6; Herbert Solomon, interview by author, Stanford University, 19 March 1990.

10. "Functions of the Applied Mathematics and Statistics Laboratory," [January 1953?], JWS papers, Box 9. See also Albert Bowker to J. Wallace Sterling, 15 March 1951; and Bowker to Clarence Faust, 23 December 1950, both in JWS papers, Box 6.

11. See Ernest Hilgard to Clarence Faust, 5 December 1949, JWS papers, Box 6; "Some Suggested Developments for the Department of Psychology," 23 November 1953, FET papers, Box 3/46/10; and "Report of the Special Committee on Research Programs to the Survey of Behavioral Sciences," [1953?], Behavioral Sciences collection, Stanford University Archives. Hilgard noted in 1949 that the salaries of 8 out of the department's 14 faculty members were paid, fully or in part, with contracts and grants.

12. See John Goheen to Sterling, 15 December 1953; Goheen to Sterling, 24 March 1953; and Goheen to Sterling, 24 March 1954, all in JWS papers, Box 4.

13. "Instruction, Research, and Libraries, Detail by Schools and Departments from All Sources of Funds," 31 August 1953, JWS papers, Box 49. See also Terman, notes on meeting with biology department, 2 December 1955, FET papers, Box 3/4/7; Eric Hutchinson, professor emeritus of chemistry, interview by author, Stanford University, 27 May 1987.

14. Charles Stein, interview by author, Stanford University, 20 March 1990; Paul Kirkpatrick, interview by author, Stanford University, 26 April 1988.

15. "Report of Special Committee on Research Programs to the Survey of Behavioral Sciences," Behavioral Sciences collection, Stanford University Archives. Members of the committee were economist Moses Abramovitz, journalist Chilton Bush, Hoover Institute scholar Nobuto Ike, historian John Johnson, anthropologist Bernard Siegel, political scientist Robert Walker, Food Research Institute director William O. Jones, and pyschologist Donald Taylor. See also "Report on Faculty Interviews to the Survey of the Behavioral Sciences, 1953–54," Behavioral Sciences collection, Stanford University Archives. According to the interviewer, who did not mention any faculty members by name, junior faculty were the most apt to comment negatively on the situation at Stanford. The special committee was formed and the interviews conducted as part of a study of the university's strengths and weaknesses in the behavioral sciences with support from the Ford Foundation.

16. Lawrence Blinks, interview by author, Hopkins Marine Station, Monterey, California, 7 March 1987; Victor Twitty to Rhinelander, 9 June 1961, FET papers, Box 3/4/8.

17. Geology department meeting, minutes, 4 January 1962, FET papers, Box 3/14/4; Eric Hutchinson, interview by author, Stanford University, 27 May 1987.

18. Edward Shaw to Clarence Faust, 2 January 1951, JWS papers, Box 2. In the succeeding years, departments were selectively requested to reduce their budgets.

19. Bowker to Sterling, 15 March 1951, JWS papers, Box 6; Goheen to Sterling, 12 December 1953; and Goheen to Sterling, 15 December 1953, both in JWS papers, Box 4.

20. See Shaw to Faust, 2 January 1951; Shaw to Sterling, 18 March 1952; Shaw to Sterling, 19 March 1952; and Shaw to Sterling, 2 December 1952, all in JWS papers, Box 2.

21. "Application of Electronic Data Processing Techniques on Administrative Decision Making at Stanford University," 12 December 1964; and Alvin Eurich, Ford Foundation, to Terman, 9 October 1956, both in FET papers, Box 3/25/4. For concerns about the efficiency of institutions of higher education and their abilities to handle the expected increase in enrollments, see Brown and Sellin, *Higher Education Under Stress*; on the NDEA, see Geiger, *Research and Relevant Knowledge*, 164–65.

22. Terman, notes on classics department, 20 December 1955, JWS papers, Box 3; Fred Glover, interview by author, Stanford University, 3 March 1987. See also Raymond Harriman to Provost Douglas Whitaker, 3 November 1952; Harriman, memo, 12 December 1952; and Philip Harsh to Ray Faulkner, acting dean of humanities and sciences, n.d., all in JWS papers, Box 3.

23. Terman, notes on conversation with Lionel I.C. Pearson, 25 November 1955, JWS papers, Box 3. See also Terman, notes on conversation with Hazel Hansen, 25 November 1955; Terman, notes on conversation with John Dodds, 5 December 1955; and Terman, notes on classics department, 20 December 1955, all in JWS papers, Box 3.

24. See Terman, notes on meeting with biology department, 2 December 1955, FET papers, Box 3/4/7; Terman, notes on conversation with John Goheen, 21 December 1955; and Terman, notes on philosophy department, 5 March 1956, both in FET papers, Box 3/45/5; Terman, notes on meeting with economics faculty, 9 May 1956, FET papers, Box 3/15/2; Terman, notes on mineral sciences, 14 March 1956; and Terman, notes on meeting with mineral sciences faculty, 14 March 1957, both in FET papers, Box 3/14/2; Eric Hutchinson, interview by author, Stanford University, 27 May 1987; and Charles Stein, interview by author, Stanford University, 20 March 1990.

25. Charles Stein, interview by author, Stanford University, 20 March 1990. In the early 1960s, Stein, in reaction to the U.S. bombing of Vietnam, stopped accepting ONR patronage.

26. Victor Twitty to Sterling, 29 November 1955, FET papers, Box 3/4/7.

27. Kenneth Arrow to Sterling, 19 December 1955, JWS papers, Box A-12.

28. Konrad Krauskopf to Terman, 7 June 1956, FET papers, Box 3/14/2. See also Krauskopf to Sterling, 21 March 1957, FET papers, Box 3/14/2; and Terman to Sterling, 4 April 1957, FET papers, Box 3/14/2. Geology chairman Levorsen had resisted the creation of the school; he left Stanford in 1952, at which time Charles F. Park became head of the geology department as well as dean of the School of Mineral Sciences.

29. See Terman, "Problems with Mineral Sciences," n.d., FET papers, Box 3/14/2; "Instruction, Research and Libraries, Detail by Schools and Departments from all sources of funds," 31 August 1943, JWS papers, Box 49; "Geology Department Minutes," 4 May 1962, FET papers, Box 3/14/4.

30. Terman, notes, 25 April 1956, FET papers, Box 3/14/2.

31. Terman, notes on conversation with Park, 13 December 1955; Terman, notes on Robert Rose appointment, 26 January 1956; Terman, notes, 14 March

1956; and Terman, notes on meeting with mineral sciences, 14 March 1957, all in FET papers, Box 3/14/2. McPhee, *Encounters with the Archdruid*, p. 12, describes an encounter between geologist Park and environmental activist David Brower: "[S]uch is Park's feeling for where ore bodies are that some of his friends think he has occult powers."

32. Terman to Sterling, n.d., FET papers, Box 3/14/2. Terman was referring to the reaction from Stanford's geologists. Sterling's comment was pencilled in the margin of Terman's letter.

33. Fred Humphrey to Sterling, 12 March 1957; and School of Mineral Sciences to Sterling, 20 March 1957, both in FET papers, Box 3/14/2. See also Krauskopf to Sterling, 21 March 1957; and Terman to Sterling, 4 April 1957, both in FET papers, Box 3/14/2.

34. Terman, notes, 24 April 1957, FET papers, Box 3/14/2.

35. "Proposed Ten Year Program in Metallurgical Engineering," 4 August 1960, FET papers, Box 3/39/2. Leslie, *Cold War and American Science*, pp. 212–23, discusses the creation of Stanford's material science program but attributes all initiative to the entrepreneurial Huggins, ignoring the role of Stanford's administrators both in developing the program and enabling Huggins to act as he did.

36. See Robert Huggins to Albert Bowker, 18 March 1960, FET papers, Box 3/39/2; and provost's meeting, notes, 4 April 1960, FET papers, Box 3/61/2.

37. See Fred Glover to Terman, 2 May 1960, FET papers, Box 3/39/2; and "Materials Science at Stanford University," October 1960, FET papers, Box 3/38/7.

38. Geology department meeting, minutes, 4 January 1962 and 4 May 1962, FET papers, Box 3/14/4; see also Terman, notes on School of Earth Sciences, 2 January 1963, FET papers, Box 3/14/5.

39. Terman to Sterling, 8 January 1963, FET papers, Box 3/14/6.

40. Heffner to Richard Jahns, 6 April 1966, FET papers, Box 3/14/5; see also Terman, notes, n.d., Terman papers, Box 3/14/4.

41. Terman to Fred Glover, n.d., FET papers, 3/4/1.

42. Bowker to Terman, 6 April 1959, FET papers, Box 3/32/1.

43. For Blinks's comments on UC-Berkeley, see Blinks to Terman, 5 May 1960, FET papers, Box 3/21/1; see also Blinks to Terman, 25 June 1959, FET papers, Box 3/32/1. For Blinks's concerns about overcollecting, see Blinks to Terman, 25 June 1959, FET papers, Box 3/32/1. For Blinks's comments about traditional fisheries interests, see Blinks to Terman, 4 July 1959, FET papers, Box 3/32/1, and Blinks to Terman, 5 May 1960, FET papers, Box 3/21/1.

44. Blinks to Terman, 11 July 1960, FET papers, Box 3/32/1.

45. Terman to Blinks, 4 November 1960; and Terman, notes on conversation with John Wilson, 2 November 1960, both in FET papers, Box 3/32/1.

46. Blinks to Terman, 8 November 1960, FET papers, Box 3/32/1.

47. For the NSF's advice about overhead charges, see Terman to Kenneth Creighton, 17 May 1961, FET papers, Box 3/32/3. For comments about Blinks, see Terman, notes on conversation with John Wilson, n.d., FET papers, Box 3/32/3. See also Terman to Blinks, 4 November 1960; and Terman, notes, 2 November 1960, FET papers, Box 3/32/1.

48. Twitty, memo, n.d., FET papers, Box 3/4/8.

49. Twitty to Philip Rhinelander, 9 June 1961, FET papers, Box 3/4/8; see also Twitty to Philip Rhinelander, 4 January 1960, FET papers, Box 3/32/1.

50. George Myers to Terman, 15 December 1960; and Twitty to Terman, 19 December 1960, both in FET papers, Box 3/4/8.

51. Donald McKernan to Terman, 6 February 1962, FET papers, Box 3/4/9.

52. Sterling to Robert Sears, dean of humanities and sciences, 15 June 1965; and Terman to Fred Glover, n.d., FET papers, Box 3/4/11.

53. See Stanford Medical School budget figures, 1961–62, FET papers, Box 3/41/5; on the Ford Foundation's interests, see Bowker to Terman, 26 December 1962, FET papers, Box 3/4/10; on the transfer of the medical school to the Stanford campus, see President Sterling to Lister Hill, n.d., FET papers, Box 3/43/5.

54. Twitty to Rhinelander, 4 January 1960, FET papers, Box 3/32/1; and Clifford Grobstein to Terman, 15 November 1963, FET papers, Box 3/4/10.

55. Donald Kennedy to Halsey Royden, 11 May 1965, FET papers, Box 3/5/1.

56. Terman, notes, 8 November 1971, FET papers, Box 3/4/11; for the concerns of Lederberg and Kornberg, see Robert Sears to Terman, n.d., Terman papers, Box 3/5/1.

57. Terman to Glover, n.d., FET papers, Box 3/4/11; see also Sterling to Sears, 15 June 1965, FET papers, Box 3/4/11.

58. Myers to Sterling, 26 June 1965, FET papers, Box 3/10/11.

59. Ibid.

60. Terman to Glover, n.d., FET papers, Box 3/4/1.

61. For Berg's demands, see Sears to Sterling, 25 April 1966, FET papers, Box 3/4/11. The information on the "fighting fund" came from Fred Glover, interview by author, Stanford University, 3 March 1987. According to Berg, his decision to withdraw his name from consideration was unrelated to the administration's willingness or unwillingness to meet his demands. (Berg did not recall making these demands, in fact.) Berg did, however, want to head a department; in 1969, Arthur Kornberg resigned as chairman of the department of biochemistry in the medical school so that Berg could replace him. Paul Berg, interview by author, telephone conversation, 17 October 1994.

62. "Stanford's Minimum Needs in the Coming Decade," 10 October 1959, Administrative Studies, Surveys and Reports by the Vice-President for Business and Finance, Stanford University Archives. Regarding Rhinelander's support of Terman's general effort, see, for example, Rhinelander to Shaw, 24 October 1960, FET papers, Box 3/15/2; and Rhinelander to Robert Wert, 23 December 1960, FET papers, Box 3/61/4.

63. See letter (draft) to President Sterling, with "possible signers" Kenneth Arrow, Felix Bloch, Leonard Schiff, Wallace Stegner, Lorie Tarshis, Virgil Whitaker, A. F. Wright, and John L. Mothershead, Jr., n.d., LS papers, Box 13. See also Philip Rhinelander to Wallace Sterling, "General Comments on Budgeting Procedures," 7 January 1959, LS papers, Box 13.

64. See Rhinelander to Kenneth Cuthbertson, 7 June 1961; and Rhinelander to Cuthbertson, 7 July 1961, both in FET papers, Box 3/4/19. See also Rhinelander to Sterling, 18 November 1959; and Rhinelander to Sterling, 7 December 1959, both in JWS papers, Box A-16.

65. Rhinelander to President Sterling, 7 January 1959, LS papers, Box 13.

66. See Terman, notes on Asian languages (copy sent to Rhinelander), 26 June 1961, FET papers, Box 3/46/20.

67. For Rhinelander's views, see Rhinelander to Terman, 30 June 1961; Rhinelander to Terman, 26 June 1961; and Rhinelander to Terman, 1 June 1961, all in FET papers, Box 3/46/20. For Terman's notes on Rhinelander, see Terman, notes, 7 July 1961, FET papers, Box 3/46/20. See also Terman to Wert, 23 June 1961, FET papers, Box 3/46/20.

68. Terman, "Notes on PHR; 'confidential,' " [July 1961?], FET papers, Box 3/49/20. Terman was also upset that Rhinelander had addressed his complaints about the university's budgeting practices directly to Cuthbertson, Stanford's financial vice-president, rather than to the provost. See provost's meeting, minutes, 14 June 1961, FET papers, Box 3/61/4.

69. See "File memo from Schiff," 4 August 1961; and letter (draft) to Sterling, with "possible signers" Leonard Schiff, et al., both in LS papers, Box 13. It is unclear whether this letter was ever sent to Stanford's president.

70. Meeting among Edward Ginzton, Leonard Schiff, Robert Hofstadter, Wolfgang Panofsky, and representatives of the Atomic Energy Commission, minutes, 19 October 1954, LS papers, Box 14/19.

71. Felix Bloch to Robert Hofstadter, 8 December 1954, FB papers, Box 1/1/12. Bloch's unhappiness with his position at CERN, which involved more administrative work than he had anticipated, led him to resign three months after arriving at CERN. For Bloch's concerns in the late 1940s that the microwave laboratory not become subject to security restrictions, see "F.B. [Felix Bloch]," memo, 21 September 1949, LS papers, Box 17/3.

72. Panofsky's dissatisfaction with conditions at Berkeley had been heightened when President Robert Sproul, in an effort to appease McCarthy sympathizers on the Board of Trustees and in the California legislature, asked that all employees of the university sign a loyalty oath. Panofsky signed the oath but was unhappy when Sproul began firing those who had not. See Wolfgang Panofsky, oral history, Niels Bohr Library, American Institute of Physics.

73. Hofstadter to Bloch, 3 November 1954, FB papers, Box 1/6/4.

74. Schiff, Hofstadter, Ginzton, and Panofsky to President Sterling, 8 October 1954, LS papers, Box 14/19; Hofstadter to Bloch, 3 November 1954, FB papers, Box 1/6/4.

75. Schiff to Sterling, "Physics Department's Five-Year Plan," December 1949, JWS papers, Box A-12.

76. Minutes of the 55th meeting of the AEC's General Advisory Committee, 30 September–2 October 1957, AEC records, General Advisory Committee collection. The various concerns of the Joint Committee on Atomic Energy (JCAE) may be found in "Stanford Linear Accelerator," *Hearings before the Subcommittee on Research and Development and the Subcommittee on Legislation of the Joint Committee on Atomic Energy,* 86th Congress, First Session (1959). For concerns within the AEC and its General Advisory Committee that a facility of the magnitude proposed could not be located on a campus without "ruining the university," see Willard Libby, AEC commissioner, "Support of Accelerator Research" (policy statement), 16 March 1955, AEC 603/24, AEC records, Secretariat collection, Box 1305.

77. Hofstadter to Schiff, 8 September 1958; and Hofstadter to Schiff, 28 September 1958, both in LS papers, Box 3/15. Hofstadter's feelings about the proposed accelerator may also have been influenced by Bloch, whom Hofstadter greatly admired. In response to Bloch's warnings about the proposed project, Hofstadter wrote in early 1955, "[M]y enthusiasm for [the accelerator] has flagged considerably" (see Hofstadter to Bloch, 13 March 1955, FB papers, Box 1/6/4). Hofstadter's ideas about academic life are expressed in Hofstadter, "Free Spirit in the Free University," CUNY commencement address, 13 June 1962, FET papers, Box 3/31/4.

78. Hofstadter to Schiff, 28 September 1958, LS papers, Box 3/15. See also Hofstadter to Schiff, 8 September 1958; Hofstadter to Schiff, 26 September 1958; and Hofstadter to Schiff, 30 September 1958, all in LS papers, Box 3/15. Regarding the administration of the Mark III, see Bowker to Terman, 13 October 1960, JWS papers, Box B-5.

79. Hofstadter to Bloch, 5 February 1959, FB papers, Box 1/6/4.

80. "Measures for Proceeding with the Proposed Stanford Accelerator," Report to the General Manager, AEC, from the Director of Research, AEC, 14 May 1958, AEC 603/42, AEC records, Secretariat collection, Box 1305. See also Greenberg, *Politics of Pure Science,* p. 227.

81. James R. Killian, "Memorandum for the President," 2 April 1959, AEC records, John McCone collection, Box 2276. See also Greenberg, *Politics of Pure Science,* pp. 228–30. The panel comprised Emmanuel Piore (member of PSAC and formerly of the ONR), Hans Bethe (Cornell physicist), Leland Haworth (director, Brookhaven National Laboratory), Jesse Beams (chair, physics department, University of Virginia), and Edward McMillan (associate director, Berkeley's Lawrence Radiation Laboratory).

Members of Congress, and some in the AEC, were not pleased with Killian's and Eisenhower's intervention. The AEC was initially reluctant to defend SLAC in appropriation hearings before Congress, fearing "pressure" from Congress to reduce other AEC activities in order to fund the accelerator without increasing the agency's budget. See Minutes of the 154th meeting of the AEC, 25 February 1960, AEC 1036/7 and 1036/8, AEC records, Secretariat collection, Box 1426. Senator Clinton P. Anderson of the JCAE was irritated that the JCAE had not been given a voice in the final decision, which he believed had not been fairly evaluated in comparison to the MURA proposal. "The Stanford people made their original deal in the White House," he complained to Robert S. Marshak, a University of Rochester physicist (11 April 1960, Clinton P. Anderson papers, Box 819/SLAC, Library of Congress).

82. In judging the feasibility of the Stanford proposal in comparison with that of the MURA proposal, MIT physicist Bruno Rossi explained that the Stanford accelerator "appears to be a fairly straight forward extension . . . of the existing Stanford accelerator [Mark III]. It does not seem likely to me that unforeseen difficulties may arise . . . to seriously jeopardize the outcome of the project. I must add that my confidence arises in part from the high technical and scientific competence of the group presenting the proposal." The opinions of other physicists solicited by the AEC and shared with the PSAC special panel were similar (see Bruno Rossi to John H. Williams, Director, Division of Research, AEC, 27 May 1958, JCAE records, SLAC/642).

Regarding the significance of the SLAC proposal to the Defense Department, see Ted Brown, advisor to the JCAE, to James T. Ramey, executive director, JCAE, 1 June 1959, JCAE records, SLAC/642; and Donald A. Quarles, deputy defense secretary, to Lewis Strauss, AEC commissioner, 3 March 1958, AEC 603/39, AEC records, Secretariat collection, Box 1305.

In addition to serving on PSAC, Panofsky was also an advisor to the AEC's Division of Military Applications.

83. John McCone, AEC chairman, to J. Wallace Sterling, 8 April 1960, AEC records, John McCone collection, Box 2276. In a 9 December 1959 meeting with President Sterling, McCone explained that the AEC was funding the construction of six accelerators, all of which were running over budget. Originally estimated to require a total of $72 million for construction, the figure had escalated to $176 million. Estimates for the total yearly operating costs had jumped from $13 million to $68 million. McCone was "very disturbed" by this trend and stated his determination to avoid similar problems with SLAC ("Summary of notes on the meeting of the [AEC] Commissioners with Dr. Sterling, President, Stanford University," 9 December 1959, AEC records, Secretariat collection, Box 1426). See also John C. Vinciguerra, director, AEC division of contracts, to A. R. Luedecke, AEC general manager, 18 December 1961, AEC records, John McCone collection, Box 2276.

84. Howard C. Brown, Jr., special assistant to the AEC chairman, 20 May 1960, AEC records, John McCone collection, Box 2276. According to Panofsky's recollection, the idea of bringing self-made millionaire David Packard to the meeting with McCone had been his. Packard's expressions of confidence in Stanford's physicists carried great weight with McCone, a wealthy California businessman. (See Panofsky, oral history, Niels Bohr Library, American Institute of Physics.)

85. Panofsky to Schiff, 22 October 1963, LS papers, Box 14. For the physicists' objections to the AEC's proposed control over design and construction of SLAC, see Wallace Sterling to A. R. Luedecke, AEC general manager, 26 February 1960, LS papers, Box 14. For the physicists' adverse reaction to the AEC's plan to require SLAC to conform to AEC security regulations, see John C. Vinciguerra to A. R. Luedecke, 18 December 1961, AEC records, John McCone collection, Box 2276. According to Vinciguerra, Panofsky "personally led the discussions in voicing the University's objections" to the security provisions.

86. See Panofsky, oral history, Niels Bohr Library, American Institute of Physics; Schiff to Bowker, 6 December 1961, LS papers, Box 14/20; and Minutes of the Graduate Division Committee, 4 January 1962, FET papers, Box 3/29/8.

87. Bloch to Schiff, 21 October 1959, LS papers, Box 17/3.

88. See Schiff to Bowker, 6 December 1961, LS papers, Box 14/20; and George Pake to the physics department, 5 March 1962, LS papers, Box 17/3.

89. Bowker to Ernest Hilgard, advisory board chair, 11 January 1962, JWS papers, Box B-3. The two physicists in question were Joseph Ballam and H. Pierre Noyes. The members of the Advisory Board were Hilgard, John Dodds, H. E. Dougall, H. S. Kaplan, John Mothershead, Leonard Schiff, and John Vennard.

90. Physics department memo, 23 May 1963, JWS papers, Box B-3. See also Sidney Drell to Schiff, 12 May 1962; Schiff to Drell, 19 May 1962; and Schiff to Drell, 25 May 1962, LS papers, Box 17/2.

91. Drell to Panofsky, 3 March 1962, SLAC records, director's office papers, "Drell." Physicist George Pake agreed with Drell that the department's opposition to salary-splitting had become untenable. Noting the "great disparity" between the amount of federal support and the amount of university support available to the physicists, Pake wrote that "any solution of dilemma must lie in the use of federal funds to broaden the faculty base upon which the university's physics program rests. I do not especially like this conclusion," he conceded; "it is simply unavoidable" (Pake to the physics department, 5 March 1962, LS papers, Box 17).

92. Bloch to Schiff, 3 August 1962; and Bloch to Walter Meyerhof, 8 January 1963, both in LS papers, Box 14/20. Meyerhof, a German-born experimentalist in atomic and molecular physics who had joined Stanford's department in 1949, warned of the dangers of granting researchers who were on the federal payroll, and thus not in "free association" with the university, the privilege of educating students (see Meyerhof to the physics department, 15 October 1962, LS papers, Box 14/20). For Terman and Bowker's response to the proposal to make SLAC a degree-granting institution separate from the physics department, see Panofsky to Drell, 31 May 1962, SLAC records, director's office papers, "Drell."

93. Physics department to Sterling, 6 December 1962, JWS papers, Box B-3.

94. Bowker to Sterling, 19 February 1963, JWS papers, Box B-3. See also Sidney Raffel, advisory board chairman, to Sterling, 6 February 1963; Bowker to Raffel, 15 February 1963; and Fred Glover to Sterling, 5 February 1963, all in JWS papers, Box B-3.

95. See Sterling to Schiff, 25 June 1963, JWS papers, Box B-3; see also, Drell to Panofsky, n.d., SLAC records, director's office papers, "Drell"; Panofsky to Meyerhof, 8 January 1963, LS papers, Box 14/20; and Drell to Bowker, 9 January 1963, LS papers, Box 14/20.

96. See Schiff to Panofsky, 18 March 1964; and Meyerhof to Panofsky, 10 February 1964, both in JWS papers, Box B-3.

97. For Panofsky's views of the quota, see Panofsky to Sterling, 11 December 1964; Panofsky to Sterling, 12 January 1965; Panofsky to Terman, 5 March 1965; and Panofsky to Schiff, 23 March 1964, all in JWS papers, Box B-3. For Terman's opinion of the quota, see Terman to Sterling, 20 March 1964, JWS papers, Box B-3. See also Schiff to Panofsky, 18 March 1964; and Schiff to Sterling, 18 March 1964, both in JWS papers, Box B-3. Hofstadter was unhappy about the suggestion that Matthew Sands, deputy director of SLAC and former Caltech physicist, be given teaching privileges. To permit this meant "yielding, in principle, so that the doors are opened to other SLAC people as well. I am afraid that the net effect is a victory by SLAC and a dishonor to the department's principles of running its own affairs" (see Hofstadter to Schiff, 2 October 1965, LS papers, Box 3/15).

98. Hubert Heffner to Sterling, 4 April 1965, JWS papers, Box B-5.

99. See Sterling to Schiff, 30 July 1965, JWS papers, Box B-3. See also

Heffner to Sterling, 20 April 1965, JWS papers, Box B-3; and Hofstadter to Schiff, 2 October 1965, LS papers, Box 3/15. For the reactions of faculty members outside the physics department to the conflict over joint appointments, see mathematics department to President Sterling, 13 March 1963; biochemist Arthur Kornberg and chemistry chairman William Johnson to Sterling, 1 September 1965; chemist Paul Flory to Sterling, 2 September 1965; and chemist Henry Taube to Sterling, 2 September 1965, all in JWS papers, Box B-3. By 1965, the chemistry and physics departments were the only ones still resisting joint appointments.

100. Virgil Whitaker to Sterling, 28 September 1965; and Schiff to Sterling, 4 August 1965, both in JWS papers, Box B-3.

101. Eric Hutchinson, interview by author, Stanford University, 27 May 1987. Hutchinson described Terman as "very unmannerly," a "workaholic," and "tiresome in the extreme." "I don't think he read a novel or went to a play in his life. But he worked until midnight. And he loved to amass detail in his mind." Hutchinson recalled conversations with Terman in which Terman, disagreeing with what Hutchinson was saying, would interrupt with the command, "Stop talking."

Chapter 7.   Private Foundations and the "Behavioral Revolution"

1. This general description of the social sciences in the early cold war may be found in a variety of sources. See, for example, Buck, "Adjusting to Military Life"; Webb, *Social Sciences,* pp. 509–11; Somit and Tanenhaus, *Development of Political Science*; McCaughey, *International Studies*; and Heims, *Cybernetics Group*.

2. For examples of this interpretation, see Klausner and Lidz, *Nationalization of the Social Sciences,* and Geiger, "American Foundations."

3. Schrecker, *No Ivory Tower,* p. 339.

4. The "status anxiety" explanation, in fact, owes much to the "behavioralist persuasion" whose dominance it seeks to explain.

5. Needell, " 'Truth is Our Weapon.' "

6. Heims, *Cybernetics Group,* p. 7.

7. See Geiger, "American Foundations," pp. 333–34, for figures on support for social science research provided by the three leading foundations to America's leading universities between 1946 and 1958.

Between 1948 and 1951, annual support for social science research from the Carnegie Corporation, Ford Foundation, and Rockefeller Foundation totaled approximately $7 million. In 1953 foundation support totaled approximately $165 million, of which the Ford Foundation contributed 40 percent or $66 million. Between 1955 and 1958, support from the three leading foundations totaled $43.6 million. See Geiger, *Research and Relevant Knowledge,* pp. 93, 105; John Riley, Jr., "Status of Social Sciences, 1950," in Klausner and Lidz, *Nationalization of the Social Sciences,* p. 115; and Bernard Berelson to H. Rowan Gaither, Donald Marquis, and Hans Speier, 14 December 1951, FF collections, Behavioral Sciences, Office Files, Bernard Berelson.

The precise amount expended by the federal government in support of academic social science research is more difficult to determine. According to the minutes of the Committee on Human Resources (HRC) of the Defense Department's Research and Development Board, in 1948 the federal government spent $662,000 for academic and nonacademic social science research (basic and applied). See minutes of the 5th meeting of the Committee on Human Resources, 7 May 1948, RDB records, Entry 341, Committee files, Box 241. According to Riley, "Status of Social Sciences, 1950," p. 115, the federal government spent a total of $52 million in 1948 for research and development in the social sciences. Riley's figures, unlike those provided by the HRC, included expenditures for development as well as research, and expenditures for statistical research as well as social scientific research. According to the estimates of Bernard Berelson of the Ford Foundation, in 1951 the federal government was contributing approximately $2.5 million annually for research in the behavioral sciences (Berelson to Gaither, Marquis, and Speier, 14 December 1951, FF collections, Behavioral Sciences, Office Files, Bernard Berelson). By FY 1953, at the height of military spending during the Korean War, the Defense Department was providing $25 million to support basic and applied research in the academic and nonacademic social sciences, 40 percent of which supported research and development of "training devices." The contribution to academic research in the social sciences was certainly no greater than $10 million that year, and possibly less. See "Status of Human Resources R and D for Assistant Secretary of Defense for R and D," 20 July 1953, RDB records, Entry 341, Committee files, Box 408.

8. Macdonald, *Ford Foundation,* pp. 42, 131–33.

9. Macdonald, *Ford Foundation,* pp. 19–21, 36–49. See also, Geiger, "American Foundations." Histories of foundation patronage in earlier periods also tend to depict the foundations as ideal patrons. See, for example, Kohler, *Partners in Science.*

In the 1930s it became accepted that a lag was developing between technical knowledge and the knowledge of how technological changes were affecting society and might best be managed. This viewpoint was promoted by the Social Science Research Council, which was seeking to make a case for the importance of social scientific research. See Kuznick, *Beyond the Laboratory,* pp. 51–56.

10. As one college president strongly supportive of Bush's view of the social sciences explained, one only had to look to Nazi Germany and other totalitarian states to understand the inevitable outcome of governmental support of the social sciences. See Bush, *Endless Frontier,* p. 118.

11. Macdonald, *Ford Foundation,* pp. 25–35.

12. Seybold, "The Ford Foundation." See also *Report of the Study for the Ford Foundation on Policy and Program,* November 1949, FF collections.

13. See, for example, Arnove's introduction to Arnove, *Philanthropy and Cultural Imperialism.* Scholarly interest in the ruling, or power, elite, may be traced to the work of C. W. Mills, especially *The Power Elite* (New York: Oxford University Press, 1956). An excellent recent example of this approach may be found in O'Connell, "Social Structure and Science." O'Connell charts the multiple informal ties between individuals involved in the Harvard Russian Research Center, the administration of Harvard University, the Carnegie

Corporation, and the air force. For example, Clyde Kluckhohn, the head of the center and of the center's air-force-funded project to interview Soviet refugees, was also an advisor to the air force and to the Committee on Human Resources, created by the Defense Department's Research and Development Board (RDB). Also on the RDB's Committee on Human Resources was Carnegie Corporation president Charles Dollard and Carnegie Corporation trustees John Gardner and Vannevar Bush. Bush, of course, was close to Harvard president James Conant, having worked with him in the Office of Scientific Research and Development during the war, and after the war, joining Conant's Committee on the Present Danger, a private group formed in 1950 to lobby Congress and to alert the public to the dangers posed to Western Europe by Soviet communism. Conant, Bush, Kluckhohn, Gardner, and Dollard all interacted socially, as well, as members of the exclusive Cosmos Club.

14. Macdonald, *Ford Foundation,* pp. 10–11 and 137–38; McCaughey, *International Studies,* p. 144; and Bernard Berelson, oral history, FF collections.

15. See Macdonald, pp. 8, 155.

16. Macdonald, *Ford Foundation,* pp. 8, 155; Bernard Berelson, oral history, FF collections.

17. Bernard Berelson, oral history, FF collections. According to Berelson, Gaither was strongly influenced by Hans Speier of RAND.

18. See Buck, "Adjusting to Military Life," p. 221: "Four years with the military had shown that prewar applied social science was insufficiently scientific to withstand the demands made on it by an army inevitably interested in getting a practical job done first." See also Katz, *Foreign Intelligence,* pp. 14–17. As Arthur Schlesinger, Jr., noted at the time, "In writing of reports, one is expected to turn out thoroughly objective and neutral intelligence. . . . [C]are should be taken about the use of color words such as 'reactionary,' 'progressive,' 'left or right,' etc." (as quoted in Katz, p. 17). See also the records of the Human Resources Committee of the RDB for a detailed picture of the Defense Department's interests in social scientific research.

More generally, the postwar political climate favored the use of depoliticized language and research of a politically uncontroversial nature. For example, under its first president, Paul Hoffman, the Ford Foundation established the Fund for the Republic as part of its "strengthening democracy" program. Headed by Robert Hutchins, the fund provided support for studies of civil liberties, including small amounts of money for the study of political blacklisting, the origins of the federal loyalty oath program, and the reaction of faculty members to McCarthyism. McCarthyites pointed to the fund, among other things, in their attacks on the Ford Foundation. See Macdonald, *Ford Foundation,* pp. 69–80.

19. "Self-Study Program," Behavioral Science Division, Ford Foundation, March 1953, attached to Bernard Berelson to President Sterling, 27 March 1953, JWS papers, Box 29.

20. Hans Speier, oral history, pp. 22–24, Archives, Division of Space History, National Air and Space Museum, Washington, D.C.; and Heims, *Cybernetics Group,* p. 202.

21. Needell, " 'Truth is Our Weapon,' " pp. 400–401 n.6; Ford Foundation Press Release, 27 June 1951, FF collections, Behavioral Sciences, Office Files, Bernard Berelson.

22. Rowan Gaither, "Program V Activities," 19 December 1951, FF collections, Behavioral Sciences, Office Files, Bernard Berelson.

23. Needell, " 'Truth is Our Weapon,' " pp. 411–16.

24. See Gaither, "Development of Program V," 27 January 1951; Gaither, "Program V Activities," 19 December 1951; and "Program V: Action of Officers on December 20, 1951," 28 December 1951, all in FF collections, Behavioral Sciences, Office Files, Bernard Berelson. See also "Draft of Report on Program V," 9 January 1952, FF collections, Report # 003264.

25. See Gaither, "Program V Activities," 19 December 1951; and Gaither, "Program V: Action of Officers on December 20, 1951," 28 December 1951, both in FF collections, Behavioral Sciences, Office Files, Bernard Berelson. See also "Communications Project at MIT—Orientation In," 23 October 1953, FF collections, William McPeak papers, Office Files, Folder 260. On the creation of CENIS, see Needell, " 'Truth is Our Weapon,' " pp. 416–17.

26. Geiger, "American Foundations," pp. 333–34.

27. Sterling to Gaither, 16 January 1950, B. J. Craig, secretary/treasurer of the Ford Foundation to Sterling, 28 July 1950; and William W. McPeak, assistant director, Ford Foundation Study Committee, to Sterling, [August 1950?], all in JWS papers, Box 49.

28. See Sterling to Paul Hoffman, [1951?], FF collections, Grant File 50–276/1; "Report on the Employment of a Grant of $100,000 by the Ford Foundation to Stanford University," November 1950–January 1955, FF collections, Grant File 50–276/3; and "Progress Report—Committee for Research in the Social Sciences," November 1951–March 1953, JWS papers, Box 29. Others involved in CRISS between 1951 and 1953 included Moses Abramovitz (economics), Arthur Coladarci (education), Alfred de Grazia (political science), Paul Hanna (education), David Harris (history), William O. Jones (Food Research Institute), Bernard Siegel (anthropology), Donald Taylor (psychology), John Troxell (business school), Robert Walker (political science), Paul Wallin (sociology), C. Langdon White (geography), and C. Leland Winder (psychology).

29. Lerner, *Psychological Warfare against Nazi Germany: The Sykewar Campaign, D-Day to VE-Day* (Cambidge: MIT Press, 1971).

30. "Report of the Planning Committee for the Ford Foundation Grant," 8 September 1951, JWS papers, Box 49.

31. "Progress Report—Committee for Research in the Social Sciences," November 1951–March 1953, JWS papers, Box 29.

32. See Schrecker, *No Ivory Tower*; and Caute, *Great Fear.*

33. Ray Lyman Wilbur to William Hansen, 24 August 1940, RLW papers, Box 105, "physics"; and Fred Glover, confidential memo to Sterling, 5 March 1953, JWS papers, Box B-1. Stanford administrators became somewhat concerned about Roberts again in 1953; although no longer in the employ of the university, Roberts was cited by the California Un-American Activities Committee, commonly referred to as the Burns Committee, as one of the most highly placed communists in California and administrators were apparently

worried that Stanford faculty members might be asked to testify before the committee.

34. For examples of the concerns of wealthy alumni, see Roy E. Naftzger to Paul Edwards, President, Stanford Board of Trustees, 10 May 1950; L. R. Weinmann to Edwards, 10 May 1950; L. H. Roseberry to Edwards, 5 August 1948; Doris A. Parks to President Sterling, n.d.; and Andrew Copp, Jr., to Edwards, 14 April 1948, all in PE papers, Box 2. Most did not question the loyalty of specific professors. But Copp sent Edwards a copy of *Alert,* a publication put out by the right wing in California, which listed professors suspected of left-wing beliefs. The editor of *Alert,* Edward Gibbons, also wrote the 1949 report on communism in America for the state's Senate Committee on Un-American Activities, at that time known as the Tenney Committee, after the state senator, Jack Tenney, who headed the committee (see Barrett, *The Tenney Committee*). And Robert Donner, in response to President Sterling's request for specific names (Donner had made vague accusations about "socialist-types" on the Stanford faculty), sent Sterling a pamphlet entitled "RED-ucators" which listed twenty-one Stanford faculty members (Donner to Sterling, 9 August 1951, JWS papers, Box B-1). The origin of "RED-ucators" is unclear; a copy of the pamphlet may be found in the Hoover Institution Library. More upsetting to Stanford's administration than the complaints of alumni about nameless, disloyal faculty members were the activities of California's Burns Committee, particularly its willingness to name faculty members suspected of disloyalty.

The administration's own efforts to eliminate radicals from the campus extended to the students. In 1949, for example, Alice Beach, a Stanford employee, was sent by the university's office of information to observe a meeting of a Stanford student group, the Young Progressives, and to report back to the Director of Information. See Boyd Haight, Assistant Director of Information, to "Tom" (most likely, Thomas Spragens), 16 August 1949, JWS papers, Box 14. Sterling's initial, and the comment, "interesting," make clear that the president read the report.

35. Stanford faculty members first learned of Sterling's stated commitment to cooperate with the Burns Committee by reading the San Francisco *Chronicle* on 8 August 1952. On reading the news, Leonard Schiff (chair, physics) contacted Stanford's provost in "a state of some alarm," according to the provost. Other faculty members distressed by the news included Bernard Haley (political science), Ernest Hilgard (psychology), and the novelist Wallace Stegner (creative writing). See Provost Whitaker to Sterling, 13 August 1952; and Schiff to Whitaker, 12 August 1952, both in JWS papers, Box B-1; Wallace Stegner, "Suggestions on the problem of investigations," [23 January 1953?]; and B. F. Haley to Sterling, 19 March 1953, both in JWS papers, Box C-9.

In his first press conference after becoming president of Stanford, Sterling made it clear that he would not tolerate members of the Communist Party on the Stanford faculty. As quoted by the *Stanford Daily* (6 April 1949, p. 1), Sterling stated, "I doubt if any member of the Communist Party is a free agent. If he isn't a free agent, he cannot be objective in his teaching. Therefore, he should be precluded from classroom instruction." By 1953 the university's policy continued to be that a member of the Communist Party could not be a member of

Stanford's faculty (although the problem remained, for Stanford as for other universities, as to how to identify members of the Communist Party).

Sterling had not yet decided what to do about faculty members who had once been, but were no longer, members of the Communist Party. This did not become an issue until 1963, when the Department of Sociology offered a research position to Jan Howard. Dean of graduate studies Albert Bowker recalled that she had been subpoenaed by the State Un-American Activities Committee and he brought her name to President Sterling's attention. According to Provost Terman's notes on the matter in June 1963, "Jan Howard still refuses to tell Wally [Sterling] if *was* a member of the Communist Party . . . [Trustee Morris] Doyle advised Wally against employing her—unless she answers his direct questions—says would hurt Wally with Board." In November 1963 Howard was willing to tell Sterling "privately" whether she had been a party member, but Sterling insisted that she must make the information public. Trustee David Packard moved that the trustees give Sterling until the end of the year to resolve the matter. Sterling resisted pressure from the board to fire Howard but recommended that her affiliation with Stanford end when her grant expired in August 1964. See Terman, notes on Jan Howard, June 1963; and Terman, notes, 23 November 1963, both in FET papers, Box 3/32/3.

36. Haley to Sterling, 22 January 1953; and Haley to Sterling, 19 March 1953, both JWS papers, Box C-9.

37. The attacks by Hoover and his associates on North, Spaeth, Rothwell, Fisher, and those involved in the Carnegie Corporation-sponsored studies of the impact of revolutions on international relations are described from a somewhat sympathetic perspective by Nash in *Herbert Hoover,* pp. 126–49. Both Fisher and Rothwell were liberal internationalists; Hoover, his friends, and wealthy benefactors of the Hoover Library objected to Fisher's outspoken criticism of McCarthy and his support for Owen Lattimore, who had been labeled by McCarthy as a "top Russian spy." Rothwell's views also irritated Hoover but Hoover did intervene with HUAC to prevent Rothwell from being subpoenaed to testify in the Hiss case. Hoover and his friends became upset with North in 1953 when he published *Moscow and the Chinese Communists,* which they regarded as insufficiently critical of the Chinese communists. The origins of Hoover's animosity toward Spaeth, who had worked during the war with Nelson Rockefeller and after the war was close to the Ford Foundation, are unclear. But Hoover attempted to prevent Spaeth's appointment as dean of the Stanford law school in 1946, and in 1955 attacked Spaeth before the Stanford board of trustees for accepting a grant from the Fund for the Republic for an "impartial" study of witnesses' testimony in hearings before legislative committees concerning communism.

Paul Hanna was first attacked in 1947, in the testimony of Aaron M. Sargent, a Palo Alto attorney, before the State Senate Committee on Education. According to Sargent's testimony, a communistic cell existed in Stanford's School of Education, of which Paul Hanna was a part (see Paul Hanna papers, Box 5, Hoover Institution Archives). Paul Baran was first attacked in the 2 July 1954 issue of *New Counter-Attack,* which came to the attention of Fred Glover, secretary to President Sterling (see Glover to Sterling, 22 July 1954, Baran files,

Pacific Studies Center, Mountain View, California). Both Ernest Hilgard and H. H. Fisher were attacked in "RED-ucators" (see JWS papers, Box B-1). Of all those suspected of unconventional political views, only Hilgard, it seems, was called to Washington to testify; he then lost his security clearance. (See Hilgard's autobiographical account in Lindzey, *History of Psychology*. I thank Sigmund Diamond for bringing this source to my attention.)

38. Nash, *Herbert Hoover*, pp. 119, 131, and 135. The employee of the Hoover Library was Witold Sworakowski.

39. As quoted in Nash, *Herbert Hoover*, p. 141.

40. There is only indirect evidence that Lerner, unlike Pool, was encouraged to leave Stanford. Shortly after their departures, political science professor Alfred de Grazia wrote to President Sterling to indicate his concern that the loss of Lerner and Pool would suggest "to the outside world" that Stanford lacked competence in the field of international affairs. While de Grazia was particularly upset over the loss of Pool, he wrote of Lerner's departure, "I am not disputing other features of that *action*" (emphasis added), which suggests that Lerner left Stanford under different circumstances than did Pool. See de Grazia to Sterling, 9 March 1953, JWS papers, Box 29.

41. See Nash, pp. 128–36, and C. E. Rothwell to Perrin, 19 November 1952, JWS papers, Box C-9. Fisher, a "Vermont Republican," had initially upset Hoover, his friends, and Hoover Library benefactors with his 1946 book, *America and Russia in the World Community,* which suggested that the U.S. and the USSR were not irreconcilably opposed but might work together in the postwar world. While Sterling was not able to withstand pressure from Hoover for Fisher's resignation, Sterling was personally supportive of Fisher, his former teacher.

42. See Fred Glover to Sterling, 22 July 1954, Baran files, Pacific Studies Center, Mountain View, California. (The files on Baran at the Pacific Studies Center are copies of material once held by the Stanford Archives.)

Among those objecting to Baran were Stanford trustee David Packard (see Packard to Editor, *Stanford Daily,* May 1961 [unsent]; a Texaco stockholder (see James T. Wood to President Sterling, 9 June 1961); Willard Chilcott, trustee, Occidental College (see H. H. Everett, regional director, university relations, to Lyle Nelson, 13 December 1961); a California attorney (see Dudley Harkleroad to Provost Terman, 28 November 1962); and the sister to the Ambassador to Argentina (see Betty McClintock Kirby to President Sterling, 13 February 1963), all in Baran files, Pacific Studies Center, Mountain View. In response to an attack on Baran as a communist in the January–February 1961 issue of *FACTS in Education,* Sterling arranged a private luncheon on 6 March 1961 with prominent donors to the university, including T. S. Peterson and S. Z. Natcher of Standard Oil of California, and John R. Beckett, of TransAmerica. See Jessie Applegarth, secretary to President of Standard Oil of California, 16 March 1961, Baran Files, Pacific Studies Center.

To those complaining about Baran, Stanford administrators explained that Baran had tenure and could not be fired. Joseph M. Vickers, California Superior Court Judge and volunteer fund-raiser for Stanford, suggested to Sterling that if the university could not fire Baran, it should make it clear to potential donors that "the University has been and is doing all it can to discourage Professor Baran from remaining at Stanford" (Vickers to Sterling, 28 March 1963, Baran files, Pacific Studies Center). While Sterling replied that to make such information available to potential donors would be unwise, as there might be "feedback to the faculty," it does appear that the university was keeping Baran's salary artificially low in order to encourage him to leave the university (see Sterling to Vickers, 22 May 1963, Baran files, Pacific Studies Center). According to Terman's notes, in the fall of 1956 Baran, one of the department's senior members, had the fourth lowest salary; by 1963 Baran was receiving the lowest salary in the department ($14,500). See salary figures (apparently jotted down by Provost Terman), Baran files, Pacific Studies Center. Despite Sterling's desire to avoid "feedback to the faculty," the members of the economics department concluded that the administration's refusal to give Baran the requested improvements in salary indicated that "professor Baran is being punished for his views." Calling this "a violation of academic freedom," the department threatened to bring the issue before the American Association of University Professors. See Kenneth Arrow to Sterling, 8 March 1963; Arrow to Sterling 7 June 1963; and economics department to Sterling, 7 June 1963, all in JWS papers, Box 2.

43. Terman to files, 16 November 1955, FET papers, Box 3/45/12; Glover to Sterling, 13 September 1955, JWS papers, Box 52; and Terman, memo, 16 November 1955, FET papers, Box 3/45/12.

44. See Bernard Berelson to Sterling, 27 March 1953; and Stanford Self-Study Proposal, 13 May 1953, both in JWS papers, Box 49. Other universities participating in the self-survey program in 1953 were Harvard, the University of Chicago, the University of North Carolina, and the University of Michigan.

45. See "Psychology—Department Self-Study," 23 November 1953; "Role of Mathematics and Statistics in Training and Research in the Behavioral Sciences," 1 December 1953; "Self-Survey—Anthropology and Sociology," n.d.; "History—Survey of," 23 November 1953; "Department Self-Study for the Behavioral Sciences—Political Science," n.d.; "Institute for Journalistic Studies," January 1954, and Visiting Committee, Ford Foundation, "Report on Anthropology," 20 April 1954, all in JWS papers, Box 49.

46. "Report on Faculty Interviews to the Survey of the Behavioral Sciences, 1953–54"; and "Report of the Special Committee on Research Programs to the Survey of the Behavioral Sciences, 1953–54," both in Behavioral Sciences collection, Stanford University Archives.

47. Ernest Hilgard to Stanley Weigel, 15 March 1954; and Hilgard to Sterling, 20 April 1955, both in JWS papers, Box 49.

48. W. Allan Wallis, chair, Ford Foundation Self-Study Program, "1953–54 Program of University Surveys of the Behavioral Sciences," 18 April 1955, FF collections, Report #002918; and "Stanford Self-Study Proposal," 13 May 1953, JWS papers, Box 49.

49. "Department Self Study for the Behavioral Sciences—Political Science," n.d., JWS papers, Box 49. See also Peter Odegard, Visiting Committee, Ford Foundation, notes on the political science department, 17 March 1954, JWS papers, Box 49.

50. Francis X. Sutton, "Memo on telephone conversation with Ernest R.

Hilgard, June 16th, 1955," 21 June 1955, FF collections, Grant File 55–113/4. See also Hilgard to Provost Douglas Whitaker, 10 June 1955; and Hilgard to Sterling, 23 December 1954, both in JWS papers, Box 49.

51. Chilton Bush to Sterling, 8 February 1955, JWS papers, Box 3.

52. See Hilgard to Whitaker, 10 June 1955, JWS papers, Box 49; Bush to Sterling, 19 November 1958, JWS papers, Box 1; International Studies Committee, minutes, 18 November 1963, FET papers, Box 3/33/5; and "International Studies, 1965," FET papers, Box 3/33/5.

The university abolished the undergraduate journalism program, and with Ford Foundation support, it inaugurated the Neiman Program, which provided fellowships to established journalists for a year of study at Stanford.

53. Bush to Philip Rhinelander, 5 October 1959, JWS papers, Box 1. By 1960 the administration had already decided that Schramm was the "key man" in the department and that it should build a program around his interests. Dean Rhinelander acknowledged that neither Weigle nor Brinton, professors associated with the journalism program, would be "very sympathetic with the project of emphasizing Communications." Rhinelander failed to anticipate the objections of Bush. See Rhinelander to Robert Wert, 21 October 1960, JWS papers, Box 1. See also Rhinelander to Wert, 25 October 1960; Clifford Weigle to Sterling, 27 April 1961; and Bush to Wert, 1 May 1961, JWS papers, Box 1.

54. Wilbur Schramm, "Notes on the Future of Communications at Stanford," 20 May 1963; and Robert Sears, dean of humanities and sciences, to Terman, 1 May 1963, both in JWS papers, Box 1. See also Terman, notes on communications department, 31 May 1963; Terman to Stanford's advisory board, 6 June 1963; and "Communications Department, Government Contracts, 1963–64," FET papers, Box 3/11/3.

55. Leavelle's position was initially filled by David Smith, a political theorist who had been hired to Stanford the previous year using funds freed from the salaries of two political science professors whose salaries were being partially supported by nondepartmental funds. Smith soon left Stanford to return to Swarthmore. See Watkins to Sterling, 23 April 1956, and Philip Rhinelander to Terman, 15 April 1957, both in JWS papers, Box 5; Hubert Marshall, interview by author, Stanford University, 20 March 1990.

56. Peter Odegard, member of the Ford Foundation visiting committee, notes on Stanford political science department, 17 March 1954, JWS papers, Box 49; Terman, notes on conversation with Philip Rhinelander, 10 April 1958, JWS papers, Box 5; and Albert Bowker to Terman, 23 May 1957, FET papers, Box 3/6/1.

57. Hubert Marshall, interview by author, Stanford University, 20 March 1990. See also *Stanford Daily*, 8 May 1958, p. 1; and Kalleberg, Moon, and Sabia, *Dissent and Affirmation*, pp. 2–4, 272–76.

58. Rhinelander to Albert Bowker, 7 March 1958, JWS papers, Box B-5; Terman to Sterling, 2 March 1958, JWS papers, Box 5. Rhinelander himself preferred the department to appoint Louis Hartz.

59. See, for example, Young, *Study of Politics*; and Charlesworth, *Contemporary Political Analysis,* which includes an essay by Mulford Q. Sibley, "The Limits of Behavioralism," pp. 51–71.

60. Jerome G. Kerwin to Bob [Robert Wert?], 17 January 1958; and Francis G. Wilson to James Watkins, 24 January 1958, both in JWS papers, Box B-5.

61. Rhinelander to Bowker, 7 March 1958, JWS papers, Box B-5. The administration got similar opinions of Sibley from Stanford economist Kenneth Arrow and Stanford psychologist and former University of Minnesota faculty member Leon Festinger. See also Rhinelander notes, 27 December 1957, JWS papers, Box 5.

62. Rhinelander explained to Bowker that, while "I am not happy about the Sibley recommendation," the department's objections to Easton were of "sufficient foundation so that we cannot properly ram him down their throats." See Rhinelander to Bowker, 7 March 1958, JWS papers, Box B-5; see also Rhinelander to Watkins, 18 March 1958, JWS papers, Box B-5. According to Hubert Marshall, Watkins was a very "proper person," whom he had never observed to be "acrimonious." But in his meeting with Rhinelander to protest the administration's rejection of Sibley, Watkins became so upset that he pushed some papers off Rhinelander's desk and onto the floor (Hubert Marshall, interview by author, Stanford University, 20 March 1990).

63. Bowker, notes, 27 March 1958, JWS papers, Box 5. Regarding the removal of Watkins as chair, see Terman, notes of conversation with Rhinelander, 27 February 1958, FET papers, Box 3/46/19; and Terman to Sterling, 2 March 1958, JWS papers, Box 5. According to Marshall, even before his row with the dean of humanities and sciences, Watkins had been tagged as a "dinosaur" by Terman. Robert Walker, who disliked Watkins's genteel anti-Semitism, also campaigned to have him removed as department chair (Hubert Marshall, interview with author, Stanford University, 20 March 1990).

64. See Terman, notes on Sibley, 28 April 1958; and Terman, notes on Sibley, 30 April 1958, both in JWS papers, Box 5.

65. Hubert Marshall, interview by author, Stanford University, 20 March 1990. Sibley was also an associate editor of *Liberation,* a journal founded in 1956 by a group of radical pacifists.

66. Francis G. Wilson to Watkins, 24 January 1958, JWS papers, Box B-5; Bowker, notes on Sibley, 27 March 1958, JWS papers, Box 5; and Terman, notes on Sibley, 30 April 1958, JWS papers, Box 5.

67. "Coe Stipulations," n.d., FET papers, Box 3/45/12. See also Diamond, "American Studies Program," which discusses the relationship between Coe and Yale's American Studies program.

68. Rhinelander accepted Walker's insistence that Sibley was the "best man available" and became "convinced that a failure to confirm the appointment would create such major problems within the Department as to face Professor Walker with very serious obstacles as he assumes the chairmanship." Rhinelander to Terman, 15 April 1958, JWS papers, Box B-5.

69. Terman, notes on Sibley, 28 April 1958; and John Darley to Ray Faulkner, 5 March 1958, both in JWS papers, Box 5.

70. See *Stanford Daily,* 18 April 1958, p. 1 and 17 April 1958, p. 2 (copies in JWS papers, Box 5). On Sibley's activism, see Fred Glover to Terman, n.d., JWS papers, Box 5. Glover's note included clippings from the local papers on Sibley's

activities. On the resurgence of the peace movement after 1957, see Wittner, *Rebels against War,* pp. 240–56; and Weart, *Nuclear Fear,* pp. 241–58.

71. Dwight Clark to Rhinelander, 8 May 1958, JWS papers, Box B-5. For the students' reactions, see *Stanford Daily,* 8 May 1958, p. 1; Jim Momson to Sterling, 22 April 1958; Susan Borman to Sterling, 23 April 1958; Robert Jones to Sterling, 8 May 1958; and Jim Messinger, Stanford student body president, to Sterling, 26 May 1958; all in JWS papers, Box 5.

Stanford administrators received 25 letters from alumni and members of the local community, 21 of which charged the administration with violations of academic freedom, and a petition with 20 signatures protesting the administration's action. See JWS papers, Box 5.

72. Lewis Terman, Terence Terman, and Bobbie and Frederick Terman, Jr., interview by author, Stanford University, 29 May 1992.

73. Terman, notes on Lerner, 27 May 1958; and Rhinelander to Sterling, 26 May 1958, both in FET papers, Box 3/45/12.

74. Terman, notes on conversation with Bruce Bliven about Max Lerner, 27 May 1958; Terman, notes on Kendall, 28 May 1958, both in FET papers, Box 3/45/12.

75. See Bowker to Terman, 23 May 1957; Terman, notes on Bunzel, 25 May 1957; and Terman, notes, 31 May 1958, all in FET papers, Box 3/6/1.

76. Fred Glover, memo on conversation with David Packard, 21 March 1962, FET papers, Box 3/6/1; Glover to Thomas Pike, 23 April 1962; and Pike to Glover, 17 April 1962, both in JWS papers, Box 5. David Packard and Frederick Terman were also on the board of directors of Granger Associates, which manufactured communications equipment for bombers. See *Resistance,* 9 March 1967 (copy of which is in JWS papers, Box 30).

Bunzel had been hired as a replacement for Thomas Barclay, who had initially been highly supportive of the appointment. By late 1959 Barclay, now an emeritus professor, had soured on Bunzel, for reasons that are not clear but were probably related to Bunzel's political views, and he had begun communicating with Provost Terman about Bunzel. See Terman, notes on conversation with Barclay, 27 November 1959; and Barclay to Terman, 23 February 1960, both in FET papers, Box 3/6/1. Terman thanked Barclay for sending a clipping from the *Stanford Daily*'s "Letters to the Editor," which complained about Bunzel's politics and his behavior during Rousselot's speech (Terman to Bradley, 21 October 1961, FET papers, Box 3/6/1).

There is no evidence that Barclay provided reports to Stanford administrators about Sibley's politics. In at least one other instance, however, he did report to the administration about a possible appointment to the political science department. In April 1963 he learned that the department had given a temporary position to Frederick L. Schuman, a professor at Williams College and expert on the Soviet Union. Barclay reported to Terman that Schuman was "biased, prejudiced, and highly subjective in his opinions and teaching" and had caused "difficulty, controversy and embarrassment" at Williams. To allow him to remain at Stanford would surely hurt Stanford's fund-raising efforts, Barclay concluded. Schuman did not remain at Stanford but it is not clear that the political science department or the Stanford administration ever considered him for a permanent appointment. See Barclay to Terman, 5 April 1963; Frank P. Adams to Stanford trustee Morris Doyle, 12 April 1963; and Curtis Tarr to Terman, 17 April 1963, all in FET papers, Box 3/45/12.

77. President Sterling's Statement to the Academic Council, 13 June 1958, Minutes of the Academic Council, Stanford University Archives.

78. Cornelius P. Cotter to Sterling, 17 April 1958, JWS papers, Box B-5.

79. Cotter to Sterling, 17 April 1958, JWS papers, Box B-5.

80. Barclay to Sterling, 4 December 1961, JWS papers, Box 5.

81. Robert Sears to Robert Wert, 27 January 1963, FET papers, Box 3/45/2.

Chapter 8. The Undergraduates

1. Farnsworth, *Mental Health*, p. 114. Among the others addressing the emotional health of college students (in contrast to the problems of adolescents and post-adolescents) and arguing for the employment of psychological counselors and psychiatrists on campus were Blaine and McArthur, *Emotional Problems*; Hanfmann, *Psychological Counseling*; Eddy, *College Influence on Student Character*; Wedge, *Psychosocial Problems*; and Whittington, *Psychiatry on the College Campus*. Articles on the subject also appeared in *Journal of Counseling Psychology* and the *Journal of the American College Health Association*. In 1956, the World Federation for Mental Health held a conference on the subject of the mental health of college students, and produced Funkenstein, *The Student and Mental Health*. The "founding father" of the student counseling movement was Yale's C. C. Fry, who drew attention to the mental health of students in 1942 with *Mental Health in College*.

2. Farnsworth, *Mental Health*, pp. 10–11, 18. The first university-based counseling program had been created in the late 1920s at Yale, but interest in the mental health of students did not become significant until after World War II.

3. Farnsworth, *Mental Health*, p. 27; see also Napoli, *Architects of Adjustment*, p. 135. On the post-World War II history of the psychological profession more generally, see Herman, *American Psychology*, and Gilgen, *American Psychology*.

4. By the mid-1960s, Graham B. Blaine, Jr., a psychiatrist with Harvard University Health Services, was arguing that postwar affluence and a resulting parental permissiveness created spoiled children unable to handle the stresses of higher education. See Blaine, *Hazards of Affluence*.

5. William D. Temby, "Suicide," in Blaine and McArthur, *Emotional Problems*, p. 136. Founder of Brandeis University's student counseling services in 1952, psychologist Eugenia Hanfmann (*Effective Therapy*, p. 14) stressed, as did Farnsworth, the impersonality of the postwar university as the main source of students' problems.

6. Farnsworth, *Mental Health*, p. 21. On p. 117, Farnsworth goes on to explain: "Teaching and counseling are in many respects similar, emphasis in formal teaching being directed toward understanding of subject-matter, and in counseling toward understanding the individual's interaction with the new ideas to which he has been exposed."

7. Paulsen, "College Students in Trouble."

8. Hoopes and Marshall, *The Undergraduate in the University,* pp. 51–52.

9. Robert Jones, sophomore, to Sterling, 8 May 1958, JWS papers, Box 5. Jones was referring to professor Thomas Bailey. The meeting between President Sterling and students was reported in the *Stanford Daily,* 14 May 1958, p. 2; a copy of this report may be found in JWS papers, Box 5. According to the students at the meeting, the best teachers at Stanford in 1958 were historian H. Stuart Hughes and Sibley.

10. Dormitory sponsors to the General Studies Committee, 10 May 1961, FET papers, Box 3/26/4.

11. See William Johnson to Halsey Royden, 3 October 1963, FET papers, Box 3/58/10.

12. Student to Fred Glover, n.d., FET papers, Box 3/26/4.

13. As quoted in Chafe, *Never Stop Running,* p. 498 n. 2. See also Chafe, pp. 167–68.

14. Bark to Robert Wert, 17 November 1960. For students' concerns about grades, see Parent to Terman, 11 January 1960; and Rexford Snyder to E. H. Brooks, 22 December 1960, both in FET papers, Box 3/26/4. See also General Studies Committee, "Freshman Attitude Survey," October 1962, FET papers, Box 3/58/10. Responses to the survey did not correlate with grade point average; successful students as well as those who were floundering reported anxiety about grades.

15. Sanford Atwood, Provost, Cornell University, to Terman, 2 July 1959; and Terman to David Faville, 4 February 1961, FET papers, Box 3/29/3. For inquiries about Stanford's grading policies from other university administrators, see John Miller, Yale University, to Albert Bowker, 24 May 1962; J. P. Elder, Harvard University, to Bowker, 14 May 1962; and Don Hamilton, Princeton University, to Bowker, 17 May 1962, all in FET papers, Box 3/29/3.

16. See Rexford Snyder to Terman, 21 October 1957, FET papers, Box 3/1/2; Snyder to Terman, 1 November 1960, FET papers, Box 3/29/3; Snyder to Terman, 27 April 1962, FET papers, Box 3/1/6; Admissions Committee minutes, 18 April 1957, FET papers, Box 3/1/2; and "Stanford Admissions," n.d., FET papers, Box 3/1/3.

For some faculty members on the admissions committee, Stanford had not gone far enough in opening the university to students on the basis of intellectual merit. The university's admissions office continued use of a ten-point scale in rating applicants although the allocation of points was changed in 1958, reducing to 3 points the weight given to "personal rating," an ill-defined category which included consideration of such things as "personality," "leadership," and extracurricular activities. (Of the remaining 7 points, SAT math score was given 1 point, SAT verbal score 2 points, and high school GPA was given 4 points.) "Discretionary" or "preference" points could also be given for other factors, such as whether one of the applicant's parents had attended Stanford. On some faculty members' concerns about the "personal rating," see Fred Glover to President Sterling, n.d.; and Admissions Committee minutes, 28 February 1957, 18 April 1957, 14 January 1958, and 12 February 1958, all in FET papers, Box 3/1/2–3.

Changes in admissions at Stanford followed developments at other elite universities. See Synnott, *The Half-Opened Door.*

17. For a discussion of the embrace, by university administrators, of the concept of meritocracy, and particularly, of Harvard president James B. Conant's role in promoting this concept in relation to university education, see Louis Menand, "The Quiet American," a review of *James B. Conant: Harvard to Hiroshima and the Making of the Nuclear Age,* by James G. Hershberg, *New York Review of Books,* 41/13 (14 July 1994), pp. 16–21.

18. This had been a socially acceptable response in the prewar years when a "gentleman's 'C'" did not bar the "gentleman" from economic success and social respectability after graduation. In the postwar university, filled with children of middle-class backgrounds whose parents saw a college education as the route to economic security, rejecting the norms of the university may not have been a widely chosen option.

19. Hoopes and Marshall, *The Undergraduate in the University,* p. 38. The Carnegie Corporation provided the support for the second year of the study.

20. Rhinelander to Sterling, 21 May 1957, JWS papers, Box A-12.

21. Rhinelander to Sterling, 21 May 1957, JWS papers, Box A-12; Bark to Wert, 17 November 1960, FET papers, Box 3/26/4; and Terman to parent, 18 January 1961, FET papers, Box 3/26/4.

22. Bark to Wert, 17 November 1960; Rexford Snyder to Terman, 29 November 1960; and Snyder to E. H. Brooks, 22 December 1960, all in FET papers, Box 3/26/4.

23. Twitty to Rhinelander, 9 January 1961, FET papers, Box 3/26/4.

24. Rhinelander to Twitty, 12 January 1961; and Twitty to Rhinelander, 2 June 1961, both in FET papers, Box 3/26/4.

25. Report, Committee on Instruction in the Freshman Year, 5 June 1961, FET papers, Box 3/26/4.

26. Rhinelander to Wert, 10 January 1961, FET papers, Box 3/58/10; and Chafe, *Never Stop Running,* p. 168.

27. According to Chafe, Stanford's top administrators, including President Sterling, quickly soured on Lowenstein and seemingly encouraged the antagonism that developed between Lowenstein and the residence hall business manager. It is likely that Stanford's administration would have dismissed Lowenstein at the end of the academic year; Lowenstein, however, left on his own accord, after being denied a permanent position in Stanford's political science department. See Chafe, *Never Stop Running,* pp. 173–74. Chafe is correct in pointing to the anti-Semitism of political scientist James Watkins but greatly overstates Watkins's influence in the department and with Stanford's administration in 1962. Further, even had Lowenstein not been a political activist who inspired students, his appointment to the political science department would have been unlikely, given the administration's determination to appoint only "star" political scientists and Lowenstein's lack of both scholarly publications and a doctorate in political science.

28. Chafe, *Never Stop Running,* pp. 174–86. See also Harris, *Dreams Die Hard.*

29. See, for example, Gingrich, *To Renew America* (New York: Harper Collins, 1995).

30. Kerr, *Uses of the University with 1994 Commentaries,* pp. 115, 126.

31. See, for example, Sykes, *Profscam.*

32. That such is the case is suggested by the tenure and promotion decisions of one major research university in 1993–1994, made public by court order. Despite claims of Ohio State University administrators that undergraduate teaching was an important factor in determining promotions, the *Chronicle of Higher Education* reported that the files relating to tenure decisions reflected mainly concerns about publications and success in obtaining external support and national recognition. In the case of one scientist, his decision not to seek federal patronage for his research counted heavily against him in the decision to deny tenure. See Douglas Lederman and Carolyn J. Mooney, "Lifting the Cloak of Secrecy from Tenure: Court Order Results in Unprecedented Access to Files at Ohio State University," *Chronicle of Higher Education*, 41/31 (14 April 1995), pp. A16-A18.

33. Katherine S. Mangan, "Hahnemann U. Angers Faculty with Threat to Fire Those Who Don't Attract Grant Money," *Chronicle of Higher Education*, 41/6 (5 October 1994), p. A20.

Bibliography

Archival Material

Academic Council of Stanford University. Minutes. Stanford University Archives.

Administration. Studies, Surveys, and Reports by the Vice-President for Business and Finance, Stanford University. Stanford University Archives.

Anderson, Clinton P. Papers. Manuscript Division, Library of Congress.

Annual Financial Statement of the University. Stanford University Archives.

Atomic Energy Commision. Papers. U.S. Department of Energy Archives, Germantown Building, Washington, D.C.

Baran, Paul. Files. Pacific Studies Center, Mountain View, California.

Behavioral Sciences. Collection. Stanford University Archives.

Birge, Raymond. Papers. Bancroft Library, University of California at Berkeley.

Blackwelder, Eliot. Papers. Hoover Institution Archives, Stanford University.

Bloch, Felix. Oral history. Niels Bohr Library, American Institute of Physics.

———. Papers. Stanford University Archives.

Bush, Vannevar. Papers. Carnegie Institute of Washington

Congressional Joint Committee on Atomic Energy (JCAE). Record Group 128. National Archives.

Davis, Paul. Oral history. Stanford University Archives.

Directory of Officers and Students of Stanford University, Stanford University Archives.

Dodds, John W. Papers. Stanford University Archives.

Edwards, Paul. Papers. Stanford University Archives.

Ford Foundation. Various collections. Ford Foundation Archives.

Ginzton, Edward. Oral history. Stanford University Archives.

Hanna, Paul. Papers. Hoover Institution Archives, Stanford University.

Hansen, William W. Papers. Stanford University Archives.

Hansen Laboratories. Papers. Stanford University Archives.

MIT President. Papers. MIT Archives.
National Advisory Committee on Aeronautics. Record Group 255. Federal Records Center, Suitland, Maryland.
Naval Research Advisory Committee Research. Records. Office of Naval Research, Ballston, Virginia.
Office of Research and Development. Record Group 227. Administrative Office, General Records: National Archives; Administrative Office, Contracts: Federal Records Center, Suitland, Maryland.
Office of the U.S. Secretary of Defense, Research and Development Board. Record Group 330, Entry 341. National Archives.
Operating Budget, Stanford University. Stanford University Archives.
Panofsky, Wolfgang. Oral history. Niels Bohr Library, American Institute of Physics.
Report of the President of Stanford University. Stanford University Archives.
Schiff, Leonard. Papers. Stanford University Archives.
Speier, Hans. Oral history. Division of Space History. National Air and Space Museum. Washington, D.C.
Stanford Lands. Scrapbooks. Stanford University Archives.
Stanford Linear Accelerator Center. Director's Office papers. Stanford Linear Accelerator Center Archives.
Stanford School of Engineering. Papers. Stanford University Archives.
Sterling, J. Wallace. Papers. Stanford University Archives.
Terman, Frederick E. Papers. Stanford University Archives.
Terman, Lewis M. Papers. Stanford University Archives.
Tresidder, Donald. Papers. Stanford University Archives.
University Services. Papers. Stanford University Archives.
Varian, Russell and Sigurd. Papers. Stanford University Archives.
Webster, David Locke. Papers. Stanford University Archives.
Wiggins, Ira Wiggins. Papers. Stanford University Archives.
Wilbur, Ray Lyman. Papers. Stanford University Archives.

Interviews by the Author

Harold Bacon, Stanford University, 22 January 1987.
Paul Berg, telephone interview, 17 October 1994.
Lawrence Blinks, Hopkins Marine Station, Monterey, Calif., 7 March 1987.
Albert Bowker, Washington, D.C., 4 April 1991.
Sidney Drell, Stanford Linear Accelerator Center, 4 September 1987.
Fred Glover, Stanford University, 3 March 1987.
Paul Hanna, Stanford University, 26 March 1986.
Robert Hofstadter, Stanford University, 5 March 1987.
Eric Hutchinson, Stanford University, 27 May 1987.
Donald Kennedy, telephone interview, 29 September 1994.
Paul Kirkpatrick, Stanford University, 26 April 1988.
Herbert Marshall, Stanford University, 20 March 1990.
Lincoln E. Moses, Stanford University, 20 March 1990.

William Rambo, Stanford University, 18 March 1987.
Philip Rhinelander, Stanford University, 22 January and 9 February 1987.
Hugh Skilling, Stanford University, 6 April 1988.
Herbert Solomon, Stanford University, 19 March 1990.
Charles Stein, Stanford University, 20 March 1990.
Lewis Terman, Terence Terman, Frederick Terman, Jr., and Bobbie Terman, Stanford University, 29 May 1992.

Published Sources

Arnove, Robert, ed., *Philanthropy and Cultural Imperialism: The Foundations at Home and Abroad*. Boston: G.K. Hall, 1980.
Auerbach, Lewis E. "Scientists in the New Deal: A Pre-War Episode in the Relations between Science and Government in the United States." *Minerva* 3: 457 (1964).
Babbidge, Homer, Jr., and Robert M. Rosenzweig. *The Federal Interest in Higher Education*. New York: McGraw-Hill, 1962.
Badger, Anthony. *The New Deal: The Depression Years, 1933–1940*. London: Macmillan, 1989.
Balogh, Brian. *Chain Reaction: Expert Debate and Public Participation in American Commercial Nuclear Power, 1945–1975*. Cambridge: Cambridge University Press, 1991.
Barrett, Edward L. *The Tenney Committee: Legislative Investigation of Subversive Activities in California*. Ithaca: Cornell University Press, 1951.
Bauman, John F. *In the Eye of the Great Depression: New Deal Reporters and the Agony of the American People*. DeKalb, Ill.: Northern Illinois University Press, 1988.
Baxter, James Phinney. *Scientists Against Time*. Boston: Little, Brown and Company, 1946.
Bell, Daniel. *The End of Ideology: On the Exhaustion of Political Ideas in the Fifties,* Rev. ed. New York: Free Press, 1965.
Ben-David, Joseph. *American Higher Education: Directions Old and New*. New York: McGraw Hill, 1972.
Bernstein, Barton J. "Four Physicists and the Bomb: The Early Years." *Historical Studies in the Physical and Biological Sciences* 18: 231 (1988).
Best, Gary Dean. *Herbert Hoover: The Postpresidential Years, 1933–1964*. Vol. 1. Stanford: Hoover Institution Press, 1983.
Blaine, Graham B., Jr. *Youth and the Hazards of Affluence: The High School and College Years*. New York: Harper Colophon Books, 1966.
Blaine, Graham B., Jr., and Charles C. McArthur, eds. *Emotional Problems of the Student*. New York: Appletone-Century-Crofts, Inc., 1961.
Blakey, Roy, and Gladys Blakey. *The Federal Income Tax*. London: Longmans, Green and Co., 1940.
Bloom, Allan. *The Closing of the American Mind*. New York: Simon and Schuster, 1987.

Boyer, Paul. *By the Bomb's Early Light: American Thought and Culture at the Dawn of the Atomic Age.* New York: Pantheon, 1985.

Bridgman, Percy. "Science and Freedom: Reflections of a Physicist." *Isis* 37: 128 (1947).

Brown, Francis J., and Thorsten Sellin, eds. *Higher Education Under Stress.* Vol. 301. Philadelphia: Annals of the American Academy of Political and Social Sciences, 1955.

Buck, Peter. "Adjusting to Military Life: The Social Sciences Go to War, 1941–1950." In *Military Enterprise and Technological Change: Perspectives on the American Experience,* edited by Merritt Roe Smith. Cambridge: MIT Press, 1985.

Bush, Vannevar. *Science, The Endless Frontier: A Report to the President on a Program for Postwar Scientific Research.* Washington, D.C.: Government Printing Office, 1945.

California. State Relief Administration. *Review of Activities of the State Relief Administration of California, 1933–1935.* Sacramento: State Printing Office, 1936.

Carlson, Bernard. "Academic Entrepreneurship and Engineering Education: Dugald C. Jackson and the MIT-GE Cooperative Engineering Course, 1907–1932." *Technology and Culture* 29: 526 (1988).

Caute, David. *The Great Fear: The Anticommunist Purge under Truman and Eisenhower.* London: Secker and Warburg, 1978.

Chafe, William. *Never Stop Running: Allard Lowenstein and the Struggle to Save American Liberalism.* New York: Basic Books, 1993.

Charlesworth, James C., ed. *Contemporary Political Analysis.* New York: Free Press, 1967.

Coffman, Lotus. *The State University, Its Work and Problems: A Selection from Addresses Delivered Between 1921 and 1933.* Minneapolis: University of Minnesota Press, 1934.

Commission on Financing Higher Education. *Nature and Needs of Higher Education.* New York: Columbia University Press, 1952.

Commoner, Barry. *Science and Survival.* New York: Viking Press, 1966.

Cuff, Robert D. *The War Industries Board: Business-Government Relations during World War I.* Baltimore: The Johns Hopkins University Press, 1973.

Davidson, Carl. "Towards a Student Syndicalist Movement, Or University Reform Revisited." In *The University Crisis Reader: Confrontation and Counter Attack,* edited by Immanuel Wallerstein and Paul Starr. New York: Random House, 1971.

Dennis, Michael A. " 'Our First Line of Defense': Two University Laboratories in the Postwar American State." *Isis* 85/3; 427 (September 1974).

Diamond, Sigmund. "The American Studies Program at Yale: Lux, Veritas, et Pecunia." *Prospects: An Annual of American Cultural Studies.* Vol. 16. New York: Cambridge University Press, 1991.

———. *Compromised Campus: The Collaboration of Universities with the Intelligence Community, 1945–1955.* New York: Oxford University Press, 1992.

Dickson, David. *The New Politics of Science.* New York: Pantheon Books, 1984.

Domhoff, William. *The Bohemian Grove and Other Retreats: A Study in Ruling-Class Cohesiveness.* New York: Harper Torchbooks, 1974.

D'Souza, Dinesh. *Illiberal Education: The Politics of Race and Sex on Campus.* New York: Free Press, 1991.

Dupree, A. Hunter. *Science in the Federal Government: A History of Policies and Activities to 1940.* Cambridge: Harvard University Press, 1957.

Eddy, E. D., Jr., et al. *The College Influence on Student Character.* Washington, D.C.: American Council on Education, 1959.

Elliott, Orrin Leslie. *Stanford University: The First Twenty Five Years, 1891–1925.* Stanford: Stanford University Press, 1937.

Embree, Edwin, R. "In Order of Their Eminence: An Appraisal of American Universities." *Atlantic Monthly* 155/6: 53 (June 1935).

Etzkowitz, Henry. "The Making of an Entrepreneurial University: The Traffic Among MIT, Industry, and the Military." In Vol. 12 of *Science, Technology, and the Military,* edited by Everett Mendelsohn, Merritt Roe Smith, and Peter Weingart. Boston: Kluwer Academic Publishers, 1988.

Farnsworth, Dana L. *Mental Health in College and University.* Cambridge: Harvard University Press, 1957.

Forman, Paul. "Behind Quantum Electronics: National Security as Basis for Physical Research in the United States, 1940–1960." *Historical Studies in the Physical and Biological Sciences* 18: 149 (1987).

Fry, C. C. *Mental Health in College.* New York: Commonwealth Fund, 1942.

Funkenstein, D. H., ed. *The Student and Mental Health—An International View.* London: World Federation for Mental Health, 1959.

Galison, Peter. "Physics Between War and Peace." In vol 12 of *Science, Technology, and the Military,* edited by Everett Mendelsohn, Merritt Roe Smith and Peter Weingart. Boston: Kluwer Academic Publishers, 1988.

Galison, Peter, and Bruce Hevly, eds. *Big Science: The Growth of Large-Scale Research.* Stanford: Stanford University Press, 1992.

Geiger, Roger. "American Foundations and Academic Social Science, 1945–1960." *Minerva* 26/3: 315 (Autumn 1989).

———. *Research and Relevant Knowledge: American Research Universities Since World War II.* New York: Oxford University Press, 1993.

———. *To Advance Knowledge: The Growth of American Research Universities, 1900–1940.* New York: Oxford University Press, 1986.

Gibson, Weldon P. *SRI: The Founding Years.* Los Altos, California: Publishing Services Center, 1980.

———. *SRI: The Take-Off Days.* Los Altos, California: Publishing Services Center, 1986.

Gilgen, Albert R. *American Psychology since World War II: A Profile of the Discipline.* Westport, Connecticut: Greenwood Press, 1982.

Gilpin, Robert, and Christopher Wright, eds. *Scientists and National Policy-Making.* New York: Columbia University Press, 1964.

Goodstein, Judith. *Millikan's School: A History of the California Institute of Technology.* New York: W.W. Norton, 1991.

Greenberg, Daniel S. *The Politics of Pure Science: An Inquiry into the Relationship Between Science and Government in the United States.* New York: New American Library, 1967.

Gruber, Carol. *Mars and Minerva: World War I and the Uses of Higher Learning in America.* Baton Rouge: Louisiana State University Press, 1975.

———. "The Overhead System in Government-Sponsored Academic Science: Origins and Early Development." *Historical Studies in the Physical and Biological Sciences* 25/2: 241 (1995).

Hagen, Raymond D. *Windows to the Origins: The Office of Naval Research.* Washington, D.C.: Office of Naval Research, 1986.

Hallion, Richard P. *Legacy of Flight: The Guggenheim Contribution to American Aviation.* Seattle: University of Washington Press, 1977.

Hanfmann, Eugenia. *Effective Therapy for College Students.* San Francisco: Jossey-Bass, 1979.

Hanfmann, Eugenia, et. al., eds. *Psychological Counseling in a Small College.* Cambridge: Schenkman, 1963.

Harris, David. *Dreams Die Hard.* New York: St. Martin's, 1982.

Hawkins, Hugh. *Between Harvard and America: The Educational Leadership of Charles W. Eliot.* New York: Oxford University Press, 1972.

Hawley, Ellis. "Herbert Hoover, the Commerce Secretariat, and the Vision of an 'Associative State,' 1921–1928." *Journal of American History* 61/1: 116 (June 1974).

———, ed. *Herbert Hoover as Secretary of Commerce: Studies in New Era Thought and Practice.* Iowa City: University of Iowa Press, 1981.

Heilbron, John, and Robert Seidel. *Lawrence and His Laboratory: A History of the Lawrence Berkeley Laboratory,* Vol. 1. Berkeley: University of California Press, 1989.

Heims, Steve J. *The Cybernetics Group.* Cambridge: MIT Press, 1991.

Herman, Ellen. *The Romance of American Psychology: Political Culture in the Age of Experts.* Berkeley: University of California Press, 1995.

Hershberg, James G. *James G. Conant: Harvard to Hiroshima and the Making of the Nuclear Age.* New York: Knopf, 1993.

Hevly, Bruce W. "Base to Campus: The Influence of Academic Science on Military Research at NRL." Paper presented at the Workshop on the Military and Postwar Science, The Johns Hopkins University, 1986.

———. *Expanding the Spectrum: Sun and Earth at the Naval Research Laboratory.* Baltimore: The Johns Hopkins University Press, forthcoming.

Hoff-Wilson, Joan. *Herbert Hoover, Forgotten Progressive.* Boston: Little, Brown, 1975.

Hofstadter, Richard and Walter P. Metzger. *The Development of Academic Freedom in the United States.* New York: Columbia University Press, 1955.

Hook, Sidney, ed. *In Defense of Academic Freedom.* New York: Pegasus Books, 1971.

Hoopes, Robert, and Hubert Marshall. *The Undergraduate in the University: A Report to the Faculty by the Executive Committee of the Stanford Study of Undergraduate Education, 1954–1956.* Stanford: Stanford University Press, 1957.

Horowitz, David A., Peter N. Carroll, and David D. Lee. *On The Edge: A New History of 20th-Century America.* St. Paul: West Publishing Company, 1990.

Judd, Charles H. *Research in the U.S. Office of Education.* Advisory Committee on Education, Staff Study 19. Washington, D.C.: Government Printing Office, 1939.

Kalleberg, Arthur L., J. Donald Moon, and Donald R. Sabia, Jr., eds. *Dissent and Affirmation: Essays in Honor of Mulford Q. Sibley.* Bowling Green: Ohio: Bowling Green University Popular Press, 1983.

Kargon, Robert W. *The Rise of Robert Millikan: Portrait of a Life in American Science.* Ithaca: Cornell University Press, 1982.

Kargon, Robert W., and Elizabeth Hodes. "Karl Compton, Isaiah Bowman, and the Politics of Science in the Great Depression." *Isis* 76/283: 301 (September 1985).

Kargon, Robert, Stuart Leslie, and Erica Schoenberger. "Far Beyond Big Science: Science Regions and the Organization of Research and Development." In *Big Science: The Growth of Large-Scale Research,* edited by Peter Galison and Bruce Hevly. Stanford: Stanford University Press, 1992.

Katz, Barry M. *Foreign Intelligence: Research and Analysis in the Office of Strategic Services, 1942–1945.* Cambridge: Harvard University Press, 1989.

Kerr, Clark. *The Uses of the University.* Cambridge: Harvard University Press, 1963.

———. *The Uses of the University with 1994 Commentaries on Past Developments and Future Prospects.* Cambridge: Harvard University Press, 1995.

Kevles, Daniel J. "K1S2: Korea, Science and the State." In *Big Science: The Growth of Large-Scale Research,* edited by Peter Galison and Bruce Hevly. Stanford: Stanford University Press, 1992.

———. *The Physicists: The History of a Scientific Community in Modern America.* New York: Knopf, 1978.

Klausner, Samuel Z., and Victor M. Lidz, eds. *The Nationalization of the Social Sciences.* Philadelphia: University of Pennsylvania Press, 1986.

Kohler, Robert. *Partners in Science: Foundations and Natural Scientists, 1900–1945.* Chicago: University of Chicago Press, 1991.

Koistinen, Paul A. C. *The Military-Industrial Complex: A Historical Perspective.* New York: Praeger, 1980.

Kolko, Gabriel. *The Triumph of Conservatism: A Reinterpretation of American History, 1900–1916.* New York: Free Press, 1963.

Koppes, Clayton. *JPL and the American Space Program: A History of the Jet Propulsion Laboratory.* New Haven: Yale University Press, 1982.

Kuznick, Peter. *Beyond the Laboratory: Scientists as Political Activists in 1930s America.* Chicago: University of Chicago Press, 1987.

Lapp, Ralph. *The Weapons Culture.* New York: W.W. Norton, 1968.

Larsen, Judith K., and Everett M. Rodgers. *Silicon Valley Fever: Growth of High-Technology Culture.* New York: Basic Books, 1984.

Layton, Edwin T., Jr. *The Revolt of the Engineers: Social Responsibility and the American Engineering Profession.* Cleveland: Case Western Reserve University Press, 1971.

Lecuyer, Christophe. "The Making of a Science-Based Technological University: Karl Compton, James Killian, and the Reform of MIT, 1930–1957." *Historical Studies in the Physical and Biological Sciences* 23/1: 153 (1992).

Leslie, Stuart W. *The Cold War and American Science: The Military-Industrial-Academic Complex at MIT and Stanford.* New York: Columbia University Press, 1993.

————. "Playing the Education Game to Win: The Military and Interdisciplinary Research at Stanford." *Historical Studies in the Physical and Biological Sciences* 18: 55 (1987).

Leuchtenburg, William. *Franklin D. Roosevelt and the New Deal, 1932–1940.* New York: Harper and Row, 1963.

Lindzey, Gardner, ed. *A History of Psychology in Autobiography.* Vol. 6. Englewood Cliffs, New Jersey: Prentice-Hall, 1974.

Lowood, Henry. "From Steeples of Excellence to Silicon Valley." *Stanford University Campus Report.* 20/23: 11 (9 March 1988).

McCaughey, Robert A. *International Studies and Academic Enterprise: A Chapter in the Enclosure of American Learning.* New York: Columbia University Press, 1984.

McConnell, Thomas R., and Malcolm Wiley, eds. *Higher Education and the War.* Vol. 231. Philadelphia: Annals of the American Academy of Political and Social Science, 1944.

Macdonald, Dwight. *The Ford Foundation: The Men and the Millions.* New York: Reynal and Company, 1956.

McDougall, Walter. *The Heavens and the Earth: A Political History of the Space Age.* New York: Basic Books, 1985.

McMahon, A. Michal. *The Making of a Profession: A Century of Electrical Engineering in America.* New York: Institute of Electrical and Electronic Engineers, 1984.

McPhee, John. *Encounters with the Archdruid.* New York: Farrar, Straus, and Giroux, 1971.

May, Elaine Tyler. *Homeward Bound: American Families in the Cold War Era.* New York: Basic Books, 1988.

Medeiros, Frank A. "The Sterling Years at Stanford: A Study in the Dynamics of Institutional Change." Ph.D. diss., Stanford University, 1979.

Melman, Seymour. *The Permanent War Economy: American Capitalism in Decline.* New York: Simon and Schuster, 1974.

Millett, John D. *Financing Higher Education in the United States.* New York: Columbia University Press, 1952.

Minton, Henry L. *Lewis M. Terman: Pioneer in Psychological Testing.* New York: New York University Press, 1988.

Mirrielees, Edith R. *Stanford: The Story of a University.* New York: G.P. Putnam's Sons, 1959.

Mitchell, Greg. *The Campaign of the Century: Upton Sinclair's Race for Governor of California and the Birth of Media Politics.* New York: Random House, 1992.

Napoli, Donald S. *Architects of Adjustment: The History of the Psychological Profession in the United States.* Port Washington, New York: Kennikat Press, 1981.

Nash, George H. *Herbert Hoover and Stanford University.* Stanford: Hoover Institution Press, 1988.

Needell Allan A. " 'Truth is Our Weapon': Project TROY, Political Warfare, and Government-Academic Relations in the National Security State." *Diplomatic History* 17/3: 399 (Summer 1993).

Nisbet, Robert. *The Degradation of the Academic Dogma: The University in America, 1945–1970.* New York: Basic Books, 1971.

Noble, David F. *America By Design: Science, Technology, and the Rise of Corporate Capitalism.* New York: Knopf, 1977.

———. *Forces of Production: A Social History of Industrial Automation.* New York: Knopf, 1984.

———. "The Selling of the University: MIT-Whitehead Merger." *Nation* 234/5: 129 (6 February 1982).

O'Connell, Charles. "Social Structure and Science: Soviet Studies at Harvard." Ph.D. diss., University of California at Los Angeles, 1990.

Orlans, Harold, ed., *Science Policy and the University.* Washington, D.C.: Brookings Institute, 1968.

Owens, Larry. "MIT and the Federal 'Angel': Academic R & D and Federal-Private Cooperation before World War II." *Isis* 81: 189 (1990).

———. "The Counterproductive Management of Science in World War II: Vannevar Bush and the Office of Scientific Research and Development." *Business History Review* 68: 515 (Winter 1994).

Paulsen, James A. "College Students in Trouble." *Atlantic Monthly* 214/1: 96 (July 1964).

President's Commission on Higher Education. *Higher Education for American Democracy, A Report.* New York: Harper and Brothers, 1948.

Price, Don. *Government and Science: Their Dynamic Relation in American Democracy.* New York: New York University Press, 1954.

Purcell, Carroll W. "The Anatomy of a Failure: The Science Advisory Board, 1933–1935." *Proceedings of the American Philosophical Society* 109: 342 (December 1965).

———. "A Preface to Government Support of Research and Development: Research Legislation and the National Bureau of Standards, 1935–1941." *Technology and Culture* 9: 145 (April 1968).

Rae, John. *Climb to Greatness: The American Aircraft Industry, 1920–1960.* Cambridge: MIT Press, 1968.

Ramo, Simon. *The Business of Science: Winning and Losing in the High-Tech Age.* New York: Hill and Wang, 1988.

Reingold, Nathan. "Vannevar Bush's New Deal for Research: Or the Triumph of the Old Order." *Historical Studies in the Physical and Biological Sciences* 17: 299 (1986).

Ridenour, Louis N. "Should the Scientists Resist Military Intrusion?" *American Scholar* 16: 213 (Spring 1947).

Ridgeway, James. *The Closed Corporation: American Universities in Crisis.* New York: Random House, 1968.

Riesman, David, and Verne Stadtman, eds. *Academic Transformation: Seventeen Institutions Under Pressure.* New York: McGraw Hill, 1973.

Roche, George. *The Fall of the Ivory Tower: Government Funding, Corruption, and the Bankrupting of American Higher Education.* Washington, D.C.: Regnery Publishing, 1994.

Roland, Alex. *Model Research: The National Advisory Committee for Aeronautics, 1915–1958.* Washington, D.C.: NASA, 1985.

Rosenzweig, Robert. *The Research Universities and Their Patrons.* Berkeley: University of California Press, 1982.

Ross, Dorothy. *The Origins of American Social Science.* Cambridge: Cambridge University Press, 1991.

Rossiter, Margaret, and Clark Elliott, eds. *Science at Harvard University: Historical Perspectives.* Bethlehem, PA: Lehigh University Press, 1992.

Sapolsky, Harvey M. *Science and the Navy: The History of the Office of Naval Research.* Princeton: Princeton University Press, 1990.

Schrecker, Ellen W. *No Ivory Tower: McCarthyism and the Universities.* New York: Oxford University Press, 1986.

Schweber, Samuel. "The Empiricist Temper Regnant: Theoretical Physics in the United States, 1920–1950." *Historical Studies in the Physical and Biological Sciences* 17: 55 (1986).

Seidel, Robert. "Accelerating Science: The Postwar Transformation of the Lawrence Radiation Laboratory." *Historical Studies in the Physical and Biological Sciences* 13: 375 (1983).

———. "Physics Research in California: The Rise of a Leading Sector in American Physics." Ph.D. diss., University of California at Berkeley, 1978.

Seidelman, Raymond. *Disenchanted Realists: Political Science and the American Crisis 1884–1984.* Albany: SUNY Press, 1985.

Servos, John W. "The Industrial Relations of Science: Chemical Engineering at MIT, 1900–1939." *Isis* 71: 531 (1980).

Seybold, Peter. "The Ford Foundation and the Triumph of Behavioralism in American Political Science." In *Philanthropy and Cultural Imperialism: The Foundations at Home and Abroad,* edited by Robert Arnove. Boston: G. K. Hall and Co., 1980.

Shaffter, Dorothy. *The National Science Foundation.* New York: Praeger Press, 1969.

Sherry, Michael S. *Preparing for the Next War: American Plans for Postwar Defense, 1941–1945.* New Haven: Yale University Press, 1977.

Shils, Edward. "The University: A Backward Glance." *The American Scholar,* 51/1: 163 (Spring 1982).

Smith, Alice K. *A Peril and a Hope: The Scientists' Movement in America, 1945–1947.* Chicago: University of Chicago Press, 1965.

Smith, Page. *Killing the Spirit: Higher Education in America.* New York: Viking, 1990.

Somit, Albert, and Joseph Tanenhaus, *The Development of Political Science: From Burgess to Behavioralism.* Boston: Allyn and Bacon, 1967.

Sykes, Charles J. *ProfScam: Professors and the Demise of Higher Education.* Washington, D.C.: Regnery Gateway, 1988.

Synnott, Marcia G. *The Half-Opened Door: Discrimination and Admissions at Harvard, Yale and Princeton, 1900–1970.* Westport, Connecticut: Greenwood Press, 1979.

Touraine, Alain. *The Academic System in American Society.* New York: McGraw-Hill, 1974.

United States Congress. Joint Committee on Atomic Energy. *Stanford Linear Accelerator. Hearings before the Subcommittee on Research and Development and the Subcommittee on Legislation of the Joint Committee on Atomic Energy.* 86th Cong., 1st sess. Washington, D.C.: Government Printing Office, 1959.

Vagtborg, Harold. *Research and American Industrial Development.* New York: Pergamon Press, 1976.

Varian, Dorothy. *The Inventor and the Pilot: Russell and Sigurd Varian.* Palo Alto, California: Pacific Books, 1983.

Veblen, Thorstein. *The Higher Learning in America: A Memorandum on the Conduct of Universities by Business Men.* New York: A.M. Kelley, 1965 (c. 1918).

Veysey, Laurence. *The Emergence of the American University.* Chicago: University of Chicago Press, 1965.

Wang, Jessica. "Science, Security and the Cold War: The Case of E.U. Condon." *Isis* 83/2: 238 (June 1992).

Weart, Spencer. *Nuclear Fear: A History of Images.* Cambridge: Harvard University Press, 1988.

Webb, William H., et al. *Sources of Information in the Social Sciences.* 3rd ed. Chicago: American Library Association, 1986.

Wedge, B. M., ed. *Psychosocial Problems of College Men.* New Haven: Yale University Press, 1958.

Whittington, H. G. *Psychiatry on the College Campus.* New York: International University Press, 1963.

Wiley, Malcolm M. *Depression, Recovery and Higher Education.* New York: McGraw-Hill, 1937.

Winkler, Allan. *Life Under a Cloud: American Anxiety about the Atom.* New York: Oxford University Press, 1993.

Wittner, Lawrence. *Rebels Against War: The American Peace Movement, 1933–1983.* Rev. ed. Philadelphia: Temple University Press, 1984.

Wolff, Robert Paul. *The Ideal of the University.* Boston: Beacon Press, 1969.

Yergin, Daniel. *Shattered Peace: The Origins of the Cold War and the National Security State.* Boston: Houghton Mifflin, 1977.

Young, Roland, ed. *Approaches to the Study of Politics: Twenty-Two Contemporary Essays Exploring the Nature of Politics and Methods by Which It Can Be Studied.* Evanston, Ill.: Northwestern University Press, 1958.

Index

Composition: Maple-Vail Book Manufacturing Group
Text: 10/13 Galliard
Display: Galliard
Printing and binding: Maple-Vail Book Manufacturing Group